Second Edition

SOCIOLOGYAS
for AQA

Stephen Moore   Dave Aiken   Steve Chapman

Collins

An imprint of ~~HarperCollins~~ Publishers

William Collins' dream of knowledge for all began with the publication of his first book in 1819. A self-educated mill worker, he not only enriched millions of lives, but also founded a flourishing publishing house. Today, staying true to this spirit, Collins books are packed with inspiration, innovation and practical expertise. They place you at the centre of a world of possibility and give you exactly what you need to explore it.

Collins. Do more.

Published by Collins
An imprint of HarperCollins*Publishers* Limited
77–85 Fulham Palace Road
Hammersmith
London W6 8JB

Browse the complete Collins catalogue
at **www.collinseducation.com**

Commissioned by Thomas Allain-Chapman
Consultant editor Peter Langley
Reader Pam Law
Project managed by Hugh Hillyard-Parker
Production by Sarah Robinson
Edited by Ros Connelly
Cover design by Blue Pig Design
Internal design by Patricia Briggs
Typesetting by Hugh Hillyard-Parker
Figures typeset by Liz Gordon
Cartoons by Oxford Designers and Illustrators
Index by Indexing Specialists (UK) Ltd, Hove, UK
Printed and bound by Printing Express, Hong Kong

Author dedications

Dave Aiken: Thanks again to Maggie for her unrelenting support – back on ironing duty I promise (and not just my own shirts, Ms Oakley). Love to the kids, Leo, Laurie and Amelia, who helped keep things in perspective, and to the Collins team for their patience. Also dedicated in loving memory of my mother (14/4/1930 to 12/6/2002), whose intelligence, sense of justice and love will always inspire me to make a positive contribution wherever I can.

Steve Chapman: For Fiona.

CONTENTS

Sociology AS for AQA

ACKNOWLEDGEMENTS

The publishers would like to thank the following for permission to reproduce photographs. The page number is followed, where necessary, by T (top), B (bottom), L (left), R (right) or C (centre).

Alamy (1); Mary Evans Picture Library (2); Rex Features (6 all); Empics (9); Corbis (10); Alamy (12); Science Photo Library (13); Alamy (20); Alamy (23L); Rex Features (23C); S & R Greenhill (23R); South American Picture Library (24); Mary Evans Picture Library (26L); Alamy (26R); Getty-Images (33); Brian Jones (34); Ronald Grant Archive/Fox Television (35); Bridgeman Art Library (40T&C); Getty-Images (40B); Alamy (44); Corbis (49TL & B); Network Photographers (46TR); Bubbles Photo Library (49, 50); Rex Features (52T); Getty-Images (52B); Getty-Images (55); Alamy (56); Photofusion (58 both); Bubbles Photo Library (59); Courtesy of NSPCC (64TL); Rex Features (64TR); Still Photos/Sebastian Bolesch (64BL); S & R Greenhill (64BR); S & R Greenhill (67); Bubbles Photo Library (70); Alamy (73); Photofusion/Crispin Hughes (79); Rex Features (80TL & BL); S & R Greenhill (80TR & BR); S & R Greenhill (83); Rex Features (85 both); S & R Greenhill (88L); Photofusion (88CT); Rex Features (88CB & R); Topfoto (90); S & R Greenhill (94L); Science Photo Library (94R); PA/Empics (97); S & R Greenhill (103); Alamy (106); Rex Features (108); Science Photo Library/Oullette & Therous/Publiphoto Diffision (110); Rex Features (115); BBC/Dave Pickthorn (124); Associated Press (129); Corbis (132); Rex Features (136); Kobal Collection (138 both); Rex Features (139); Advertising Archives (142TL); Kobal Collection (142TR); BBC/Adam Pensotti (142 BL); Sky Sports (142 BR); Roger Scruton (145); Advertising Archives (148); Rex Features (150); PA/Empics (155); John Walmsley/Education Photos (161); S & R Greenhill (162 all); Mary Evans Picture Library (163); John Walmsley/Education Photos (164); Still Pictures/Edward Parker (170); Photofusion/Stan Gamester (174TL); S & R Greenhill (174TR); Network Photographers/Mike Abrahams (174B); Rex Features (177); John Walmsley/Education Photos (178); S & R Greenhill (180); John Walmsley/Education Photos (183); S & R Greenhill (186TL); Bubbles Photo Library (186TR & BR); Rex Features (186BL); S & R Greenhill (188); Network Photographers (192L); Bubbles Photo Library (192R); Photofusion (195); Alamy (198 both); Rex Features (205); Photofusion/David Montford (206); Corbis (208); Hugh Hillyard-Parker (212T & B); Alamy (212C); Photofusion/Crispin Hughes (218); Network Photographers (221); Rex Features (224); Photofusion/Paul Doyle (227); Corbis (230L); Photofusion/Lisa Woollett (230C); Alamy (230R); Science Photo Library (233); Corbis (239); Getty-Images/ Imagebank (245); Photofusion (246); Topfoto (247); Rex Features (252); S & R Greenhill (253); Alamy (258); Getty-Images (259TL & TR); Getty-Images/Imagebank (259BL); Empics (259BR); Rex Features (261); Alamy (267); Mary Evans Picture Library (270); Hugh Hillyard-Parker (272); Science Photo Library (273); Stephen Bourne (275 all); Corbis (281, 282).

Every effort has been made to contact copyright holders, but if any have been inadvertently overlooked, the publishers will be pleased to make the necessary arrangements at the first opportunity.

The organization of the book

The book is divided into a series of units, each linking into AQA AS-level modules. Each unit consists of a number of topics, which divide the unit into manageable parts. Each topic starts by building on your prior knowledge; it then goes on to provide all the knowledge you need, before giving you the chance to check your understanding and reinforce key concepts. There is then an opportunity to apply the knowledge, practise an exam-style question and build wider skills. Finally, there are research- and internet-based extension activities, creating opportunities to explore issues further.

Features of the textbook

Each topic contains a number of features designed to help you with learning, revision and exam-preparation. These are illustrated and described on the following two pages.

In addition to regular topic features, each unit ends with a Unit summary in the form of a 'spider diagram'. This provides an attractive visual overview of the whole unit and identifies important connections between the topics. This feature should prove particularly useful for revision. See, for example, pp. 30–1.

Sociology for AS Level: A guide for AQA candidates

The table below shows how the units in this book relate to the AQA AS-level specification. Turn to Unit 8: *Preparing for the AS exam* (pp. 278–83) for more detail and an explanation of the courses and their assessment.

How this textbook covers the AQA AS specification

Texbook unit	AQA AS
Unit 1 Introduction to Sociology: key themes and perspectives	Core themes*: ● Socialization, culture and identity ● Social differentiation, power and stratification
Unit 2 Families and households	**AS Module 1** Families and households
Unit 3 Health	**AS Module 1** Health
Unit 4 Mass media	**AS Module 1** Mass media
Unit 5 Education	**AS Module 2** Education
Unit 6 Wealth, poverty and welfare	**AS Module 2** Wealth, poverty and welfare
Unit 7 Sociological methods	**AS Module 3** Sociological methods

* There are two 'core themes' within the AQA specification, as listed here. These themes run through all the topics in the specification and all the units in this book.

Getting you thinking

The opening activity draws on your existing knowledge and experiences to lead in to some of the main issues of the topic. The questions are usually open and, although suitable for individual work, may be more effectively used in discussion in pairs or small groups, where experiences and ideas can be shared.

Main text

The important sociological concepts, debates and the latest research are all covered. A careful balance between depth and accessibility is maintained in every unit.

TOPIC 3

The content of the mass media: making the news

gettingyouthinking

1 Which aspects of the above screen shots suggest that the news:
- is 'up to the minute'?
- comes from around the world?
- employs the latest technology?

2 Think of the music that introduces news broadcasts. What impression does it give?

News: a 'window on the world'?

For most of us, TV news is the most important source of information about what is going on outside our day-to-day experiences. We rely on TV news to help us make sense of a confusing world. As you probably worked out from the questions above, news broadcasts are carefully managed to give an impression of seriousness and credibility. But do they really represent a 'window on the world'? How do TV journalists and editors decide which of the millions of events that occur in the world on any day will become 'news'?

Critics of the media have pointed out that the news is most certainly not a 'window on the world'. Instead, they argue that it is a manufactured and manipulated product involving a high degree of selectivity and bias. What causes this? Three important elements are:

1 institutional factors both inside and outside the newsrooms (such as issues of time and money)

2 the culture of news production and journalism (how news professionals think and operate)

3 the ideological influences on the media (the cause and nature of bias).

Institutional factors

The 'news diary'

Rather than being a spontaneous response to world events, many news reports are planned well in advance. Many newspapers and TV news producers purchase news items from press agencies (companies who sell brief reports of world or

---

focusonresearch

Tony Sewell

Black masculinities and schooling

How Black boys survive modern schooling

Sewell (1996) found that Black pupils belonged to a range of both pro- and antischool subcultures as a result of the lack of positive recognition of their culture and stereotyped views held by many teachers. He found that Black pupils were disciplined excessively by teachers who were socialized into racist attitudes and

who were scared of these students' masculinity, sexuality and physical skills. The Black boys adapted in various ways, some of which reinforced these stereotyped views, and behaved in ways that could be interpreted as violent and disruptive. Sewell adapts Merton's typology of deviance in describing the subcultural responses that emerged:

1 *Conformists* – Black boys who were often praised for their positive behaviour and attitude who were said to be adopting White values at the expense of losing their African-Caribbean identities – the largest group though still less than half the cohort

2 *Innovators* – accepted the goals of the school, but maintained a rebellious and antischool posture, while avoiding trouble through their adoption of 'intelligent strategies'

3 *Retreatists* – a small group of loners who kept themselves to themselves

4 *Rebels* – who adopted the signs and signals of aggressive African-Caribbean masculinity and rejected the school. Their behaviour was aggressively masculine and they perceived masculinity in terms of sex and money. Their favoured term of abuse was 'pussy', which used to imply homosexuality or femininity and low status. Other pupils perceived them to be bullies.

Adapted from Blundell, J. and Griffiths J. (2002)
Sociology since 1995, Lewes: Connect Publications

1 What, according to Sewell, is the cost of Black boys' lack of acceptance by the school?

2 What is the difference between 'innovators' and 'rebels'?

3 What do you think Sewell might mean by the 'intelligent strategies' adopted by innovators?

4 How does each subculture's behaviour relate to the traditional goals of education (academic success and progression to further education) and the accepted means of achieving them (hard work, cooperation and intellectual development)?

Focus on research activities

A recent piece of interesting and relevant research is summarized, followed by questions that encourage you to evaluate the methods used as well as the conclusions drawn.

Check your understanding

These comprise a set of basic comprehension questions – all answers can be found in the preceding text.

Check your understanding

1. What have been the overall trends in male and female achievement in the last 20 years?

2. How might changes in the economy affect both female and male attitudes towards education?

3. How may changes in both the organization of the education system and classroom practices have benefited the education of females?

4. How may aspects of boys' socialization explain why they underachieve at school?

5. What characteristics do male antischool cultures possess that undermine educational success for boys?

6. Explain how class and ethnicity may be just as important as gender in explaining the current achievement patterns of boys.

Web tasks

Activities using the worldwide web to develop your understanding and analysis skills. This feature also serves to identify some of the key websites for each topic.

web.task

The government's concern about gender and achievement is demonstrated by their creation of a website devoted to the issue. Visit it at www.standards.dfee.gov.uk/genderandachievement for statistical data and summaries of research.

Key terms

There are simple definitions of important terms and concepts used in each topic, linked to the context in which the word or phrase occurs. Most key terms are sociological, but some of the more difficult but essential vocabulary is also included. Each key term is printed **in bold type** the first time it appears in the main text.

KEY TERMS

Girls into Science and Technology a pre-National Curriculum initiative designed to encourage females to opt for science and technology.

Manufacturing industry industries that actually make goods. Most of the work in such industries is manual and based in factories.

Peer group status being seen as 'big' or important in the eyes of friends and other people around you.

PSE Personal and Social Education. Sometimes known as PSHE (including Health Education) or PSME (including Moral Education).

Service sector a group of economic activities loosely organized around finance, retail and personal care.

research ideas

- Conduct a content analysis of two science and technology textbooks used at your school or college. One should be significantly older than the other, if possible. Count the number of times that males and females appear in diagrams, photographs, etc., and record how they are shown. Find examples that are gender specific. What roles do they suggest as typical for each gender? Is there a change over time?

- Interview a sample of boys and girls. Try to find out if they have different expectations about future success. Are there differences in the amount of time they spend on homework?

Research ideas

Suggestions for small-scale research which could be used as the basis for AS or A2 coursework, or for class or homework activities.

---

exploring explanations of poverty

Item A The undeserving poor

<< So, let us get it straight from the outset: the underclass does not refer to a degree of poverty, but to a type of poverty.

It is not a new concept. I grew up knowing what the underclass was; we just didn't call it that in those days. One class of poor people was never even called poor – they simply lived with low incomes. Then there was another set of poor people … these poor people didn't lack just money. They were defined by their behaviour. Their homes were littered and unkempt. The men in the family were unable to hold a job for more than a few weeks at a time. Drunkenness was common.

The children grew up ill-schooled and ill-behaved and contributed a disproportionate share of the local juvenile delinquents.>>

Murray, C. (1990) *The Emerging British Underclass*, London: IEA (Health and Welfare Series), p. 1

Item B Look after yourself

The British labour market has many of the worst features of the USA – ranging from high turnover of staff to inequality of income – but without the compensating virtues of mobility and managerial dynamism. In the UK, the search for maximum and immediate profit to meet the demands of shareholders, means that firms are less willing to offer lifetime employment and less willing to undertake training, as both of these are costly. The result is that employees are paid the lowest possible wages, while the social benefits of pensions, health care, holidays and a general sense of caring for workers, both as employees and citizens, are largely absent. The underlying belief is that, in this kind of market economy, everybody looks after themselves.

Adapted from Hutton, W. (1995) *The State We're In*, London: Vintage, pp. 281–4

Item C From disadvantage to social exclusion

The problems of social exclusion are often linked and mutually reinforcing. The risk of social exclusion is highest for those with multiple disadvantages. The figure on the right illustrates this, showing that the likelihood of being out of work increases with the number of disadvantages experienced by an individual. For example, more than 50 per cent of those with three or more labour-market disadvantages are nonemployed, compared with 3 per cent without any of these characteristics.

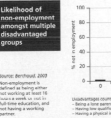

Likelihood of non-employment amongst multiple disadvantaged groups

Source: Berthoud, 2003

Non-employment is defined as being either not working at least 16 hours a week or not in full-time education, and not having a working partner.

Disadvantages counted:
– Being a lone parent or single person
– Having low qualifications or skills
– Having a physical impairment
– Being over 50
– Being from an ethnic minority group
– Living in a region of high unemployment

Source: Social Exclusion Unit (2004) *Tackling Social Exclusion: Taking stock and looking to the future*, London: Office of the Deputy Prime Minister

1. Explain what is meant by an 'underclass' (Item A). (2 marks)
2. Suggest two characteristics that Murray might associate with the underclass. (4 marks)
3. Identify three ways in which 'the search for maximum and immediate profit' may help harm the workforce (Item B). (6 marks)
4. Identify and briefly explain two reasons why there is a relationship between multiple disadvantage and unemployment (Item C). (8 marks)
5. Examine the view represented by the statement: 'What thoughtful rich people call the problem of poverty, thinking poor people call, with equal justice, the problem of riches'. (20 marks)
6. Using material from the Items and elsewhere, assess the extent to which the existence of an underclass is a key cause of poverty. (20 marks)

Exploring …

Data response activities which follow the format of AQA AS-level exam papers. They reflect the structure of AQA questions for each module and can be used to assess your progress at the end of each topic, as well as providing regular exam practice.

WHERE DO YOU BEGIN to look at a subject whose subject matter covers some of the most complicated and controversial issues facing humankind? Not an easy task. This introductory unit begins by focusing on two key themes in the study of human societies. The first theme, covered in Topic 1, explains how societies are created and identifies some of the forces that bind people together into social groups. Next, in Topic 2, comes an exploration of some of the inequalities that divide people and create tension in societies. These first topics cover the two 'core themes' that run through every part of the AQA Sociology specification that you are following.

Given the wide-ranging and controversial nature of the subject, it's not surprising that when sociologists look at societies, they focus on different things. For example, some see shared values and agreement, while others see conflict and inequality. The last four topics introduce you to the key sociological perspectives – perspectives that will reappear throughout your Sociology course.

Introduction to Sociology: key themes and perspectives

Socialization, culture and identity

gettingyouthinking

Feral children

Feral or 'wild' children are those who, for whatever reason, are not brought up by humans. One famous example of feral children is that of two infant girls, Kamala and Amala, who were lost in the jungle in India in about 1918. The girls had been found living with wolves, in a cave-like den. The older girl was 6 or 7 years old and the other, who died a year later, perhaps a year younger.

When captured, the girls were like animals. They were naked and ran in a sort of stooped crouch.

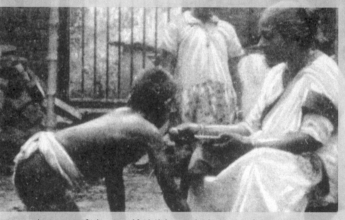

Kamala, one of the 'wolf children', being taught to accept food and drink by hand

They were afraid of artificial light. They were afraid of humans and kept a good distance. They did not display any characteristically human qualities. For example, they did not use tools of any kind, not even a stick. They did not know how to make a shelter. They did not walk upright. They did not laugh. They did not sing. They did not show any affection or attraction or curiosity towards humans. But what is especially striking is that the girls used no language. They used no noises or gestures to communicate. They didn't point at things or directions, or nod their head in agreement or disagreement. They preferred to eat with the dogs in the compound, who seemed to accept them. They ate by pushing their faces into the food, the way dogs do, and they drank by lapping from a bowl.

Adapted from Singh, J.A. and Zingg, R.N. (1942)
Wolf Children and the Feral Man, New York: Harper

Shirbit culture

The Shirbit culture believes that the human body is ugly and that its natural tendency is to feebleness and disease. The Shirbit therefore indulge in rituals and ceremonies designed to avoid this, and consequently every household has a shrine devoted to the body. The rituals associated with the shrine are private and secret. Adults never discuss the rituals and children are told only enough for them to be successfully initiated. The focal point of the shrine is a box built into the wall in which are kept charms and magical potions for the face and body. These are obtained from the medicine men who write down the ingredients in an ancient and secret language which is only understood by the herbalist who prepares the potion. These potions are kept in the charm-box for many years. Beneath the charm-box is a small font. Every day, twice a day, every member of the family enters the shrine room in succession and bows his or her head before the charm-box, mingles different sorts of holy water in the font and proceeds with a brief rite of ablution.

The Shirbit have an almost pathological horror of and fascination with the mouth, the condition of which is believed to have a supernatural influence on all social relationships. Were it not for the rituals of the mouth, they believe their teeth would fall out, their friends would desert them and their lovers would reject them. Finally, men and women indulge in barbaric acts of self-mutilation. Men engage in a daily body ritual of scraping and lacerating their faces with a sharp instrument, while women bake their heads in a small oven once a month.

Based on Levine, R. (1956) 'Body language of the Nacirema',
American Anthropologist, 58

1. Make a list of the things that the feral girls could not do and compare them with what you were capable of at the age of 6 or 7 years.

2. In your opinion, what skills were the feral girls likely to have that you lack?

3. What does the first extract tell us about the behaviour of human beings?

4. What aspects of Shirbit cultural behaviour seem alien to you?

5. In what ways might Shirbit behaviour be thought to resemble British culture?

Defining culture

What would you be like if all human influences were removed from your life? Tragic stories of **feral children**, such as that described on the left, show us very clearly that being human is about contact with other people. Without that contact we are reduced to basic and **instinctive** behaviour. But when humans work together – as they usually do – they create **cultures** that are complex, fascinating and utterly different. Our own culture always appears to be the most 'normal', while other cultures may seem strange, different and even inferior in some cases (a view known as **ethnocentrism**). Did you notice that the odd culture of the 'Shirbit' (described on the left) was actually a description of 'British' behaviour, especially our obsession with cleanliness, as it might appear to someone from a very different culture? ('Shirbit' is an anagram of 'British'.)

The idea of 'culture' is very important for sociologists. Culture is commonly defined as the way of life of a social group. More specifically, the term refers to 'patterns of belief, **values**, attitudes, expectations, ways of thinking, feeling and so on' which people use to make sense of their social worlds (Billington *et al.* 1998).

Some sociologists argue that culture also consists of **customs** and rituals, **norms** of behaviour, **statuses** and **roles**, language, symbols, art and material goods – the entire way in which a **society** expresses itself. Culture brings people together because it is shared and taken for granted. The idea of culture helps us to understand how individuals come together in groups and identify themselves as similar to or different from others.

When societies become larger and more complex, different cultures may emerge in the same society. Think of Britain today, where there are cultures based on different ages, genders, classes, ethnic groups, regions and so on – a situation known as **cultural diversity**. Sociologists refer to these 'cultures within cultures' as **subcultures**. They share some aspects of what we think of as 'British culture' – maybe eating with a knife and fork and speaking English – but they also possess distinctive cultural features that are all their own, for example, ways of dressing, accents and attitudes to the family.

The formation of culture

Culture is made up of several different elements, including values, norms, customs, statuses and roles.

Values

Values are widely accepted beliefs that something is worthwhile and desirable. For example, most societies place a high value on human life – although during wartime this value may be suspended. Other examples of British values include fair play, democracy, free speech, achievement, tolerance, wealth, property, romantic love, marriage and family life.

Norms

Norms are values put into practice. They are specific rules of behaviour that relate to specific social situations, and they govern all aspects of human behaviour. For example, norms govern the way we prepare and eat food, our toilet behaviour and so on. Norms also govern how we are supposed to behave according to our gender – that is, there are rules governing what counts as masculine or feminine behaviour. These norms have changed in recent years – for example, only 40 years ago, women with young babies going out to work or wearing trousers to work would have met with social disapproval.

Customs

Customs are traditional and regular norms of behaviour associated with specific social situations, events and anniversaries which are often accompanied by rituals and ceremonies. For example, in Britain many people practise the custom of celebrating Bonfire Night on November 5th, and this usually involves the ritual of burning a Guy Fawkes effigy and setting off fireworks.

It is also the social custom to mourn for the dead at funerals, and this usually involves an elaborate set of ritualistic norms and a ceremony. For example, it is generally expected that people wear black at funerals in Britain. Turning up in a pink tuxedo would be regarded as **deviant**, or norm-breaking, behaviour.

Statuses

All members of society are given a social position or status by their culture. Sociologists distinguish between 'ascribed' statuses and 'achieved' statuses. Ascribed statuses are fixed at birth, usually by inheritance or biology. For example, gender and race are fixed characteristics (which may result in women and ethnic minorities occupying low-status roles in some societies). Achieved statuses are those over which individuals have control. In Western societies, such status is normally attained through education, jobs and sometimes marriage.

Roles

Society expects those of a certain status to behave in a particular way. A set of norms is imposed on the status. These are collectively known as a role. For example, the role of 'doctor' is accompanied by cultural expectations about patient confidentiality and professional behaviour.

Culture and biology

Some people, known as **sociobiologists**, believe that human behaviour is largely the product of nature, so we can learn much about humans by studying animals. Most sociologists reject this view. If human behaviour were biologically determined, they argue, we could expect to see little variation in how people behave, whereas human behaviour is actually richly diverse. For example, if we look at other societies, we can see very different values and norms relating to gender roles, marriage, family and bringing up children. If human behaviour is influenced by biology at all, it is only at the level of physiological need – for example, we all need to sleep, eat and go to the toilet. However, when you look more closely, you find that even these biological influences are shaped by culture. Cultural values and norms determine what we eat. For example, insects are not popular as a food in Britain, and cannibalism would be regarded with horror. Cultural norms also determine *how* we eat. For example, eating behaviour is accompanied by a set of cultural norms called 'table manners', while the binge eating associated with bulimia is normally conducted in secret because of cultural disapproval.

Socialization and the transmission of culture

At birth, we are faced with a social world that already exists. Joining this world involves rapidly learning 'how things are done' in it. Only by learning the cultural rules of a society can a human interact with other humans. Culture needs to be passed on from generation to generation in order to ensure that it is shared. Shared culture allows society's members to communicate and cooperate. The process of learning culture is known as **socialization**. This involves learning the norms and values of a culture so that ways of thinking, behaving and seeing things are taken for granted or **internalized**.

Primary socialization

The family, and specifically parents, are central to **primary socialization**, the first stage in a lifelong process. Children learn language and basic norms and values. These can be taught formally, but they are more likely to be picked up informally by children imitating their parents. Parents may use **sanctions** to reinforce approved behaviour and punish behaviour defined as unacceptable. Such processes develop children's roles within the family and society so that children

learn how they are expected to behave in a range and variety of social situations.

Feral children

We can illustrate the importance of primary socialization and contact with culture by examining feral children (children brought up in the wild by animals) to see what cultural characteristics they lack. If we consider the case of Kamala and Amala (see p. 2), we can see that they lacked toilet training, table manners and any sense of decorum. They had no sense of humour and consequently did not know how to laugh. They had no sense of music and could not sing. They did not know how to show affection. All of these things are cultural products which we pick up within the family.

Secondary socialization

Other institutions and groups also participate in the socialization of children. These are often referred to as agents of **secondary socialization**. Schools, religion and the mass media all play a role in teaching society's members how to behave in particular situations and how to interact with people of a different status.

Socialization in all its varied forms involves children interacting with others and becoming aware of themselves as individuals. It is the process through which children acquire both a personal and a social **identity**.

Culture, socialization and history

Norbert Elias (1978) argues that the process of socialization has grown more influential throughout history, so that culture exerts a greater civilizing influence over our behaviour now than in any other historical age. He points out that in the Middle Ages, there were fewer cultural constraints on individual behaviour. People ate with their fingers, urinated and defecated in public, and engaged in explicit sexual behaviour that today would be defined as indecent and obscene. Moreover, burping, breaking wind, spitting and picking one's nose in public were regarded as perfectly normal forms of behaviour.

KEY TERMS

Cultural diversity describes a society in which many different cultures exist.

Culture the way of life of a particular society or social group.

Customs traditional forms of behaviour associated with particular social occasions.

Deviance rule-breaking behaviour.

Ethnocentrism the belief that one culture is 'normal' and others inferior.

Feral children children brought up with limited contact with humans.

Identity the sense of who we are.

Instinct a genetic or biological code in animals that largely determines their behaviour.

Internalize accept something so that it becomes 'taken for granted'.

Norms rules of behaviour in social situations.

Primary socialization socialization in the very early years of life, normally through parents.

Roles positions in society such as 'mother' or 'police officer'. Roles are made up of norms.

Sanctions actions that encourage or discourage particular behaviour, such as smiling or frowning at a young child.

Secondary socialization socialization that continues throughout life. Education, the media and religion are all important influences.

Socialization the process by which we learn acceptable cultural beliefs and behaviour.

Society a social system made up of social institutions such as the family, education, law, politics, the media, religion, peer groups, and so on.

Sociobiology the study of similarities between the natural and social worlds.

Status social position.

Subculture a group within a larger culture that shares aspects of that culture but also has some of its own values, customs and so on.

Values widely accepted beliefs that something is worthwhile.

Culture and society

The concept of 'culture' is often used interchangeably with the concept of 'society', but it is important to understand that they do not mean exactly the same thing. Culture forms the connection between the individual and society – it tells the individual how to operate effectively within social institutions such as the family, marriage, education and so on. Zygmunt Bauman (1990) notes that socialization into culture is about introducing and maintaining social order in society. Individual behaviour that lies outside the cultural norm is perceived as dangerous and worth opposing because it threatens to destabilize society. Consequently, societies develop cultural mechanisms to control and repress such behaviour.

Culture and identity

Culture plays an important role in the construction of our identity. Identity is made up of two components – how we see ourselves and how others see us. It involves some choice on our part – that is, we often actively identify with aspects of our culture in regard to particular groups or activities, e.g. a football team, a friendship network, a fashion or trend. However, our identity is partly imposed on us by our culture. We are born into particular cultural positions or statuses – we do not choose our social class, gender, ethnic group, age, religion and nationality. Social forces like these shape our identity.

Check your understanding

1. Using examples, define what is meant by the terms 'values' and 'norms'.
2. Give an example of an ascribed status in Britain.
3. Why do sociologists believe that human behaviour is not biologically determined?
4. What is the difference between primary and secondary socialization?
5. What role does culture play in the construction of identity?

exploring culture and socialization

Item A Active socialization

Socialization is the process whereby the helpless infant gradually becomes a self-aware, knowledgeable person, skilled in the ways of the culture into which she or he is born. Children obviously learn a great deal from their parents but they also learn basic values, norms and language, from a range of people, including grandparents (especially grandmothers), childminders and baby-sitters, siblings and neighbours who act as 'aunts', etc. There are other secondary influences, such as playgroups and nurseries, as well as television, video and computer games and traditional media such as comics or storybooks. Children do not passively absorb these influences. They are from the very beginning active beings. They 'make sense' of their experience and decide for themselves how to react.

Adapted from Giddens, A. (1997) *Sociology* (3rd edn), Cambridge: Polity Press, p. 25 and Bernardes, J. (1997) *Family Studies: An Introduction*, London: Routledge, p. 112

1. Explain what is meant by 'culture'. (2 marks)
2. Identify two social institutions that are responsible for the transmission of culture. (4 marks)
3. Identify three norms that are important in British culture today. (6 marks)
4. Identify and briefly illustrate two cultural influences on our sense of identity. (8 marks)

research idea

- Draw up a questionnaire to give to other students which aims to find out the extent to which culture is shared. You might ask about aspects of culture such as mealtimes and food customs, leisure activities, values and beliefs, and taste in music. Carry out the survey and analyse your results.

web.task

Visit **www.feralchildren.com**

Choose a child and write a report on them detailing how the child differs from children who have experienced normal socialization.

Social differentiation, power and stratification

gettingyouthinking

Where you rate in the new social order

1 Higher managerial & professional occupations

1.1 Employers & managers in large organizations
Company directors, corporate managers, police inspectors, bank managers, senior civil servants, military officers

1.2 Higher professionals
Doctors, barristers and solicitors, clergy, librarians, social workers, teachers

2 Lower managerial & professional occupations
Nurses and midwives, journalists, actors and musicians, prison officers, police, soldiers (NCO and below)

3 Intermediate occupations
Clerks, secretaries, driving instructors, computer operators, telephone fitters

4 Small employers & own account workers
Publicans, playgroup leaders, farmers, taxi drivers, window cleaners, painters and decorators

5 Lower supervisory, craft & related occupations
Printers, plumbers, butchers, bus inspectors, TV engineers, train drivers

6 Semi-routine occupations
Shop assistants, traffic wardens, cooks, bus drivers, hairdressers, postal workers

7 Routine occupations
Waiters, road sweepers, cleaners, couriers, building labourers, refuse collectors

8 Never worked/long-term unemployed

Source: *The Guardian*, 15 January 1999

1 The *Guardian* cartoon above shows the government's new social classification of the population, which is based on eight job categories. Examine it carefully and try and work out what has been used to distinguish the categories.

2 Where would the Royal Family fit into this classification?

3 Using the occupational examples listed in each category, allocate David and Victoria Beckham, and Richard Branson (owner of Virgin) to a social class.

4 What problems have you identified with this classification system?

Despite being a wealthy country that can offer its citizens a very good standard of living, the UK is still characterized by great inequalities in wealth and income that affect people's opportunities in life (known as **life chances**), such as their level of educational qualification and life expectancy. In the words of Tony Blair, in the UK, a great number of people are 'socially excluded' from taking part in activities which the rest of society takes for granted. For example, in 2001, it was estimated that five million children were living in poverty. What these inequalities tell us is that the UK is a society characterized by social **stratification** – people are ranked hierarchically according to social and economic factors such as wealth, income, qualifications, skills and so on.

One way in which the government attempts to keep tabs on the extent of these inequalities is through the use of the occupational classification illustrated in the cartoon on the left known as the National Statistics: Socio-Economic Classification (NS-SEC). This was introduced in 2000. This system is based on a rather complex collection of criteria, e.g. levels of skill, authority over others, salary, promotion prospects, control over the work process, hours worked and so on. However, many sociologists are unhappy with this system for reasons which you may have spotted when you attempted to allocate Her Majesty to it. The system fails to account for those wealthy enough not to have to work – in other words, a significant proportion of the rich who live off inherited wealth, share dividends, rents and so on are not covered by it. Moreover, you will have seen that it was also difficult to allocate our 'celebrities' to these occupational categories. By rights, Victoria Beckham (as 'Posh Spice') should have been allocated to social class 2, while David Beckham doesn't fit in any of categories, so their extreme wealth makes a mockery of this system.

Other sociologists point out that social class, i.e. our socio-economic position in society, is only one form of inequality and stratification that exists in UK society. It is argued by feminists that gender is an important source of inequality while other sociologists point out that the UK is a **multicultural** society in which racism and, consequently, ethnic inequalities are a daily fact of life. More recently, sociological research has focused on disability, age and sexuality as producing newer forms of inequality and stratification.

Whatever forms of stratification exist, we can see that those at the top of the system experience many more benefits in terms of life chances and standard of living than those beneath them. We have already identified inequalities in education and health, but we can also see differences in political **power**. Those at the top of the stratification system are often in a position to maintain inequality against the will of others and to generate further economic and social advantages for themselves.

Differentiation and stratification

Social differences exist in every society. Social **differentiation** may take the form of variations in aspects of culture such as dress, language or customs, or in the degree of power, wealth and status accorded to individuals and groups. Stratification refers to the process by which groups of people are ranked hierarchically into strata or layers which come to share specific characteristics, such as being wealthy or poor, powerful or powerless, and so on.

There are a number of different types of stratification. The oldest form is probably **slavery**. Many ancient societies practised slavery and, as recently as the early 19th century, the slave trade – the transportation to the New World of millions of Africans – was dominated by the British. Slave labour still continues in varied forms around the world today. Some sociologists see it as the basis of inequalities that exist around race and ethnicity in contemporary Britain.

Another type of stratification is **feudalism**. This medieval system was based on a hierarchical system of land ownership, with the king at the top lending land in return for services and loyalty from his nobles. At the bottom of this system was the peasant who had few rights – for instance, they often could not marry without permission of the local lord of the manor.

Caste is a stratification system found in India and among minority ethnic groups that migrated to Britain from South Asia. It is usually associated with Hinduism (although Sikhs and Muslims also practise forms of caste). In the Hindu version, people are born into closed groups called *varna* which are ranked on the basis of religious purity achieved in a previous life. If you were especially bad in a previous life, you might be born into the non-caste group called 'untouchables', who have the least **status** in Hindu society.

Some sociologists point out that many societies often stratify on the basis of belonging to particular tribes or clans – as in Scotland until the late 18th century. Others stratify along racial or ethnic lines. The system of segregation formerly found in the Southern states of the USA and the South African system of apartheid, which was only dismantled in the late 1980s, are good examples of stratification based on notions of racial superiority.

Social class

In the UK, social class is regarded as the main form of stratification. However, it differs from the previous forms described in that the UK is regarded as an open rather than closed society. In other words, in the UK it is possible to achieve **upward mobility** through acquiring qualifications, hard work, and even marriage. Class societies are therefore regarded as achievement-orientated or **meritocratic** systems, although some sociologists disagree on this point by pointing out that some people, especially those from upper-class backgrounds educated in public schools and Oxbridge, have more opportunities to succeed than the majority of the population. Certainly, Tony Blair believes we are an open society – in 1999, he said: 'I believe we will have an expanded middle class, with ladders of opportunity for those of all backgrounds.' Sociologists such as Marxists are sceptical of this claim, as you will see in Topic 4.

The class structure

It is generally agreed that four broad social classes exist in the UK.

The upper class

The upper class is thought to be made up of three categories of rich people in Britain:

1 *the jet-set rich* – includes film stars, rock stars and sports professionals
2 *landowners* – people whose wealth in the form of land and property has been largely inherited
3 *the entrepreneurial rich* – those who wealth is wrapped up in stocks and shares. Some, e.g. the Sainsbury family, have inherited their wealth, whereas others, e.g. Richard Branson (shown on p. 6), are self-made millionaires.

The middle classes

This term refers to a number of **non-manual** social groups. The term implies that they have a great deal in common when there are often distinct differences between them:

● *Professionals* – Doctors, solicitors, teachers, lecturers, etc. This group is characterized by high levels of education which equips them with **cultural capital**, i.e. the knowledge, attitudes and skills required so that their children can also take advantage of further and higher education.
● *Managers* – This group tends to have worked its way up from the shop or office floor and tends to have skills specific to particular organizations. The job security of this group is constantly under threat from economic recession.
● *White-collar workers* – Clerks, secretaries, etc., carrying out routine tasks and employed by organizations such as banks, building societies and insurance firms. Some sociologists argue that the pay and working conditions of this group have deteriorated so much that they have more in common with the working classes than the middle class.
● *The petit-bourgeoisie* – The self-employed, such as farmers and hauliers. There are signs that this group is increasingly adopting radical methods to protect their interests, which they see as under threat.

The working classes

This concept refers to skilled, semi-skilled and unskilled **manual workers** who make up about 50 per cent of the workforce. They generally enjoy fewer privileges than middle-class workers in terms of holidays, sick pay, opportunities for promotion, pensions, etc., and their jobs are generally less secure. There are also major differences in educational qualifications, life expectancy, infant mortality, housing and leisure pursuits between the working class and other social classes.

The underclass

Recently, some sociologists have claimed that an **underclass** has appeared at the bottom end of the working class. This group is supposed to be deviant in that it is workshy, happy to live off state benefits, involved in criminal activities and promiscuous. Critics of this idea suggest that it stereotypes the poor as 'undeserving'. They argue that the number of people in poverty through no fault of their own – because of economic recession, cuts in welfare spending and so on – has actually increased in the last 10 years.

Social status

Some sociologists argue that social differences are just as important as class differences in the UK. It is argued that social status does not always derive from economic factors such as wealth and income. It can also derive from education, occupation, speech, dress, age, gender and race. For example, people do not look up to doctors and follow their orders unquestioningly because doctors are wealthy or earn more than they do. Rather, we respect doctors because they have spent years in training, learning what the rest of us see as very difficult skills. This issue of status has led sociologists to explore a range of social differences which they suggest are just as important as social class differences.

Gender

Feminists see British society as **patriarchal** (i.e. male dominated). They claim that men have used their economic and cultural power to define women and women's interests as subordinate to men and men's interests. They claim that in every sphere of social life, patterned gender inequalities can be seen. These ideas are explored in further detail in Topic 4.

Race and ethnicity

It can be argued that inequalities are also stratified across ethnic lines in the UK. If we examine the evidence, we can see that White children generally do better in education than children from minority ethnic groups (with the exception of Indian and Chinese children, who do slightly better on average than Whites). With regard to indicators such as unemployment, low-skilled and low-paid jobs, life expectancy, infant mortality rates and housing, people from African-Caribbean, Pakistani and Bangladeshi backgrounds do substantially worse than White people. Moreover, there is evidence that the police and courts treat these groups more harshly than White offenders.

These inequalities and the lack of power that results from them have led some sociologists to conclude that institutional racism exists across a range of British institutions, including the police, the judicial system, the prison service and the NHS. It is suggested that such institutions discriminate against ethnic minorities because they are organized around a set of often unconscious stereotypes and discriminatory practices that are taken for granted, habitual and often not recognized as racism.

Disability

In recent years, we have increasingly recognized that disability is not only a medical condition, but also a social condition, in that the way that society reacts to the disabled can have a negative effect on them. In other words, they have been 'disabled by society'. It is argued that disabled people have been socially marginalized and discriminated against by social attitudes. This has led to exclusion from mainstream employment, education, housing, and leisure opportunities. A growing number of disabled people have challenged negative stereotypes and

Mike Oliver
The politics of disablement

Oliver's (1990) research questions the dominant social attitude that the inequalities that disabled people face lie in their lack of physical and mental capabilities. Oliver was very critical of questions aimed at the disabled in the 1985 Office of Population Census Studies. This questionnaire included the following:

(a) Can you tell me what is wrong with you?

(b) What complaint causes your difficulty in holding, gripping or turning things?

(c) Does your health problem/disability mean that you need to live with relatives or someone else who can help look after you?

(d) Does your health problem/disability make it difficult for you to travel by bus?

(e) Does your health problem/disability affect your work in any way at present?

Oliver argues that the questions above are discriminatory because they assume personal inadequacy. Oliver argues that these questions are typical of a society whose attitudes are mainly responsible for bringing about social barriers that make it hard for disabled people to experience normal lives.

1 Taking each question in turn, how does each one presuppose that disability is the problem?

2 How would you modify these to reflect Oliver's view that social attitudes and practices are the main reason that the disabled find it difficult to lead normal lives?

discriminatory social policies by organizing pressure groups to develop positive identities among the disabled and to petition for fairer treatment.

Ageism

Age is another source of status inequality. The young and elderly both lack status in modern British society. In many societies around the world, the elderly acquire status as they get older. They are revered as wise and society feels a strong duty to care for them. This is not the case in the UK, where the elderly often experience **ageism** – prejudicial attitudes and discriminatory practices which dismiss them as a problem or burden. In 2003, the government announced plans to make ageism illegal.

Sexuality

Finally, sexuality may be another source of inequality. It is certainly the case that gay men and lesbians do not enjoy equal status with heterosexual people, despite nearly 40 years of legalization. There is still a strong tendency in society that defines these types of sexuality as deviant and unnatural. Moreover, this **homophobia** (dislike of homosexuality) has extended to erroneous media coverage of Aids as a 'gay plague', despite Aids being overwhelmingly a heterosexual problem worldwide. It has also led to discrimination in the form of physical attacks on – and the murder of – people solely because they are homosexual.

KEY TERMS

Ageism discrimination based upon negative stereotypes, usually focusing on the elderly.

Cultural capital cultural skills, such as knowing how to behave, speak and learn, passed on by middle-class parents to their children.

Differentiation ways of distinguishing between social groups, e.g. the NS-SEC distinguishes between occupational groups.

Feudalism medieval system of stratification based on the ownership of land.

Homophobia prejudice and discrimination against gay people.

life chances opportunities or lack of them to acquire material, social and cultural rewards, such as jobs, qualifications or good health.

Manual work physical labour.

Meritocratic rewards on the basis of achievement, i.e. effort, ability and intelligence.

Multicultural characterized by a variety of ethnic groups.

Non-manual work work which mainly involves mental labour.

Patriarchal male dominated.

Power the ability to maintain inequality against the will of others.

Social exclusion missing out on opportunities and activities that most other people take for granted because of poverty or other factors beyond your control.

Status prestige.

Slavery form of stratification where people are either owned by others or are forced to work for no or very little pay.

Stratification hierarchical ranking based on social status, resulting in patterns of inequality.

Underclass a social group in poverty which (depending on your perspective) is a product of workshy attitudes and an overgenerous benefit system or a product of economic recession.

Upward social mobility the ability to move upwards through the class system, e.g. from working class to middle class.

Paxton and Dixon (2004)
The State of the Nation: Inequality in the UK

Poverty

- In 1998, the UK was bottom of the European league, with the highest child poverty rate in the EU, but by 2001, the UK had risen to 11th out of 15. Yet compared to the best-performing European countries, the UK still has a poor record.

Inequality

- Although the gender pay gap has narrowed, only very slow progress has been made since 1994. In 1994, women in full-time work earned on average 79.5 per cent of what men earned. By 2003, this had only increased to 82 per cent.
- Wealth distribution has continued to widen in the last decade. Between 1990 and 2001, the percentage of wealth held by the wealthiest 10 per cent of the population increased from 47 per cent to 54 per cent.
- Regional inequalities remain large. In the South East, 17 per cent of people are in the poorest 20 per cent of the population, compared with 26 per cent of people in the North East.

Education

- Between 1989 and 2002, there has been a general improvement in educational attainment, but a class gap remains. 74 per cent of children from the highest social classes achieved five or more GCSEs at grades A* to C in 2002, more than twice the proportion of children in the lowest social classes.

- Entry to higher education has increased from 19 per cent in 1990 to 31 per cent in 2000, but it has benefited the well-off more than the poor. In 2002, while just over 40 per cent of teenagers from higher professional backgrounds were in higher education, the figure for those from the lowest social class was just 11 per cent.

Citizenship

- Interest in politics has fallen slightly across all social classes, but there is a growing class divide. Between 1991 and 1999 for the lowest social classes, interest in politics halved.
- People's sense of empowerment – the feeling that they could influence decisions if they wanted to – is lower among the more deprived. Fifty-one per cent of the top social class felt they could influence decisions at a local level in 2003, compared to just 33 per cent of the bottom social class.

Quality of life

- Since 1996, levels of life satisfaction appear to have declined for the poor.
- Between 1996 and 2003, the proportion of those on low incomes satisfied with family life fell by 15 per cent from 60 to 45 per cent.
- Perceived levels of antisocial behaviour have risen since 1992 with concerns particularly felt in deprived areas. Twenty-eight per cent of households earning less than £5000 perceived antisocial behaviour to be a 'very or fairly big problem' in their area in 2002/3, compared to just 18 per cent of those earning above £30 000.
- The poorest continue to be more likely to fear and suffer from crime. In the most disadvantaged areas, 5.7 per cent of households were victims of violent crime, compared with 2.9 per cent of households in the least disadvantaged.
- Life expectancy in different social classes at the age of 65 has polarized. The difference between men from the highest and lowest social class in 1997/9 was 4.1 years, an increase from a difference of 2.6 years in 1972/6.
- Deprived communities suffer worse effects of environmental degradation.
- Industrial sites are disproportionately located in deprived areas: in 2003, there were five times as many sites in the bottom 10 per cent of wards, and seven times as many emission sources, than in the top 10 per cent of wards.

Adapted from Paxton, W. and Dixon, M. (2004), *The State of the Nation*, Institute for Public Policy Research

---

Choose any two of the points outlined above.

1 How might the data have been collected? How accurate do you think it is? Explain your answer.

2 Suggest ways in which any two of these inequalities might be reduced.

Check your understanding

1 What is the NS-SEC used for?

2 Explain why the caste system is 'closed' and class systems are 'open'.

3 What groups make up the upper class and the middle class?

4 What is meant by social status?

5 Identify five sources of social status that exist in modern Britain, apart from social class.

research idea

- Conduct a survey to find out the extent of class identity among a sample of young people.
  - What classes do they think exist?
  - Do they believe that class is still important?
  - Do they feel that they belong to any particular class?
  - Do they feel that their gender, ethnicity, age or sexuality is more important?

web.task

Visit the following websites and document the types of different inequalities experienced by a variety of status groups:

- **The Disability Archive of the Centre for Disability Studies at Leeds University** includes a range of resources written by disabled sociologists, including Colin Barnes and Tom Shakespeare **www.leeds.ac.uk/disability-studies**

- **Help the Aged – www.ageconcern.org.uk –** this site contains details of the different forms that ageism takes today

- **Outrage is an organization which fights discrimination against gay people – www.outrage.org.uk**

- **The Commission for Racial Equality documents inequality relating to ethnic minorities in the UK – www.cre.gov.uk/ –** as does The Runnymede Trust – **www.runnymedetrust.org/**

- **The Equal Opportunities Commission documents Inequalities experienced by women – www.eoc.org.uk**

exploring social differentiation, power and stratification

Item A The importance of social class

Sociologists typically approach the unequal distribution of scarce resources as a study of stratification. The term 'stratification' refers to the fact that there is inequality of resources between groups of people, and that these form a structured, or systematic, hierarchy. As a matter of fact, on average, men have more resources than women; property owners more than employees; professional workers more than unskilled manual workers; White people more than Black; older people more than younger ones, and so on.

Class divisions remain the most important of inequalities in British society. Class continues to exert a great influence on our lives, and inequalities between the poor and wealthy have increased in the last 20 years. Gender and ethnicity are increasingly important but it is important to acknowledge that middle-class women enjoy more opportunities than working-class men and women, whilst the middle-class members of minority ethnic groups are advantaged compared to working-class people of any ethnicity.

1 Explain what is meant by 'stratification'. (2 marks)

2 Identify two advantages in terms of life chances that the middle class enjoy over the working class. (4 marks)

3 Identify three sources of inequality associated with age. (6 marks)

4 Identify and briefly describe two ways in which disabled people might be disabled by society. (8 marks)

Consensus, culture and identity

<< Examining the homes in an English suburb, Nigel Barley noticed how organized they are. They begin with front gardens which must be kept in good order but never sat in; it is only permissible to sit in back gardens. Front doors, often elaborately furnished, open into a hall and various public rooms. Rooms are segregated according to functions relating to human bodily functions, such as eating, washing and defecating. Dinner, for example, will only be served in a bedroom if someone is ill. Access to rooms is regulated, so that access to the sitting room implies more formality than the kitchen, and lavatories can be used by visitors with permission. Bedrooms, where the most private undressing and sexual functions are performed, are considered to be the most personal rooms, and people knock on bedroom doors. The ideal is for each individual or sexual couple to have their own bedroom, and for new couples to have a new house. Bedrooms are individually furnished or decorated by their inhabitants, but it is never difficult to identify which member of the family owns a particular bedroom or their age or sex.>>

Billington, R. *et al.* (1998) *Exploring Self and Society*, Basingstoke: Macmillan, pp. 38–9

1 Can Barley's description of the suburban home be applied to your experience of home?

2 Do you think this description is typical of most homes in the UK?

3 Barley is describing a very ordered and structured world. What do you think is the reason for all this order and predictability? Where does it come from?

We learn from an early age to see our status as wrapped up with our home, and to see a happy family and home as important goals. In other words, there exists a great deal of agreement in society about how we ought to organize our daily lives. Sociologists refer to this agreement among members of society as **consensus**. This consensus means that we have a good idea of how we should behave in most situations. It also means that we can anticipate pretty accurately how other people are going to behave, just as we can guess the layout of their house or flat. Some sociologists see this order and predictability as the key to understanding society. If this order did not exist – if we were always confused and uncertain about our own and others' values and behaviour – then, they believe, chaos and anarchy would be the result. This theory of society is known as **functionalism** or consensus theory.

Functionalism

Functionalism is a **structuralist theory**. This means that it sees the individual as less important than the **social structure** or organization of society. It is a 'top-down' theory that looks at society rather than the individuals within it. Society is more important because the individual is produced by society. People are the product of all the social influences on them: their family, friends, educational and religious background, their experiences at work, in leisure, and their exposure to the media. All of these influences make them what they are. They are born into society, play their role in it and then die. But their deaths do not mean the end of society. Society continues long after they are gone.

Social order

Functionalists study the role of different parts of society – social institutions – in bringing about the patterns of shared and stable behaviour that they refer to as **social order**. They might study, for example, how families teach children the difference between right and wrong, or how education provides people with the skills and qualifications needed in the world of work. For functionalists, society is a complex system made up of parts that all work together to keep the whole system going. The economic system (work), the political system, family and kinship, and the cultural system (education, mass media, religion and youth culture) all have their part to play in maintaining a stable society from generation to generation.

A major function of social institutions is to socialize every individual into a system of norms and values that will guide their future behaviour and thinking. People need to be taught the core values of their society and to internalize them, so that they become shared and 'taken for granted'. The end result of this process is **value consensus** – members of society agree on what counts as important values and standards of behaviour. Such consensus produces a sense of **social solidarity**, i.e. we feel a sense of belonging to a group that has something in common. We feel a sense of common **identity**.

Another important foundation stone of social order in modern societies is the specialized division of labour. This refers to the organization of jobs and skills in a society. All members of society are dependent upon this division of labour, which supplies a vast and invisible army of workers to maintain the standard of living we take for granted. For example, hundreds of unskilled and skilled manual workers, professionals and managers are involved in supplying us with essential services such as electricity, gas, water, sewage systems, transport, food in supermarkets, and so on. The fact that you are able to sit in a classroom and read this book is also the product of hundreds of workers you will never see or meet. For example, someone has decided that your area needs a school or college, somebody has hired a caretaker to open and maintain the building, cleaners to clean, secretaries to run the office, teachers to teach and managers to decide to put on AS Sociology. The presence of this book in front of you required an author, editors, proofreaders, graphic designers, picture researchers, illustrators, a publisher, printers, people involved in the production of paper and ink, lorry drivers to transport the finished product to warehouses and bookshops, and someone behind the counter or a computer to sell it on to schools, teachers and students. Note, too, that you are already part of this division of labour. Without students, educational institutions would be pointless. The list of people we are dependent upon is endless. Think about how your life would change if all electricity workers were abducted by aliens overnight!

The specialized division of labour, therefore, is crucial because without it, society would soon descend into chaos. Consequently, another function of **social institutions** is to prepare young people to take their place in the division of labour by transmitting the idea that education, qualifications, working hard and a career are all worthwhile things. This ensures that young people will eventually come to replace workers who have retired or died, and so social order is maintained.

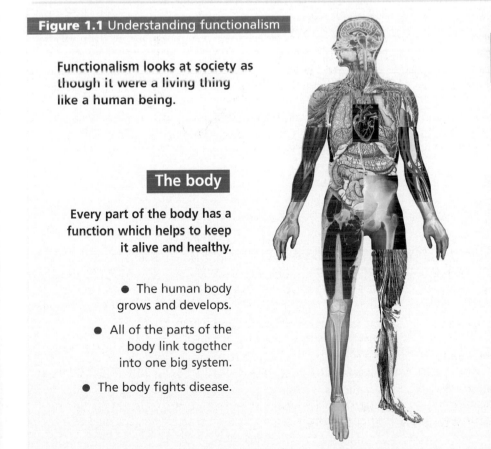

Figure 1.1 Understanding functionalism

Functionalism looks at society as though it were a living thing like a human being.

How is society like a human body?

The body

Every part of the body has a function which helps to keep it alive and healthy.

- The human body grows and develops.
- All of the parts of the body link together into one big system.
- The body fights disease.

Society

Every part of society helps to keep society going – for example, the family helps by bringing up the next generation.

- Societies gradually develop and change.
- All of the parts of society work together and depend on each other – they are interdependent.
- Society has mechanisms to deal with problems when they occur, such as the police and the legal system.

Talcott Parsons

Talcott Parsons (1902–79) was a key functionalist thinker. He argued that socialization is the key to understanding human behaviour patterns. The role of social institutions, such as the family, education, religion and the media, is to ensure the passing on, or reproduction, of socially acceptable patterns of behaviour. Social institutions do this in a number of ways:

● They socialize people into key values of society, such as the importance of nuclear family life, achievement, respect for authority and hierarchy, and so on. The result is that most members of our society share common values and norms of behaviour (value consensus) and consequently, we can predict how people are going to behave in the vast majority of social situations. The family, education and the mass media are primarily responsible for this function.
● They give some values and norms a sacred quality, so that they become powerful formal and informal moral codes governing social behaviour. These moral codes underpin our definitions of criminal, deviant and immoral behaviour. An example of a formal moral code is 'do not steal', because it is embodied in the law, while examples of more informal moral codes are 'do not lie' or 'do not commit adultery'. The social institutions of religion and the law are primarily responsible for the transmission of these codes, although media reporting of crime and deviance also contributes by reminding members of society about what counts as normality and deviance, and publicizing the punishments handed out to those who indulge in behaviour that lies outside the consensus.
● They encourage social solidarity (a sense of community) and **social integration** (a sense of belonging). For example, the teaching of history is an important means of achieving this goal, because it reminds members of society about their shared culture.

So, our behaviour is controlled by the rules of the society into which we are born. The result is that we don't have to be told that what we are doing is socially unacceptable. We will probably feel inhibited from indulging in such behaviour in the first place because we are so successfully immersed in the common values of society by our experience of socialization.

Identity

Identity is the way we feel about ourselves, which is partly shaped by how others view us. People's identity as fathers, mothers and children, for example, is controlled by a value consensus. This defines and therefore largely determines what roles each status has to adopt if it is to fit successfully into society. In other words, there is a clear set of expectations about what makes a 'good' mother or father, son or daughter. For example, people defined as 'normal' parents will engage in socially approved behaviour – they will protect their children from harm rather than neglect them or inflict excessive physical punishment on them; they will give them unconditional love; they will support them economically, and so on. Note that these expectations may change according to gender – hence the commonly held belief that working mothers, rather than working fathers, may be a cause of psychological damage in children. Functionalists point out that our experience of socialization and social control ensures that most of us will attempt to live up to those social and cultural expectations without question.

Criticisms of functionalism

Functionalism is far less popular in sociology today than it was in the 1950s. Part of its decline in popularity is probably linked to the problems it had attempting to explain all the diversity and conflict that existed in society from the 1960s onwards. Criticism of functionalism has therefore been widespread:

● Functionalism has been criticized for overemphasizing consensus and order, and failing to explain the social conflicts that characterize the modern world. We see clear differences in behaviour all around us every day, and there may be clear cultural differences present in the same society. For example, behaviours on which most of society might have been agreed 50 years ago, such as women with young children going out to work, cohabitation, abortion or homosexuality (which were all regarded as wrong), now attract a range of differing opinions. Some functionalists have attempted to explain this by reference to subculture. This can be defined as a way of life subscribed to by a significant minority who may share some general values and norms with the larger culture, but who may be in opposition to others. For example, in a

Sociology AS for AQA

KEY TERMS

Consensus a general agreement.

Functionalism a sociological perspective that focuses on understanding how the different parts of society work together to keep it running smoothly.

Identity the way we feel about ourselves.

Social institution a part of society such as education or the family.

Social integration a sense of belonging to society.

Social order patterns of shared and predictable behaviour.

Social solidarity a sense of community.

Social structure an alternative term for the social organization of society.

Structuralist theory a theory that believes that human behaviour is influenced by the organization of society.

Value, or moral, consensus an agreement among a majority of members of society that something is good and worthwhile.

multicultural society like the UK, some minority ethnic groups may retain very traditional ideas about women's roles, marriage, homosexuality, etc.

- Functionalism has also been accused of ignoring the freedom of choice enjoyed by individuals. People choose what to do – they do what makes sense to them. Their behaviour and ideas are not imposed on them by structural factors beyond their control. In this sense, functionalism may present 'an oversocialized' picture of human beings.
- There may also be problems in the way functionalists view socialization as a positive process that never fails. If this were the case, then delinquency, child abuse and illegal drug-taking would not be the social problems they are.
- Finally, functionalism has been accused by Marxists of ignoring the fact that power is not equally distributed in society. Some groups have more wealth and power than others and may be able to impose their norms and values on less powerful groups. The next few topics focus on this process.

Check your understanding

1 Using your own words, explain what is meant by value consensus.

2 What are the key values of society according to Parsons, and what agencies are mainly responsible for their transmission?

3 What agencies are responsible for turning key values into powerful moral codes that guide our most basic behaviour?

4 Why do social agencies such as the law and the media need to regulate our behaviour?

5 How might the teaching of British history encourage a sense of community and integration in British schools?

exploring consensus, culture and identity

Item A Key social institutions

Durkheim believed that the function of social institutions was to promote and maintain social cohesion and unity. The family is one of the key institutions binding the individual into the fabric of social life. It provides society with an orderly means of reproduction and provides physical and economic support for children during the early years of dependence. The child learns the essential ideas and values, patterns of behaviour and social roles (such as gender roles) required for adult life. Education develops both values and the intellectual skills needed by children to perform the role in the specialized division of labour and society to which they are allocated. The discipline structure and socialization of children in schools function to maintain consensus and ensure that society operates smoothly. Religion provides a set of moral beliefs and practices which socially integrates people into a common identity and community.

Adapted from Chapman, K. (1986) *The Sociology of Schools*, London: Routledge, p. 38; Thompson, I. (1986) *Religion*, London: Longman, pp. 4–5; and Wilson, A. (1991) *Family*, London: Longman, pp. 9–10

1 Explain what is meant by 'the specialized division of labour'. (2 marks)

2 Identify two functions of religion (Item A). (4 marks)

3 Identify three examples which suggest that socialization is not as successful as functionalists claim. (6 marks)

4 Identify and briefly explain two reasons why functionalists might be criticized for overemphasizing consensus and order. (8 marks)

research idea

- Interview a sample of people of different ages and genders about their values. To what extent do they share similar values?

web.task

Search for the website 'Dead Sociologists' Society'. Use it to find out about the ideas of the founding father of functionalism, Emile Durkheim.

Conflict, culture and identity

getting you thinking

Imagine that we could illustrate the distribution of income in the UK by getting the population to take part in a parade that will take an hour to pass by. Imagine, too, that we can somehow magically alter the height of individuals in the parade so that it reflects how much money they have. Those with an average income will have a height of 5ft 8in. Our parade begins with those with the lowest incomes – in other words, the shortest people – and ends with those with the highest incomes – in other words, the tallest people.

The first people to pass by are tiny. For example, after three minutes, an unemployed single mother living on welfare goes by. She is about 1ft 10in high. Six minutes later a single male pensioner, owning his own home and claiming income support, passes by. He is about 2ft 6in high. After 21 minutes, semi-skilled manual workers start to pass by – they are 3ft 9in high. After 30 minutes, there is still no sign of the people

earning average incomes. We don't see these until 62 per cent of the population have gone by. After about 45 minutes skilled technicians pass – they are 6ft 10in tall. With ten minutes to go, heights really start to grow. Middle-class professionals pass by – they are 11 feet high. However, the real giants only appear in the last minute of the parade. Chief executives of companies over 60 feet high. In the last seconds, there are amazing increases in height. Suddenly, the scene is dominated by colossal figures, people as high as tower blocks. Most of them are businessmen, owners of companies, film stars and a few members of the Royal Family. Robbie Williams and Prince Charles are nearly a mile high. Britain's richest man is the last in the parade, measuring four miles high.

Adapted from Penn, J., quoted in Donaldson, P. (1973) *A Guide to the British Economy*, Harmondsworth: Penguin

1. What does this parade tell us about the way income is divided in the UK?
2. Give examples of how long it took for people on different incomes to appear in the parade.
3. Does the parade surprise you in any way? Is Britain more, or less, unequal than you thought?

Lots of students have part-time jobs. Perhaps you have. If so, you sell your time and your ability to work to an employer who, in return, gives you money. But is this a fair exchange? Think about why they employ you. It's not to do you a favour, but because they benefit: the work you do is worth more to them than the amount they pay you. They would benefit even more if they paid you less for the same work or got you to do more

work for the same pay. Of course, it would be better for you if you were paid more for the same work or worked less for the same pay. To put it another way, what is good for your boss is bad for you, and vice versa. There's a very basic conflict of interest between you and your employer. This conflict occurs not because you are unreasonable or your boss is money-grabbing. It occurs simply because the system works that way.

Marxism

This is the starting point for **Marxism**, a sociological perspective based on the ideas of Karl Marx (1818–83). For Marxists, the system we live in (which he called **capitalism**) divides everyone up into two basic classes: bosses and workers. Marx called the bosses the **bourgeoisie** or ruling class (because they controlled society), and the workers he called the **proletariat**. The ruling class benefit in every way from how society operates, while the workers get far less than they deserve.

Like functionalism, Marxism is a structuralist theory – that is, it sees the individual as less important than the social structure of society. In particular, Marxism sees the economic organization of societies as responsible for the behaviour of individuals. This is because Marxism claims that individuals are the products of the class relationships that characterize economic life.

Society is based on an exploitative and unequal relationship between two economic classes. The bourgeoisie are the economically dominant class (the ruling class) who own the **means of production** (machinery, factories, land, etc.). The proletariat or working class, on the other hand, own only their ability to work. They sell this to the bourgeoisie in return for a wage. However, the relationship between these two classes is unequal and based on conflict because the bourgeoisie aim to extract the maximum labour from workers at the lowest possible cost.

According to Marxists, the result is that the bourgeoisie exploit the labour of the working class. The difference between the value of the goods and services produced by the worker and the wages paid is pocketed by the capitalist class and lies at the heart of the vast profits made by many employers. These profits fuel the great inequalities in wealth and income between the ruling class and the working class. For example, according to the Inland Revenue, in 1994, 53 per cent of financial wealth in the UK was owned by 5 per cent of the population. Even if we add property ownership to financial wealth, the least wealthy 50 per cent of the population only own about 10 per cent of all wealth in the UK. These figures are also likely to be underestimates, because people generally do not declare the full sum of their wealth to the tax authorities – for instance, they may keep wealth abroad.

If society is so unfair, how come the working class go along with it? Why aren't there riots, strikes and political rebellion? Why does society actually appear quite stable, with most people pretty content with their position?

Ideology

Marxists argue that the working class rarely challenge capitalism because those who control the economy also control the family, education, media, religion – in fact, all the cultural institutions that are responsible for socializing individuals. Louis Althusser (1971) argued that the function of those cultural institutions is to maintain and **legitimate** class inequality. The family, education, the mass media and religion pass off ruling-class norms and values as 'normal' and 'natural'. Marxists refer to these ruling-class ideas as **ideology**.

Socialization is an ideological process in that its main aim is to transmit the ruling-class idea that capitalist society is **meritocratic** – that is, if you work hard enough, you can get on – despite the fact that the evidence rarely supports this view. This ideological device is so successful that the majority of the working class are convinced that their position is deserved. In other words, they are persuaded to accept their lot and may even be convinced that capitalism has provided them with a decent standard of living.

Marxists argue that capitalist ideology shapes the way of life of a society – its culture. A good example of this, say Marxists, is the way that the mass media convince us through advertising and popular culture – television, cinema, pop music, tabloid newspapers, etc. – that our priority should be to buy more and more material goods (see Figure 1.2 below). We want to be rich so that we can buy more and more and more, and, somehow, this will make us happy. What is more, while we are all watching soap operas and reading the latest celebrity gossip, we're not noticing the inequalities and exploitation of the capitalist system.

This means that most of us are not aware of our 'real' identity as exploited and oppressed workers. We experience what Marxists describe as **false class consciousness**. Eventually though, Marxists believe, we will learn the real truth of our situation and rebel against the capitalist system.

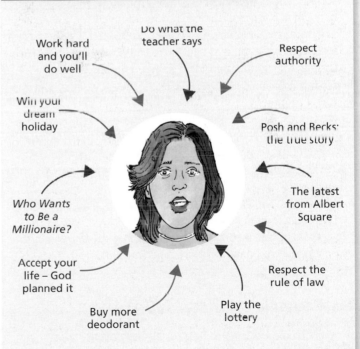

Figure 1.2 Brainwashed by ideology

Do what the teacher says
Work hard and you'll do well
Respect authority
Win your dream holiday
Posh and Becks: the true story
Who Wants to Be a Millionaire?
The latest from Albert Square
Accept your life – God planned it
Respect the rule of law
Buy more deodorant
Play the lottery

Criticisms of Marxism

- The notion of 'false class consciousness' has been undermined by surveys such as those conducted by Marshall et al. (1988) and the government in the form of the British Social Attitudes survey (Jowell et al. 1995). The British Social Attitudes survey found that 69 per cent of people thought their opportunities were influenced by their social class 'a great deal' or 'quite a lot'. Marshall argued that over 70 per cent of his survey sample believed that social class was an inevitable feature of British society and over 50 per cent felt that class conflict existed in the UK between a ruling class that monopolized economic and political power and a lower class that could do little to change its position. Marshall noted that most people were aware of social injustices, especially relating to inequalities in the distribution of wealth and income, but felt there was little they could do practically to bring about more equality. However, in support of the concept of ideology, Charlesworth's (2000) study of working-class people in Rotherham blames the educational system for this indifference and cynicism. He argues that the working-class experience of education results in them devaluing themselves and restricting their ambitions to 'being disappointed' in life.

- Like functionalism, Marxism has been accused of ignoring the freedom of choice enjoyed by individuals. People choose what to do and think – they are not 'brainwashed' by ideology. In this sense, Marxism too may present an 'oversocialized' picture of human beings.
- This criticism is not true of all Marxists. Some have argued that **oppositional subcultures** can exist within the capitalist system. For example, Hall and Jefferson (1976) argued that youth subcultures are often a means by which young people can express dissatisfaction with the capitalist system. They argued that the value systems, dress codes and behaviour of groups such as mods, skinheads and punks are a form of symbolic and temporary resistance to society. Their resistance is symbolic in that their behaviour often shocks society, but temporary in that they eventually become passive adults.
- Marxism may put too much emphasis on conflict. After all, despite all its inequalities, capitalism has managed to improve most people's standard of living. Perhaps Marxism also ignores common interests that employers and workers have. If workers work well, then the business does well and employers can afford to increase wages.
- Marxism, in general, has been criticized for claiming that all cultural activity is geared to class interests. Consequently, Marxists neglect the fact that culture may reflect religious, patriarchal, nationalistic and ethnic interests.

The work of Max Weber

Another sociologist who took a conflict perspective was Max Weber (1864–1920). He agreed with Marx that social class was an important source of inequality but argued that inequality could also be rooted in influences that have nothing to do with economics. Weber stressed the concept of 'status differences' as being at the heart of inequality – class was only one form of status. For example, Weber pointed out that in many societies, power is acquired from being born into a particular tribe or ethnic group. Inequality between Blacks and Whites in apartheid South Africa in the period 1950 to 1990 stemmed from status rather than social class, in that even the

poorest White was regarded as having more status and power than educated and economically successful Black people.

In Hindu India, the caste system (even though illegal) still exerts a strong influence on inequality. In this system, every person is born into one of four closed status groups or, situated below these, the non-caste group known as 'untouchables'. This system of status differences is based upon religious purity – the better the life you lead, the more likely you will be reborn (reincarnated) as a member of a higher caste. Meanwhile, you cannot work your way out of your caste, your job is determined by it and you must marry within it.

Feminism

Feminists argue that another important status difference and source of inequality and conflict is gender. They point out that the UK is a patriarchal or male-dominated society – that is, men generally have more power and prestige than women across a range of social institutions. Women generally have less economic power than men. In 2003, women working full time earned on average 18 per cent less than men working full time and they were more likely to be in poverty. Natasha Walter, in *The New Feminism* (1999), notes that women do not enjoy equality of access to jobs, especially the top jobs in the city. Males still monopolize professional and managerial positions – for example, in 2000, only 18 per cent of hospital consultants, 7 per cent of university professors and 4.5 per cent of company directors were women. Moreover, women are still expected to be predominantly responsible for the upkeep of the home and child-rearing – surveys continue to indicate that family life is not yet characterized by equality between the sexes in terms of household labour.

Feminists believe that sexual discrimination is still a problem today and Walter argues that women still need to achieve financial, educational, domestic and legal equality with men.

KEY TERMS

Bourgeoisie (or capitalists) the owners of businesses, and the dominant class in capitalist societies.

Capitalism an economic system associated with modern societies, based on private ownership of businesses.

False class consciousness the state of not being aware of our true identity as exploited workers.

Ideology the norms and values that justify the capitalist system.

Legitimate make something appear fair and reasonable.

Marxism a sociological perspective based on the writings of Karl Marx. It believes that societies are unequal and unfair.

Means of production the land, factories, machines, science and technology, and labour power required to produce goods.

Meritocratic based on ability and effort.

Oppositional subcultures social groups whose value systems and behaviour challenge the dominant capitalist value system.

Proletariat the working class in capitalist societies.

Liberal feminists are optimistic that this will eventually happen. They believe that there has been a steady improvement in the position of women, as old-fashioned attitudes break down, more girls do well in education and more women have successful careers.

Other types of feminists are not so hopeful. Marxist-feminists argue that patriarchy suits the capitalist system as well as men, because women are unpaid domestic labourers who service the male labour force, making them fit and healthy for work, and who produce and rear the future workforce. True equality between the sexes can only occur when the capitalist system is dismantled.

Radical feminists believe that the patriarchal oppression and exploitation of women is built into every aspect of the way society is organized. In particular, the family is identified as the social institution in which patriarchy is rooted. Radical feminists argue that, through gender-role socialization, women are socialized into accepting female subordination and into seeing motherhood as their main goal in life. Moreover, radical feminists argue that men aggressively exercise their physical, economic and cultural power to dominate women in all areas of social life, and particularly in personal relationships, such as marriage, domestic labour, childcare and sex. All men benefit from this inequality – there are no good guys!

research idea

- Conduct a small survey to see how aware people are of (a) their social class and (b) inequalities in income and wealth in the UK.

Check your understanding

1 **What is the relationship between the bourgeoisie and the proletariat?**

2 **What is the function of ideology?**

3 **Describe two important criticisms of Marxism.**

4 **What is the purpose of socialization according to Marxists?**

5 **How do youth subcultures challenge capitalism?**

6 **What other sources of inequality exist, apart from social class, according to Weber and feminist sociologists?**

web.tasks

1 **Using the website of the Office for National Statistics at www.statistics.gov.uk, try to find statistics that give an indication of the extent of inequality in Britain. You might look for figures on income, wealth, education and health.**

2 **Search for the website 'Dead Sociologists' Society'. Use it to find out about the ideas of Karl Marx.**

exploring conflict, culture and identity

Item A Transmitting capitalist values

Marxists believe that social institutions such as the education system, the media, the legal system and religion are agents of capitalism which transmit ruling-class ideology. For example, the education system socializes the working class into believing that their educational failure is due to lack of ability and effort, when, in reality, the capitalist system deliberately fails them so that they will continue to be factory workers. Television socializes the working class into believing that consensus is the norm and that serious protest about the way society is organized is 'extremist'. The law socializes the working class into believing that the law is on their side when, in reality, it mainly supports and enforces the values and institutions of the capitalist ruling class.

Adapted from Brown, C. (1979) *Understanding Society: An Introduction to Sociological Theory*, London: John Murray, p. 75; and Moore, S. (1987) *Sociology Alive*, Cheltenham: Stanley Thornes, p. 274

1 Explain what is meant by the term 'ideology'. (2 marks)

2 Identify the two basic classes that characterize capitalist societies. (4 marks)

3 Identify three ways in which the working class are socialized into accepting inequality. (6 marks)

4 Identify and briefly describe two trends or patterns that suggest that the UK is a society characterized by economic inequality. (8 marks)

Social action, culture and identity

gettingyouthinking

I have known Rachael for four years. She is a mature young woman who takes her responsibilities seriously. Consequently, she has a conscientious and industrious approach to her academic studies and can be trusted to work independently and with initiative. She also works well as a member of a team and is well liked and respected by both her peers and teachers. I have no doubt that you will find Rachael to be a thoroughly honest and reliable person. I was always impressed by her enthusiasm, persistence, motivation and ability to work under pressure. I have no hesitation in recommending her to your institution.

DRIVING LICENCE   A030019

1 Surname
   PAYNE MR
2 Other names
   JAMES   Town of birth
3 Date of birth   Worcester
   24 03 1988
4 Permanent Address
   14 Roseacre Drive
   Worcester WR8 9LA
5 Issued by DVLA SWANSEA

6 Valid from   Valid until
   17 09 2005   23 03 2058
7 No
   PAYN 785288 B87VU

Signature   James Payne

EUROPEAN UNION

UNITED KINGDOM OF
GREAT BRITAIN
AND NORTHERN IRELAND

PASSPORT

My mother loves me.
I feel good.
I feel good because she loves me.

I am good because I feel good
I feel good because I am good
My mother loves me because I am good.

My mother does not love me.
I feel bad.
I feel bad because she does not love me
I am bad because I feel bad
I feel bad because I am bad
I am bad because she does not love me
She does not love me because I am bad.

R.D. Laing (1970) *Knots*,
Harmondsworth: Penguin

1 What do these documents tell us about a person? What do they not tell us?

2 What does the reference tell us about Rachael's identity? What doesn't it tell us?

3 What does the poem tell us about this person's identity?

4 How does the self-identity apparent in the poem contrast with the picture of the individual in the reference?

Official documents tell us about the identity we present to the world – our date and place of birth, age, nationality, address, marital status and so on. References, like the example on the left, give us some insight into **social identity** – how well we perform our social roles, such as our jobs. However, poems, like the one on the left, can tell us about the way we see ourselves – our **self-identity** – and how this is often the result of how we interpret other people's reactions to us.

Think about a small child. Children try out different sorts of behaviour and then watch other people react. By doing this, they learn about themselves and about what is acceptable and unacceptable. In other words, people find out about themselves through the reactions of others.

Social action theory

What has just been described is the view of **social action** or **interactionist** sociologists. They reject the structuralist assumption that social behaviour is determined, constrained and even made predictable by the organization of society. They see people as having a much more positive and active role in shaping social life. If structuralist theory is a 'top-down' theory, then social action theory is 'bottom-up', as it starts with people rather than society.

Social action theorists reject the view that people's behaviour is the product of external forces over which they have little control. Most people do not feel themselves to be puppets of society. Rather, as Chris Brown (1979) notes:

> ≪they feel they are living their own lives, making their own decisions and engaging, for the most part, in voluntary behaviour. There may be things they have to do which they resent, but resentment is, of course, tangible evidence of an independent self, forced to comply, but unwillingly and under protest.≫

However, although we operate as individuals, we are aware of other people around us. Social action theorists argue that the attitudes and actions of those other people influence the way we think and behave – that society is the product of people coming together in social groups and trying to make sense of their own and each other's behaviour.

People are able to work out what is happening in any given situation because they bring a set of **interpretations** to every interaction and use them to make sense of social behaviour. In particular, we apply meanings to symbolic behaviour. For example, gestures are symbols – putting up two fingers in a V-sign may be interpreted as insulting, because it has an obscene meaning. When we are interacting with others, we are constantly on the lookout for symbols, because these give us clues as to how the other person is interpreting our behaviour – for instance, if they are smiling, we might interpret this as social approval, and if they maintain prolonged, intense eye contact, we might interpret this as a 'come on'.

Our experience of this 'symbolic interaction' means we acquire a stock of knowledge about what is appropriate behaviour in particular situations. We learn that particular contexts demand particular social responses. For example,

I might interpret drinking and dancing at a party as appropriate, yet the same behaviour at a funeral as inappropriate. It is likely that other people will share my interpretations and so it is unlikely that the behaviour described would occur at the funeral.

Socialization and identity

Socialization involves learning a stock of shared interpretations and meanings for most given social interactions. Families, for example, teach us how to interact with and interpret the actions of others; education brings us into contact with a greater range of social groups and teaches us how to interpret social action in a broader range of social contexts. The result of such socialization is that children acquire an identity.

Social action theorists suggest that identity has three components:

1 Personal identity refers to aspects of individuality that identify people as unique and distinct from others. These include personal name, nickname, signature, photograph, address, National Insurance number, etc.

2 Social identity refers to the personality characteristics and qualities that particular cultures associate with certain social roles or groups. For example, in our culture, mothers are supposed to be loving, nurturing and selfless. Therefore, women who are mothers will attempt to live up to this description and hence acquire that social identity. As children grow up, they too will acquire a range of social identities, such as brother, sister, best friend, student. Socialization and interaction with others will make it clear to them what our culture expects of these roles in terms of obligations, duties and behaviour.

3 The individual has a **subjective** (internal) sense of their own uniqueness and identity. Sociologists call this the 'self'. It is partly the product of what others think is expected of a person's social identity. For example, a mother may see herself as a good mother because she achieves society's standards in that respect. However, 'self' is also the product of how the individual interprets their experience and life history. For example, some women may have, in their own mind, serious misgivings about their role as mother. The self, then, is the link between what society expects from a particular role and the individual's interpretation of whether they are living up to that role successfully.

The concept of self has been explored extensively by social action sociologists. Some have suggested that the self has two components – the 'I' and the 'me'. The 'I' is the private inner self, whereas the 'me' is the social self that participates in everyday interaction. When a person plays a social role as a teacher or student, it is the 'me' that is in action. The 'me' is shaped by the reactions of others – that is, we act in ways that we think are socially desirable. However, the 'I' supplies the confidence or self-esteem to play the role successfully.

Goffman (1959) argues that interaction is essentially about successful role-playing. He suggests that we are all social actors engaged in the drama of everyday life. Stage directions are symbolized by the social and cultural context in which the action takes place. For example, the classroom as a stage symbolizes particular rules that must be followed if the interaction is to be successful, e.g. students sit at desks while teachers can move around the room freely. Sometimes the script is already in place, e.g. we adhere to cultural rules about greeting people – 'Good morning, how are you?' – although often the script has to be improvised. Goffman argues that the public or social identity we present to the world is often simply a performance designed to create a particular impression. This makes sense if we think about how we behave in particular contexts or company, e.g. your behaviour in front of your grandparents is likely to be very different compared with your behaviour in front of friends. Therefore, you have a catalogue of different identities you can adopt.

Goffman invents a number of concepts that he claims people as social actors use in everyday action to assist in the management of other people's impression of them. Some people will use 'front' to manage an interaction. This refers to items of physical or body equipment that a social actor uses to enhance their performance – for example, teachers who want to convey authority may wear formal clothing to distance themselves from students. Another concept is 'region' – the classroom is the front region where the teacher 'performs', while the staffroom is where they relax and become another person, such as the colleague or friend.

Labelling theory

Labelling theory is closely linked to the social action approach and helps us to understand how some parts of society may be responsible for socializing some people into identities that may have negative consequences. Take education as an example.

Interactionists believe that the social identity of pupils may be dependent on how they interact with teachers. If teachers act in such a way that pupils feel negatively labelled – as 'lazy' or 'thick', for example – then this will seriously affect their behaviour and progress.

Howard Becker (1963) pointed out that labels often have the power of a **master status**. For example, the master status of 'criminal' can override all other statuses, such as father, son or husband. In other words, deviant labels can radically alter a person's social identity. For example, someone labelled as 'criminal' may be discriminated against and find it difficult to get employment, make new friends and be accepted into their community. They may end up seeking others with similar identities and values, and form deviant subcultures. A **self-fulfilling prophecy** is the result, as the reaction to the label makes it come true.

Think about how the experience of streaming or setting may affect the self-esteem of a pupil. How do pupils who are placed in low streams or sets feel? They may well accept a view of themselves as 'failures' and stop trying – after all, what's the point if you're 'thick'? Or what if a pupil feels labelled as a 'troublemaker' because they are Black? The negative label may be internalized (accepted) and a self-fulfilling prophecy may occur. The self sees itself as a 'failure' or as 'deviant' and reacts accordingly. The label becomes true (see Figure 1.3 below).

Goffman (1961) illustrated the power of such labelling in his ethnographic study of inmates in a mental hospital in the USA. Goffman refers to such hospitals as 'total institutions' because they attempt to shape all aspects of their inmates lives, e.g. by organizing their routine. Goffman argues that total institutions deliberately break down a person's sense of self through a process he calls 'mortification' – they are stripped, given a common uniform to wear and referred to by a serial number.

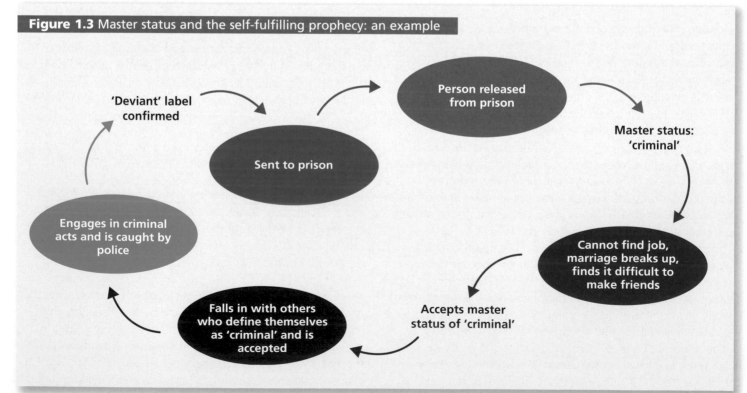

Figure 1.3 Master status and the self-fulfilling prophecy: an example

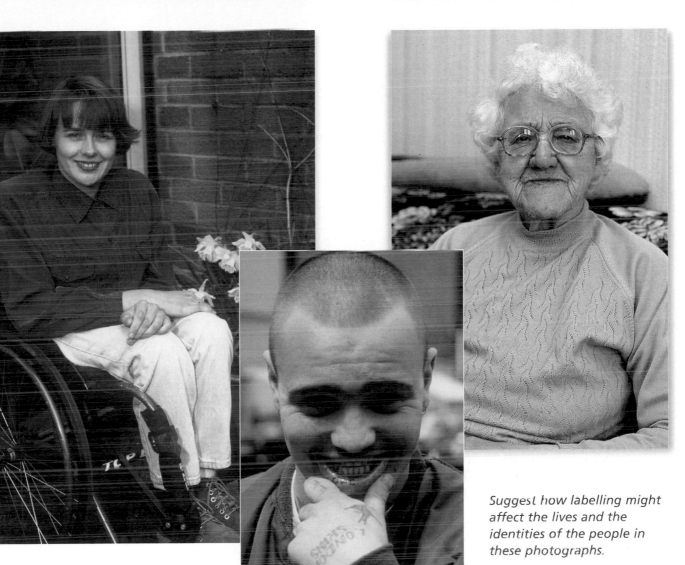

Suggest how labelling might affect the lives and the identities of the people in these photographs.

In other words, the institution sets about destroying individuality. The institution then attempts to rebuild the self in its own collective image. However, Goffman notes that the inmates he studied reacted in various ways to this process. Some conformed to the institution's demands; some even became institutionalized – they became so completely dependent on the institution that they could no longer survive in the outside world. Some, however, hung on to their individuality by giving the impression that they were conforming, while others openly opposed the system. What Goffman's work indicates is that the self and self-esteem can be very resilient and that labelling does not always have to be such a destructive process. Those who have been labelled can actually resist the definitions of the powerful.

Recent studies in a social action context have focused on how we interpret our bodies. It is argued that the way people view themselves and others is shaped by the dominant cultural ideas and images about ageing, body shape, weight and beauty that we see in media products such as magazines, advertisements, television and films. It is argued by feminist commentators that British culture sees the slim or thin female form as the ideal goal, with the result that young girls are socialized into seeing the slim figure as a source of status and success, while 'too much' weight is unattractive and socially inadequate. It is suggested that eating disorders, such as anorexia and bulimia, may be the outcome of these dominant cultural ideas, as female identity is often bound up with how women perceive their bodies. Research on female eating disorders suggests that those with the disorders often have low self-esteem and often subscribe to distorted images about their weight and attractiveness.

A recent symbolic interactionist study focused on shyness. Scott (2003) carried out in-depth interviews with 16 'shy' individuals in the South Wales area who volunteered after responding to an advertisement. She also set up a website about 'shyness and society' that included an email distribution list. Over a period of nine months, a virtual community composed of 42 individuals was created which exchanged ideas and discussed online the social aspects of shyness.

Scott found evidence of the notion of an 'I' and a 'me', in that shyness was often experienced as a conflict between a desire to be part of a social scene and the fear of being negatively judged or criticized. The shy 'I' was often beset by feelings of 'anxiety, uncertainty and inhibition', while the shy 'me' was concerned about how other people would view them that is, they were afraid of making a fool of themselves or not

Douglas Yu
The Matsigenka

Douglas Yu (1998) carried out a study with the Matsigenka tribe, who lived in a remote area of South-Eastern Peru and had not been exposed to television and advertising. He showed male members of the tribe pictures of females with different body shapes. He found that the Matsigenka men favoured more 'rounded' female shapes, i.e. plump women. They often remarked that the slim-waisted females looked skinny or pallid – and were perhaps recovering from a bout of diarrhoea. The researchers then tested the perceptions of men who used to live in the same area but had since moved to towns, where advertising and television were more common. These males when shown the same images preferred the slimmer forms.

Adapted from Senior, M. (1999) 'With the body in mind',
Sociology Review, 8(4)

1 What was the main cause of the difference in male perception in your view?

2 What do you think is the ideal body image, according to Matsigenka women?

3 What might be the effect on the Matsigenka women's body image and identity when television finally comes to that part of Peru?

---

fitting in. Many participants felt plagued by 'what if' feelings, such as 'what if they don't like me?'. Scott's sample often felt shy in particular social contexts in which the reactions of others were perceived as important. Scott notes that shyness is often seen as a 'deviant' activity, although society is likely to interpret it as 'normal' in particular social groups, e.g. among girls. She argues that there is a lot of moral pressure put on shy people to overcome their 'problem' through the use self-help books, miracle drugs and shyness clinics.

Criticisms of social action theory

Social action theories have been criticized because they tend to be very vague in explaining who is responsible for defining acceptable norms of behaviour. They do not explain who is responsible for making the rules that so-called deviant groups break. In this sense, they fail to explore the origin of power and neglect potential sources such as social class, gender and ethnicity. For example, Marxists argue that the capitalist ruling class define how social institutions such as education and the law operate. In other words, social action theories tend to be descriptive rather than explanatory.

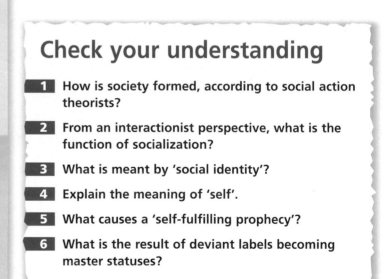

Check your understanding

1 How is society formed, according to social action theorists?

2 From an interactionist perspective, what is the function of socialization?

3 What is meant by 'social identity'?

4 Explain the meaning of 'self'.

5 What causes a 'self-fulfilling prophecy'?

6 What is the result of deviant labels becoming master statuses?

KEY TERMS

Interpretations the meanings that we attach to particular objects or situations, e.g. we usually interpret classrooms as learning environments and act accordingly.

Labelling theory the idea that categorizing or stereotyping individuals or groups can seriously affect their behaviour. Used especially in the fields of education and deviance.

Master status a label or status that can override all others (e.g. criminal, child abuser).

Self-identity refers to how we see ourselves, usually in reaction to how we think others see us.

Self-fulfilling prophecy a prediction that makes itself become true.

Social action theory or **interactionism** a sociological perspective that focuses on the ways in which people give meaning to their own and others' actions.

Social identity refers to how society sees us, in terms of whether we live up to the cultural expectations attached to the social roles we play.

Subjective personal, based on your own view.

Item A 'All the world's a stage'

Individuals, like actors, are performing for an audience. Speech, acts and gestures all require someone else to be watching or listening. Our identities, therefore, are the product of how we present ourselves and how others perceive us. For example, you have to persuade your tutor that you have seriously adopted the identity and role of student. Your tutor may respond by according you an 'ideal' student label or identity. If you fail to convince, you may be labelled as a 'deviant' student, i.e. as idle or troublesome. This 'deviant' label is a 'master status' which overshadows other aspects of identity. Often, people who are considered deviant in one respect are assumed to be deviant in other respects. For example, other teachers may judge you negatively in staffroom discussions.

Those labelled as 'deviants' often experience stigma – people behaving differently towards them. In reaction, those labelled may pursue a deviant career by adopting a lifestyle which confirms their deviant status. In other words, a self-fulfilling prophecy results.

Adapted from Woodward, K. (ed.) (2000) *Questioning Identity: Gender, Class, Nation*, London: Routledge, pp. 14–15 and Croall, H (1998) *Crime and Society in Britain*, Harlow: Longman pp. 61–2

1 **Explain what is meant by the term 'self-fulfilling prophecy'.** (2 marks)

2 **Identify two aspects of your own identity.** (4 marks)

3 **Identify three possible consequences of being labelled by an institution, such as a school, the police or a mental hospital.** (6 marks)

4 **Identify and briefly describe two criticisms of the concept of 'labelling'.** (8 marks)

research ideas

- Observe an everyday situation involving interaction between people. It could be in a library, at a bus stop, in a common room or a pub.
  - What is going on?
  - Does everyone share the same interpretation of the situation?
  - How do people try to manage the impression they give of themselves?

- Find two groups of students: one group who have experience of being placed in a high stream, and one group who have experience of being placed in a low stream. Give a questionnaire to, or interview, each group in order to find out how streaming affected their self-image, motivation and progress. Compare the responses of the two samples.

web.task

Visit the following websites on shyness and write a brief report detailing how it may affect a person's self-esteem and identity:

- **Susie Scott's 'Shyness and Society' website at www.cf.ac.uk/socsi/shyness**

- **The Shyness Institute, a major shyness research centre at www.shyness.com/shyness-institute.html**

- **The Shyness Home Page detailing the work of the American sociologists, L. Henderson and P.G. Zimbardo, at www.shyness.com**

Postmodernism

gettingyouthinking

Try to imagine the life ahead for the woman from the 1930s in the first photograph.

1 What sort of family life do you think she would have had?

2 Might she have had paid employment? What problems might she have faced in pursuing a career?

3 What about the roles played by her and her husband?

Now think about the future for the young woman of today.

4 What sort of family life do you think she is likely to have?

5 Is she likely to have paid employment?

6 What about her relationship with her husband?

You may well have found it fairly straightforward to plot out the future for the young woman of 70 years ago. Attempting the same task for a woman today is much more difficult. Maybe she will choose not to marry or live in a family. Maybe she won't have children. Alternatively, she could devote her life to a family, but then again she might decide to focus on following a career – or she could do both. The choices appear endless. Being a woman today seems much more flexible and uncertain – and less predictable – than in the past.

Sociologists have watched recent social changes with great interest. Some have reached the conclusion that society has experienced such major upheavals that the old ways of explaining it just won't work any more. They believe that we are entering a new sort of society, which they refer to as the postmodern world or **postmodernity**. But before we can consider this, we need to head back to the beginnings of sociology.

Have you ever wondered why sociology came about? History tells us that sociology developed in order to explain the rapid social changes associated with **industrialization** and **urbanization** during the 19th century. Lives changed so drastically during this period that, not surprisingly, people began to look for theories and explanations that would help make sense of the bewildering changes taking place. Families left the rural communities where they had lived for centuries, to find work in the new cities. They had to adjust to a different lifestyle, different work, different bosses and different kinds of relationships with family and community.

On the whole, early sociologists approved of these changes and the kind of society they created – now commonly referred to as **modernity** or the modern world. They set out to document the key features of what they saw as an exciting new order.

The nature of the modern world

Sociologists have identified four major characteristics of the modern world:

1 *Industrialization* – Production is industrial and economic relationships are capitalist. Factories produce goods, bosses own factories, and workers sell their labour to bosses. Social class is therefore the basic source of difference and identity in modern societies.
2 *Urbanization* – Early modernity was associated with great population movement to the cities, known as urbanization. Twentieth-century theories of modernity have tended to celebrate the bright lights and innovation of the city while ridiculing rural culture as living in the past.
3 *Centralized government* – Government is characterized by a **bureaucratic** state that takes a great deal of responsibility both for the economy and for the welfare of its citizens.
4 *Rational, scientific thinking* – What really made modern society stand apart from premodern societies was the revolution in the way people thought about the world. Before industrialization, tradition, religion and superstition had provided the basis for views of the world. The modern world adopted a new way of thinking, shaped by science and reason.

New ideas and theories (referred to by postmodernists as '**big stories**' or **meta-narratives**) competed with each other to explain this constantly changing modern world and these theories frequently called for more social progress. Some of these theories were political (e.g. socialism), while others were cultural (e.g. the ideas of feminism). To paraphrase Marx, one of the leading modernist thinkers, their job was not just to explain the world – the point was to change it.

Sociology and the modern world

Sociologists were caught up in this excitement about modernity, and attempted to create scientific theories that would explain the transition from the traditional to the modern. One of the founding fathers of sociology, Auguste Comte, believed that sociology was the science of society. This **positivist** view argued that sociological research based upon scientific **rationality** could rid the world of social problems such as crime.

Marx, too, celebrated modernity, despite his criticism of its economic relationships, because he believed that science had given people the power to change the world. Sociological theories, therefore, also developed into meta-narratives as they attempted to provide us with knowledge or 'truth' about the nature of modernity

The postmodern world

In the past 20 years or so, some sociologists have identified trends and developments which, they claim, show that modernity is fragmenting or dissolving. They argue that it is being replaced by a postmodern world in which many sociological ideas and concepts are becoming irrelevant.

Characteristics of postmodernity have been identified in aspects of work, culture, identity, globalization and knowledge.

Work

The nature of work and economic life has changed. Work is no longer dominated by mass factory production in which thousands of people work alongside each other. Work today is mainly located within the **service sector**, and is dominated either by jobs that mainly involve the processing of information (e.g. the financial sector), or by jobs that involve the servicing of **consumption** (e.g. working in a shop).

Our ideas about work have also changed. People today are less likely to expect a job for life, and are more willing to accept a range of flexible working practices, such as part-time work, working from home and job-sharing.

Culture

As our society has grown wealthier, so the media and other cultural industries – such as fashion, film, advertising and music – have become increasingly central to how we organize our lives. It is suggested that we are a 'media-saturated' society in which media advice is available on how we can 'make over' our homes, gardens, partners and even ourselves. Look, for example, at the lifestyle magazines ranged on the shelves of bookshops and newsagents, advising you on skin care, body size and shape, hair colour and type, fitness, cosmetic surgery and so on. What these trends tell us is that consumption is now a central defining feature in our lives.

Postmodern culture is also about mixing and matching seemingly contradictory styles. Think about the way in which different music from different times and different styles is 'sampled', for example.

Identity

Our identities are now likely to be influenced by mainstream popular culture which celebrates **diversity**, consumerism and choice. In other words, the old 'me' was about where I came from in terms of my family and class background, the area I lived in and so on. The new postmodern 'me', however, is about designer labels, being seen in the right places, the car I drive, listening to the right music and buying the right clothes. Style has become more important than substance. As Steve Taylor (1999) argues, society has been transformed into:

>> *something resembling an endless shopping mall where people now have much greater choice about how they look, what they consume and what they believe in.*>>

Globalization

The global expansion of **transnational companies** – such as McDonald's, Sony, Coca-Cola and Nike – and the global marketing of cultural forms – such as cinema, music and computer games – have contributed to this emphasis on consumption. Such globalization has resulted in symbols that are recognized and consumed across the world. Images of Britney Spears and Eminem are just as likely to be found adorning the walls of a village hut in the interior of New Guinea as they are a bedroom wall in Croydon. Brands like Nike and Coca-Cola use global events like the World Cup and the Olympic Games to beam themselves into millions of homes across the world.

It is therefore no wonder that this global culture is seen to be challenging the importance of national and local cultures, and challenging **nationalism** as a source of identity. Information technology and electronic communication such as email and the internet have also been seen as part of this process.

Knowledge

In the postmodern world, people no longer have any faith in great truths. In particular, people have become sceptical, even cynical, about the power of science to change the world, because many of the world's problems have been brought about by technology. In the political world, ideologies such as **socialism** – which claimed they were the best way of transforming the world – have been discredited in many people's eyes, with the collapse of communism in Eastern Europe. Postmodernists insist that truth is both unattainable and irrelevant in the postmodern world. Instead, they stress the **relativity** of knowledge, ideas and lifestyles, such that many different yet equally authentic values are possible.

Postmodernism and sociology

Steve Taylor argues that these developments have three main consequences for sociology:

1   Most sociology is concerned with explaining the nature and organization of modern societies and social institutions. However, the key relationships that underpin such societies – class, family, gender – are no longer relevant.

2   Sociologists can no longer claim to produce expert knowledge about society, because in postmodern societies, relativity and uncertainty have replaced absolute judgements about what is or should be. As Swingewood (2000) argues, in postmodern societies 'knowledge is always incomplete, there are no universal standards, only differences and **ambiguity**'. The big sociological stories, such as functionalism and Marxism, have become redundant, because 'knowledge' is now judged in terms of its usefulness rather than its claim to be a universal 'truth'.

3   Sociologists can no longer make judgements or claim that they know what is best for societies. Sociology is only one set of ideas competing with others. All have something relevant to offer. If people want to listen to sociologists and act upon their findings, it is up to them. It is equally relevant not to do so.

Endless choice in the postmodern world

IF DISSATISFIED WITH ANY PRODUCT SIMPLY RETURN IT AND EXCHANGE IT FOR ANOTHER.

GENDER ROLES / RELIGIONS / WORK / VALUES / FAMILY LIFE

Criticisms of postmodernism

Critics of postmodernism suggest that it is guilty of making too much of recent social changes. Evidence suggests that aspects of the postmodernist argument – especially the decline of social class, ethnicity and nationalism as sources of identity – are exaggerated. For example, surveys indicate that people still see social class as a strong influence in their lives, and use aspects of it to judge their success and status and that of others. There is no doubting that consumption has increased in importance, especially among young people, but it is pointed out that consumption does not exist in a vacuum. The nature of your consumption – what and how much you consume – still very much depends upon your income, which is generally determined by your occupation and social class. Similarly, our ability to make choices is still also constrained by our gender and ethnicity, because of the influence of patriarchy and institutional racism.

Check your understanding

1   What term is used by postmodernists to describe theories of society?

2   What was the role of sociology, according to Auguste Comte?

3   Identify two social changes that have led some sociologists to argue that we are entering a postmodern world.

4   How do the media contribute to our sense of identity?

5   What is the relationship between globalization and postmodernism?

6   How did the collapse of communism in Eastern Europe contribute to people's cynicism about meta-narratives?

7   What is the role of the internet in postmodern society?

Ambiguity the state of being open to a range of interpretations – the meaning is not clear.

Bureaucratic based on rules and procedures.

Consumption the use of goods and services, especially as part of forming an identity.

Diversity variety.

Industrialization the transformation of societies from being agricultural to industrial, which took place in the 18th and 19th centuries (see also Unit 2, Topic 2).

Meta-narratives or **'big stories'** the postmodernist term for theories like Marxism and functionalism, which aim to explain how societies work.

Modernity period of time starting with the industrial revolution, associated with industrial production, urban living, rational thinking and strong central government.

Nationalism belief system or political view that stresses shared geographical location, history and culture.

Positivism the view that sociological research based upon scientific principles could rid the world of social problems such as crime.

Postmodernity term used by postmodernists to describe the contemporary period, which is characterized by uncertainty, media-saturation and globalization.

Rationality actions decided by logical thought.

Relativity the idea that no one example of something (e.g. political view, sociological theory, lifestyle, moral) is better than any other.

Service sector a group of economic activities loosely organized around finance, retail and personal care.

Socialism a political belief system based on the idea of collective ownership and equal rights for all.

Transnational companies companies that produce and market goods on a global scale.

Urbanization the trend towards living in towns and cities rather than in rural areas.

exploring postmodernism

Item A An endless shopping mall

A good deal of postmodern theory in sociology (and popular culture) is an attempt to come to terms with some of the effects of living in a media-saturated society. Postmodernists argue, in opposition to most sociological theories of the media, that the 'information explosion' of the last two or three decades has not led to increasing conformity and acceptance of 'dominant values', but rather, has led to greater choice and diversity. We are now bombarded with a mass of different media images.

The effect of this, according to postmodern theorists, has been to transform society into something resembling an endless shopping mall where people now have much greater choice about how they look, what they consume and what they believe in.

A consequence of this, postmodernists argue, is that what most sociologists call societies, or social structures, have become fragmented and have become much less important in influencing how people think and act.

For postmodernists, our sense of identity – that is, our ideas of who we are – comes less from things like where we live, our family, our class and our gender, and much more from the images we consume via the media. In a postmodern world, people define themselves much more in terms of the choices they make about their clothes, cars, football teams and so on.

Taylor, S. (1999) 'Postmodernism: a challenge to sociology', 'S' Magazine, 4, p. 14

1 **Explain what is meant by a 'media-saturated society'. (2 marks)**

2 **Identify two sources of identity in modern societies. (4 marks)**

3 **Identify three characteristics of postmodern society. (6 marks)**

4 **Identify and briefly describe two ways in which postmodernism may challenge sociological thought. (8 marks)**

web.task

Use the world wide web to search for information on:

- **postmodernism – find out about its influence on art, architecture and literature**
- **Jean Baudrillard, a key postmodern thinker.**

research idea

- Interview a sample of 16 to 19 year olds about their expectations of the future (jobs, relationships, family, etc.). To what extent are they uncertain or clear about their future?

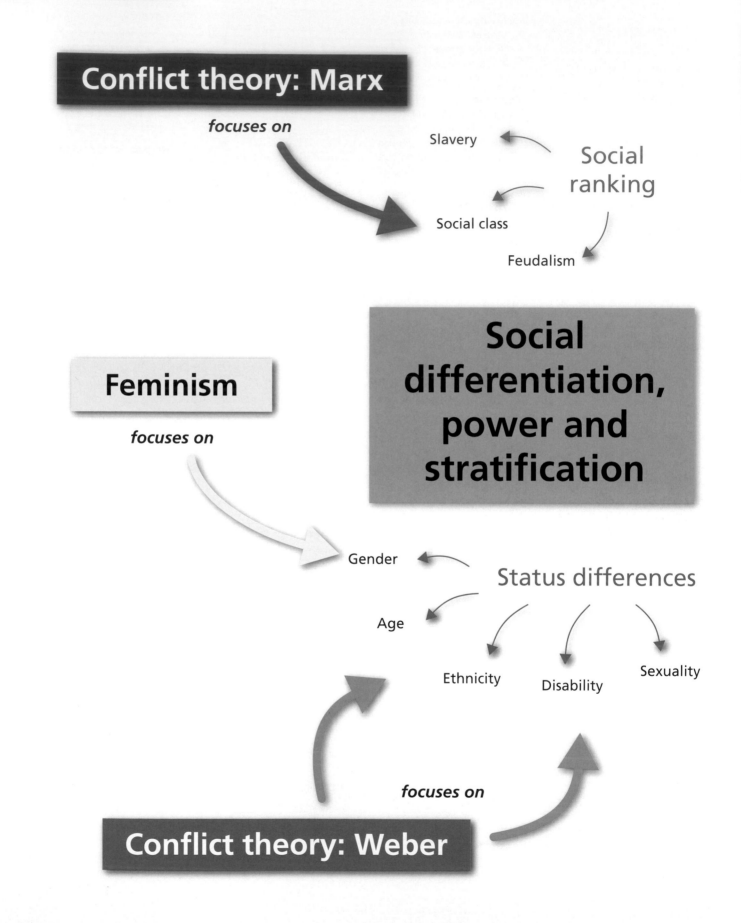

Conflict theory: Marx

focuses on

Slavery

Social ranking

Social class

Feudalism

Social differentiation, power and stratification

Feminism

focuses on

Gender

Status differences

Age

Ethnicity

Disability

Sexuality

focuses on

Conflict theory: Weber

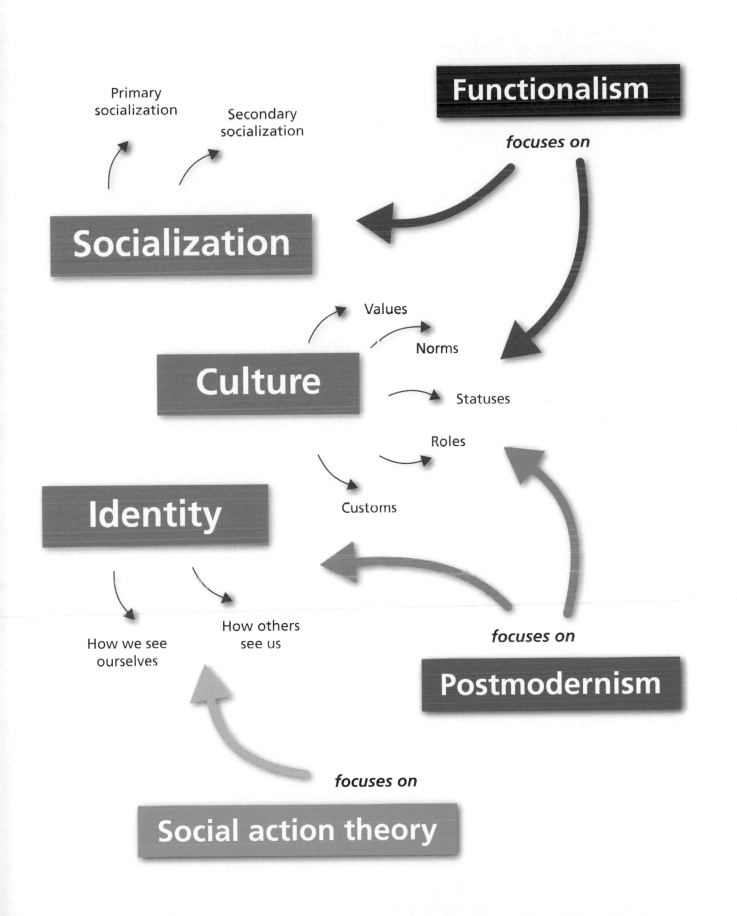

EVERYONE THINKS THEY KNOW SOMETHING ABOUT FAMILIES AND HOUSEHOLDS. This is not surprising, as virtually all of us will live in a family at some point in our lives. We often assume that most people share our experience of family life and that most families are organized along the lines of our own. Also, because family life is often intense and emotional, we often feel strongly about the family setup and find it difficult to understand why other people don't do things as we do. The study of families and households can sometimes be difficult because we find it hard to set aside our own experiences. However, as you study this unit, you must try to be objective and impartial – a good sociologist puts aside their own prejudices and emotions, and makes judgements purely on the basis of evidence.

This is particularly important with regard to Topic 1, in which we examine what is meant by the 'family' and how definitions of what constitutes 'proper' or 'ideal' family life have been dominated by particular perspectives.

In Topic 2, we critically explore the modern family's relationship with industrialization, and in particular, functionalist, Marxist and feminist conceptions of the family.

In Topic 3, we examine the view that the modern family is under attack and in decline, and that the state is partially responsible for this situation.

In Topic 4, this theme is continued through an examination of a range of family changes that are seen by New Right commentators as responsible for a so-called 'crisis in family life'. This crisis has supposedly led to a number of social problems, including a rise in crime, male underachievement at schools and teenage pregnancy. We look at the evidence with regard to marriage, cohabitation and divorce.

Topic 5 continues on this trail because family traditionalists also argue that the appearance of alternative types of families in recent years is yet more evidence of family decline. This section, therefore, examines the facts about one-parent families, reconstituted families, ethnic minority families and other forms of diversity. Some sociological theories argue that such family diversity is actually healthy for society and individuals.

Topic 6 deals with childhood, which many people assume is a biological state of age. However, this topic will show that childhood is, in fact, socially constructed, as experiences of it differ from society to society, as well as *within* societies. How we treat children is yet another concern of those who believe that society is in moral decline.

Finally, Topic 7 focuses on power and control in the family and critically examines the view that relationships between men and women in families have become more equal. It looks at a range of different aspects of family life including domestic labour, emotional labour, fathering and domestic violence, in order to work out the degree of change in family relationships.

AQAspecification	topics	pages
Candidates should examine:		
Different conceptions of the relationship of the family to the social structure, with particular reference to the economy	Covered in Topic 1	34–39
The relationship between the family and state policy	Covered in Topic 3	46–51
Changes in family structure and household structure and their relationship to industrialization and urbanization	Covered in Topic 2	40–45
Changing patterns of marriage, cohabitation, separation, divorce and child bearing	Covered in Topic 4	52–57
The diversity of contemporary family and household structures	Covered in Topic 5	58–63
Changes in the status of children and childhood	Covered in Topic 6	64–69
The nature and extent of changes within the family relating to gender roles, domestic labour and power relationships	Covered in Topic 7	70–75

Families and households

Defining the family

Left: an Ik village clings to the hillside

Below: an Ik child called Lokiira

The family does not feature heavily in the culture of the Ik of Northern Uganda. In fact, as far as the Ik are concerned, the family means very little. This is because the Ik face a daily struggle to survive in the face of drought, famine and starvation. Anyone who cannot take care of him- or herself is regarded as a useless burden by the Ik and a hazard to the survival of the others. Families mean dependants such as children who need to be fed and protected. So close to the verge of starvation, family, sentiment and love are regarded as luxuries that can mean death. Children are regarded as useless appendages, like old people, because they use up precious resources. So the old are abandoned to die. Sick and disabled children too are abandoned. The Ik attitude is that, as long as you keep the breeding group alive, you can always get more children.

Ik mothers throw their children out of the village compound when they are 3 years old, to fend for themselves. I imagine children must be rather relieved to be thrown out, for in the process of being cared for he or she is grudgingly carried about in a hide sling wherever the mother goes. Whenever the mother is in her field, she loosens the sling and lets the baby to the ground none too slowly, and laughs if it is hurt. Then she goes about her business, leaving the child there, almost hoping that some predator will come along and carry it off. This sometimes happens. Such behaviour does not endear children to their parents or parents to their children.

Adapted from Turnbull, C. (1994) *The Mountain People*, London: Pimlico

1 How do the Ik define the family?

2 Given your own experience of family life, think of three features of the family that you would expect to find in all families, wherever they are. How do these three features differ from the Ik?

3 In what ways might some British families share some of the characteristics of the Ik?

You probably reacted to the description of the Ik with horror. It is tempting to conclude that these people are primitive, savage and inhuman, and that their concept of the 'family' is deeply wrong. However, sociologists argue that it is wrong simply to judge such societies and their family arrangements as unnatural and deviant. We need to understand that such arrangements may have positive functions. In the case of the Ik, with the exceptional circumstances they find themselves in – drought and famine – their family arrangements help ensure the survival of the tribe. Moreover, you may have concluded that family life in the UK and for the Ik have some things in common. British family life is not universally experienced as positive for all family members. For some members – young and old alike – family life may be characterized by violence, abuse and isolation.

The problem with studying the family is that we all think we are experts. This is not surprising, given that most of us are born into families and socialized into family roles and responsibilities. It is an institution most of us feel very comfortable with and regard as 'natural'. For many of us, it is the cornerstone of our social world, a place to which we can retreat and where we can take refuge from the stresses of the outside world. It is the place in which we are loved for who we are, rather than what we are. Family living and family events are probably the most important aspects of our lives. It is no wonder then that we tend to hold very fierce, emotional, and perhaps irrational, views about family life and how it ought to be organized. Such 'taken-for-granted' views make it very difficult for us to examine objectively family arrangements that deviate from our own experience – such as those of the Ik – without making critical judgements.

Defining 'the family'

The experiences of the Ik suggest that family life across the world is characterized by tremendous variation and diversity. However, we can see that, until fairly recently, popular definitions of 'the family' in modern UK society were dominated by a traditional view that the **nuclear family** was the ideal type of family to which people should aspire. It was generally accepted that this family, which was the statistical norm until the 1980s, should have the following characteristics:

- It should be small and compact in structure, composed of a mother, father and usually two or three children who are biologically related.
- The relationship between the adults should be **heterosexual** and based on romantic love. Children are seen as the outcome of that love.
- The relationship between the adults should be reinforced by marriage, which, it is assumed, encourages **fidelity** and therefore family stability.
- Marriage should be companionate, i.e. based on husband and wives being partners. There is an overlap between male and female responsibilities as men get more involved in childcare and housework. However, some 'natural' differences persist. It is taken for granted that women want to have children and that they should be primarily responsible for **nurturing** and childcare. The male role is usually defined as the main economic breadwinner and head of the household.

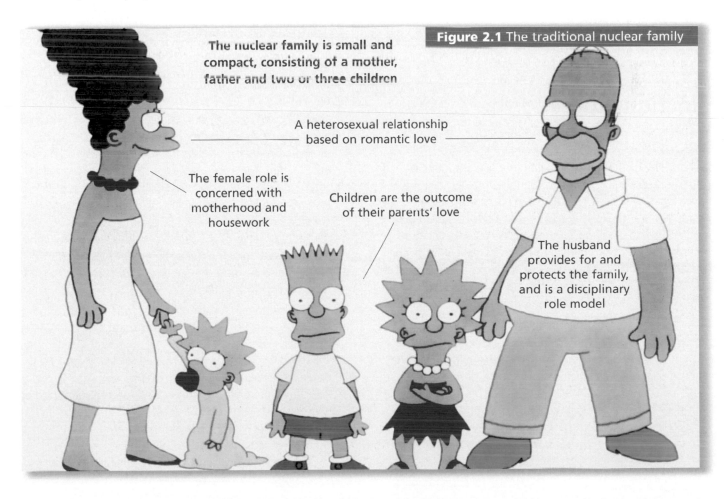

Figure 2.1 The traditional nuclear family

The nuclear family is small and compact, consisting of a mother, father and two or three children

A heterosexual relationship based on romantic love

The female role is concerned with motherhood and housework

Children are the outcome of their parents' love

The husband provides for and protects the family, and is a disciplinary role model

The influence of the traditional view of the family

Despite recent changes in the structure of families, and the liberalization of attitudes towards family life, we can still see the influence of traditional beliefs about family life in the UK. It can be argued that they constitute a powerful 'ideology' about what families should look like and how family members should behave. For example, the belief that the main responsibility for parenting lies with mothers is still very influential.

We can see this dominant set of ideas about family life reflected in government **social policy** – for example, in the assumption that there is no need for state provision of free childcare because women are happy to give up work to look after children. Traditional beliefs are also reflected in the pronouncements of religious leaders, politicians and editors of newspapers, which regularly state that certain types of relationships (e.g. homosexual ones) and certain types of living arrangements (e.g. lone parents and **cohabitation**) are not worthy of being called families. We can even see such views reflected in our own everyday behaviour and attitudes, as Jon Bernardes argues:

>> *It is not just that many people think of women as the most appropriate carers of children but rather that we all act on this belief in our daily lives. Men may hesitate or not know how to engage in certain tasks or, in public, men may be discouraged from comforting a lost child whilst a woman may 'naturally' take up this role. Examples of family ideology can be found in a wide range of everyday practices, from images on supermarket products to who picks up dirty laundry (or who drops it in the first place).>>*

Bernardes, J. (1997) *Family Studies: An Introduction*, London: Routledge, p. 31

Functionalism and the family

For many years, the sociology of the family was dominated by the theory of functionalism. Functionalist sociologists see the family as one of the most important social institutions. In particular, functionalists see the family as the cornerstone of society because it is functional or beneficial both for the individual and for society. It meets the needs of individuals for emotional satisfaction, social support, personal development, identity and security. It meets the needs of society for social order and stability. It plays a key role in making individuals feel part of society.

Functionalists have identified a number of functions of the family that contribute to the well-being of society:

1 The family is the *primary agent of socialization* – It socializes new generations into the culture of society by teaching them common values, norms, traditions and roles. For example, children learn the patterns of behaviour expected of their gender, i.e. what is regarded as appropriate masculine and feminine behaviour. Parsons (1955) argued that families are 'personality factories', producing children who are committed to shared norms and values and who

have a strong sense of belonging to society. In these ways, the family is central to the creation of value consensus, **social integration** and, therefore, social order.

2 *The family is an important agent of social control* – It polices society's members on a daily basis, in order to maintain the consensus and social order brought about by socialization. For example, the family defines what is socially acceptable behaviour with regard to sex and regulates behaviour such as dating, pre-marital sex, marital sex and extra-marital sex. These family controls prevent the potential anarchy and disorder that might result if people were allowed to engage in unregulated sex. Furthermore, marriage results in emotional stability for the couple. As regards children, primary socialization involves the development of a conscience that allows the individual to know the difference between 'right' and 'wrong'. This is backed up through parental use of positive sanctions (e.g. rewards) and negative sanctions (e.g. punishments).

3 *Marriage* is regarded as *the most appropriate setting for* **procreation** – In fact, children are seen as the natural outcome of romantic love. Reproduction is an essential function because the family provides new members of society to replace those who have died.

4 The family also has a number of *economic functions* – It provides children with economic support, not only during their early years of dependence, but often well after they have flown the family nest, e.g. to go on to university or to set up homes of their own. The family also provides the economy with workers. The family, along with education, functions to ensure that its members are willing to take on occupational duties and obligations. Families also play a central role as consumers of the material goods and services produced by the economy. An examination of television advertising reveals the family to be the central unit of economic consumption.

5 Parsons argued that the *family functions to relieve the stress of modern-day living* – He claimed that family life 'stabilizes' adult personalities. This is sometimes referred to as the 'warm bath' theory, in that the family provides a relaxing environment for the male worker to immerse himself in after a hard day at work (see Fig. 2.2 above right). Romantic love and the unconditional love parents have for their children provide family members with the means to cope with the anxieties of modern life. In this sense, the family is 'home sweet home', a 'haven in a heartless world'.

6 Families also perform a number of *miscellaneous functions to support their members*:

– The economic, social and educational resources the family offers us give us our social status in the eyes of other members of society, e.g. our social-class position. These resources can determine whether or not we experience upward social mobility.

– Family members are often cared for and supported by other family members if they are ill, disabled or in poverty. The family, therefore, plays important health and welfare functions, and works alongside social institutions such as the National Health Service.

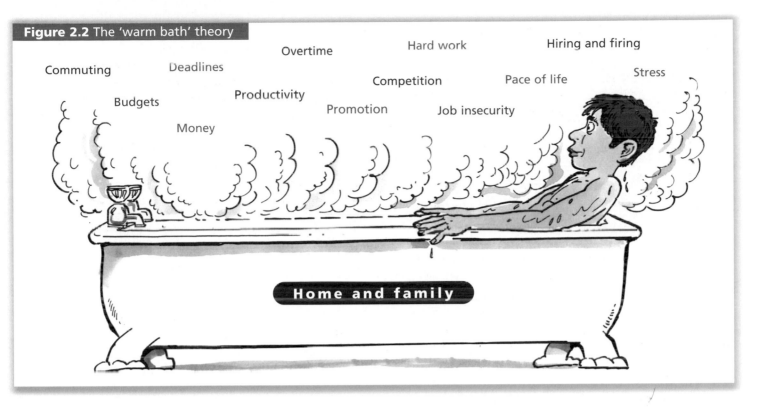

Figure 2.2 The 'warm bath' theory

Commuting Deadlines Overtime Hard work Hiring and firing
Budgets Productivity Competition Pace of life Stress
Money Promotion Job insecurity

Home and family

- Most children are taught to read and write by family members before they go to school. The family also often provides children with a number of cultural and material supports throughout their educational careers.
- Other sociologists point out that the family is important for both political and religious socialization. Many of our beliefs, prejudices and anxieties may be rooted in the strong emotional bonds we forge with our parents.
- The family is often an important site of leisure and recreation for its members.

Functionalists, therefore, see the family as a crucial social institution functioning positively to bring about healthy societies and individuals. Murdock (1949) went as far as to claim that the nuclear family is a biological necessity because it is universal, i.e. it can be found in all human societies.

Criticisms of functionalist views of the family

- The idea that families benefit all the individuals in them has been strongly attacked, especially by feminist sociologists, who argue that the family serves only to exploit and oppress women. Moreover, the rosy and harmonious picture of family life painted by functionalists ignores social problems such as increases in the divorce rate, child abuse and domestic violence.
- Functionalist analyses of the nuclear family tend to be based on middle-class and American versions of family life and, as a result, neglect other influences such as ethnicity, social class and religion. For example, Parsons does not consider the fact that wealth or poverty may determine whether or not women stay at home to look after children.

Since Parsons wrote in the 1950s, many Western societies, including the UK, have become multicultural. Religious and cultural differences may mean that Parsons' version of the family is no longer relevant in contemporary society.

- Functionalists also tend to see socialization as a one-way process, with children as passive recipients of culture. However, this view underestimates the role of children in families – they may have more choice in accepting or rejecting the attempts to mould their personalities than functionalists give them credit for.
- Functionalist thinking on the family suggests that the domestic **division of labour** is both 'natural' and unchangeable because it is based on biological differences. However, there is a lack of scientific evidence to support this view.
- Finally, social and cultural changes may mean that some of the functions of the family have been modified or even abandoned altogether, as demonstrated in Table 2.1 on the following page.

KEY TERMS

Cohabitation unmarried couples living together as man and wife.

Division of labour the organization of work.

Extended kin relations beyond the nuclear family, such as aunts, uncles and grandparents.

Fidelity faithfulness.

Heterosexual attracted to the opposite sex.

Nuclear family a family consisting of two parents and their children.

Nurturing caring for and looking after.

Procreation having children.

Social policy the measures the government takes to address social issues.

Social integration the sense of belonging to society.

Table 2.1 Changes in the functions of the family

Family function	Recent social trends – have these undermined or supported family functions?
Procreation	The size of families has declined as people choose lifestyle over the expense of having children. Many women prefer to pursue careers and are making the decision not to have children. The UK birth rate has consequently fallen.
Regulating sex	Sex outside marriage is now the norm. Alternative sexualities, e.g. homosexuality, are becoming more socially acceptable.
Stabilizing personalities	A high percentage of marriages end in divorce. However, some argue that divorce and remarriage rates are high because people continue to search for emotional security.
Economic	Although welfare benefits are seen by some as undermining family economic responsibilities, the family is still a crucial agency of economic support, especially as the housing market becomes more expensive for first-time buyers, and young people spend longer periods in education with the prospect of debt through student loans.
Welfare	A decline in state funding of welfare in the 1980s led to the encouragement of 'community care', in which the family – and especially women – became responsible for the care of the elderly, the long-term sick and the disabled.
Socialization	This is still rooted in the family, although there are concerns that the mass media and the peer group have become more influential, with the result that children are growing up faster.
Social control	Power has shifted between parents and children as children acquire more rights. This trend, alongside attempts to ban smacking in England and Wales, is thought by some sociologists to undermine parental discipline. Some sociologists argue that families need fathers and see the absence of fathers in one-parent families as a major cause of delinquency.

Check your understanding

1 Identify four features of the traditional family.

2 How influential is biology in shaping the traditional family?

3 What has been the impact of the traditional model of the family on popular thinking?

4 What is the 'warm bath' theory?

5 How have functionalist views of the family been criticized by feminists?

research ideas

- Conduct a survey amongst your classmates to find out about other families and their lifestyles. Focus particularly on size of family, whether parents work, who takes responsibility for domestic duties in the home, contact with **extended kin** such as grandparents and cousins, the role and responsibilities of children, and so on. How much do their accounts differ from your own experience of family life?

- Make a list of the functions that your family performs. Think about how family functions change according to how old you are and what gender you are. For example, think about how the family functioned for you as a baby. Compare that with how you think the family will function for you when you are 20.

web.task

Visit websites dedicated to the family such as www.familyeducation.com and www.familiesonline.co.uk

Look at the content of these sites in terms of advice, news and letters from parents. What functions should families be performing according to these sites? Do such functions support the functionalist theory of the family?

exploring defining the family

Item A   The five sentiments of the nuclear family

There are five sentiments that underpin traditional ideas about the nuclear family. First, marriage is regarded as the climax of romantic love, and children are seen as symbolic of the couple's commitment to each other. Second, it is assumed that the ultimate goal of women is to have children, stay at home and gain satisfaction through the socialization of their children. Women who choose not to have children may be viewed as 'unnatural'. Third, it is assumed that the family is a positive and beneficial institution in which family members receive **nurturing**, care and love. Fourth, the male is expected to be head of the household and to provide for the family. Finally, it is assumed that the immediate family comes first and all other obligations and relationships come second.

Adapted from Chapman, S. and Aiken, D. (2000) 'Towards a new sociology of families', *Sociology Review*, 9(3)

Item B   Questioning the functionalist view

The existence of 'the family' has been taken for granted by many sociologists. For functionalist sociologists, in particular, any query over the use of 'the family' appears trivial and tends to be dismissed. The failure by functionalists to question the idea of 'the family' has allowed all sorts of mistaken ideas to persist, such as the naturalness of monogamy (whereas many societies permit more than one marriage), the inevitability of female inferiority (which many feminists dispute), the right of men to control and abuse women (which many women dispute), and the right of parents to smack children (which is banned in some European countries, including Scotland).

Adapted from Bernardes, J. (1997) *Family Studies: An Introduction*, London: Routledge, pp. 4–5

Item C   Essential and non-essential functions of the family

Ronald Fletcher distinguishes between 'essential' and 'non-essential' functions of the family. He argues that, while other agencies have become responsible for six 'non-essential' functions, the family still performs three 'essential' functions that only it can perform. These are the stable satisfaction of sexual needs, the production and rearing of children, and the provision of a home. Fletcher argues that the state actually supports the family in fulfilling these essential functions through the provision of health care, child benefit, council housing, etc. Fletcher argues that the family is no longer primarily responsible for production of housing, clothing and food for its own needs, education, recreation, religion, health and welfare, although he stresses that the family still continues to play an important role in most of these areas of social life.

Adapted from Steel, E. and Kidd, W. (2001) *The Family*, Palgrave

1 **Explain what is meant by 'monogamy' (Item B).** (2 marks)

2 **Suggest two ways in which the traditional family is supposed to benefit adults, according to Item A.** (4 marks)

3 **Identify three functions associated with the traditional family by functionalist sociologists (Items A and C).** (6 marks)

4 **Identify and briefly describe two 'mistaken ideas' that have arisen out of the failure to question the idea of the family, according to Bernardes in Item B.** (8 marks)

5 **Examine the view that popular definitions of the family are dominated by a traditionalist nuclear family ideal.** (20 marks)

6 **Using information from the Items and elsewhere, assess the functionalist theory of the family.** (20 marks)

The family and industrialization

gettingyouthinking

'Summer', by Italian painter Bassano (c. 1570–80)

'The Common Method of Beetling, Scutching and Hackling the Flax', from 'The Linen Manufactory of Ireland', 1791 by William Hincks

1 What roles appear to be played by men, women, children and members of the extended family in these pictures?

2 Compare these with the roles they typically play today.

3 What reasons can you think of to explain the changes in roles?

The pre-industrial family

Parsons (1965) argued that the economic systems of **pre-industrial** societies were largely based on **extended kinship networks**. Land and other resources were commonly owned by a range of relatives extending well beyond the nuclear family unit. For example, it was not uncommon to live with and work alongside cousins. This extended family was responsible for the production of food, shelter and clothing, and would trade with other family groups for those things they couldn't produce themselves. Very few people left home to go to work. Home and workplace were one and the same thing.

Roles in these families were the product of **ascription** rather than **achievement**. This means that both family status and job were the product of being born into a particular extended family known for a particular trade or skill. For example, if the family were pig farmers, then there was a strong likelihood that all members of the family – men and women, old and young alike – would be involved in some aspect of pig farming. Moreover, these roles would be passed down from generation to generation. Few family members would reject the roles, because duty and obligation to the family and community were probably the key values of pre-industrial society.

In return for this commitment, the extended family network probably performed other functions for its members:

- The family equipped its members with the skills and education they needed to take their place in the family division of labour, although this socialization rarely extended to literacy and numeracy.
- The family functioned to maintain the health of its members, in the absence of a system of universal health care. However, the high infant mortality rates and low life expectancy of the pre-industrial period tell us that this was probably a constant struggle.
- The family also provided welfare for its members. For example, those family members who did make it into old age would be cared for, in exchange for services such as looking after very young children.
- The extended family was expected to pursue justice on behalf of any wronged family member.

The effects of industrialization

Parsons argued that the industrial revolution brought about four fundamental changes to the family:

1 **Industrialization** demanded a more **geographically mobile** workforce. At the same time, achievement became more important than ascription as mass education was introduced. People were, therefore, less likely to defer to their elders or feel a strong sense of obligation to remain near to kin. Parsons argued that nuclear families were formed as people moved away from their extended kin in the countryside in order to take advantage of the job opportunities brought about by industrialization in the towns.

2 The nuclear unit which evolved out of the pre-industrial extended family became 'isolated' from kin. They had less contact with kin and so were less reliant on them for economic and social supports. This was partly the result of geographical mobility which meant that nuclear units often moved away from the areas in which their extended family had lived for generations. Parsons saw the nuclear family as 'privatized', meaning that it was less likely to be subjected to pressures from extended kin or the immediate community. The nuclear family was 'home-centred' and more focused on the needs of its immediate members.

3 Specialized agencies developed which gradually took over many of the functions of the family. Parsons referred to this process as 'structural differentiation'. For example, after the industrial revolution, families could buy food and clothing mass produced in factories. Companies developed that specialized in the mass production of homes. The result of these processes was that the family became less important as an agency of production. The home and the workplace became separated as people become wage earners in the factory system. Moreover, the state also eventually took over the functions of education, health and welfare. This left the nuclear family to specialize in two essential functions – the primary socialization of children and the stabilization of adult personalities. Parsons claimed that structural differentiation resulted in the family becoming a more streamlined and effective unit.

4 The new nuclear unit provided the husband and wife with very clear social roles. The male is the '**instrumental leader**', responsible for the economic welfare of the family group and protection of family members. He goes out to work and earns money. The female is the '**expressive leader**', primarily responsible for the socialization of children and the emotional care and support of family members. It is clearly implied that this sexual division of labour is 'natural' because it is based on biological differences. For example, women's **maternal instincts** made them best suited to be emotional caretakers of both children and their spouses. Parsons saw relationships between husbands and wives as complementary, with each contributing to the maintenance of the family in a qualitatively different way.

Parsons concluded that only the nuclear unit could effectively provide the achievement-orientated and geographically mobile workforce required by modern industrial societies.

Historical criticisms of Parsons' view

Historians suggest that Parsons was far too simplistic in his interpretation of the history of the family. They point out that the evidence suggests that industrialization may follow different patterns in different industrial societies. The Japanese experience, for example, has been quite different from that of the UK and, consequently, extended families have remained important in Japan.

Laslett's (1972) study of English parish records suggests that only 10 per cent of households in the pre-industrial period contained extended kin. In other words, most pre-industrial families may have been nuclear, and not extended as Parsons claimed. Such small families were probably due to late marriage, early death and the practice of sending children away to become servants or apprentices. It may also be the case that industrialization took off so quickly because nuclear families already existed – and so people could move quickly to those parts of the country where their skills were in demand. However, Laslett's data has been criticized as unreliable because statistics do not give us any real insight into the quality of family life, i.e. how people actually experienced the family or the meaning they attached to family life. For example, people may have lived in nuclear units but may have seen and spent quality time with other relatives on a daily basis.

Michael Anderson's historical study (1971) of the industrial town of Preston, using census records from 1851, also contradicts Parsons' view that after industrialization, the extended unit was replaced by the nuclear family. Anderson found a large number of households shared by extended kin. These probably functioned as a **mutual support system** in a town in which unemployment and poverty were common. In other words, people probably pooled their low wages in order to share the cost of high rents and to help out those who were sick, disabled and elderly.

The British sociologists Young and Willmott (1957) take issue with Parsons over the speed of change. They suggest that the movement towards the nuclear unit was not as sudden as Parsons suggests, but rather that it was more gradual in nature. Their empirical research, conducted in the 1950s in the East End of London (Bethnal Green), showed that extended families existed in large numbers even at this advanced stage of industrialization. This extended kinship network was based upon emotional attachment and obligation. It was also a mutual support network, offering its members assistance with money, jobs, childcare and advice.

Young and Willmott (1973) argue that the extended family unit went into decline in the 1960s, when working-class communities were rehoused in new towns and on council estates after extensive slum clearance. Moreover, the welfare state and full employment in the 1950s undermined the need for a mutual support system. Bright working-class young men made the most of the opportunities and qualifications made available by the 1944 Education Act and were less likely to follow their fathers into manual work. Their social mobility into white-collar and professional jobs often meant geographical mobility, i.e. moving away from traditional working-class areas, and less frequent contact with kin. Young and Willmott therefore concluded that the nuclear or symmetrical family (see Topic 7) only became the universal norm in Britain in the late 20th century.

Marxist views

Marxists generally see the nuclear family as serving the interests of the ruling class because it promotes capitalist values and discourages dissent and criticism of inequality and the way capitalism is organized.

In particular, the nuclear family unit is seen as an **ideological apparatus** that promotes values and ways of thinking essential to the reproduction and maintenance of capitalism. It helps to ensure that the working class remain ignorant of the fact that they are being exploited by the capitalist system (see Unit 1, Topic 3). For example, nuclear families encourage their members to pursue the capitalist-friendly goals of materialism, consumerism and 'keeping up with the Joneses'. Marcuse (1964) claimed that working-class families are encouraged to pursue 'false needs' in the form of the latest consumer goods and to judge themselves and others on the basis of their acquisitions. He noted that this served the interests of capitalism rather than consumers, because it both stimulated the economy and distracted workers from the need to seek equality and justice.

Marxists argue that the family reproduces and maintains this 'false' class consciousness through primary socialization, which also stresses to children that the main route to happiness and status lies in material possessions. In addition, the way in which nuclear families are traditionally organized (e.g. the male as the head of the household) encourages passive acceptance of authority, obedience, hierarchy and inequality – qualities that are well suited to a conformist factory workforce. In these ways, the nuclear family benefits the capitalist class, rather than benefiting the whole of society as functionalists suggest.

Marxists argue that the working-class extended family has been deliberately discouraged by the capitalist ruling class, because its emphasis on a mutual support system and collective shared action encourages its members to be aware of their social-class position and hence inequality. Such class consciousness (see Unit 1, Topic 6) is regarded as threatening, because it may eventually challenge the wealth and power of the capitalist class.

Marxist-feminist views

Marxist-feminists are sceptical about Parsons' claim that the nuclear family meets the needs of industrial society. They, too, suggest that the nuclear family benefits capitalist society and therefore the bourgeoisie at the expense of the working class. Marxist-feminists have focused on the contribution of domestic labour, i.e. housework and childcare, to capitalist economies. They point out that such work is unpaid but has great value for capitalist economies. In other words, capitalism exploits women. Moreover, men benefit from this exploitation.

Margaret Benston (1972) suggested that the nuclear family is important to capitalism because it rears the future workforce at little cost to the capitalist state. Women's domestic labour and sexual services also help to maintain the present workforce's physical and emotional fitness. Mothers and housewives are also a useful reserve army of labour that can be hired cheaply as part-time workers in times of economic expansion and let go first in times of recession. Finally, it can be argued that the capitalist class directly exploit women's domestic labour by hiring women as cleaners, nannies and cooks. This enables the wealthy of both sexes to pursue careers outside the home.

Marxist-feminists agree that a traditional **familial ideology** exists and this benefits capitalism in three main ways:

- The focus on women as mothers puts considerable cultural pressure on women to have children and take time out of the labour market to bring up those children. This benefits capitalism by ensuring the creation of a future workforce. It also benefits men, because women do not compete on a level playing field for jobs or promotion opportunities.
- The socialization of children ensures that the pattern of male dominance and female subordination (symbolized by men's traditional role as main economic earner and head of household and women's as domestic labour) is reproduced generation after generation.
- The social policies of the state support traditional roles within the home and, in particular, women's responsibility for domestic labour. For example, women are given rights to maternity pay and maternity leave, while men's paternity rights are far fewer, reinforcing the view that children are mainly the responsibility of mothers rather than both parents.

Some feminists suggest that the nuclear family may also be useful to capitalism and men because it provides an emotionally supportive retreat for male workers who may be frustrated at their treatment in the workplace. The focus on a comfortable home and attaining a good standard of living may distract workers from their workplace problems and reduce the possibility of industrial unrest. However, some men may attempt to make up for their lack of power and control in the workplace by exerting control within the family. This may have negative consequences for some females, in the form of domestic violence (see Topic 7).

Radical feminist views

Radical feminists argue that the main beneficiaries of women's domestic labour are men. They argue that the main effect of industrialization was that women's prime function was defined as mother/housewife, allowing men to dominate paid work. They argue that both men and women are socialized into a set of ideas that largely confirm male power and superiority. In other words, familial ideology is **patriarchal ideology**. The family is the main arena for transmitting this ideology through the socialization of children into gender roles. Such socialization encourages the notion that the sexual division of labour is 'natural' and unchangeable. It is argued that women are also primarily portrayed by patriarchal familial ideology as sexual objects when single and mothers/housewives once married.

Radical feminists therefore suggest that the emergence of the modern nuclear family meets the needs of men rather than the needs of all members of society. The family is essentially a patriarchal institution which exploits and oppresses women.

However, these feminist criticisms of the family have been criticized for three main reasons:

1 Like functionalism, they have dated fairly badly, because they fail to account for recent economic and social changes, such as the feminization of the economy, the educational success of young females, women's use of divorce and many women's rejection of domestic labour as their unique responsibility.

2 They portray women as passively accepting their lot – the reality, however, is that women can adopt a range of active social identities today, many of which do not involve playing a secondary role to men. In other words, many young women are resisting traditional male definitions of what their role should be.

3 There is an implicit assumption that all male–female relationships involve male exploitation of women. However, the bulk of male–female relationships are probably based on mutual love and respect rather than domination and subordination.

KEY TERMS

Achievement the allocation of roles and status on the basis of individual merit, e.g. through the acquisition of qualifications.

Ascription the allocation of roles and status on the basis of fixed characteristics, e.g. on the basis of gender or what family you are born into.

Expressive leader Parsons' term for the female function of mother/housewife.

Extended kinship networks relationships between family members beyond the nuclear family, e.g. grandparents, cousins.

Familial ideology the view that a particular type of family (e.g. the nuclear family) and particular living arrangements (e.g. marriage, men as breadwinners, women as mothers and housewives, etc.) are the ideals that people should aspire to.

Geographical mobility the ability to move quickly around the country.

Ideological apparatus according to Marxists, any institution that is involved in the transmitting of ruling-class ideas, e.g. education, mass media.

Industrialization the process (occurring during the 18th and 19th centuries in Britain) whereby societies moved from agricultural production to industrial manufacturing. It had a huge impact, creating cities (urbanization), changing the sort of work people did, and fundamentally altering their social experiences and relationships.

Instrumental leader Parsons' term for the male breadwinner.

Maternal instinct a 'natural' instinct to desire motherhood and want to care for children.

Mutual support system a system in which family members work to support each other.

Patriarchal ideology ideas that support and justify male domination of society.

Pre-industrial before the industrial revolution.

The isolated nuclear family?

Parsons argued that nuclear families have little need for contact with wider kin. However, recent sociologists note that relatively self-sufficient nuclear families still feel a strong sense of obligation to extended kin in times of family crisis, despite distance (see Focus on Research below). Isolation from kin, therefore, is not a characteristic of many modern families.

focus on research

McGlone, Park and Smith (1998)
Families and kinship

Every year the British Social Attitudes study takes place. This survey uses structured interviews to discover the attitudes of a large sample of the British public. In 1998, Francis McGlone, Alison Park and Kate Smith compared the results of the 1986 and the 1995 studies with regard to the experiences of families with children. They concluded that, although contact had reduced over those 10 years, 'relatives remain important in the lives of most young parents, with the majority of people with dependent children remaining in frequent contact with their immediate family'. The authors discovered that unemployment and poverty, community care for the elderly, the increasing number of young people electing to live at home for longer periods and women going out to work all create a greater need for family mutual support systems.

1 How might the use of structured interviews in research aimed at discovering attitudes be criticized?

2 Suggest reasons why contact between members of the extended family may have declined in recent years.

Check your understanding

1 In Parsons' view:

(a) What functions did the pre-industrial family perform?

(b) What happened to the functions of the family after industrialization?

2 In what ways do historians challenge Parsons' ideas about family change?

3 From a Marxist perspective, whom does the nuclear family benefit? How?

4 Whom does the nuclear family benefit according to radical feminists? How?

research idea

● Visit your local reference library and ask to see a copy of the 1851 census for your area. Randomly choose a couple of streets and work out how households were organized. Does this evidence support Parsons or Anderson?

web.task

Use the worldwide web to research yours or a friend's family history. Start at www.familyrecords.gov.uk

You could also interview older relatives. How has your family changed? Do the changes in your family fit any of the patterns described in this topic?

exploring the family and industrialization

Item A From pre-industrial to industrial society

Functionalist view of the evolving family

PRE-INDUSTRIAL SOCIETY

Agricultural economy

Extended family

Labour-intensive production

Family as producers

→ Industrialization and urbanization →

→ Technological development →

INDUSTRIAL SOCIETY

Manufacturing economy

Nuclear family

Machine-intensive production

Family as consumers

Source: Jorgensen, N. (1995) *Investigating Families and Households*, London: Collins Educational, pp. 14–15

Item B The isolation of the nuclear family

According to functionalists, industrialization led to greater geographical mobility and loss of regular contact with extended kin. The wider family network was no longer required, as emotional and personal needs were met by the nuclear unit. However, a number of sociological studies of the 1950s and 1960s suggested that the isolation of the nuclear family from the wider family had been exaggerated. The study of Bethnal Green in London by Young and Willmott (1957) found extended families with frequent and strong contact between kin. By the late 1960s, studies of new council estates and factory workers with high incomes were suggesting that contact with kin, although not totally severed, was in decline. Research indicated that people were mainly living in nuclear families which were more inward-looking, home-centred and less inclined to be sociable outside the home with kin and friends.

Adapted from Abercrombie, N. and Warde, A. (2000) *Contemporary British Society* (3rd edn), Cambridge: Polity Press, pp. 302–9

Item C Feminism and unequal power relationships

During the 1970s and 1980s, feminist perspectives dominated most debates and research on the family. Many feminist writers questioned the functionalist vision that the family is a cooperative unit based on common interests and mutual support. They have sought to show that the presence of unequal power relationships within the family means that men benefit more than women from family life. They have emphasized two main themes. First, they argue that there exists a domestic division of labour in which women are exploited by men. Some feminists see this as a product of capitalism, while others claim that families were characterized by patriarchy well before industrialization came along. Second, feminists have drawn attention to the unequal power relationships that exist in many families that they see as responsible for domestic violence.

Adapted from Giddens, A. (2001) *Sociology* (4th edn), Cambridge: Polity Press, pp. 175–7

---

1 Explain what is meant by 'patriarchy' (Item C). (2 marks)

2 Suggest two ways in which extended kinship networks benefit their members. (4 marks)

3 Identify three ways in which industrialization affected the family. (6 marks)

4 Identify and briefly explain two reasons why families may have become isolated and privatized. (8 marks)

5 Examine the view that the nuclear family did not exist in the UK before industrialization. (20 marks)

6 Assess the view that the nuclear family exists primarily to benefit the powerful rather than society as a whole. (20 marks)

The family, morality and the state

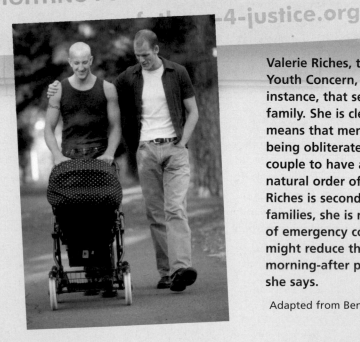

gettingyouthinking

Valerie Riches, the founder president of a body called Family and Youth Concern, is a woman of conviction. She is convinced, for instance, that sex education harms the young and undermines the family. She is clear that sending childless housewives out to work means that men's 'masculine role as the provider and father' is being obliterated. She has also criticized the decision of a gay couple to have a child by a surrogate mother. 'It's against the natural order of things', she says. Interestingly, although Ms Riches is second to none in her opposition to single-parent families, she is none the less firmly opposed to the introduction of emergency contraception – the morning-after pill – which might reduce the creation of more such faulty units. 'Taking a morning-after pill will encourage girls to be easy and carefree', she says.

Adapted from Bennett, C. (2000) 'Valerie's moral lead', *Guardian*, 14 December

1 Look carefully at the images above. How might some people see them as threatening the traditional family?

2 In the article, five things are identified that Valerie Riches thinks are undermining the family. What are they? Do you agree that these things are harming the family unit?

3 Think of any ways in which the government influences your family life. In your opinion, should it play a greater or a lesser role? What role, if any, should it play?

In the UK over the last 50 years, public debate about the family has focused on the changing nature of family life and its impact on society. This debate has often been dominated by those who, like Valerie Riches, take the view that the traditional nuclear family and the moral character of the young are under attack from a number of 'threats', including sex education, contraception, working mothers, homosexuality, divorce and single-parent families. Moreover, the state is accused of not doing enough to protect the traditional family. In fact, some commentators have suggested that liberal state policies, especially those introduced in the 1960s, are responsible for starting the perceived decline in traditional family values.

The golden age of family life

Those who claim that the family is in decline can be grouped under the label '**New Right**', in that they are usually conservative thinkers and politicians who believe very strongly in tradition. These commentators often assume that there was once a 'golden age' of the family, in which husbands and wives were strongly committed to each other for life, and children were brought up to respect their parents and social institutions such as the law.

Many New Right thinkers see the 1960s and early 1970s as the beginning of a sustained attack on traditional family values, particularly by the state. They point to social policies, such as the legalization of abortion in the 1960s and the NHS making the contraceptive pill available on prescription, as marking the beginning of family decline. The sexual freedom that women experienced as a result of these changes supposedly lessened their commitment to the family. At the same time, equal opportunities and equal pay legislation distracted women from their 'natural' careers as mothers. The 1969 Divorce Reform Act was seen as undermining commitment to marriage. The decriminalization of homosexuality and the lowering of the homosexual age of consent have been interpreted as particularly important symbols of moral decline, because the New Right see homosexuality as 'unnatural' and deviant.

Familial ideology

New Right views on the family reflect a **familial ideology** – a set of ideas about what constitutes an 'ideal' family. Their preferred model is the traditional nuclear family with a clear sexual division of labour, as described in Topic 1 (see p. 37). This ideology is transmitted by sections of the media and advertising, politicians, religious leaders, and pressure groups such as 'Family and Youth Concern'.

Family decline and the 'New Right'

This familial ideology also makes a number of assumptions about how not to organize family life. In particular, it sees the declining popularity of marriage, the increase in cohabitation, the number of births outside marriage, and teenage pregnancy as symptoms of the decline in family morality. Homosexuality, single parenthood, liberal sex education, abortion and working mothers are all seen as threats, both to family stability and to the wellbeing of society itself.

A good example of the New Right approach to the family can be seen in the view that there exists an underclass of criminals, unmarried mothers and idle young men who are responsible for rising crime. It is argued that this underclass is welfare-dependent, and that teenage girls are deliberately getting pregnant in order to obtain council housing or state benefits. To make things worse, this underclass is socialising its children into a culture revolving around crime and delinquency, and anti-authority, antiwork and antifamily values.

State policy and the family

Britain, unlike other European countries, does not have a separate minister for family affairs. However, three broad trends can be seen in state policy which suggest that the ideology of the traditional nuclear family has had, despite New Right misgivings, some positive influence on government thinking:

1 Tax and welfare policies have generally favoured and encouraged the heterosexual married couple rather than cohabiting couples, single parents and same-sex couples. Graham Allan (1985) goes as far as to suggest that these policies have actively discouraged cohabitation and one-parent families.

2 Policies such as the payment of child benefit to the mother, and the government's reluctance to fund free universal nursery provision, have reinforced the idea that women should take prime responsibility for children.

3 The lack of a coordinated set of family policies may reflect the fact that the state has tended to see the family as a **private institution** and is therefore reluctant to interfere in its internal organization. Despite being accused of being a 'nanny state' by its critics, the Labour government of Tony Blair has generally not directly intervened with legislation in family affairs. For example, in 2004, the state shied away from making the smacking of children by parents illegal.

Nevertheless, New Right thinkers still believe that grave damage has been inflicted on the nuclear family ideal by misguided government policy. For example, they claim that governments have encouraged mothers to return to work and, consequently, generations of children have been 'damaged' by **maternal deprivation**. There have been few tax or benefit policies aimed at encouraging mothers to stay at home with their children. The New Right argue that commitment to marriage has been weakened by governments making divorce too easy to obtain. Morgan (2000) even suggests that the government is 'antimarriage'. The New Right also claim that 'deviant' family types such as single-parent families have been encouraged by welfare policies.

Criticisms of the New Right

Government policy has generally been aimed at ensuring that the family unit does not overwhelm the rights of the individuals within it. Therefore, legislation has focused on improving the social and economic position of women. For example, the Conservative government made marital rape illegal in 1991. The Labour government introduced the 'New Deal' in April 1998, which aimed to encourage single mothers back to work. The same government also instructed police forces to get tough on domestic violence. The rights of children have also been enhanced through successive Children's Acts. There is no doubt that such legislation has undermined traditional male dominance in families, but many people believe that improved rights for women and children strengthen the family rather than weaken it.

The traditional nuclear family is still central to state policy. Feminist sociologists and other radical critics argue that the state generally supports familial ideology, as can be seen in Table 2.2 below.

There is also evidence that the Labour Government supports the familial ideology. Despite recognition of other family types, especially single-parent families, and sympathetic noises about improving the rights of gay people, cabinet ministers have regularly stated that married parents create the best environment for bringing up children.

Evaluating familial ideology

Feminists have claimed that familial ideology is merely patriarchal ideology – a set of ideas deliberately encouraged by men that ensure male dominance in the workplace. For example, Oakley points out that if society subscribes to the view that women have a maternal instinct, it follows on that society will believe that women who elect not to have children are somehow deviant, that 'real' women are committed to giving up jobs to bring up children, and that working mothers are somehow 'damaging' their children. Oakley argues that this aspect of familial ideology benefits men because it results in women withdrawing from the labour market – they do not compete with men for jobs which results in men enjoying advantages in promotion and pay. This ideology ties women to men, marriage, the home, children and, for a while, economic dependence. Moreover, such family ideology permeates gender-role socialization – girls are taught from infancy that motherhood is their ultimate goal.

Other sociologists have argued that familial ideology has led to the nuclear family being over**idealized**. It fails to acknowledge that divorce and one-parent families might be 'lesser evils' than domestic violence and emotional unhappiness. The ideology also neglects key cultural changes, such as the changing roles of men and women and, especially, cultural and ethnic diversity, as well as social and economic problems such as poverty, homelessness, racism, etc.

The view that the family is a private institution has led to the general neglect of severe social problems, such as child abuse and domestic violence. Until the late 1980s, for example, only as a very last resort would social workers break up families in which they suspected abuse. It took a series of abuse-related child deaths to change this policy.

A similar theme suggests that the ideology results in the worsening of family problems, such as domestic violence, because women believe that their husbands 'punish' them for being 'bad' wives and mothers. They therefore see themselves as deserving of punishment and believe that they should stick

Table 2.2 State policy and familial ideology

	State policy	Familial ideology
Care in the community	The state has encouraged families to take responsibility for the elderly and long-term sick and disabled. Female members of the family often carry the burden of this care, which means they are less likely to work full time and are more likely to be economically dependent upon a male.	The traditional sexual division of labour is reinforced; women as emotional and physical caretakers, and men as breadwinners.
Housing Policy	Fox Harding (1996) argues that the best council housing is often allocated to married couples with children and the worst housing on problem estates is allocated to one-parent families. Housing in the UK is overwhelmingly designed for the nuclear family.	The traditional nuclear family is clearly the dominant family type. Other types of family are 'punished' or discouraged.
Parenting	Fathers have only two days paid leave from work on the birth of a child – they have no legal rights for paid or unpaid leave for longer periods. The Child Support Agency (CSA) was set up to pursue absent fathers in order that they take financial responsibility for their children. Mothers are often awarded custody of children after divorce and fathers are often denied access to children by the law. Unmarried fathers have few legal rights over their children compared with married men.	It is assumed that women's primary role is motherhood and childcare rather than paid work. It is implied that men have no childcare skills. The function of the CSA is to ensure women's continuing economic dependence on men. Marriage is seen as superior to cohabitation.

by their man through thick and thin. This theme is explored further in Topic 7.

Barrett and McIntosh (1982) argue that familial ideology is antisocial because it dismisses alternative family types as irrelevant, inferior and deviant. For example, as a result of the emphasis on the nuclear family ideal and the view that families need fathers, one-parent families are seen as the cause of social problems, such as rising crime rates and disrespect for authority. This theme will be further explored in Topic 4.

The family: in decline or just changing?

New Right politicians strongly believe that the family – and therefore family ideology – is in decline, and that this is the source of all our social problems. However, it may simply be that family ideology is evolving rather than deteriorating, as we realize that the traditional family denies women and children the same rights as men. People today may be less willing to tolerate these forms of inequality and the violence and abuse that often accompany them. Increasing acceptance and tolerance of a range of family types may be healthy for society, rather than a symptom of moral decay.

focus on research

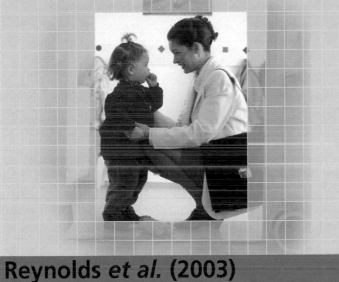

Reynolds et al. (2003)
Caring and counting

The researchers interviewed 37 mothers and 30 fathers in couples who had at least one pre-school child (Reynolds et al. 2003). The mothers were working in a hospital or in an accountancy firm. All the mothers in the study had strong, traditional views about what being a 'good mother' and a 'good partner' was about. Employment did not necessarily lead to more egalitarian relationships with their partners.

In fact, most of the mothers and fathers interviewed subscribed to highly traditional and stereotypical views about the gendered division of labour within the home. The mothers had primary responsibility for the home and the conduct of family life. Mothers who worked full time were just as concerned as those working part time to 'be there' for their children and to meet the needs of their children and their family.

The researchers found no evidence of mothers becoming more 'work centred' at the expense of family life. Those who worked full time were just as concerned to 'be there' for their children and their partner as those working part time.

Apart from increasing the family income, mothers also felt their employment was helping them to meet their children's emotional and social development. Separate interviews with the women's partners revealed widespread agreement that the mother's work was having a positive impact on family relationships. Most fathers felt their children had benefited from their mothers' work, which provided a positive role model for their children.

Some mothers, nevertheless, expressed concern that their job had a negative impact on the family, particularly when they were overstretched at work, felt tired or had trouble 'switching off' from a bad day at work. A number of fathers also felt uneasy about the demands placed on their partners at work and the effect that work-related stress could have on their children and their relationship with each other.

Adapted from the website of the Joseph Rowntree Foundation (www.jrf.org.uk)

1 **Comment on the sample used in the study.**

2 **How did parents feel that mothers' employment was having a positive effect on their families?**

3 **What concerns were expressed about mothers' employment?**

Jonathan Gershuny (2000)
Standards of parenting

A major theme of those who believe that the family is in decline is working parents and particularly working mothers. However, research illustrates the complexity of the debate about whether standards of parenting have fallen. In 2000, Jonathan Gershuny, using data from the diaries of 3000 parents, suggested that the quality of parenting had significantly improved compared with the past. He noted that the time British parents spent playing with and reading to their children had increased fourfold and this was the case for both working and non-working parents.

1 How could the use of diaries in Gershuny's research be criticized?

Check your understanding

1 What legislation introduced in the 1960s and 1970s is seen as damaging to the family, according to New Right commentators?

2 What is the attitude of the Labour government towards the family?

3 What are the main symptoms of the decline in family morality, according to the New Right?

4 In what ways has familial ideology had an impact on state policy?

5 In what ways has state policy been good for family members?

researchideas

● Conduct a mini-survey of teenagers and old-age pensioners to see whether there is any major difference in how they perceive family life and so-called 'threats' to it, such as homosexuality, cohabitation and illegitimacy.

● Observe the media and other institutions for signs of familial ideology. You could, for example:
  – study television commercials at different times of the day
  – examine the content of specific types of programmes, such as soap operas or situation comedies
  – analyse the content of women's magazines
  – stroll through family-orientated stores, such as Mothercare, Boots and BHS, to see whether familial ideology is apparent in their organization, packaging, marketing, etc.

web.tasks

1 Visit the websites of organizations dedicated to protecting family life, such as the Family Matters Institute at www.familymatters.org.uk and Family and Youth Concern at www.famyouth.org.uk and make a list of the family issues they consider to be important. In what ways do these issues support familial ideology?

2 Visit the websites of the major political parties and find out what their policies are towards the family.

Item A Conservative views of the family

Conservative thinkers have tended to define what the traditional family should be in terms of a heterosexual conjugal unit based on marriage and co-residence. A clear segregation of tasks based on sexual differences is seen as the 'traditional', 'natural' and 'God-given' way of ordering our lives. It is assumed that the man is the 'natural' head of the family. The family's key tasks are the reproduction of the next generation, the protection of dependent children and the inculcation of proper moral values in children. The family also disciplines men and women in economic and sexual terms: it keeps us in our proper place. Order, hierarchy and stability are seen as the key features of the 'healthy' family and the 'healthy' society. However, conservative commentators see this traditional family as under threat and in decline. This is seen as one of the main causes of the claimed wider moral decay in society.

Adapted from Sherratt, N. and Hughes, G. (2000) 'Family: from tradition to diversity?' in G. Hughes and R. Fergusson (eds) *Ordering Lives: Family, Work and Welfare*, London: Routledge, p. 60

Item B State interference in the family

<< The state has intervened significantly in families for a considerable length of time, whether by providing support (such as family income credits for those earning low wages and with dependent children) or in overseeing the bringing up of children (if social workers think this is not being done properly, then children may be put temporarily or more permanently into the care of the local authority). This interference has not lessened – indeed, as politicians and the media have come together to discuss what they see as the decline of the family, so the extent of that interference has increased. However, conservative thinkers tend to believe that there has not been enough state input into protecting the traditional family, or that state interference has actually contributed to its decline by encouraging the development of 'deviant' living arrangements.>>

Abercrombie, N. and Warde, A. (2000) *Contemporary British Society* (3rd edn), Cambridge: Polity Press, pp. 287–8

Item C Same-sex couples are families too

The House of Lords has ruled that a homosexual couple in a stable relationship can be defined as a family. One of the law lords, Lord Nicholls defined a family as follows: 'The concept underlying membership of a family is the sharing of lives together in a single family unit living in one house. It seems to me that the bond must be one of love and affection, not of a casual nature, but in a relationship which is permanent, or at least intended to be so. As a result of that permanent attachment, other characteristics will follow, such as a readiness to support each other emotionally and financially, to care for and look after each other in times of need, and to provide a companionship in which mutual interests and activities can be shared'. Dr. Adrian Rogers of the pressure group, Family Focus, deplored the ruling and said 'homosexual couples cannot be defined as families – the basis of true love is the ability to procreate and have children'.

Adapted from the *Guardian*, 29 October 1999.

1 **Explain what is meant by the phrase 'the traditional family' (Item A).** (2 marks)

2 **Identify two ways in which the state intervenes in family life (Item B).** (4 marks)

3 **Suggest three ways in which the traditional family might be seen as being 'under threat and in decline' (Item A).** (6 marks)

4 **Identify and briefly explain two problems that may be caused by the overidealization of the nuclear family.** (8 marks)

5 **Examine the view that the traditional nuclear family is no longer valued.** (20 marks)

6 **Using information from Item B and elsewhere, assess the argument that state policy has largely failed to protect the institution of the family.** (20 marks)

Marriage and marital breakdown

gettingyouthinking

A summary of changes over time
Marital status and cohabitation

Living in Britain
The 2002 General
Household Survey

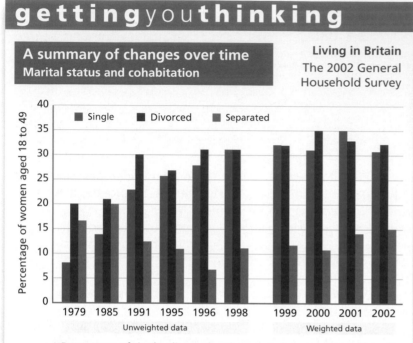

- ■ Single ■ Divorced ■ Separated

Percentage of women aged 18 to 49

Unweighted data
Weighted data

Percentage of single, divorced and separated women aged 18 to 49 cohabiting, by legal marital status: Great Britain, 1979 to 2002
Widows have not been included because their numbers are so small.

Divorces

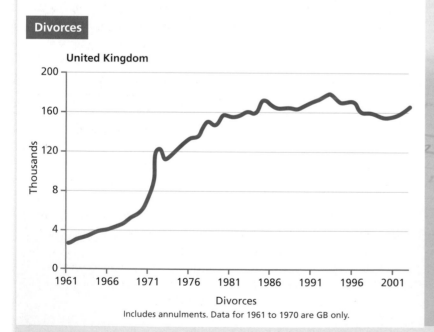

United Kingdom

Thousands

Divorces
Includes annulments. Data for 1961 to 1970 are GB only.

Above: Marriage in the 21st century? A couple on the escalator on their way to tying the knot in the clothing department at the supermarket where they work

Below: Is marriage still a lifelong commitment?

1 What has been the general trend for divorce since 1961?

2 What does the bar chart tell us about the marital status of cohabiting women since 1979?

3 Suggest possible explanations for the trends illustrated above.

4 Why might the images above and the statistical trends be alarming for supporters of the traditional family?

It is not difficult to see why supporters of the traditional family, such as the New Right, are so alarmed by figures and images such as those on the left. They believe that they indicate a crisis in the family, which will inevitably result in increasing antisocial behaviour and moral breakdown. Many postmodernists and feminists look at the figures and images in a very different way – they see them as indicators of greater personal choice in our private lives, and as evidence of a rejection of patriarchal family arrangements. So who is right?

Marriage

The latest statistics indicate that fewer people are getting married than at any other time in the last century. There were just fewer than 250 000 weddings in 2001, compared with 426 000 in 1972, although this improved to 254 000 in 2002. Only 34 per cent of marriages involved a religious ceremony in 2002 compared with 51 per cent in 1991.

In 1996, only one third of all British women in their late twenties were married with children, compared with two thirds in 1973. Berthoud (2000) has observed ethnic differences in the marriage statistics. For example, he notes that about three quarters of Pakistani and Bangladeshi women are married by the age of 25, while Black British people are the group least likely to get married.

These figures have recently provoked a keen debate between New Right commentators and feminists. New Right commentators express concerns about the decline in marriage. Patricia Morgan (2000) argues that marriage involves unique 'attachments and obligations' that regulate people's behaviour. For example, she claims that married men are more likely to be employed than unmarried or cohabiting men and earn more (i.e. 10 to 20 per cent more in 2001) because they work harder than any other male group. Furthermore, married people live longer than single people.

However, fears about what these statistics reveal are probably exaggerated for three reasons:

1 People are delaying marriage rather than rejecting it. Most people will marry at some point in their lives. However, people are now marrying later in life, probably after a period of cohabitation. The average age for first-time brides in 2001 was 28.4 years and for all grooms 30.6 years, compared with 22 for women and 24 for men in 1971. Women may delay marriage because they want to develop their careers and enjoy a period of independence.
2 British Social Attitude Surveys indicate that most people, whether single, **divorced** or cohabiting, still see marriage as a desirable life-goal. People also generally believe that having children is best done in the context of marriage. Few people believe that the freedom associated with living alone is better than being married to someone.
3 More than 40 per cent of all marriages are remarriages (in which one or both partners have been divorced). These people are obviously committed to the institution of marriage despite their previous negative experience of it. An interesting new trend is the number of young men – aged

under 25 – who are marrying women significantly older than them, i.e. 'toy-boy' marriages. One in three of first-time grooms are younger than their brides, more than double what it was in 1963.

Wilkinson (1994) notes that female attitudes towards marriage and family life have undergone a radical change or 'genderquake'. She argues that young females no longer prioritize marriage and children, as their mothers and grandmothers did. Educational opportunities and the feminization of the economy have resulted in young women weighing up the costs of marriage and having children against the benefits of a career and economic independence. The result of this is that many females, particularly middle-class graduates, are opting out of marriage and family life altogether.

Other feminist sociologists are sceptical about the value of marriage. Smith (2001) argues that marriage creates unrealistic expectations about **monogamy** and faithfulness in a world characterized by sexual freedom. She argues that at different points in people's life cycles, people need different things which often can only be gained from a new partner. Campbell (2000) suggests that marriage is promoted because of fears about lack of discipline among young people. Moreover, she suggests that marriage benefits men more than it does women.

Cohabitation

A constant source of concern to the New Right has been the significant rise in the number of couples cohabiting during the last decade. In 1998, 28 per cent of men and 26 per cent of women living in Britain, aged between 25 and 29, cohabited. New Right commentators claim that cohabitation is less stable than marriage. A report by the Institute for the Study of Civil Society (Morgan 2000) claimed that cohabiting couples were less happy and less fulfilled than married couples, and more likely to be abusive, unfaithful, stressed and depressed.

However, surveys indicate that few people see cohabitation as an alternative to marriage. Rather, it is merely seen as a prelude to marriage, i.e. as a test of compatibility, and consequently tends to be a temporary phase, lasting on average about five years, before approximately 60 per cent of cohabiting couples eventually marry – usually some time after the first child is born. Although cohabitation marks a dramatic change in how adults live together – it was met with extreme moral disapproval as recently as the 1960s – cohabiting couples with and without children only account for 6 per cent of all households. Cohabitation is also linked to the rising divorce rate, i.e. a significant number of people live together quite simply because they are waiting for a divorce.

Births outside marriage

New Right commentators have been especially disturbed by the fact that one in three babies is now born outside marriage. In particular, media **moral panics** have focused on the fact that the UK has the highest rate of teenage pregnancy in Europe.

For example, in 2002, there were 44 100 pregnancies in the 16-to-18 age group and 7875 among the under 16s.

However, according to the National Council for One Parent Families, the under-16 conception rate has fallen considerably, compared with the 1960s, and it has fallen slightly over the last ten years to approximately 8 per 1000 girls. Only 3 per cent of unmarried mothers are teenagers, and most of them live at home with their parents. Experts are generally sceptical that such teenagers are deliberately getting pregnant in order to claim state housing and benefits. Moreover, four out of five births outside marriage are registered to both parents, and three-quarters of these are living at the same address. Most births outside marriage, therefore, are to cohabiting couples. It should also be pointed out that a significant number of marriages break up in the first year after having a child, which suggests that marriage is not always the stable institution for procreation that the New Right claim it is.

Some sociologists argue that we should be more concerned about the trend towards childlessness that has appeared in recent years. The Family Policy Studies Centre estimates that one woman in five will choose to remain childless, and this figure is expected to double in the next 20 years (McAllister 1998). In 2000, one in five women aged 40 had not had children compared with one in ten in 1980, and this figure is expected to rise to one in four by 2018. There is no doubt that fewer children are being born. Current fertility patterns suggest that women today have an average of 1.7 children each. This is not sufficient to replace the population lost due to death and emigration. Moreover, women are having children later in life, e.g. births to women aged between 35 and 39 have dramatically increased in the last 20 years.

Marital breakdown

Types of marital breakdown

Marital breakdown can take three different forms: divorce, separation and **empty-shell marriages**:

- *Divorce* refers to the legal ending of a marriage. Since the Divorce Reform Act of 1969, divorce has been granted on the basis of '**irretrievable** breakdown' and, since 1984, couples have been able to petition for divorce after the first anniversary of their marriage. 'Quickie' divorces are also available, in which one partner has to prove the 'fault' or 'guilt' of the other, for matrimonial 'crimes' such as adultery, although these tend to be costly.
- *Separation* is where couples agree to live apart after the breakdown of a marriage. In the past, when divorce was difficult to obtain or too expensive, separation was often the only solution.
- *Empty-shell marriages* are those in which husband and wife stay together in name only. There may no longer be any love or intimacy between them. Today, such marriages are likely to end in separation or divorce, although this type of relationship may persist for the sake of children or for religious reasons.

The divorce rate

Britain's divorce rate is high, compared with other industrial societies. Within Europe, only Denmark has a higher rate. In 1938, 6000 divorces were granted in the UK. This figure had increased tenfold by 1970, and in 1993, it peaked at 165 000 but fell thereafter. However, in 2002, divorce rose for the first time in seven years to 148 000. People who had been divorced before constituted about 20 per cent of this total. There are now nearly half as many divorces as marriages.

By the late 1980s, almost 25 per cent of all women who had married when under 20 years of age were separated after only five years of marriage. If present trends continue, about 40 per cent of current marriages will end in divorce.

New Right sociologists argue that such divorce statistics are a symptom of a serious crisis in the family. They suggest that, because of the easy availability of divorce, people are no longer as committed to the family as they were in the past. This view was partly responsible for the government abandoning the section of the Family Law Act (1996) that intended to replace existing divorce procedures with a single ground for divorce. Under this new legislation, divorce would have been granted to couples with children after a compulsory cooling-off period of 18 months, if both parties agreed after counselling that their marriage had ended. However, fears that this was an easier way out of marriage than the present system prompted the Labour government to abandon the proposal in 2001.

Why is the divorce rate increasing?

Changes in divorce law have generally made it easier and cheaper to end marriages, but this is not necessarily the cause of the rising divorce rate. Legal changes reflect other changes in society, especially changes in attitudes. In particular, sociologists argue that social expectations about marriage have changed. Functionalist sociologists even argue that high divorce rates are evidence that marriage is increasingly valued and that people are demanding higher standards from their partners. Couples are no longer prepared to put up with unhappy, 'empty-shell' marriages. People want emotional and sexual compatibility and equality, as well as companionship. Some are willing to go through a number of partners to achieve these goals.

Feminists note that women's expectations of marriage have radically changed, compared with previous generations. In the 1990s, most **divorce petitions** were initiated by women. This may support Thornes and Collard's (1979) view that women expect far more from marriage than men and, in particular, that they value friendship and emotional gratification more than men do. If husbands fail to live up to these expectations, women may feel the need to look elsewhere.

Women's expectations have probably changed as a result of the improved educational and career opportunities they have experienced since the 1980s. Women no longer have to be unhappily married because they are financially dependent upon their husbands. Moreover, Hart (1976) notes that divorce may be a reaction to the frustration that many working wives may feel if they are responsible for the bulk of housework and childcare. Similarly, it may also be the outcome of tensions produced by women taking over the traditional male role of breadwinner in some households, especially where the male is unemployed and the 'crisis of masculinity' might result from the male feeling that his role has been usurped.

Divorce is no longer associated with stigma and shame. This may be partly due to a general decline in religious practices. The social controls, such as extended families and **close-knit communities**, that exerted pressure on couples to stay together and that labelled divorce as 'wicked' and 'shameful', are also in decline. Consequently, in a society dominated by **privatized nuclear families**, the view that divorce can lead to greater happiness for the individual is more acceptable. It is even more so if divorce involves escaping from an abusive relationship or if an unhappy marriage is causing emotional damage to children. However, it is important to recognize that such attitudes are not necessarily a sign of a casual attitude towards divorce. Most people experience divorce as an emotional and traumatic experience, equivalent to bereavement. They are usually also aware of the severe impact it may have on children.

Beck and Beck-Gernsheim (1995) argue that rising divorce rates are the product of a rapidly changing world in which the traditional rules, rituals and traditions of love, romance and relationships no longer apply. In particular, they point out that the modern world is characterized by individualization, choice and conflict.

- *Individualization* – We are under less pressure to conform to traditional collective goals set by our extended family, religion or culture. We now have the freedom to pursue individual goals.

- *Choice* – Cultural and economic changes mean that we have a greater range of choices available to us in terms of lifestyle and living arrangements.
- *Conflict* – There is now more potential for antagonism between men and women because there is a natural clash of interest between the selfishness encouraged by individualization and the selflessness required by relationships, marriage and family life.

Beck and Beck-Gernsheim argue that these characteristics of the modern world have led to personal relationships between men and women becoming a battleground (they call it the 'chaos of love') as evidenced by rising divorce rates. However, Beck and Beck-Gernsheim are positive about the future because they note that people still generally want to find love with another in order to help them cope with a risky, rapidly changing world. In particular, love helps compensate for the stress and, particularly, the impersonal and uncertain nature of the modern world. Love is the one thing people feel is real and that they can be sure of. Divorce and remarriage may simply be signs that people still have faith that they will one day find the true love they need to help them cope with the complexity of modern life.

Divorce trends suggest that monogamy (one partner for life) will eventually be replaced by **serial monogamy** (a series of long-term relationships resulting in cohabitation and/or marriage). However, the New Right panic about divorce is probably exaggerated. It is important to remember that although four out of ten marriages may end in divorce, six out of ten succeed. Over 75 per cent of children are living with both natural parents who are legally married. These figures suggest that society still places a high value on marriage and the family.

Figure 2.3 Reasons for increasing divorce rate

Changes in divorce law have generally made it easier and cheaper to end marriages but legal changes reflect other changes in society, especially changes in attitudes.

Divorce may be the outcome of tensions produced by women taking over the traditional male role of breadwinner in some households.

Divorce is no longer associated with stigma and shame. The view that divorce can lead to greater happiness for the individual is more acceptable.

Functionalist sociologists argue that high divorce rates are evidence that marriage is increasingly valued and that people are demanding higher standards from their partners.

Beck and Beck-Gernsheim (1995): rising divorce rates are the product of a rapidly changing world in which the traditional rules, rituals and traditions of love, romance and relationships no longer apply.

Thornes and Collard: women value friendship and emotional gratification more than men do. If husbands fail to live up to these expectations, women may feel the need to look elsewhere.

Hart: divorce may be a reaction to the frustration that many working wives may feel if they are responsible for the bulk of housework and childcare.

Women's improved educational and career opportunities mean that they no longer have to be unhappily married because they are financially dependent upon their husbands.

Smart and Stevens (2000)

Cohabitation: testing the water?

Smart and Stevens (2000) carried out interviews with 20 mothers and 20 fathers who were separated from cohabiting partners with whom they had had a child. They found that most of the sample were either indifferent to marriage or had been unsure about marrying the person with whom they had lived. Many of the female respondents had wanted their partners to become more 'marriage-worthy', especially in terms of expressing emotional commitment and helping more with the children. Cohabitation, then, was generally a test of their own and their partner's commitment. Many felt that their level of commitment to each other was the same as married couples but they believed it was easier to leave a cohabiting relationship than it was to leave a marriage.

1 What does this research tell us about the meaning of cohabitation?

2 What effect might the choice of sample have had on the findings?

KEY TERMS

Close-knit community a community in which there are close relationships between people (everyone knows everyone else).

Divorce the legal ending of a marriage.

Divorce petition a legal request for a divorce.

Empty-shell marriage a marriage in which the partners no longer love each other but stay together, usually for the sake of the children.

Irretrievable unable to be recovered. Broken down for ever.

Monogamy the practice of having only one partner.

Moral panic public concern over some aspect of behaviour, created and reinforced in large part by sensational media coverage.

Privatized nuclear family a home-centred family that has little contact with extended kin or neighbours.

Serial monogamy a series of long-term relationships.

web.tasks

1 **Use the archives of either the *Guardian* or the *Daily Telegraph* websites to research the debate about divorce. The latter is excellent for links to relevant sites such as www.divorceon-line.com, the family law consortium and the Lord Chancellor's Department.**

2 **Visit the websites of the following organizations and work out whether they support familial ideology:**

– **www.themothersunion.org**

– **www.civitas.org.uk – this site has a collection of interesting fact sheets on the family plus excellent links to traditionalist family sites**

– **www.oneplusone.org.uk**

Check your understanding

1 Why have marriage rates declined in recent years?

2 What has been the trend in the number of births outside marriage?

3 Why are teenage mothers not the problem the media make them out to be?

4 Why is cohabitation not a threat to marriage?

5 Why are women more likely to initiate divorce proceedings than men?

research ideas

● Carry out a mini-survey across three different age groups (e.g. 15 to 20, 25 to 30, and 35 to 40), investigating attitudes towards marriage, cohabitation, childlessness, births outside marriage, etc.

● Interview two males and two females to find out what characteristics they are looking for in a future partner. Do your findings support the view that females set higher standards in relationships?

exploring marriage and marital breakdown

Item A The changing family

The family seems to be dwindling as a social institution. The stark figures would suggest that British society has turned its back on those things normally associated with the idea of 'the family'. Within one generation, we have seen the following changes: only half as many people are getting married, lone-parent families have increased threefold, children born outside marriage have quadrupled in number, and the number of divorces has trebled. However, there is strong evidence that these things indicate a change in the nature of the family, rather than its death. The family remains a cornerstone of British society in terms of people's lives and their sense of identity. Families are still a crucial source of care and support for the elderly and the disabled. Nearly two in three working mothers turn to relatives for help with childcare. Most people are in regular contact with relatives and see them at least once a month. At Christmas, more than four in five people join in some form of family gathering.

Adapted from Denscombe, M. (1998) *Sociology Update*, Leicester: Olympus Books, p. 20

Item B Deferring motherhood

Marriage is a normal and expected part of women's lives in Western society. However, although the vast majority of women will expect to marry at some time and at least once, in recent years there has been some decline in the popularity of marriage. In 1971, only 4 per cent of women remained unmarried by the age of 50, but by 1987, the proportion had grown to 17 per cent. Women today are marrying older and marrying less. The Family Policy Studies Centre estimates that one in five young women will remain childless. Typically, those who defer motherhood are educated women. A recent study showed that women who have qualifications are twice as likely as those with no qualifications to say they expect to have no children.

Adapted from Chandler, J. (1993) 'Women outside marriage', *Sociology Review*, 2(4), and Jorgensen, N. *et al.* (1997) *Sociology: An Interactive Approach*, London: Collins Educational, pp. 100–1

Item C Married with children

Despite all the arguments about the decline of marriage, the increase in illegitimacy and so on, it continues to be the case that most people in Britain grow up, get married and form a nuclear family for part of their adult life. Nine out of ten people get married at some time in their lives; 90 per cent of women are married by the age of 30 and over 90 per cent of men before the age of 40. Most couples who get married (or have stable cohabitation relationships) have children. Thus nine out of ten married women have children, and four out of five children live with their two natural parents. Seventy-nine per cent of families with children are headed by a married couple.

Adapted from Abbott, P. and Wallace, C. (1997) *An Introduction to Sociology: Feminist Perspectives* (2nd edn), Routledge

1 Explain in your own words what is meant by the term 'serial monogamy'. (2 marks)

2 Identify two trends that suggest that the family remains a 'cornerstone of society' (Item A). (4 marks)

3 Identify three reasons why some women are choosing voluntary childlessness (Item B). (6 marks)

4 Identify and briefly explain two reasons why cohabitation is increasing. (8 marks)

5 Examine criticisms of the view that the increase in divorce is due to its easy availability. (20 marks)

6 Using information from the Items and elsewhere, assess the argument that the recent trends in marriage, cohabitation, divorce and births outside marriage are significant threats to the stability of the family. (20 marks)

Family diversity

getting you thinking

The Immediate Family...

Ann's stepsister
Ann's stepMum
Ann's stepgran
Ann's stepsister
Ann's Stepdad
Ann's Gran
Ann's Mum
Ann's brother
Ann
Ann's Dad
Phil
Phil's Mum & Dad
Phil's Stepmother
Phil's Gran's bloke
Phil's Gran
Phil's stepfather & stepsister
Phil's step brother
Phil's Grandad
Phil's step Grandmother
Ann's ½ sisters
Phil's ½ brother & sister

Single Parent Family | Advertising Family | Lesbian Family | Child-free Family | Gay Family | Step Family | Divorced Family | Socially Excluded | Nuclear Family | We're no longer in love but we decided to stay together for the children's sake... | Long term Family

1 Examine the Posy Simmonds cartoon above – which of these family setups fit the traditional view of the family?

2 Which family setups are furthest from the ideal? Explain why.

3 In what way do the images of family life above support the view that familial ideology is out of touch with reality?

The nuclear family is by no means the only way to organize living arrangements. Rapoport *et al.* (1982) are very critical of the functionalist and New Right view that the typical family is nuclear. They point out that even back in 1978, only 20 per cent of families fitted this ideal. Rapoport and colleagues argue that family life in Britain is actually characterized by **diversity**. A range of family types exist, with diverse internal setups reflecting the changing nature of British society.

Organizational or structural diversity

In 1999, only 23 per cent of households were made up of couples with dependent children. In other words, the nuclear unit seems to be in the minority. However, household statistics give us only a static picture of family life. Other categories, such as married-couple and single-person households, may have evolved out of nuclear units, or may evolve into nuclear units in the near future. It is important, therefore, not to dismiss the nuclear unit as irrelevant. If we look at the statistics in another way, a different picture emerges – for example, two-parent families make up 74 per cent of all families. However, there is no doubt that other family structures – such as cohabiting couples with children, one-parent families and reconstituted families – are growing in importance. Denscombe notes that 41 per cent of children live in a non-traditional family today in 2004.

One-parent families

The number of one-parent families with dependent children tripled from 2 per cent of UK households in 1961 to 7 per cent in 2003. There are now approximately 1.75 million lone-parent families in Britain, making up about 25 per cent of all families. About 26 per cent of people under the age of 19 live in a one-parent family.

Ninety per cent of single-parent families are headed by women. Most of these are ex-married (divorced, separated or widowed) or ex-cohabitees. The fastest growing group of single parents is made up of those who have never married or cohabited. Haskey estimated this group to be 26 per cent of all single mothers in 2002. Contrary to popular opinion, most single mothers are not teenagers – teenage mothers make up just 3 per cent of lone parents. The average age of a lone parent is actually 34.

Ford and Millar (1998) note that lone parenthood is seen by some as an inherently second-rate and imperfect family type, reflecting the selfish choices of adults against the interests of children. For example, New Right thinkers see a connection between one-parent families, educational underachievement and delinquency. They believe that children from one-parent families lack self-discipline and can be emotionally disturbed, because of the lack of a firm father figure in their lives. In addition, New Right thinkers are concerned about the cost of one-parent families to the state. Public expenditure on such families increased fourfold in the 1990s. It is suggested that the state offers 'perverse incentives', such as council housing and benefits, to young females to get pregnant.

Ford and Millar note that the 'perverse incentives' argument is flawed when the quality of life of lone parents is examined. Many experience poverty, debt and material hardship, and try to protect their children from poverty by spending less on themselves. Ford and Millar also suggest that poverty may be partly responsible for lone parenthood. Single women from poor socio-economic backgrounds living on council estates with higher than average rates of unemployment are more likely than others to become solo mothers. Motherhood is regarded as a desired and valued goal by these women and may be a rational response to their poor economic prospects. Surveys of such women suggest that children are a great source of love and pride, and most lone parents put family life at the top of things they see as important.

Feminist sociologists maintain that familial ideology causes problems for the one-parent family because it emphasizes the nuclear family ideal. This ideal leads to the **negative labelling** of one-parent families by teachers, social workers, housing departments, police and the courts. Single parents may be **scapegoated** for inner-city crime and educational underachievement, when these problems are actually the result of factors such as unemployment and poverty. The New Right also rarely consider that single parenthood may be preferable to the domestic violence that is inflicted by some husbands on

focus on research

Burghes and Brown (1995)
Teenage single mothers

A qualitative study using unstructured interviews with 31 mothers who were teenagers at conception and who have never been married was carried out by Burghes and Brown in 1995. They found that most of the pregnancies were unintended. However, nearly all the respondents expressed strong anti-abortion views and adoption was rarely considered. Most of the mothers reported that their experience of lone motherhood was a mixture of hard work and enormous joy. For the most part, the mothers interviewed preferred to be at home caring for their children. All the mothers intended to resume training or employment once their children were in school. Marriage was also a long-term goal.

1 How does this research challenge stereotypes about teenage mothers?

their wives and children – or that the majority of one-parent families bring up their children successfully.

Reconstituted families

The **reconstituted** or stepfamily is made up of divorced or widowed people who have remarried, and their children from the previous marriage (or cohabitation). Such families are on the increase because of the rise in divorce. In 2003, it was estimated that 726 000 children were living in this type of family.

Reconstituted families are unique because children are also likely to have close ties with their other natural parent. An increasing number of children experience co-parenting, where they spend half their week with their mother and stepfather and spend the other half with their father. Some family experts see co-parenting as a characteristic of binuclear families – two separate post-divorce or separation households are really one family system as far as children are concerned.

De'Ath and Slater's (1992) study of step-parenting identified a number of challenges facing reconstituted families. Children may find themselves pulled in two directions, especially if the relationship between their natural parents continues to be strained. They may have tense relationships with their step-parents, and conflict may arise around the extent to which the step-parent and stepchild accept each other, especially with regard to whether the child accepts the newcomer as a 'mother' or 'father'. Strained relations between step-parents and children may test the loyalty of the natural parent and strain the new marriage. These families may be further complicated if the new couple decide to have children of their own, which may create the potential for envy and conflict among existing children.

Kinship diversity

There is evidence that the **classic working-class extended family** continues to exist. The study *Villains*, by Janet Foster (1990) – of an East End London community – found that adults were happy to live only a few streets away from their parents and close relatives, and visited them regularly. Ties between mothers and children were particularly strong, and contacts between mothers and married daughters were frequent. Close kinship ties also formed the major support network, providing both emotional and material support.

Brannen (2003) notes the recent emergence of four-generation families – families that include great-grandchildren – because of increasing life expectancy. However she points out that as people are having smaller families because of divorce or women pursuing careers, we are less likely to experience horizontal intragenerational ties, i.e. we have fewer aunts, uncles and cousins. Brannen argues that we are now more likely to experience vertical intergenerational ties, i.e. closer ties with grandparents and great-grandparents. Brannen calls such family setups 'beanpole families'. She argues that the 'pivot generation', i.e. that sandwiched between older and younger family generations is increasingly in demand to provide for the needs of both elderly parents and grandchildren. For example, 20 per cent of people in their fifties and sixties currently care for an elderly person, while 10 per cent care for both an elderly person and a grandchild. Such services are based on the assumption of 'reciprocity', i.e. the provision of babysitting services is repaid by the assumption that daughters will assist mothers in their old age.

There is also evidence that extended kinship ties are important to the upper class, in their attempt to maintain wealth and privilege. The economic and political **elite** may use marriage and family connections to ensure 'social closure' – that is, to keep those who do not share their culture from becoming part of the elite.

Cultural diversity

There are differences in the lifestyles of families with different ethnic origins and religious beliefs. Research carried out at Essex University in 2000 indicates that only 39 per cent of British-born African-Caribbean adults under the age of 60 are in a formal marriage, compared with 60 per cent of White adults (Berthoud 2000). Moreover, this group is more likely than

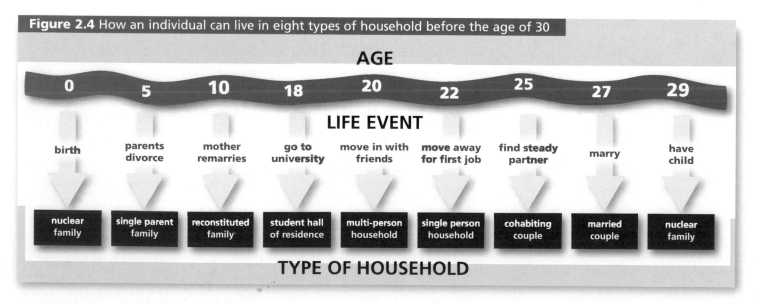

Figure 2.4 How an individual can live in eight types of household before the age of 30

AGE

| 0 | 5 | 10 | 18 | 20 | 22 | 25 | 27 | 29 |

LIFE EVENT

| birth | parents divorce | mother remarries | go to university | move in with friends | move away for first job | find steady partner | marry | have child |

| nuclear family | single parent family | reconstituted family | student hall of residence | multi-person household | single person household | cohabiting couple | married couple | nuclear family |

TYPE OF HOUSEHOLD

any other group to intermarry. The number of mixed-race partnerships means that very few African-Caribbean men and women are married to fellow African-Caribbeans and only one-quarter of African-Caribbean children live with two Black parents. Ali (2002) notes that such marriages result in interethnic families and mixed-race (sometimes called 'dual heritage') children. Some sociologists have suggested that these types of families have their own unique problems, such as facing prejudice and discrimination from both White and Black communities. Children too may feel confused about their identity in the light of such hostility.

There is evidence that African-Caribbean families have a different structure to White families. African-Caribbean communities have a higher proportion of one-parent families compared with White communities – over 50 per cent of African-Caribbean families with children are one-parent families. Rates of divorce are higher but there is also an increasing tradition in the African-Caribbean community of mothers choosing to live independently from their children's father. Berthoud notes two important and increasing trends:

- 66 per cent of 20-year-old African-Caribbean mothers remain single compared with 11 per cent of their White peers, while at 25 years, these figures are 48 per cent and 7 per cent respectively.
- At the age of 30, 60 per cent of African-Caribbean men are unattached, compared with 45 per cent of their White peers.

These trends indicate that African-Caribbean women are avoiding settling down with the African-Caribbean fathers of their children. Berthoud (2003) suggests that the attitudes of young African-Caribbean women are characterized by 'modern individualism' – they are choosing to bring up children alone for two reasons:

- African-Caribbean women are more likely to be employed than African-Caribbean men. Such women rationally weigh up the costs and benefits of living with the fathers of their children and conclude that African-Caribbean men are unreliable as a source of family income and are potentially a financial burden. Surveys indicate that such women prefer to be economically independent.
- Chamberlain and Goulborne (1999) note that African-Caribbean single mothers are more likely to be supported by an extended kinship network in their upbringing of children – interestingly, African-Caribbean definitions of kinship often extends to including family friends and neighbours as 'aunts' and 'uncles'.

The Essex study also found that the Pakistani and Bangladeshi communities are most likely to live in old-fashioned nuclear families, although about 33 per cent of Asian families – mainly Sikhs and East African Asians – live in extended families. East African Asian extended families are likely to contain more than one generation, while Sikh extended units are organized around brothers and their wives and children.

Berthoud argues that South Asians tend to be more traditional in their family values than Whites. Marriage is highly valued and there is little divorce (although this may indicate

empty-shell marriages). Marriage in Asian families – whether Muslim, Hindu or Sikh – is mainly arranged and there is little intermarriage with other religions or cultures. There is also evidence that Bangladeshi and Pakistani women have more children than Indian and White women, and at younger ages. Relationships between Asian parents and their children are also very different from those that characterize White families. Children tend to respect religious and cultural traditions, and they feel a strong sense of duty to their families, and especially to their elders. South Asian families, particularly, feel a strong sense of duty and obligation to assist extended kin in economic and social ways. This is important because Bangladeshi and Pakistani families in the UK are more likely to be in poverty compared with Indian and White families. Such obligations often extend to sending money to relatives abroad on a regular basis and travelling half way around the world to nurse sick or dying relatives.

Lone households

Berthoud and Gershuny (2000) identify a number of people who do not live with any member of their nuclear family, i.e. not with parents, spouse or children. This group is composed of elderly widows and young people in their twenties. For example, 9 per cent of adults aged 20 to 29 lived entirely alone in 1996, while 9 per cent lived with non-relatives (who were not a partner or spouse).

Class diversity

The Rapoports suggest that there may be differences between middle-class and working-class families in terms of the relationship between husband and wife and the way in which children are socialized and disciplined. Some sociologists argue that middle-class parents are more child-centred (see Topic 6) than working-class parents. They supposedly take a greater interest in their children's education, and consequently pass on cultural advantages in terms of attitudes, values and practices (i.e. cultural capital – see Unit 1, Topic 6) which assist their children through the educational system. However, critical sociologists argue that working-class parents are just as child-centred, but that material deprivation limits how much help they can give their children. Therefore, the working-class child's experience is likely to be less satisfactory – because of family poverty, poor schools, lack of material support, greater risks of accidents both in the home and in the street, and so on.

Sexual diversity

As discussed earlier in this unit, the New Right have expressed concern at the increasing number of same-sex couples who are cohabiting – and particularly the trend of such couples to have families through adoption, artificial insemination and surrogacy. In 1999, the law lords ruled that a homosexual couple can be legally defined as a family, and the Government is now looking to introduce legislation which will mean that long-term same-sex partners will have similar rights to heterosexual married couples with regard to inheritance (of property and pensions, for example) and next-of-kin status. New Right commentators have suggested that such family setups are 'unnatural' and that children will either be under pressure to experiment with the lifestyles of their parents or will be bullied at school because of the sexuality of their parents. In the courts, such fears have meant that in the past mothers who have come out as lesbians have lost custody of their children.

There have been a number of sociological studies of homosexual couples and children. Studies of couples suggest that relationships between partners are qualitatively different from heterosexual partners in terms of both domestic and emotional labour because they are not subject to gendered assumptions about which sex should be responsible for these tasks. There may, therefore, be more equality between partners. It is also suggested that same-sex couples work harder at relationships in terms of commitment because they face so many external pressures and criticisms, e.g. disapproval by other members of their family. However, recent research indicates that they may face the same sorts of problems as heterosexual couples in terms of problems such as domestic violence.

Studies of children brought up in single-sex families show no significant effects in terms of gender identification or sexual orientation. For example, Gottman (1990) found that adult daughters of lesbian mothers were just as likely to be of a heterosexual inclination as the daughters of heterosexual mothers. Dunne (1997) argues that children brought up by homosexuals are more likely to be tolerant and see sharing and equality as important features of their relationships with others.

Postmodernism and family diversity

Postmodernists argue that postmodern family life is characterized by diversity, variation and instability. For example, women no longer aspire exclusively to romantic love, marriage and children. Pre-marital sex, serial monogamy, cohabitation, economic independence, single-sex relationships and childlessness are now acceptable alternative lifestyles. Men's roles too are no longer clear cut in postmodern society, and the resulting 'crisis of masculinity' (see p. 55) has led to men redefining both their sexuality and family commitments. Beck and Beck-Gernsheim (1995) argue that such choice and diversity have led to the renegotiation of family relationships as people attempt to find a middle ground between individualization and commitment to another person and/or children. Others disagree with this view. They argue that family diversity is exaggerated, and that the basic features of family life have remained largely unchanged for the majority of the population since the 1950s.

There is no doubt that nuclear families are still very common, but the increasing number of other family types – especially single-parent families and reconstituted families – indicates a slow but steady drift away from the nuclear ideal.

Check your understanding

1 How might reconstituted family life differ from that experienced in nuclear families?

2 Why do feminist sociologists think that one-parent families are seen as a 'problem'?

3 In what sense might working-class and upper-class families be similar in terms of their contact with extended kin?

4 What differences might exist between working-class and middle-class families?

5 What types of families are African-Caribbeans and South Asians likely to be living in?

KEY TERMS

Classic working-class extended family a family in which sons and daughters live in the same neighbourhood as their parents, see each other on a regular basis and offer each other various supports.

Diversity difference, variation.

Elite the most powerful, rich or gifted members of a group.

Negative labelling treating something as being 'bad' or 'undesirable'.

Reconstituted families stepfamilies.

Scapegoated unfairly blamed.

research ideas

- If you know people from ethnic or religious backgrounds different from your own, ask them if you can interview them about their experience of family life. Make sure your questionnaire is sensitive to their background and avoids offending them.

web.task

Use the web to research one-parent families. The following websites contain a range of useful data and information:

www.gingerbread.org.uk

www.opfs.org.uk

www.oneparentfamilies.org.uk

www.apsoc.ox.ac.uk/fpsc/

Item A Postmodern family life

Postmodern family life is clearly pluralistic, i.e. characterized by diversity, variation and instability rather than by some universal nuclear ideal. In the postmodern world, we can see such diversity in the fact that women no longer view romantic love and marriage as their primary goals. Premarital sex and serial monogamy are socially acceptable. More young women are electing not to have children in favour of having careers. Reproductive technology and developments in genetics mean that non-traditional women, e.g. lesbians, women in their sixties etc can have children. The increase in dual-career families means greater emphasis on fathering and the appearance of alternative masculinities symbolized by househusbands. In the past we set rules and limits for children. We are now more likely to set lists and schedules and to make deals with them as equals.

Adapted from Chapman, S. and Aiken, D. (2000) 'Towards a new sociology of families?', *Sociology Review*, 9(3)

Item B Postmodern lifestyles

Fuelled by media moral panics about rising crime, low standards in education, the young lacking a work ethic, the rise of illegitimacy, divorce and single-parenthood, politicians and other 'opinion formers' appear to give support to the traditional nuclear family. Family diversity, from this view, is a 'social problem' to be solved. However, postmodernists suggest that we cannot say that one type of family is better than another because absolute meaning or truth has collapsed in social life. In postmodern societies, we are free to choose the lifestyles we wish since this is the only way to search for meaning in a society that offers choice, fragmentation and diversity. Claims that some family forms are 'better' or more 'natural' or more 'normal' than others are a leftover from modernist thought, which attempted to establish truths about ideal family forms. In a postmodern society, we cannot even say what constitutes a 'family'.

Adapted from Kidd, W. (1999) 'Family diversity in an uncertain future', *Sociology Review*, 9(1)

Item C Poverty and single-parent families

Controversy surrounds the issue of how children are affected by living in single-parent families. Poorer educational achievement and behavioural problems have been highlighted. However, only a minority of children in separated families experience such outcomes. Above all, such problems are caused by poverty and poor housing rather than inadequate socialization. In the absence of poverty, children from one-parent families fare no worse than children in other families. Ninety per cent of lone parents say they would like to work at some point, although many find it difficult to combine work with caring for children alone.

Adapted from *One Parent Families Today: The Facts*, National Council for One Parent Families, March 2000

1 Explain what is meant by 'househusbands' (Item A). (2 marks)

2 Suggest two ways in which family structures or relationships have changed according to postmodernist sociologists (Items A and B). (4 marks)

3 Identify three variations in family life which are the product of cultural differences. (6 marks)

4 Identify and briefly describe two problems faced by one-parent families (Item C). (8 marks)

5 Examine the view that successful families need two loving heterosexual parents. (20 marks)

6 Assess the argument that the basic features of family life have remained largely unchanged for the majority of the population since the 1950s. (20 marks)

Childhood

gettingyouthinking

Image used in an NSPCC campaign against child abuse

Funeral of a Palestinian child killed in an Israeli attack

Gun-toting children in Sierra Leone

Friendship in childhood

1 What does the cartoon on the right tell us about family life in the Middle Ages?

2 How does the experience of medieval childhood differ from that of today?

3 What do the images above tell us about the experience of childhood today?

Children dressed like their parents

In the Middle Ages, young and old played together in games and festivals, as in this scene based on Brueghel's painting, the 'Battle between Carnival and Lent', where the children are depicted as small adults.

Everyone worked together

At 8 years, I was put out as an apprentice

So he could learn his trade from me.

Everyone was held responsible

Tudor law says a 7 year old can be hanged for stealing

In many cases, houses were not split up into special rooms for eating, sleeping, working or cooking

So children could not escape from the adult world

What is a child? Innocent, cute, funny? That's certainly the popular image suggested by birthday cards, magazines and so on. However, the cartoon above and some of the images on the left give a different impression. We can see that ideas about childhood appear to vary between different societies and different historical periods. This means that childhood is a **social construction** – something created by society, rather than simply a biological stage.

Childhood in pre-industrial society

The social historian Philippe Aries (1962) suggested that what we experience today as childhood is a recent social invention. He claimed that, in pre-industrial society, childhood as we know it today did not exist. Children were 'little adults' who took part in the same work and play activities as adults. Toys and games specifically for children did not exist. Moreover, Aries argued

that children were regarded as an **economic asset** rather than as a symbol of people's love for one another. Investing emotionally in children was difficult when their death rate was so high.

Aries's evidence for this view of childhood has been questioned, but other historians agree that the pre-industrial family was a unit of production, working the land or engaged in crafts. Children were expected to help their parents from a very young age. Those who did not help with domestic production usually left home to become servants or apprentices.

Childhood and industrialization

After industrialization these attitudes continued, especially among the working classes, whose children were frequently found working in factories, mines and mills. Aries argued that middle-class attitudes towards children started to change during this period. There was a growth in marital and parental love in middle-class families as the **infant mortality rate** started to fall.

Social attitudes towards children really started to change in the middle of the 19th century. Children were excluded from the mines and factories where thousands of them had been killed or injured. Some working-class parents, however, resisted these moves, because they depended on their children's wages.

Many 19th-century campaigners were concerned about juvenile delinquency, beggars and child prostitution, and consequently wanted to get children off the streets. However, there is considerable evidence that children continued to be badly treated in this period, and child prostitution and abuse were common features of most cities. It was not until the turn of the 20th century that the age of sexual consent was raised to 16.

Childhood in the 20th century

The 20th century saw the emergence of a **child-centred** society. This was probably the result of improved standards of living and nutrition in the late 19th century, which led to a major decline in the infant mortality rate. The higher standard of living also meant that having children became more expensive. The increased availability and efficiency of contraception allowed people to choose to have fewer children. Consequently, parents were able to invest more in them in terms of love, socialisation and protection.

Childhood and adolescence were consequently seen as separate categories from adulthood. Children were seen as being in need of special attention and protection.

Children and the state

Concern over the rights of children can be seen in greater state involvement in protecting them. Parents' rearing of children is now monitored through various pieces of legislation, such as the 1989 Children Act. The role of social services and social workers is to police those families in which children are thought to be at risk. The state also supervises the socialization of children through compulsory education, which lasts 11 years. It also takes some economic responsibility by paying child benefit and children's tax credits to parents.

Increasingly, children have come to be seen as individuals with rights. The Child Support Act (1991) deals with the care, bringing up and protection of children. It protects children's welfare in the event of parental separation and divorce, emphasizing that the prime concern of the state should be the child, and what children themselves say about their experiences and needs. Some children have recently used the act to 'divorce' their parents, while others have used it to 'force' their separated/divorced parents to see them more regularly.

Theoretical approaches to childhood

The conventional approach

Many functionalists and New Right thinkers tend to subscribe to what has been termed a 'conventional' approach to childhood. This sees children as a vulnerable group – both under threat from and in need of protection from adult society. This approach suggests that successful child-rearing requires two parents of the opposite sex, and that there is a 'right' way to bring up a child. Such views often 'blame' working mothers or single mothers, and/or inadequate parents, for social problems such as delinquency. They also see children as in need of protection from 'threats' such as homosexuality and media violence.

Melanie Phillips' book *All Must Have Prizes* (1997) is typical of this conventional approach to childhood. She argues that the culture of parenting in the UK has broken down and the 'innocence' of childhood has been undermined by two trends:

1 The concept of parenting has been distorted by liberal ideas, which have given too many rights and powers to children. Phillips argues that children should be socialized into a healthy respect for parental authority. However, she argues that children's rights have undermined this process, and parents are increasingly criticized and penalized for resorting to sanctions such as smacking.
2 Phillips believes that the media and the peer group have become more influential than parents. She sees the media in the form of magazines aimed at young girls, pop music videos and television as a particular problem, because they encourage young girls to envisage themselves as sexual beings at a much younger age.

These trends mean that the period of childhood has been shortened – it is no longer a sacred and innocent period lasting up to 13 or 14 years. Phillips complains that adulthood encroaches upon the experiences of children a great deal earlier than in the past. She argues that many children do not have the emotional maturity to cope with the rights and choices that they have today. The result, she believes, is an increase in social problems such as suicide, eating disorders, self-harm, depression and drug/alcohol abuse.

The assumptions contained in conventional approaches to childhood have been very influential on social policy. For example, in family law and especially the divorce courts, children are portrayed as potential victims in need of protection from the law and the state. They tend not to be given any say in the decisions made by parents, judges and politicians. It is assumed that they lack the maturity and experience to contribute to the debate about their futures.

An alternative view

This conventional approach has been criticized by sociologists who have researched children's perspectives on society and family. They suggest that functionalist and New Right

Neil Postman (1982)

Is childhood disappearing?

Postman argues that childhood is disappearing. His view is based on two related ideas.

1 The growth of television means that there are no more secrets from children. Television gives them unlimited access to the adult world. They are exposed to the 'real world' of sex, disaster, death and suffering.

2 'Social blurring' has occurred so there is little distinction between adults and children. Children's games are disappearing and children seem less childlike today. They speak, dress and behave in more adult ways, while adults have enjoyed looking more like their kids and youth generally. Over time, nearly all the traditional features that mark the transition to adulthood – getting a job, religious confirmation, leaving home, getting married – no longer apply in any clear way.

Postman's analysis has been heavily criticized. His arguments do not appear to be based on solid evidence, while recent studies indicate that adults are actually taking more and more control of their children's lives. For example, David Brooks (2001) diagnoses parents today as obsessed with safety, and ever more concerned with defining boundaries for their kids and widening their control and safety net around them.

Perhaps it is children that are disappearing rather than childhood. Children are a smaller percentage of our overall population today and are diminishing in relative proportion to other age groups.

Adapted from Allen, D. (2001) 'Is childhood disappearing?', *Studies in Social and Political Thought,* 6(1), 2001

1 What methods could be used to collect data about the impact of television on children?

2 To what extent do you believe that childhood is disappearing? What evidence can you use to support your view?

arguments assume that children are simply empty vessels. Family life is presented as a one-way process in which parenting and socialization aim to transform children into good citizens. However, this view ignores the fact that children have their own unique interpretation of family life, which they actively employ in interaction with their parents. In other words, the relationship between parents and children is a two-way process in which the latter can and do influence the nature and quality of family life. For example, research by Morrow (1998) found that children can be constructive and reflective contributors to family life. Most of the children in Morrow's study had a pragmatic view of their family role – they did not want to make decisions for themselves but they did want a say in what happened to them.

Conventional approaches are also criticized because they tend to generalize about children and childhood. This is dangerous because, as we saw earlier, childhood is not a fixed, universal experience. Historical period, locality, culture, social class, gender and ethnicity all have an influence on the character and quality of childhood. This can be illustrated in a number of ways:

● In many less developed nations, the experience of childhood is extremely different from that in the industrialized world. Children in such countries are constantly at risk of early death because of poverty and lack of basic health care. They are unlikely to have access to education, and may find themselves occupying adult roles as workers or soldiers. In many countries, children are not regarded as special or as in need of protection. For example, in Mexico, it is estimated that 1.9 million children live rough on the streets – 240 000 of these have been abandoned by their parents. In Brazil, 1000 homeless children are shot dead every year by people who regard them as vermin.

● Even in a country such as Britain, experience of childhood may differ across ethnic and religious groups. For example, there is evidence that Muslim, Hindu and Sikh children generally feel a stronger sense of obligation and duty to their parents than White children. Generational conflict is therefore less likely or is more likely to be hidden.

● Experiences of childhood in Britain may vary according to social class. Upper-class children may find that they spend most of their formative years in boarding schools. Middle-class children may be encouraged from an early age to aim for university and a professional career, and they are likely to receive considerable economic and cultural support from their parents. Working-class childhood may be made more difficult by the experience of poverty. For example, research by Jefferis et al. (2002) found that children who experienced poverty had significantly fallen behind children from middle-class backgrounds in terms of maths, reading and other ability tests by the age of 7.

● Experiences of childhood may differ according to gender. Boys and girls may be socialized into a set of behaviours based on expectations about masculinity and femininity. For example, there is some evidence that girls are subjected to stricter social controls from parents compared with boys when they reach adolescence.

We also need to acknowledge that some children's experiences of childhood may be damaging. Different types of child abuse have been rediscovered in recent years, such as neglect and physical, sexual and emotional abuse. The NSPCC points out that each week at least one child will die as a result of an adult's cruelty, usually a parent or step-parent, while 30 000 children are on child protection registers because they are at risk of abuse from family members. The negative effects of divorce have been documented in several surveys of teenagers. In conclusion, not all children experience the family or their parents as positive – for many children and teenagers, the family is exploitative and dangerous.

focus on research

Morrow (1998)
Children's views of the family

A qualitative study of 183 children aged between 8 and 14, carried out by Morrow in 1998, found that children's views do not necessarily conform to stereotypical images of the nuclear family. The research asked pupils to draw and write about 'who is important to me?', and to complete a sentence on 'what is a family?' and 'what are families for?'. They were also given a short questionnaire asking whether or not five one-sentence descriptions of family type counted as family. Group discussions also took place which explored their responses to the questionnaire. The children were found to have a pragmatic view of family life – love, care and mutual respect were regarded by them as the essential characteristics of family life. They also had a very inclusive view of who was family – absent relatives and pets were regarded as family members. This research can be downloaded from www.jrf.org.uk.

1 In what ways did the children's views about the family not conform to the 'typical' nuclear family?

Check your understanding

1 What do sociologists mean when they describe childhood as a 'social construction'?

2 How does Aries believe children were treated in pre-industrial society?

3 What were the main causes of society becoming more child-centred at the end of the 19th century?

4 How does the conventional approach to childhood view children?

5 What problems are associated with this approach?

KEY TERMS

Child-centred treating the needs of children as a priority.

Economic asset something that brings money in.

Infant mortality rate the number of babies who die in their first year of life, as a proportion of all live births.

Social construction something that is created by society.

research ideas

● In order to document the changing experience of and attitudes towards childhood, design a survey asking three generations about their experience of family.

● Using textbooks, CD-Roms and government websites, such as those of the Home Office and Lord Chancellor's department (accessible via www.open.gov.uk), compile a detailed time-line outlining state intervention in children's lives and the rights children now have.

web.task

Visit the website www.child-abuse.com/childhouse

This contains links to a number of excellent sites that look at childhood and children's rights across the world.

Alternatively, visit the NSPCC website www.nspcc.co.uk to get an idea of the degree of child abuse in UK society.

exploring childhood

Item A The social construction of childhood

Most of us tend to think of childhood as a clear and distinct stage of life. 'Children', we suppose, are distinct from 'babies' or 'toddlers'. Childhood intervenes between infancy and the onset of adolescence. Yet the concept of childhood, like so many other aspects of our social life today, has only come into being over the past two or three centuries. In traditional and pre-industrial cultures, the young move directly from a lengthy infancy into working roles within the community. Right up to the start of the 20th century, in the UK and most other Western countries, children as young as 7 or 8 years old were put to work at what now seems a very early age. There are many countries in the world today, in fact, in which young children are engaged in full-time work, often in physically demanding circumstances (coal-mines, for example). The idea that children have distinctive rights, and the notion that the use of child labour is morally wrong, are quite recent developments.

Giddens, A. (1997) *Sociology* (3rd edn),
Cambridge: Polity Press, p. 38

Item B Childhood and the law

The changing nature of legislation concerning children has reflected the changing views towards children over time. In the 19th century, the idea gradually developed that children were not simply little adults, but were vulnerable members of society who needed care and protection. This concept of the child as vulnerable dominates 20th-century thinking. For example, the Children Act of 1908 resulted in the criminal justice system treating and punishing criminal adults and children in different ways for the first time. In 1952, local authorities were given the duty to investigate cases of neglect or cruelty with regard to children, while the 1989 Children Act made it clear that the child's best interests must be central to any decision made about the welfare of the child. The child's views are therefore sought and taken into account. Such legislation reflects the fact that we are now a child-centred society.

Adapted from Moore, S. (1998)
Social Welfare Alive (2nd edn),
Cheltenham: Stanley Thornes, pp. 366–7

Item C Diversity of childhood experiences

Childhood is tremendously varied, from the sheltered pre schooler of Western nations to the maimed street beggar or gun-carrying 'freedom fighter' of less industrialized nations. Even in the UK, children may grow up in a wide variety of different and potentially damaging situations. There are occasional alarming reports of child prostitution linked to runaway children and drug use. We know from recent studies that many children of less than 10 years old may be the main carer in family situations where their parent is chronically ill or disabled. For many children, childhood may involve the direct experience of oppression, abuse, exploitation, not to mention parental divorce, poor health and poverty. Childhood experience, then, is extremely diverse by way of region, social class, housing quality, income, culture and ethnicity, prejudice, diet, disease and abuse.

Adapted from Bernardes, J. (1997)
Family Studies: An Introduction,
London: Routledge, p. 115

1 Explain what is meant by the phrase 'a child-centred society' (Item B). (2 marks)

2 Suggest two ways in which the experience of being a child in a less developed nation may differ from the experience of a British child (Item C). (4 marks)

3 Identify three ways in which the state protects the rights of children today (Item B). (6 marks)

4 Identify and briefly describe two differences between childhood in pre-industrial society and childhood in contemporary industrial society. (8 marks)

5 Examine the view that childhood today is not a fixed universal experience. (20 marks)

6 Using information from the Items and elsewhere, assess the argument that Britain has evolved into a successful child-centred society. (20 marks)

Power and control in the family

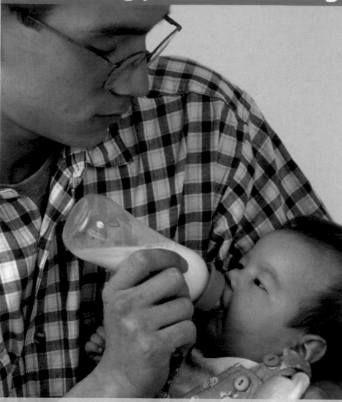

gettingyouthinking

(a) Making sure that you had sandwiches for lunch or the money to pay for a school dinner.

(b) Making sure that your favourite food was in the fridge.

(c) Arranging with other parents for you to go to a party or around to somebody's house for tea.

(d) Making sure that you had a clean swimming costume and towel on the days of school swims.

(e) Changing the sheets on your bed.

(f) Supervising your bath-time.

(g) Picking you up from school.

(h) Buying a present for you to take to another child's birthday party.

(i) Reassuring you if you had a bad dream in the night.

(j) Anticipating that you needed a new pair of shoes because you were about to grow out of your old pair.

1 Consider the list of tasks above. Which adult in your home was mainly responsible for each when you were aged 5 to 7?

2 What other aspects of power and control in the home are neglected if we only focus on household tasks?

3 Who exercises power in your home and what forms does this take?

In 1973, Young and Willmott claimed that the traditional **segregated division of labour in the home** – men as breadwinners and women as housewives/mothers – was breaking down. The relationship between husband and wife (the **conjugal relationship**) was becoming – at least in middle-class families – more joint or **symmetrical**. This trend towards **egalitarian** marriage was caused by the decline in the extended family, and its replacement in the late 20th century by the privatized nuclear family, as well as by the increasing opportunities in paid employment for women. Some media commentators were so convinced by these arguments that in the 1980s, it was claimed that a 'new man' had appeared, i.e.

males who were in touch with their feminine side and who were happy to meet women's emotional and domestic needs.

However, the exercise above should have shown you that much of women's labour in the home is neglected by studies that focus only on obvious and highly visible tasks. A good deal of what women do in the home is mental and emotional as well as physical, involving anticipating and fulfilling the needs of family members. These more subtle responsibilities tend to be missed by researchers, some of whom have concluded that men and women are becoming more equal in the home – on the basis of their sharing some of the more glamorous domestic tasks, such as cooking. These sorts of surveys can also miss other influences that ensure that power and control in the home remain firmly in male hands – violence, the lack of status associated with the mother/housewife role, the belief that working mothers damage children, the fact that being a mother limits job opportunities, and so on.

Studies of housework and childcare

The idea that equality is a central characteristic of marriage is strongly opposed by feminist sociologists. Studies of professional couples indicate that only a minority genuinely share housework and childcare. For example, Dryden's (1999) qualitative study of 17 married couples found that women still had major responsibility for housework and childcare. Similarly, studies of unemployed men indicate that, although they do more around the home, their wives, even when working full time, do the lion's share of housework and childcare. As Young comments on the findings of the British Household Panel Survey:

> << Women do more when they are working and the man unemployed, when they are working longer hours than the man, when they are both employed full time – whatever the setup. >>

Some sociologists have suggested that unemployed men resist increased involvement in housework because it threatens their masculinity, especially if their wife is the main income earner.

A survey carried out for the insurance firm Legal & General in April 2000 found that full-time working mothers spent 56 hours per week on housework and childcare, compared with men's 31 hours. This increased to 84 hours if the women had children aged 3 and under. The Future Foundation survey of October 2000 was more positive. It found that women were receiving more help in the home from husbands and boyfriends. Two-thirds of men said they did more around the home than their fathers. However, even at this rate, women will have to wait until at least 2015 before tasks are shared equally!

The quantifiable evidence, therefore, indicates that women are still likely to have a **dual burden** – they are expected to be mainly responsible for the bulk of domestic tasks despite holding down full-time jobs. Dryden found that such inequality was a constant source of friction between couples and a number of studies of marriage, notably by Hart (1976), have argued that this is a major cause of marital breakdown.

Women are also responsible for the emotional well-being of their partners and children. Studies such as that carried out by Duncombe and Marsden (1995) have found that women felt that their male partners were lacking in terms of 'emotional participation', i.e. men found it difficult to express their feelings, to tell their partners how they felt about them and to relate emotionally to their children. Duncombe and Marsden argue that this increases the burden on women because they feel they should attempt to compensate and please all parties in the home. Women consequently spend a great deal of time soothing the emotions of partners and children. This leads to the neglect of their own psychological well-being, and can have negative consequences for their mental and physical health. For example, Bernard's study of marriage (1982) confirms this – she found that the men in her study were more satisfied with their marriage than their wives, many of whom expressed emotional loneliness. Moreover, these men had no inkling that their wives were unhappy.

Decision-making

Some sociologists have focused on the distribution of power within marriages. Edgell (1980) discovered that middle-class wives generally deferred to their husbands in decision-making. Edgell concluded that the men in his sample were able to demand that the interests of their wives and families be subordinated to the man's career, because he was the main breadwinner. Similarly, surveys of young married couples with children conclude that the decision to have children, although jointly reached, dramatically changes the life of the mother rather than the father. However, Gillian Leighton (1992) discovered that the power to make decisions changed when males became unemployed. In her study of professional couples, working wives often took over responsibility for bills and initiated cutbacks in spending.

Fatherhood

An important part of the New Right critique of one-parent families is the view that most of them lack fathers. Dennis and Erdos (2000), for example, suggest that fatherless children are less likely to be successfully socialized into the culture of discipline and compromise found in nuclear families and so are less likely to be successful parents themselves. It is suggested that such children lack an authority figure to turn to in times of crisis and as a result the peer group and mass media have increased in influence. It is argued that such influence is likely to lead to an increase in social problems, such as delinquency, sexual promiscuity, teenage pregnancy and drug use.

There is no doubt that de-partnering, whether from marriage or cohabitation, leads to some degree of de-parenting, i.e. one or other parent, usually the father in the UK, becomes less involved in the parenting of a child. The law in the UK tends to uphold traditional ideas about gender roles and custody of children is mainly awarded to the mother. Bernardes notes that the Children Act clearly states that the mother should have parental responsibility for a child if the parents are not married. It is estimated that 40 per cent of fathers lose complete touch with their children after two years; others will experience irregular contact or conflict with their ex-partners about access arrangements. The recent publicity campaign by Fathers4Justice has aimed to draw attention to what they see as an unjust mother-centred legal system which denies fathers their right of access to their children.

Other commentators have suggested that we should focus on the quality of fathering. In the early 1990s, many sociologists concluded that the role of fathers was changing. For example, men in the 1990s were more likely to attend the birth of their babies than men in the 1960s, and they were more likely to play a greater role in childcare than their own fathers. Burghes (1997) found that fathers were taking an increasingly active role in the emotional development of their children. Beck (1992) notes that, in the postmodern age, fathers can no longer rely on jobs to provide a sense of identity and fulfilment. Increasingly, they look to their children to give them a sense of identity and purpose.

Warin et al. (1999), in their study of 95 families in Rochdale, found that fathers, mothers and teenage children overwhelmingly subscribed to the view that the male should be the breadwinner, despite changes in employment and family life, and that mothers were the experts in parenting. Fathers in this study felt under considerable pressure to provide for their families and this was intensified by demands from teenage children for consumer goods and designer-label fashion items. Men who were in low-paid jobs, sick, disabled or unemployed expressed feelings of frustration and sadness, and were likely to see themselves as failures for being unable to supply their children with what they wanted. The study claims that the contributions of fathers to families often goes unrecognized. Fathers were aware that they were expected to do more than previous generations and they expressed this by acting as a taxi service for their children, sharing in the shopping, carrying out informal sports coaching and going to watch children at sporting events. The researchers imply that fathers today are under considerable pressure, attempting to juggle the role of provider with the emotional support role traditionally provided by mothers. They conclude that the pressures of work and family were turning men into 'all-singing, all-dancing superdads'.

However, despite Warin and colleagues' conclusions, it is important not to exaggerate men's role in childcare. Looking after children is still overwhelmingly the responsibility of mothers, rather than jointly shared with fathers. Recent research has also focused on the pressures of work in the 21st century. It suggests that these may be negatively impacting on the ability of fathers to bond effectively with their children and spend time with them. For example, in 2003, a survey by Dex noted that half her sample of fathers reported that 30 per cent (as well as 6 per cent of mothers) worked more than 48 hours a week on a regular basis. It is unlikely that fathers in this situation will be spending quality time interacting with their families.

Patriarchal ideology

Feminists have highlighted the influence of patriarchal ideology (see Unit 1, Topic 7) on the perceptions of both husbands and wives. Surveys indicate that many women accept primary responsibility for housework and childcare without question, and believe that their career should be secondary to that of their husband. Such ideas are also reflected in state policy, which encourages female economic dependence upon men. Moreover, patriarchal ideology expects women to take on jobs

that are compatible with family commitments. Surveys suggest that a large number of mothers feel guilty about working. Some actually give up work altogether because they believe that their absence somehow damages their children.

The housewife experience

The housewife role has low status compared with paid work, and this may lead to feelings of boredom, loneliness and dissatisfaction. As a result, some housewives may see themselves as worthless or as mere extensions of their husbands and children. They may see themselves as redundant when their children grow up and leave home. Such feelings may be responsible for the high levels of depression experienced by women in modern industrial societies. Feminists would argue that these findings are yet further evidence of inequalities within marriage.

The mother/housewife role and work

Some feminist sociologists have concluded that women's participation in the labour market is clearly limited by their domestic responsibilities. Because of these responsibilities, very few women have continuous full-time careers. Mothers, then, tend to have 'jobs', while their husbands have 'careers'. As a result, women don't have the same access to promotion and training opportunities as men. Some employers may believe that women are unreliable because of family commitments and, consequently, discriminate against them.

Modern marriages appear far from equal. On all the criteria examined so far – the distribution of housework and childcare tasks, decision-making, and the impact of being a mother/housewife on employment – we see women at a disadvantage compared with men.

Violence in families

Another important aspect of power within marriage is domestic violence – the power of men to control women by physical force. This type of violence is estimated to be the most common type of violence in the UK, although because it takes place behind closed doors, often without witnesses, it is notoriously difficult to measure and document. It is also difficult to define – as Sclater (2000) notes, some behaviour, such as kicking and punching, is easily recognizable as violent, but behaviours such as threats, verbal abuse, psychological manipulation and sexual intimidation are less easy to categorize and may not be recognized by some men and women as domestic violence.

The official statistics tell us that violence by men against their female partners accounts for a third of all reported violence. Stanko's (2000) survey found that one incident of domestic violence is reported by women to the police every minute in the UK. Mirrlees-Black (1999), using data from the British

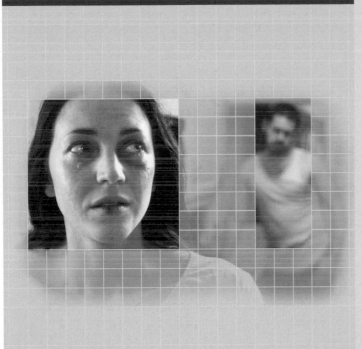

British Crime Survey
Computer-assisted interviewing

Questions on domestic violence are now part of British Crime Surveys which aim to gain an insight into the true amount of crime in society by talking to victims. The designers of this survey realized that face-to-face interviewing was an unreliable method because victims are often too embarrassed to talk about their experiences of violence. The 1996 survey was the first to use the alternative method of computer-assisted interviewing in which a lap-top is passed over to the respondent, who reads the questions on screen and enters their answers directly onto the computer without the interviewer being involved. It is thought that the confidentiality factor associated with this type of interviewing on such a sensitive issue has improved both the reliability of the method (and produced on average a 97 per cent response rate) and the validity of the data collected, i.e. people are more willing to open up.

1 What is computer-assisted interviewing?

2 Identify the advantages and disadvantages of computer-assisted interviewing.

3 To what extent is computer-assisted interviewing likely to achieve valid and reliable data about domestic violence?

Crime Survey, found that women were more likely to suffer domestic violence than men – 70 per cent of reported domestic violence is violence by men against their female partners. These figures are thought to be an underestimate because many women are reluctant to come forward because they love their partners and think they can change them, or because they blame themselves in some way for the violence. Many women fail to report violence because they feel they may not be taken seriously or because they are afraid of the repercussions. Some sociologists have reported increases in female violence on men, but it is estimated that this only constitutes at best 5 per cent of all domestic violence. Moreover, as Nazroo's (1999) research indicates, wives often live in fear of men's potential domestic violence or threats, while husbands rarely feel frightened or intimidated by their wives' potential for violence.

Feminists suggest that domestic violence is a problem of patriarchy. In particular, research indicates that men's view that women have failed to be 'good' partners or mothers is often used to justify attacks or threats. These gendered expectations may be particularly reinforced if a woman goes out to work and earns more than her partner. Many boys and men are still brought up in traditional ways to believe that they should have economic and social power as breadwinners and heads of household. However, the feminization of the economy and male unemployment has led to some sociologists suggesting that men are undergoing a 'crisis of masculinity'. Violence may be an aspect of the anxiety men are feeling about their economic and domestic role, an attempt to re-exert and maintain power and control in a rapidly changing world.

Feminists also point out that society has, until fairly recently, condoned male violence in the home. Both the state and the criminal justice system have failed to take the problem seriously, although there are now positive signs that the Labour government and police forces are now willing to condemn and punish such violence. Whatever the explanation, some feminists would argue that as long as men have the capacity to commit such violence, there can never be equality within marriage.

Theoretical explanations of inequalities in power and control in families

There are four major theoretical perspectives on the distribution of power and control in the family:

1 *Functionalists* see the sexual division of labour in the home as biologically inevitable. Women are seen as naturally suited to the caring and emotional role, which Parsons terms the 'expressive role'.

2 *Liberal feminists* believe that women have made real progress in terms of equality within the family and particularly in education and the economy. They generally believe that men are adapting to change and, although they culturally lag behind women in terms of attitudes and behaviour, the future is likely to bring further movement towards domestic and economic equality.

3 *Marxist–feminists* argue that the housewife role serves the needs of capitalism in that it maintains the present workforce and reproduces future labour-power (see Topic 2, p. 42).

4 *Radical feminists* such as Delphy (1984) believe that 'the first oppression is the oppression of women by men – women are an exploited class'. The housewife role is, therefore, a role created by patriarchy and geared to the service of men and their interests (see Topic 2, p. 43). Like functionalism, both Marxist and radical forms of feminism see women's exploitation and oppression as rooted in their biological role as mothers.

Criticisms of these theories

● These theories fail to explain why women's roles vary across different cultures. For example, the mother/housewife role does not exist in all societies.

● Feminism may be guilty of devaluing the mother/housewife role as a 'second-class' role. For many women, housework and childcare, like paid work, have real and positive meaning. Such work may be invested with meaning for women because it is 'work done for love' and it demonstrates their commitment to their families. Thus, boring, routine work may be transformed into satisfying, caring work.

● Feminists may underestimate the degree of power that women actually enjoy. Women are concerned about the amount of housework men do, but they are probably more concerned about whether men show enough gratitude or whether men listen to them, etc. The fact that many women divorce their husbands indicates that they have the power to leave a relationship if they are unhappy with it. Catherine Hakim (1996) suggests that feminists underestimate women's ability to make rational choices. It is not patriarchy or men that are responsible for the position of women in families. She argues that women choose to give more commitment to family and children, and consequently they have less commitment to work than men have.

Whatever your favoured perspective, it appears that the view that a 'new man' is emerging – sharing domestic tasks, engaging emotionally with women and showing interest in developing his fathering skills – is an overoptimistic picture of life in many conjugal relationships.

Check your understanding

1 What did Willmott and Young claim about conjugal roles in the 1970s?

2 What have recent surveys concluded about the distribution of domestic tasks between husbands and wives?

3 In what circumstances might wives acquire more power over decision-making in the home?

4 What do studies generally conclude about women's experience of the mother/housewife role?

5 What effect does the mother/housewife role have on women's job opportunities?

KEY TERMS

Conjugal relationship the relationship between married or cohabiting partners.

Dual burden refers to wives taking responsibility for the bulk of domestic tasks as well as holding down full-time jobs.

Egalitarian based on equality.

Segregated division of labour in the home a traditional sexual division of labour in which women take responsibility for housework and mothering, and men take responsibility for being the breadwinner and head of the household.

Symmetrical similar or corresponding.

research ideas

● Conduct a survey of parents using the list of tasks in the 'Getting you thinking' exercise on p. 70. An interesting variation is to ask parents separately whether they think they and their partner are doing enough around the home.

● Interview a selection of mothers in different social situations – e.g. full-time mothers, those who have full-time or part-time jobs, those who have children who have left home, etc. Try to construct an interview schedule that measures how they feel about the mother/housewife role.

web.task

Use the web to research domestic violence. The following websites contain a range of useful data and information:

● www.homeoffice.gov.uk/crime/domesticviolence/

● www.womensaid.org.uk

● www.metpolice.uk/enoughisenough

● www.womenandequalityunit.gov.uk/domestic_violence

exploring power and control in the family

Item A Working mothers

<< Working mothers spend more hours a week on housework than on their full-time job, a survey revealed yesterday. The survey of 543 parents of children under 18 was carried out for Legal & General. It found that full-time working mothers spend 56 hours a week on housework, part-time working mothers do 68 hours and housewives put in 76 hours, while fathers do only 31. Mothers spend around 14 hours a week cooking, compared with fathers' four hours, and 21 hours washing and ironing, compared with eight-and-a-half hours for men. Mothers clean for 13 hours a week, compared with their husbands' four hours, and women spend about an hour sewing compared with 10 minutes for men. Fathers do four hours a week of gardening, an hour more than mothers.>>

Guardian, 10 March 2000

Item B Why don't men do more housework?

Why does such a pronounced division of domestic labour persist? Women who continue to see housework and childcare as an essential part of being a 'good wife and mother' are more likely to be satisfied with an unequal domestic division of labour than women who reject such roles. Baxter and Western (1998) argue that women may deal with situations over which they have little control by defining them as 'satisfactory'. Men may have inflexible and demanding work schedules that make it difficult for them to meet family obligations. However, in criticism of this, men do tend to have greater control and freedom over how they spend their time outside of work. Women are often unable to 'clock on and off' from their caring responsibilities. The most plausible explanation for the persistence of an unequal domestic division of labour is that it suits men and so they resist change.

Adapted from Leonard, M. (2000) 'Back to the future: the domestic division of labour', *Sociology Review*, 10(2)

Item C Fatherhood

<< The report 'Fathers and Fatherhood in Britain' by Louie Burghes directly challenges the idea that men are abandoning a role in the family. The report found that, increasingly, fathers are taking an active involvement in the emotional side of child-rearing. Despite continuing to be the main earner in the family and working long hours, fathers are tending to spend more time with their children. The amount of time fathers spent with children was found to have increased fourfold over a generation between 1961 and 1995.>>

Denscombe, M. (1998) *Sociology Update*, Leicester: Olympus Books

---

1 Explain what is meant by the phrase 'unequal domestic division of labour' (Item B). (2 marks)

2 Identify two ways in which Item A confirms that a traditional sexual division of labour still exists in the modern family. (4 marks)

3 Identify three reasons why the sexual division of labour continues to persist, according to Item B. (6 marks)

4 Identify and briefly describe two ways in which the mother/housewife role may limit women's employment opportunities. (8 marks)

5 Examine the view that the distribution of domestic tasks between family members has become equal. (20 marks)

6 Using information from the Items and elsewhere, assess explanations for inequalities in the domestic division of labour. (20 marks)

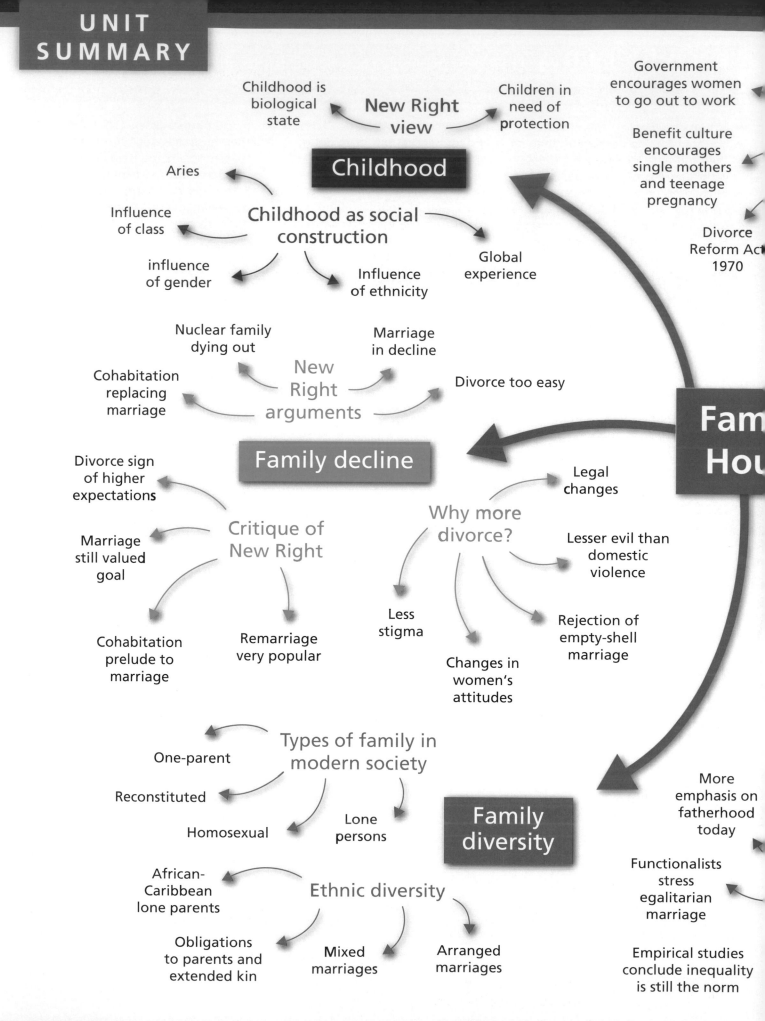

New Right view

Childhood is biological state

Children in need of protection

Childhood

Childhood as social construction

Aries

Influence of class

influence of gender

Influence of ethnicity

Global experience

Government encourages women to go out to work

Benefit culture encourages single mothers and teenage pregnancy

Divorce Reform Act 1970

New Right arguments

Nuclear family dying out

Marriage in decline

Cohabitation replacing marriage

Divorce too easy

Family decline

Critique of New Right

Divorce sign of higher expectations

Marriage still valued goal

Cohabitation prelude to marriage

Remarriage very popular

Why more divorce?

Legal changes

Lesser evil than domestic violence

Less stigma

Changes in women's attitudes

Rejection of empty-shell marriage

Fam Hou

Types of family in modern society

One-parent

Reconstituted

Homosexual

Lone persons

Family diversity

African-Caribbean lone parents

Ethnic diversity

Obligations to parents and extended kin

Mixed marriages

Arranged marriages

More emphasis on fatherhood today

Functionalists stress egalitarian marriage

Empirical studies conclude inequality is still the norm

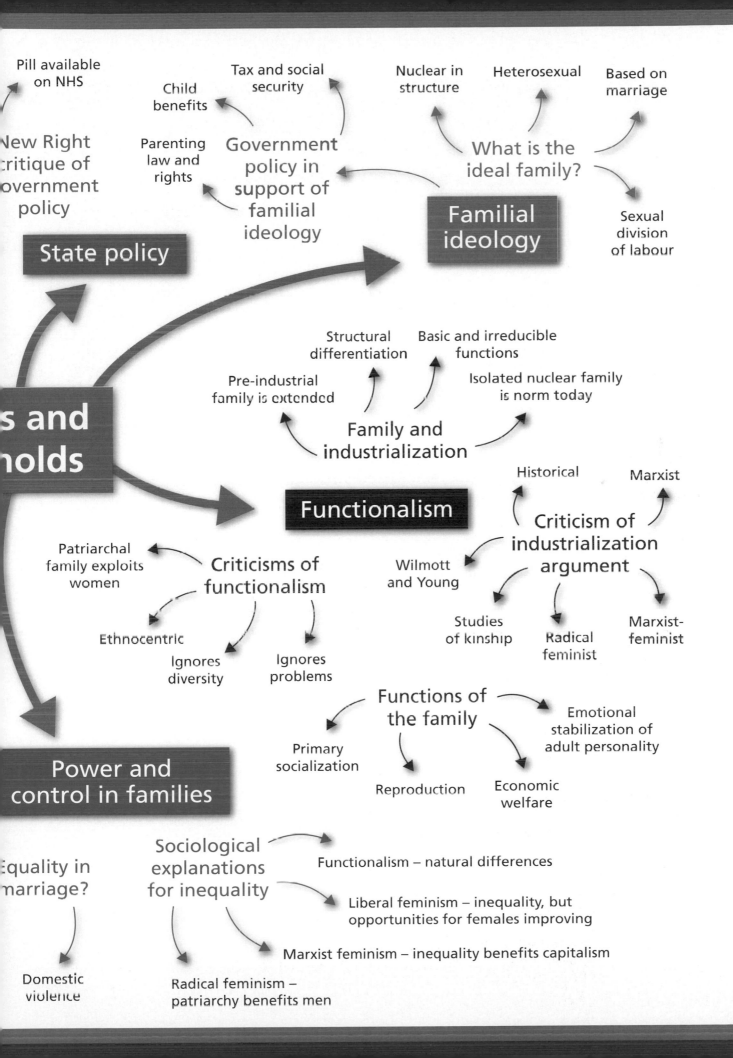

Pill available
on NHS

Child
benefits

Tax and social
security

New Right
critique of
government
policy

Parenting
law and
rights

Government
policy in
support of
familial
ideology

State policy

Nuclear in
structure

Heterosexual

Based on
marriage

What is the
ideal family?

**Familial
ideology**

Sexual
division
of labour

s and
holds

Structural
differentiation

Basic and irreducible
functions

Pre-industrial
family is extended

Isolated nuclear family
is norm today

Family and
industrialization

Functionalism

Historical

Marxist

Criticism of
industrialization
argument

Patriarchal
family exploits
women

Criticisms of
functionalism

Wilmott
and Young

Studies
of kinship

Radical
feminist

Marxist-
feminist

Ethnocentric

Ignores
diversity

Ignores
problems

Functions of
the family

Emotional
stabilization of
adult personality

Primary
socialization

Reproduction

Economic
welfare

**Power and
control in families**

Sociological
explanations
for inequality

Functionalism – natural differences

Equality in
marriage?

Liberal feminism – inequality, but
opportunities for females improving

Marxist feminism – inequality benefits capitalism

Domestic
violence

Radical feminism –
patriarchy benefits men

FOR MANY STUDENTS STUDYING SOCIOLOGY for the first time, it seems strange that we should investigate health and illness. Surely, they argue, this is something that is obviously biological rather than social. However, as we proceed through the various topics, it becomes clear that what appears at first sight to be completely natural and biological is heavily influenced by society. In Topic 1, for example, we see that some sociologists argue that the very concepts 'health', 'illness' and 'disease' are actually socially constructed, varying across societies, time and different social groups.

It is not just definitions of health and illness, however, which vary. Studies of health and illness of the British population suggest that these are not randomly distributed, but are closely linked to social class, geographical location and gender. In Topic 2, we examine the distribution of health and illness across the population and explore the contrasting explanations suggested by sociologists.

Inequalities are not found solely in the variations in health across the British population; they are also found in the provision of health services. Topic 3 explores this phenomenon of variation in the amount and quality of care within the NHS.

In the first three topics, we concentrate on the social dimensions of physical health, but in Topic 4, we look at the contribution of sociologists to the study of mental health. As many as one in five of the population suffer at some point in their lives from mental illness, so the distribution of mental illness – and the impact of being labelled as mentally ill – are important issues for sociologists.

Finally, in Topic 5, we examine the role of the medical professions. In particular, we explore how doctors have obtained the power they hold in society and who actually benefits from it. Some sociologists argue that the main beneficiary of how medicine is organized in Europe and the USA is likely to be the medical profession, rather than patients.

AQA specification	topics	pages
Candidates should examine:		
Health, illness and disability as both social and biological constructs	Covered in Topic 1	80–87
Different explanations of the unequal social distribution of health and illness	Covered in Topic 2	88–93
Different explanations of inequalities in the provision of, and access to, health care	Covered in Topic 3	94–99
Different approaches to the study of mental health and illness	Covered in Topic 4	100–105
Different explanations of the role of medicine and the health professions	Covered in Topic 5	106–111

Health

Defining health, illness and disability

gettingyouthinking

Look at the four photos on this page and then answer the following questions.

1 Which of these people are, in your opinion, 'abnormal' and which are 'normal'?

2 What suggestions can you make for helping 'abnormal' people make themselves 'normal'?

3 Next, indicate which of these people, if any, are 'ill'.

4 In small groups, compare your answers and explain how you made your decisions.

5 Do you think that health and illness and normal bodies have anything to do with society, or are they just natural, biological states?

This topic investigates the ways in which **health**, **illness** and **disability** are defined in our society and the implications for people who are defined as ill or disabled. The majority of the population pass most their lives taking for granted the normal, routine state of their bodies, until this 'normality' is disrupted in some way. At this point, people often say they are 'ill'. However, it is very unclear just what illness is. Surely, such an important concept does not vary simply according to how each individual feels? Anyway, how does anyone know what is 'normal'?

A second, linked area is the notion of 'abnormality'. If there is such a thing as 'normality', then there must be something which is 'abnormal'. This category might include those suffering from chronic (long-term) illness, such as multiple sclerosis, those with a 'mental illness' or those with a physical 'disability'.

Sociologists also want to understand how terms such as 'abnormality' and 'disability' are constructed and what implications there are for the people so labelled.

We begin by looking at how health and illness are defined and the implications of these definitions for society. We then extend our analysis to issues of disability and mental illness, and their implications for people labelled with these terms.

Definitions of health and illness

At some time, most of us will have woken up in the morning not really feeling very well. Despite telling our parents this, it may have been difficult to persuade them that we really were too ill to go to school or college (particularly if there was an exam that day or a particular lesson they knew we loathed). Only when we produced some real evidence, such as vomiting or a rash, were we believed. Our parents may also be rather less than supportive when it turns out that we have been drinking pretty heavily the night before. Ill or just hung over? And anyway, why is being hung over not being ill – after all, we feel

Talcott Parsons

The sick role: sickness as deviance

According to Talcott Parsons (1975), being sick is a deviant act which can prevent a person undertaking their normal social functions. Society therefore controls this deviance through a device known as 'the sick role'. This is illustrated in the diagram below.

Figure 3.1 The sick role

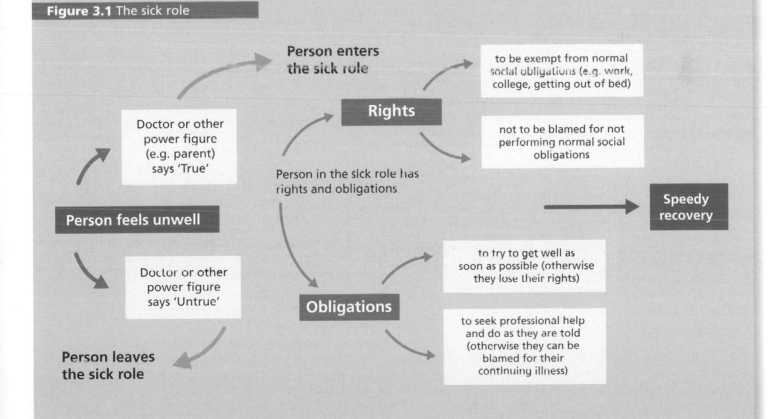

awful? The answer from disapproving parents might well be that being hung over is the price we pay for a night's drinking and that it therefore does not count as a 'real' illness.

This situation illustrates a number of issues. First, it is not clear exactly what we mean by being 'healthy' and being 'unwell'. It seems that these concepts may well have different meanings depending upon who is defining them. In this case, us and our parents. Furthermore, there is a 'moral' element involved. If feeling ill is a result of having drunk too much, then this may be classified as just a 'hangover' and hence our own fault.

Definitions of illness and their consequences (get the day off college or have to endure a miserable day attending) form the starting point for the sociology of medicine.

To unravel this complex issue, we will look first at how ordinary, or **lay**, people construct their definitions of health and illness. We will then move on to look at the competing models amongst health practitioners themselves.

Lay definitions of health and illness

In the survey *Health and Lifestyles* (1990), Mildred Blaxter asked almost 10 000 people how they defined health. She discovered that three clear types of definition emerged:

1 *Positive definitions* – where health is defined as feeling fit and able to undertake any reasonable task.
2 *Negative definitions* – where health is defined in terms of being free from pain and discomfort.
3 *Functional definitions* – where people define health in terms of being able to perform a range of tasks.

Blaxter concludes that these different definitions mean that a particular level of discomfort for one person may indicate that they are ill, whilst, for another person, it may have no such meaning. Health and illness then seem less like objective, physical states than socially defined states, varying from person to person.

Factors influencing lay definitions of health and illness

If definitions of health and illness vary, then we need to know just what factors appear to influence the way in which individuals define their sense of being healthy or ill. Sociologists have suggested that culture, age, gender and social class are particularly important.

Cultural differences

Different social groups have differing ideas of what constitutes illness. For example, Krause (1989) studied Hindu and Sikh Punjabis living in Bedford, and in particular focused on their illness called 'sinking heart' (*dil ghirda hai*) which is characterized by physical chest pain. According to Krause, this illness is caused by a variety of emotional experiences – most

importantly, public shame of some sort. No such illness exists in other mainstream cultures in Britain.

Age differences

Older people tend to accept as 'normal' a range of pains and physical limitations which younger people would define as symptoms of some illness or disability. As we age, we gradually redefine health and accept greater levels of physical discomfort. In Blaxter's national survey of health definitions, she found that young people tend to define health in terms of physical fitness, but gradually, as people age, health comes to be defined more in terms of being able to cope with everyday tasks. She found examples of older people with really serious arthritis, who nevertheless defined themselves as healthy, as they were still able to carry out a limited range of routine activities.

Gender differences

According to Hilary Graham (2002), men have fewer consultations with doctors than women and appear to have lower levels of illness. This is partly due to the greater number of complications associated with childbirth and menopause which women face, but it is also partly due to the fact that men are less likely to define themselves as ill, or as needing medical attention. The idea of 'masculinity' includes the belief that a man should be tough and put off going to the doctor.

Despite the greater propensity of men to define themselves as healthy and to visit **GPs** less often, men have considerably higher mortality (death) rates than women.

Social class differences

Blaxter's research also showed that working-class people were far more likely to accept higher levels of 'illness' than middle-class people. Blaxter describes working-class people as 'fatalistic' – that is, they accepted poor health as 'one of those things'. As a result, people from lower social classes are less likely to consult a GP than middle-class people. This may be because they will accept a higher level of pain and discomfort before considering themselves ill enough to visit a doctor.

Medical definitions of health and illness

There is a distinction in most people's minds between those who think they are ill and those who really are ill. In contemporary society, the role of deciding whether the person is truly ill lies with doctors. If they decide that a person is ill, then a series of benefits flow, both formal (in the provision of medical help, or time off work or college) and informal (such as sympathy, release from household tasks and so on).

However, if they decide that you are not really ill, then you receive no benefits and may, in fact, be open to accusations of **malingering**.

Doctors use a particular 'scientific' measure of health and illness in order to decide whether someone really is ill or not. This model is known as the **biomedical model**, and it is the

Lesley Cooper
ME: real or imagined illness?

Myalgic Encephalomyelitis (Chronic Fatigue Syndrome) has been the centre of a debate as to whether it is a real illness or not. Cooper wanted to explore the way that doctors responded to people who presented themselves at the surgery claiming to be suffering from ME. Cooper used the 'narrative method', where people were encouraged to tell their story (rather than being asked questions). Their stories were recorded and then analysed. The narratives were those of doctors, patients, researchers and psychiatrists.

What Cooper found was that individuals suffering from ME would experience a wide range of debilitating symptoms which they were unable to explain. When they were seen by doctors, their experiences were very different. Some people were diagnosed as having ME and received help and support. Others saw doctors who did not believe that ME exists as a specific illness and would either suggest that the symptoms were in the mind of the patient or that they had a virus and needed rest. Where doctors made a diagnosis of ME, sufferers were treated with some respect and concern by employers and family. However, where the diagnosis of ME was refused, this led to considerable trouble with employers and lack of support from family and friends.

Cooper's work illustrates the way that physical symptoms alone are not as important as definitions by doctors in being defined as ill.

Source: Cooper, L. (1997) 'Myalgic Encephalomyelitis and the medical encounter', *Sociology of Health and Illness*, 19(2)

1 What method did Cooper use to find out about people's experiences of ME?

2 How is this approach different to that normally used by doctors?

3 What was the effect of a doctor's decision whether or not to diagnose ME?

basis of all Western medicine. The elements of this model include the following:

- Illness is always caused by an identifiable (physical or mental) reason and cannot be the result of magic, religion or witchcraft.
- Illnesses and their causes can be identified, classified and measured using scientific methods.
- If there is a cure, then it will almost always be through the use of drugs or surgery, rather than in changing social relationships or people's spiritual lives.
- This is because the cause almost always lies in the actual physical body of the individual patient.

At its simplest, this model presents the human body as a type of machine and, just as with a machine, parts can go wrong and need repairing. Over time, the body 'wears out' just as a machine does and will eventually stop working completely. This is why the contemporary medical model is sometimes referred to as the 'bio-*mechanical*' model.

Illness and disease

What emerges from the discussion of health and illness is that individuals, using lay concepts of health, may define themselves as 'ill' or not, depending upon a range of social factors. On the other hand, doctors claim that they can scientifically determine, via medical tests, whether or not a person is ill. Eisenberg (1977) has therefore suggested that we should make a distinction between illness and disease. Illness is an individual's subjective experience of symptoms of ill health, whilst diseases are clinical conditions defined by medical professionals.

It is therefore perfectly possible, as Blaxter has pointed out, to have an illness without a disease and a disease without an illness!

Traditional and non-Western definitions of health and illness

The biomedical model contrasts markedly with concepts of illness in traditional and non-Western societies, where illness is seen as the result of a wider range of factors than just the body itself.

In traditional societies, for example, these factors could include witchcraft – where the blame for the illness lies in the bad wishes of others, or possibly the 'will of God'. A more complex model of health exists in non-Western societies, where the body and the mind are seen as completely linked. Any understanding of the body must be linked with the person's mental state, and the two need to be treated together.

However, over the last two hundred years, the biomedical model of health has come to dominate health care and has excluded other approaches. This supremacy is linked to the wider development of science and scientific methods as the predominant form of knowledge in modern societies.

Complementary medicine

In recent years, there has been a major growth in alternative or **complementary** forms of health provision. These include therapies such as homeopathy, herbal medicines and acupuncture. Following the ideas of Giddens (1991) about the development of new ways of thinking and acting in contemporary society, which he characterizes as **late modernity** (see p. 109), Hardey (1998) has argued that in late modernity, there has been a decline in the uncritical acceptance of the authority of professionals such as doctors. A second relevant feature of late modernity has been the growth in self-expression and individual choice. The idea that some people should give themselves completely into the power of doctors, and subject themselves to treatments which they may not even understand has therefore become increasingly questioned.

The result of this has been a partial rejection of the traditional biomedical model, in favour of seeking alternative therapies from the wide range available.

Criticisms of the biomedical and complementary models of health

According to Coward (1989), both the biomedical and the complementary models of health tend to stress that health problems are individual, both in terms of the causes and the cures. Coward argues that this ignores the wider social factors which cause ill health, such as poverty, poor housing, job-related stress and pollution, amongst others.

Defining disability

The dominance of medical definitions of health and ill health has had important implications for people with disabilities. According to Friedson (1965), the common perception of disability is that disabled people have some impediment that prevents them from operating 'normally'. This perception starts from the assumption that there is a clear definition of the 'normal' body, and a 'normal' range of activities associated with it.

However, it has been pointed out by critics such as Michael Oliver (1996) that the impediments imposed by society are at least as great as those imposed by the physical impairment. In other words, disability is a social construction, rather than just a physical one.

Not everyone is able to do everything as well as others – for example, run, catch or throw a ball – yet we do not describe those who are less able as being 'disabled'. We just accept these differences as part of the normal range of human abilities. This range of normality could be extended to include those defined as 'disabled'. This could occur, it is argued, if physical facilities and social attitudes were adjusted to include those with disabilities – for example, by altering the way we construct buildings, and by regarding sport played by disabled people as equal to 'traditional' types of sport.

It is with this in mind that the World Health Organization has distinguished between impairment, disability and handicap:

- *Impairment* refers to the abnormality of, or loss of function of, a part of the body.
- *Handicap* refers to the physical limits imposed by the loss of function.
- *Disability* refers to the socially imposed restriction on people's abilities to perform tasks as a result of the behaviour of people in society.

According to this approach, disability has to be understood as much in social terms as physical ones; so, a person can have an impairment without being disabled.

The origins of disability

If disability is a socially constructed concept, how did it come about? According to Finkelstein (1980), the modern idea of the dependent disabled person is largely the result of industrialization and the introduction of machinery. People with impairments were excluded from this type of work and came to be viewed as a burden. The rise of the medical profession in the early 19th century led them to become labelled as sick and in need of care.

Oliver (1990) takes Finkelstein's analysis further, by suggesting that the medical profession not only imposed the label of sickness and abnormality on people with impairments, but also helped to construct a way of looking at disability which saw it as a **personal tragedy**.

This concept of personal tragedy stresses that the individual disabled person has to be 'helped' to come to terms with the physical and psychological problems which they face. According to Oliver, this draws attention away from the fact that impairment is turned into disability by the wider economic, physical and social environment which discriminates against disabled people.

Stigma, illness and disability

Stigma is an important term in helping us to understand how people with disabilities are excluded from social activities. The idea of 'stigma' does not just apply to disabled people, but also to those with certain illnesses, such as Aids. The concept was first used in sociology by Erving Goffman (1963), who suggested that certain groups of people are defined as 'discredited' because of characteristics that are seen as 'negative'.

Types of stigma

Goffman suggested that there are two types of stigma.

1 *Discrediting* – These are obvious types of stigma, such as being in a wheelchair. People find it awkward to have normal social relations with those who are 'discredited'.

They may be embarrassed, avoid eye contact or ignore the 'obvious' disability.

2. *Discreditable* – Here, the stigma is one of potential, dependent on whether other people find out about the discreditable illness or disability. Examples of this might include HIV status or epilepsy. In this situation, the person with the illness may find it difficult to act 'normally' in case they are 'found out'.

The concept of 'master status'

When the discrediting or discreditable status becomes the main way in which people are seen by others, then Goffman calls this a 'master status'. The stigma then completely dominates the way the person is treated, and any other attributes are seen as less important. The person who is unable to walk unaided is seen simply as 'wheelchair-bound' (not as an intelligent, articulate woman, for example), and the happy family man is seen as an 'Aids victim'. Finally, Goffman points out that the

individuals themselves may accept this master status and come to see themselves solely in terms of their stigmatized status.

However, Goffman's argument that the individuals with stigma may well accept this as a master status has been criticized by other sociologists. According to Scambler and Hopkins (1986), for example, people with stigma may react in a number of different ways, using different tactics to manage their stigma:

- *Selective concealment* – If the stigmatizing condition is not obvious, the person may only tell a few trusted friends and family.
- *Covering up* – The person may tell no one.
- *Medicalizing the behaviour* – If the person cannot hide (or does not choose to hide) the condition, they could emphasize the medical aspect of it, as opposed to the social or moral aspect, and thus make a bid for sympathy (a link to the sick role here – see p. 81).

web.task

Search for obituaries of Christopher Reeve, who played Superman in a number of films. What happened to him? In what ways was he unusual in his attitude and behaviour towards disability?

- *Condemning the condemners* – This is where people with a stigmatized condition take on those who impose the stigma and engage in forms of political action to have the stigma reviewed. Examples of this include the activities of HIV/Aids pressure groups and of pressure groups set up by disabled people.

The origins of stigma

Goffman never explained the origins of stigma, that is, why some people are stigmatized and others not. His main interest was in the effect of stigma on people and their interactions with others. However, other writers have suggested reasons why certain categories of people come to be stigmatized.

Clarke (1992) conducted a content analysis survey of magazines over a 20-year period and concluded that certain illnesses are linked to leading the 'wrong' sorts of lifestyles. HIV/Aids is viewed as discreditable, as are lung cancer and **obesity**. However, heart disease had no negative image.

Oliver (1990), as discussed earlier, sees the role of the medical profession as being crucial in defining how certain conditions are viewed.

Check your understanding

1 How does the public define health?

2 Identify and explain any three factors that affect the definition of health and illness.

3 Who 'sanctions' illness (officially approves it), and what are the benefits of being 'sanctioned' as ill?

4 Construct a table summarizing the three types of medical models: biomedical, traditional and complementary.

5 What is the difference between 'impairment' and 'disability'?

6 Explain the difference between stigma and disability.

7 Why might certain types of people become stigmatized?

Sociology AS for AQA

research ideas

- Conduct interviews with a small sample of your peers at school or college. Who sanctions their 'illness' when they feel too ill to come in to school or college? How does the process of 'negotiating' absence work?

- Select a small sample of people, ideally from different generations, and ask them to rate their degree of sympathy on a scale of 1 to 5 for people with the following 'illnesses': hangover, headache (not caused by a hangover!), impotence, cirrhosis of the liver (caused by drinking too much alcohol), anorexia, heart disease, breast cancer, lung cancer caused by smoking, sexually transmitted disease.

Do your results show any different attitudes to illness and disease amongst people? What explanations can you suggest for your findings?

KEY TERMS

Biomedical model of health the conventional Western model. It sees the body as very much like a biological machine, with each part of the body performing a function. The doctor's job is to restore the functions by solving the problem of what is wrong. Ideas about the environment or the spiritual health of the person are not relevant.

Complementary medicine alternative forms of health intervention, such as homeopathy.

Disability the socially imposed restriction on people's abilities to perform tasks as a result of the behaviour of people in society.

General practitioner (GP) a local doctor who deals with general health issues.

Health a person's perception of the state of their body's wellbeing.

Illness perception of feeling unacceptably worse than normal body state.

Late modernity a term used to describe contemporary society where choice and individuality have become more important than conformity and group membership.

Lay definitions of health 'lay' refers to the majority of the public who are not medical practitioners and who therefore use common-sense ideas about health and illness.

Malingering pretending to be ill in order to avoid work or other responsibilities.

Obesity a medical term for being overweight.

Personal tragedy a term used by Oliver to describe the way disability is seen as a personal as opposed to a social problem.

Item A The Ndembu

The Ndembu explain all persistent or severe health problems by reference to social causes, such as the secret malevolence of sorcerers or witches, or punishment by the spirits of ancestors. These spirits cause sickness in an individual if his or her family and kin are 'not living well together', and are involved in grudges or quarrelling.

The Ndembu traditional healer, the chimbuki, conducts a séance attended by the victim, their kin and neighbours. By questioning these people and by shrewd observation, he builds up a picture of the patient's social situation and its various tensions. The diviner calls all the relatives of the patient before a sacred shrine to the ancestors, and induces them 'to confess any grudges and hard feelings they may nourish against the patient'. By this process all the hidden social tensions of the group are publicly aired and gradually resolved. Treatment involves rituals of exorcism to withdraw evil influences from the patient's body. It also includes the use of certain herbal and other medicines, manipulation and cupping and certain substances applied to the skin.

Adapted from Helman, C. (2000) *Culture, Health and Illness*, Oxford: Butterworth/ Heinemann, pp. 197–8 (adapted)

Item B The biomedical model

In the biomedical model, information is gathered by means of indicators like X-rays, blood sugar levels, electroencephalograph readings or biopsies, which are thought to measure these biological processes directly. This framework is closely associated with developments in Western science. Physicians can readily reach agreement on the operation of the body by reference to well-defined criteria which are known to all members of the medical profession and which become progressively more precise with advances in scientific knowledge. The doctor will be able to use signs derived from these tests as objective indicators of biological malfunction or irregularity – regardless of whether the supposed patient actually feels ill.

Adapted from Dingwall, R. (1976) *Aspects of Illness*, Basingstoke: Palgrave

1 Explain what is meant by the 'biomedical model' (Item B). (2 marks)

2 Identify two characteristics of the biomedical model of health (Item B). (4 marks)

3 Identify three factors that the Ndembu healer sees as being important in the diagnosis of illness (Item A). (6 marks)

4 Identify and briefly explain two ways in which the Western model of health and illness (Item B) is different from the traditional model described in Item A. (8 marks)

5 Discuss the view that it is societies themselves that create 'disability'. (20 marks)

6 Using information from the Items and elsewhere, assess the view that definitions of health and illness are social constructions. (20 marks)

web.task

1 RADAR is an educational and campaigning organization for people with disabilities. Visit their website at www.radar.org.uk

The website has information sheets which are worth exploring for information on disability.

2 Search online for information and advice on health – for example, *Men's Health Magazine* at www.menshealth.co.uk

Does the advice make an assumption about what is normal and abnormal in terms of body shape and styles of life?

3 Search the world wide web for examples of traditional models of health and illness. Compare them with conventional Western models.

Health inequalities

gettingyouthinking

SMRs by social class for men aged 15/20 to 64 (England & Wales)

Year	I	II	III		IV	V	Ratio V:I
			IIIN	IIIM			
1921–3	82	94	95		101	125	1.52
1930–2	90	94	97		102	111	1.23
1949–53	86	92	101		104	118	1.37
1959–63	76	81	100		103	143	1.91
1970–2	77	81	99	106	114	137	1.78
1979–80/82–3	66	76	94	106	116	165	2.50
1991–3	66	72	100	117	116	189	2.86

Note: for 1921 to 1972, men aged 15 to 64 are included;
for 1979 to 1993, men aged 20 to 64 are included

Source: Shaw, M., Dorling, D., Gordon, D. and Davey Smith, G. (1999)
The Widening Gap, Bristol: Policy Press, p. 132

SMR stands for 'standardized mortality ratio'. This is a guide to the relative chances of dying for specific age ranges (in this case men aged 15/20 to 64). In this model, average chances of death are 100 and any figures above this indicate above-average chances of death. Any figures below indicate below-average chances. The letters 'I' to 'V' stand for social classes, 'I' being the highest and 'V' the lowest.

Remember when answering these questions that SMRs are *relative* figures – that is, they show differences between groups. It is not possible to make any statements about the *absolute* figures over time.

1 In 1921–3, what were the SMRs for social class I and social class V?

2 What changes happened in the relative SMRs of the social classes:
   (a) between 1921 and 1953?
   (b) after 1972?

3 What long-term impact, if any, did the introduction of the National Health Service in the late 1940s have on inequalities in the SMR?

4 What reasons can you suggest for all the changes you have identified from the table?

5 Look at the photographs above and make a list of the reasons why, in your opinion, people in the 'lower' social classes are more likely to die young. Do you think the government could do anything about these issues?

In 1979, the Labour government of the time commissioned a report on health and illness in Britain. Shortly afterwards, they lost the election and a new Conservative government came into power. The following year, the committee reported back on their findings. The new government was so embarrassed by these findings that they only printed 260 copies and gave the report no publicity, in the hope that no one would notice. Unfortunately for the government, they did, and what the press and the public read was quite shocking: after 35 years of a free health service, health and life expectation were still very closely linked to social class. Despite this revelation, a further report ('Independent Inquiry into Inequalities in Health'), commissioned by the next Labour government almost 20 years later, found that the 'health gap' between the poorest and the richest had actually widened.

Research has shown that health is closely linked to a number of social factors, including geography, social class, gender and ethnicity. We will look at each area in turn.

Geographical differences

In 1999, a team of researchers led by Mary Shaw looked at the **parliamentary constituencies** in Britain and gathered information on the health of the people living in each constituency. They compared the one million people living in the constituencies that had the very worst health records with the one million people living in the constituencies that had the very best health records. The gap between these groups surprised even the researchers themselves.

The comparison showed that, in the worst health areas:

- children under the age of 1 are twice as likely to die
- there are ten times more women under the age of 65 who are permanently sick (including those who are disabled)
- adults are almost three times as likely to state that they have a serious 'chronic' (long-term) illness or disability
- adults have a 70 per cent greater chance of dying before the age of 65.

These geographical differences generally reflect differences in income and levels of deprivation. However, they are not simply a reflection of these, because poorer people living in the richer areas tend to have higher standards of health. It seems that quality of life in poorer areas is generally lower and, as a result, health standards are worse.

Social class

Mortality

Over the last 20 years, **death rates** have fallen for both men and women, in all social classes. But they have fallen faster for those in the higher social classes, so that the difference in rates between those in the higher and those in the lower social classes has actually grown. For example, in the early 1970s, the death rate among men of working age was almost twice as high for those in class V (unskilled) as for those in class I (professional). By the 1990s, it was almost three times as high.

Men in social class I can expect to live for almost nine years longer than men from social class V, while women in social class I can expect to live six years longer than their social class V counterparts.

Morbidity

Although death rates have fallen and life expectancy has increased, there is little evidence that the population is experiencing better health than 20 years ago. In fact, there has actually been a small increase in **self-reported** long-standing illness, and differences between the social classes are still quite clear. However, as we saw in Topic 1, what is defined as 'health' changes over time. So it may be that people are actually in better health but don't believe it.

Bearing this in mind, among the 45 to 64 age group, 17 per cent of professional men reported a limiting long-standing illness, compared to 48 per cent of unskilled men (1999). For women, the figures were 25 per cent for professional women and 45 per cent for unskilled women.

In adulthood, being overweight is a measure of possible ill health, with obesity a risk factor for many chronic diseases. There is a noticeable social-class gradient in obesity, which is greater for women than men. About 25 per cent of women in class V are classified as obese, compared to 14 per cent of women in class I.

Explanations for differences in health between social classes

Different ways of explaining class differences in **mortality** and **morbidity** have been suggested.

The artefact approach

An artefact is something observed in a scientific investigation that is not naturally present, but occurs as a result of the investigative procedure. Perhaps the link between class and health is not real but a statistical illusion. Illsley (1986) argues that the statistical connection between social class and illness exaggerates the situation. For example, he points out that the number of people in social class V has declined so much over the last 30 years that the membership is just too small to be used as the basis for comparisons with other social classes.

However, the recent 'Independent Inquiry into Inequalities in Health' showed that, even when the classes were regrouped to include classes IV and V together, significant differences remained. For example, in the late 1970s, death rates were 53 per cent higher among men in classes IV and V, compared with those in classes I and II.

Social selection

This approach claims that social class does not cause ill health, but that ill health may be a significant cause of social class. For example, if a person is chronically ill (i.e. has a long-term illness) or disabled in some way, it is usually difficult for them to obtain a secure, well-paid job. The fit and healthy are more likely to be successful in life and upwardly mobile in terms of social class.

The problem with this approach is that studies of health differences indicate that poor health is a result of poverty rather than a cause of it.

Cultural explanations

This approach stresses that differences in health are best understood as the result of cultural choices made by individuals or groups in the population.

● *Diet* – Manual workers consume twice as much white bread as professionals, and have higher sugar consumption and eat less fresh fruit.
● *Cigarette-smoking* – Over 40 per cent of males and 35 per cent of females in social classes IV and V regularly smoke, whereas only about 12 per cent of males and females in social class I smoke.
● *Leisure and lifestyle* – Middle-class people are more likely to take exercise and have a wider range of social activities than the working classes. These reduce levels of stress and help maintain a higher standard of health.
● *Alcohol* – Alcohol consumption is directly related to social class, with much higher consumption amongst the 'lower' social classes.

The cultural approach, however, fails to ask why these groups have poor diets and high alcohol- and cigarette-consumption. Critics point out that there may be reasons why people are 'forced' into an unhealthy lifestyle. These critics have put forward an alternative **structural explanation**.

Structural explanations

Some analysts see a direct relationship between differences in health and the unequal nature of British society. Supporters of this approach accept the behavioural differences pointed to earlier, but claim that this behaviour has to be seen within a broader context of inequality. So, poor health is the result of 'hazards to which some people have no choice but to be exposed given the present distribution of income and opportunity' (Shaw *et al.* 1999).

● *Poverty* – This key factor links a range of health risks. Poorer people have worse diets and worse housing conditions. They are more likely to be unemployed and generally to have a more highly stressed, lower quality of life. According to the British Regional Heart Survey (cited in Shaw *et al.* 1999) – a study of 8000 middle-aged men – over half of those who did not own a car or a home were reported to be in poor health, compared to a tenth of those who did own both.
● *Position at work* – Workers with little power or control over their work are likely to experience worse health than those given more responsibility. Research on civil servants (Davey Smith *et al.* 1990) has shown that routine clerical workers are much more likely to die young than workers in higher grades. If the lowest and highest grades are compared, those in the lowest grades are actually three times more likely to die before reaching the age of 65.
● *Unemployment* – According to Moser's long-term study of the relationship between income and wealth (Moser *et al.* 1990), unemployed men and their wives are likely to die younger than those in employment.

focus on research

Wilkinson
Health and social capital

In one of the most famous studies to uncover the relationship between social factors and health, Wilkinson compared the health and economic data for 23 different countries. He found very strong evidence to link the overall health of the population with the degree of economic inequality. Once a certain basic level of overall economic wealth had been attained by a country, then the greater the economic inequality which existed, the wider the health differentials. Interestingly, no matter how high the general standard of living became, as long as there were economic inequalities, there was no increase in the general standards of health. This meant that a country with a high standard of living, but considerable economic inequality, actually had lower standards of health for the majority of the population than a poorer country with greater social equality. Cuba, for example, despite being much poorer than the USA, has better standards of health and expectation of life overall than the USA.

Wilkinson's conclusions were that societies with low levels of inequality had high levels of 'social capital' – that is a sense of belonging and place in a society. This sense of belonging had the effect of increasing the sense of wellbeing, which in turn improved standards of health.

Wilkinson, R.G. (1996) *Unhealthy Societies: The Afflictions of Inequality*, London: Routledge

1 What is Wilkinson's explanation for the fact that Cuba has higher life expectancy than the USA?

2 What does Wilkinson mean by 'social capital'? How does it improve health?

● *Types of industry* – industries vary in how dangerous they are to their employees. For example, respiratory diseases are common amongst those working in road- and building-construction, as a result of the dust inhaled, while various forms of cancer are associated with chemical industries.

The structural approach has the advantage of explaining why there are cultural differences in behaviour between various groups in society. The argument advanced by those who support this approach is that people may make choices about their behaviour, but that the circumstances within which they make their choices are strongly affected by the extent of inequality existing in Britain.

Gender and health

Women live longer than men, but are more likely to visit their GPs for treatment. They also have higher levels of mental illness. This apparently contradictory pattern – higher morbidity combined with a longer life span – has led some observers to argue that it is not that women are more likely to be ill than men, but that they are more willing to visit the doctor. Yet MacIntyre (1993) shows that women are, in fact, no more likely than men to report symptoms. The answer lies perhaps in a combination of biological factors and social roles.

Explanations for the link between gender and health

Biology

There is some evidence to suggest that women are biologically stronger than men (for instance, female foetuses are less likely to die than male foetuses) and they have a greater biological possibility of living longer. However, this does not mean that they are less immune to illness. In addition, they can suffer from a range of health problems associated with reproduction and the menopause.

Social role

Women may also live longer because their social role tends to prevent them from taking risks. Their social role discourages them from violence, fast driving and excess alcohol-consumption. Women are also less likely to smoke than men. However, the social role that limits their activities also places considerable stress upon women, by restricting opportunities in employment and in life in general. Furthermore, women are

more likely than men to be living in poverty. They are also more likely to be lone parents. Both place considerable burdens upon their health.

Work

According to Ellen Annandale (1998), women who go out to work have better levels of health than those who do not. Annandale argues that this is not just because of the financial benefits, but also because work gives women a sense of independence and a wider social network. Both of these have the effect of lowering stress levels – and stress is closely related to standards of health.

Ethnicity and health

Surprisingly, there is only limited information available on ethnicity and illness. This is partly because of the complex make-up of ethnic groups in the UK and the difficulty of making generalizations across these groupings. However, some specific health problems can be linked with particular groups – for example, those of Afro-Caribbean origin are much more likely to suffer from sickle cell disease.

The research that has been done (mainly by the Health Education Authority) shows that members of minority ethnic groups are more likely to define themselves as having poor health than the majority population. For example, just under 50 per cent of ethnic minority members described themselves as having fair or poor health. This compared with just under 30 per cent of the majority population.

As for mortality, all ethnic minority groups have a shorter life expectancy than the majority population. Patterns in the causes of death do seem to vary, with groups from the **Indian subcontinent** having the highest levels of coronary heart disease of the whole population, while those from the **Caribbean commonwealth** have the lowest levels of death from this cause. Although, overall, health levels are worse and life expectancy is lower, one striking difference is that all of the

Figure 3.2 Influences on health

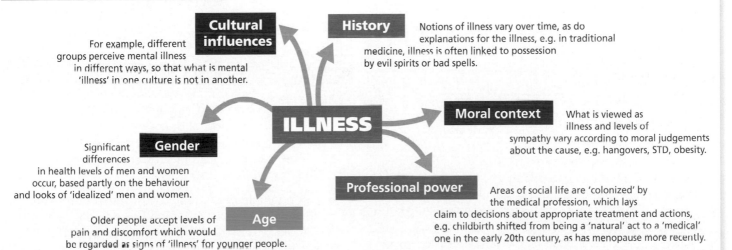

For example, different groups perceive mental illness in different ways, so that what is mental 'illness' in one culture is not in another.

Cultural influences

History Notions of illness vary over time, as do explanations for the illness, e.g. in traditional medicine, illness is often linked to possession by evil spirits or bad spells.

ILLNESS

Moral context What is viewed as illness and levels of sympathy vary according to moral judgements about the cause, e.g. hangovers, STD, obesity.

Significant differences in health levels of men and women occur, based partly on the behaviour and looks of 'idealized' men and women.

Gender

Professional power Areas of social life are 'colonized' by the medical profession, which lays claim to decisions about appropriate treatment and actions, e.g. childbirth shifted from being a 'natural' act to a 'medical' one in the early 20th century, as has menopause more recently.

Older people accept levels of pain and discomfort which would be regarded as signs of 'illness' for younger people.

Age

ethnic minority groups have lower rates of deaths from cancers than the majority population.

Explanations for the link between ethnicity and health

'Race' and inequality

We saw earlier the profound effects of inequality in helping to explain different levels of health. Minority ethnic groups have some of the lowest incomes, worst housing and highest unemployment rates in Britain. Even without any specific explanations related to 'race', the higher levels of morbidity and higher early mortality rates could largely be explained by their relative social deprivation.

'Race' as a specific factor

Some analysts have gone further than this, however, and have argued that 'race' is important by itself. First, much of the poverty and exclusion is actually caused by racism. Second, the experience of living in a racist society can place great stress upon people and this may impact upon health levels.

Culture and ethnicity

The final approach argues that cultural differences, in terms of diet and lifestyle, may influence health. For example, diets using large amounts of 'ghee' (clarified butter) can help cause heart disease amongst those of South Asian origin. Asian diets also tend to lack vitamin D. Long work hours and relatively little physical leisure activity may also lower the health levels of some minority ethnic groups.

Check your understanding

1. Identify four factors that are closely linked to health.

2. Why might some areas of Britain have worse health than others?

3. Give one example of health differences between the social classes.

4. What explanations have been suggested for health differences between the social classes?

5. Explain, in your own words, the meaning of the 'artefact approach'.

6. Do biological factors alone explain the differences in health between men and women?

7. What three explanations have been given for the differences in health between the various ethnic minorities and the majority of the population?

KEY TERMS

Artefact approach an approach that believes that the statistics about class and health exaggerate the real situation.

Caribbean commonwealth parts of the West Indies that are in the Commonwealth, such as Barbados.

Cultural explanations explanations that emphasize lifestyle and behaviour.

Death rate the number dying per 1000 of a population per year.

Indian subcontinent the section of south Asia consisting of India, Pakistan and Bangladesh.

Morbidity refers to statistics about illness.

Mortality refers to statistics of death.

Parliamentary constituency an area that elects one MP. The country is divided into over 600 constituencies.

Self-reported the result of asking people themselves.

SMR (standardized mortality ratio) a guide to the relative chances of dying for a specified age range (usually 20 to 65). Average chances of death are 100, and figures above and below indicate above-average and below-average chances.

Structural explanations explanations that focus on the make-up of society: for example, on inequalities of income and wealth.

web.tasks

1. Find the government website with information on 'Tackling Health Inequalities: A programme for action':

www.dh.gov.uk/PolicyAndGuidance/HealthAndSocial CareTopics/HealthInequalities/ProgramForAction/fs/en

What are the key actions that the government is taking? How do they relate to what you have studied here?

2. Compare the health statistics in your local area with the national picture at the government's Neighbourhood Statistics site:
www.neighbourhood.statistics.gov.uk

What differences and similarities exist? How can you explain them?

research ideas

- Conduct a survey on smoking and drinking alcohol in your school or college. Can you find any differences by gender? Do people think that smoking or alcohol consumption affects their health? Do they care?

- Ask a sample of 20 people how much fresh fruit they eat each day. You might wish to divide the sample by gender or by age or even by parental occupation. Do any differences emerge?

exploring health inequalities

Item A Smoking and social class

Prevalence of cigarette smoking: by sex and socio-economic group[1]

Great Britain	Males (%)		Females (%)	
	1998	2000	1998	2000
Professional	16	17	14	14
Employers and managers	22	23	21	20
Intermediate/junior non-manual	25	27	24	26
Skilled manual	34	33	30	26
Semi-skilled manual	39	36	33	32
Unskilled manual	44	39	31	35
All non-manual	22	23	22	22
All manual	36	34	31	29
All aged 16 and over	30	29	26	25

[1] Socio-economic group of the household reference person (excluding those in the Armed Forces and full-time students)

Source: *General Household Survey*, Office for National Statistics

Item B Illness and disability

Percentage of people in England and Wales reporting long-term illness or disability which restricts daily activities: data from Census 2001

Great Britain	Males (%)	Females (%)
White British	15.9	15.3
White Irish	17.7	15.7
Other White	13.7	13.7
Mixed	18.3	17.8
Indian	16.5	19.8
Pakistani	22.1	25.4
Bangladeshi	23.6	24.9
Other Asian	16.7	18.6
Black Caribbean	17.9	19.3
Black African	14.1	16.7
Other Black	18.8	19.9
Chinese	11.4	12.1
Any other ethnic group	14.7	14.0
All ethnic groups	16.0	15.4

Source: ONS www.statistics.gov.uk/cci/nugget.asp?id=464
www.empho.org.uk/products/ethnicity/inequalities.htm

Item C The health costs of living in an unequal society

<< Alongside these material and behavioural determinants, research is uncovering the psychosocial [social and psychological] costs of living in an unequal society. For example, perceiving oneself to be worse off relative to others may carry a health penalty, in terms of increased stress and risk-taking behaviour. Attention has also focused on the health effects of the work environment and particularly on the control that individuals exercise over the pace and content of work.

Material, behavioural and psychosocial factors cluster together: those in lower socio-economic groups are likely to be exposed to risks in all three domains. Health-damaging factors also accumulate together: children born into poorer circumstances clock up more by way of material, behavioural and psychosocial risks as they grow up and grow older. For example, girls and boys born into social classes IV and V are more likely than those in higher social classes to grow up in overcrowded homes, to develop health damaging habits like smoking and to be exposed to stressful life-events and work environments. >>

Graham, H. (ed.) (2000) *Understanding Health Inequalities*, Buckingham: Open University Press

---

1 Explain what is meant by 'material factors' (Item C). (2 marks)

2 Using Item B, identify the ethnic group:
   (a) with the highest level of female long-term illness
   (b) with the highest level of male long-term illness. (4 marks)

3 Give three examples of 'risk-taking behaviour' (Item C). (6 marks)

4 Identify and briefly explain two reasons why people from lower social classes may be more likely to smoke cigarettes (Item A). (8 marks)

5 Using information from the Items and elsewhere, examine the links between health and inequality in society. (20 marks)

6 Using information from the Items and elsewhere, assess the view that class inequalities in health are the result of cultural factors. (20 marks)

Inequalities in the health service

gettingyouthinking

GP Health promotion claims, by Jarman (UPA) score of health authority, London Boroughs, October 1995

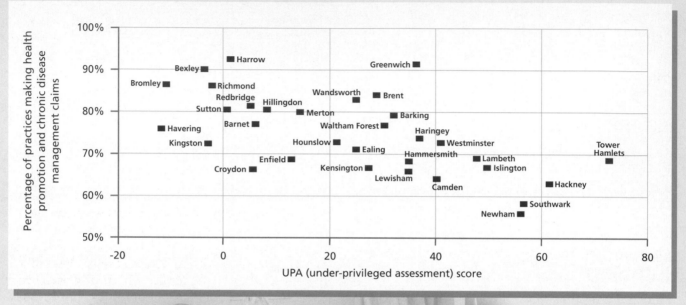

Source: www.archive.official-documents.co.uk/document/doh/ih/fig17.gif

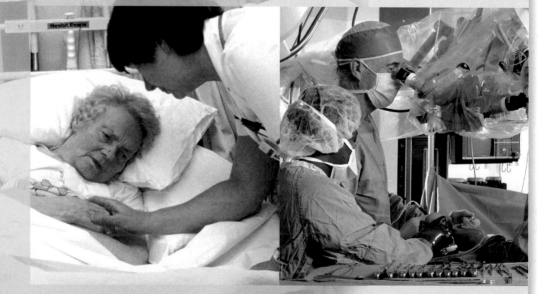

The graph above shows the amount of preventative health work done by GPs in the boroughs of London in relation to the extent of deprivation in those boroughs. The higher the position of the borough on the vertical axis, the more preventative work it is doing. The more deprived the borough is, the further to the right it is along the horizontal axis.

1. Identify the two boroughs in the graph which have the lowest levels of health prevention carried out. What other social characteristic do they share?

2. 'If more money is spent on health in poorer areas then more affluent areas are deprived.' Do you agree with this statement? Give your reasons.

3. Look at the photographs above. Which of these sorts of medical work do you think doctors would prefer to be involved in? Explain your answer.

Despite the National Health Service (NHS) being free to users, and despite taxpayers spending over £115 million *each day* on paying for the NHS, it is a fact that some groups in the population are more likely to receive medical help than others. This contradicts the fundamental notion of 'equity' – the principle that provision of services is based solely upon need. According to this principle, the health services serving disadvantaged populations should not be of poorer quality or less accessible than those serving the more affluent groups in society. Furthermore, it implies that more resources should be allocated to the poorer groups in society, as they have worse levels of health. However, sociologists argue that there is not actually equity in the NHS, for two reasons:

1   The NHS fails to provide equal services for all in relation to their relative needs.
2   Certain groups are less likely to demand services than others.

Issues of provision

The NHS is the main provider of health care for the population and it needs to plan how best to provide this care. Provision is influenced by several factors, discussed below.

Geographical and social inequalities

Each area is allocated a certain amount of money by the government to provide health care for its residents. The amount of money given to each **health authority** is based on the principle of giving more money to poorer areas and less to richer areas. Unfortunately, this has never worked out as planned, and the poorer areas have never received adequate funding. Reasons for this include:

- *Specialist teaching hospitals* – These are usually located in the richer areas of the country and have traditionally been given considerably higher levels of funding than other hospitals.

- *Political pressures* – Certain areas, such as London, have historically received more money than other regions. Over time, the reasons for this extra funding have disappeared – with shifts in population, for example. Each time plans have been put forward to reallocate money to other areas, the politicians have blocked them for fear of losing votes.

An example of this is provided by the Healthcare Commission, an official government body set up to oversee equity in health care. Easington in County Durham, a very deprived area, should be receiving an additional £26.5 million a year in funding while Kensington and Chelsea, one of the richest places in Britain is receiving £30.3 million a year, more than the official government funding formula requires.

The Healthcare Commission also found variations between England and Wales, with patients more likely to wait longer for hospital appointments in Wales than in England. In March 2004, 50 people were waiting more than nine months for an operation in England, yet in Wales, 8457 patients had been waiting longer than 12 months, of whom over 1000 had been waiting longer than 18 months.

The medical professions

The medical professions are extremely influential in determining how the different areas or specialisms of health care are funded. There are some specialisms that are seen as much more important and **prestigious**, whilst others are viewed as less important or less attractive. In general, chronic illness (that is, long-term illnesses for which there is no cure), mental health and geriatric (elderly people's) health care are seen as much less attractive areas than surgery, pharmaceuticals and high technology medicine.

Hospital and primary care trust quality

Different hospitals and **primary care trusts** appear to be organized in very different ways, which results in great differences in the chances of survival from serious operations,

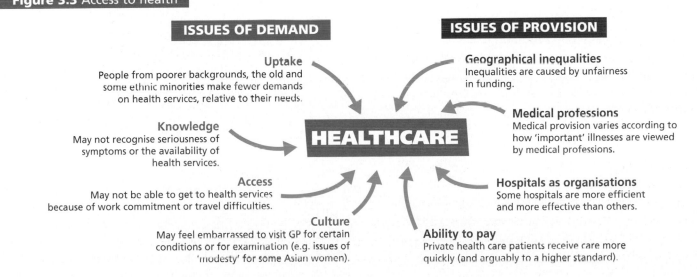

Figure 3.3 Access to health

ISSUES OF DEMAND

Uptake
People from poorer backgrounds, the old and some ethnic minorities make fewer demands on health services, relative to their needs.

Knowledge
May not recognise seriousness of symptoms or the availability of health services.

Access
May not be able to get to health services because of work commitment or travel difficulties.

Culture
May feel embarrassed to visit GP for certain conditions or for examination (e.g. issues of 'modesty' for some Asian women).

HEALTHCARE

ISSUES OF PROVISION

Geographical inequalities
Inequalities are caused by unfairness in funding.

Medical professions
Medical provision varies according to how 'important' illnesses are viewed by medical professions.

Hospitals as organisations
Some hospitals are more efficient and more effective than others.

Ability to pay
Private health care patients receive care more quickly (and arguably to a higher standard).

and in the chances of catching some form of infection in hospital (known as **iatrogenesis**). In a study of all English hospitals in 2000, the researchers found that 17 people were likely to die in the worst hospitals for every 10 in the best. For instance, the death rate from cancer is 60 per cent higher in Liverpool than in east Dorset.

Private health care

Although there is much evidence of inequalities within the NHS, greater inequalities in access to health care exist between those who rely upon the NHS and those who use the private sector.

Private health care is used by those who pay directly for medical services or who have private health insurance. The total spending on private health care in Britain is about £2.5 billion each year, and those doctors who provide private health care earn about £550 million each year.

Private health care increases inequalities in health care by:

- allowing those who can pay to have treatment without waiting, whereas NHS patients have to join a waiting list
- giving private patients access to a range of medical services that may not be available on the NHS
- limiting the number of hours worked by some consultants (senior specialists) in the NHS, who prefer to earn more money in the private sector
- employing nurses and other specialists who have been trained by the NHS – thus contributing to the shortage of trained staff.

Issues of demand

Social class variations

Although the health of the population as a whole has improved, there is no evidence to show that inequalities between the social classes have decreased. As we saw in Topic 2, despite the fact that members of the working class are more likely to be ill and to have accidents, they are actually less likely to attend doctors' surgeries. They are also less likely to take part in any form of **screening programme** that can discover disease (such as certain forms of cancer) at an early stage. They are, however, more likely to use accident and emergency services – often because conditions that have not been attended to have become acute.

The reasons for this are not that they care less about illness, but that there are more barriers to them accessing health care. They are less likely to be able to:

- afford to take time off work
- travel a considerable distance to a GP's surgery – this is a particular problem because there are far fewer GPs in poorer areas, in proportion to the population, than in more affluent areas
- notice signs of health problems.

Gender

Women live approximately seven years longer than men, but they do not necessarily do so in good health. In fact, on average, they have only two extra years of healthy life without significant chronic illness. During their lifetimes, too, women appear to have higher levels of illness and higher rates of attendance at doctors' surgeries. But this needs to be set against women's needs. Women give birth, and also take on the main childcare role, both of which put great strain upon their bodies.

Feminist sociologists argue that women actually under-use the health services, if their use is compared to their actual needs. They argue that, instead, the health services spend much of their resources on controlling women, by turning many 'normal' physical activities, such as giving birth, into medical ones. This takes power away from women and hands it to men, who form the majority of doctors.

As a result of these concerns, a national screening programme for breast cancer was introduced in 1988, and for cervical cancer in 1995. However, within these programmes, considerable differences in attendance have occurred, related to social class and ethnicity. Overall, the take-up rates have been approximately 75 per cent, but the poorer the social group, the less likely women are to attend. Similarly, the attendance rates for those of Bangladeshi and Pakistani origin are particularly low.

Ethnicity

There is a lower use of medical services by certain ethnic minority groups. Several reasons have been suggested for this:

- *Language barriers* – Until recently, there was little attempt to provide translation facilities or to publicize the NHS in minority languages.
- *Cultural differences* – The traditional acceptance of male doctors has been challenged by many women from ethnic minorities, whose ideas of modesty have meant that many are unwilling to be seen by male doctors.
- *Poverty* – Ethnic minorities contain some of the lowest-income families in Britain, and so the factors that limit working-class use of health services (time off work and public transport difficulties) apply equally to them.

Age

Older people's approach to health-care provision is different from that of middle-aged and younger people. Although they are the age group who are most in need of health services and who use them most, they tend to under-use them relative to their needs. Older people see themselves as 'wasting the doctor's time' if they consider that they may be consulting the doctor unnecessarily. What is more, geriatric medicine (the care of older people) is seen by doctors and nurses as an area of low prestige, and staffing and funding levels are extremely low. Therefore, both in terms of demand

and provision, older people do particularly badly. However, stratification by class and geography also cuts across age lines – for example, the proportion of older people in the population receiving flu vaccinations varies from 49 per cent to 78 per cent across England.

Theoretical approaches

So far, we have seen how patterns of inequalities in the usage of the NHS can best be grasped in terms of provision of services on the one hand and demand for health care on the other. However, some writers have suggested that these explanations can also be included within wider theoretical perspectives. In particular, Ham (1999) has suggested the following as the best way of understanding the inequalities in health provision and use:

● Marxism
● pluralism
● structuralism.

Marxist approaches to inequalities in health provision

Marxist writers on health, such as Doyal (1979) and O'Connor (1973), argue that the health service exists for two reasons. First, it has a 'legitimation' role, in that it persuades the bulk of the population that capitalism 'cares' for them. In this role, it acts to limit class conflict and social unrest by creating a sense of harmony. The health service therefore legitimates capitalism and is a subtle form of social control. However, the second role of health services helps the capitalist economy more directly. The health service maintains a healthy and hardworking – and therefore productive – workforce. Workers who are ill or injured are returned to work and therefore continue to make profits for the owners of capital.

Using this approach, inequalities in health provision are directly related to how productive people are. This explains why there are low levels of expenditure on people with mental illness, people with learning difficulties and the oldest and frailest members of society. The low levels of expenditure on the working class is explained by the presence of social-class

focus on research

Hilary Graham
Health ideology and government policy

Professor Hilary Graham's research was based on a detailed examination of the British government's policy documents for health provision in England between 1997 and 2004 (Welsh and Scottish health policies are run by the devolved parliaments). Graham found that the policy documents were written in a manner so vague that they could be interpreted by different groups in different ways. This vagueness meant that the Labour government was able to claim that they were tackling inequalities in health, without actually dealing with the real underlying problems which caused the differences in standards of health in the population.

Graham claims the government accepted the argument that differences in health were a reflection of inequality in society. For many analysts this means that the only way to eradicate differences in health is to eradicate the social and economic differences in society. This would involve ensuring that wage levels, educational opportunities, standards of housing and levels of wealth were all more or less equal across the population as a whole. However, achieving this would involve dramatic social upheaval. Instead, the government has chosen to put increased resources into health care for the poorer groups in society, and to undertake health education campaigns. The result has been an enormous increase in expenditure on health and a wide range of changes in how health services are provided. According to Graham, these policies are bound to fail as they ignore the simple fact that health inequalities mirror wider social and economic inequalities and little will change until these are tackled.

Graham, H. (2004) 'Tackling inequalities in health in England: Remedying health disadvantages, narrowing health gaps or reducing health gradients?', *Journal of Social Policy* 33(1), pp.115-31

1 What source of data is used by Graham?

2 What advantage did the government gain by making their policy documents vague?

3 How do most analysts believe inequalities in health can be reduced?

4 Why does Graham feel the government's policies will fail to reduce inequalities in health significantly?

divisions throughout society, whereby working-class people consistently receive worse treatment across the range of services in housing, education and health.

There are a number of problems with the Marxist analysis. It could equally be argued that, rather than being a form of social control, the National Health Service provides a very powerful alternative message to that of capitalism. The NHS is based on the socialist principle of giving to people in need, irrespective of income. Capitalism is based on people choosing to buy services, which depends upon their levels of income.

Also, some of the largest areas of NHS expenditure are actually with groups who are not 'productive'. For example, the largest group of users of the NHS are older, retired people.

Pluralist approaches

This approach suggests that the best way to understand any society (or large organization) is to examine the way that power is distributed within it. More powerful groups will be more likely to gain benefits compared to less powerful groups. This differs from the Marxist model in a number of ways, but, most importantly, pluralism argues that no one group has all the power – instead, there are numerous ('plural') competing groups who need to accommodate each other. The resulting social inequalities will be much more complex and fragmented than in the ruling-class/working-class division in Marxist theory.

Applying pluralist theory to inequalities in health service provision, we can understand these (both of provision and demand) in terms of the differences in power between the various groups. In terms of the provision of services, there is the interplay between the various professional groups (surgeons, dentists, nurses, pediatricians, geriatricians) and between managers and, finally, political interests. Demand for services consists of competing demands from the various 'illness

categories' (mentally ill, children, older people, cancer patients, etc.) and from groups stratified according to ethnicity, age, gender and class.

The outcome in terms of provision and use will constantly vary according to shifts in power between these groups.

Structuralist approaches

Alford (1975) has suggested that both the Marxist and the pluralist approaches are useful, but that combining elements of both produces a better theory.

According to Alford there are three groups of interested parties in the health service:

- dominant
- challenging
- repressed.

These groups operate on different levels and there is conflict both *between* them and *within* them. The dominant group consists of the established medical professions who vie with each other for dominance. Whatever the outcome of their struggles, the winners will have greater power over decision-making than the next 'challenging' group – which consists of senior health managers and health-service policy planners. The third group, the 'repressed' consists of patients and other consumer groups. Different categories of patients compete for their health needs to be addressed, but they do so within the framework set out by the dominant and challenging groups.

This may seem rather complex, but Alford is essentially arguing that the competing interest groups in the health service can be grouped together in terms of the power they hold. In doing so, Alford presents a modified version of pluralism. The elements of Marxism incorporated into his theory include the point that the dominant and challenging groups draw their power from established social hierarchies and so the divisions in the health-service provision reflect the divisions in the wider capitalist society.

Check your understanding

1 What do we mean by 'issues of provision and demand' when discussing inequalities in access to health care?

2 What impact can doctors and hospitals have on inequalities of provision?

3 What three factors help to restrict the use of health services by ethnic minorities?

4 How does the medical profession view geriatric medicine?

5 Explain what impact private medicine may have on health inequalities?

6 Explain the structuralist explanation of inequalities in health-care provision, using examples from the main text where appropriate.

KEY TERMS

Health authorities the National Health Service is actually a system of local health services. Health authorities are the bodies responsible for ensuring that local people get adequate health services by overseeing the local health care trusts which actually provide the health services.

Iatrogenesis illness caused by the medical professions (e.g. as a result of poor care or inaccurate diagnosis).

Prestigious of high status.

Primary care trusts the NHS organizations responsible for local health- and social-care services (including GPs).

Private health care health care that is not provided by the NHS, but which people pay for themselves.

Screening programmes programmes where particular sections of the population are tested to see if they have signs of a particular disease.

Specialist teaching hospitals very prestigious hospitals which train new doctors.

Item A The inverse prevention law

<< Strong evidence exists to support what might be called the 'Inverse Prevention Law' in primary care, in which those communities most at risk of ill health have least access to a range of effective preventive services, including cancer screening programmes, health promotion and immunization.>>

Gordon, D., Shaw, M., Dorling, D. and Davey Smith, G. (1999) *Inequalities in Health*, Bristol: Policy Press, p. 105

Item B Race, inequality and health

<<The way that [health] services are organized and offered is based on indigenous British culture and is often inflexible so that members of ethnic minority groups may find vital provision irrelevant, offensive, unhelpful or threatening.

Aspects of racism that are implicated here include the failure to provide health information in appropriate languages, the failure to make knowledge of religious, dietary and cultural imperatives basic to health professional training, and the failure to provide amenities to support cultural beliefs in the importance of running water for washing, death rites, prayer in hospital, visiting times, food in hospital, etc., as an automatic inclusion in health service budgets.>>

Culley, L. and Dyson, D. (1993) '"Race", inequality and health', *Sociology Review*, 3(1)

1 **Explain what is meant by the 'Inverse Prevention Law' (Item A).** (2 marks)

2 **Give two reasons why members of ethnic minorities might find going into hospital an 'offensive, unhelpful or threatening' experience (Item B).** (4 marks)

3 **Suggest three ways in which hospitals could be more sensitive towards ethnic minority patients (Item B).** (6 marks)

4 **Identify and briefly explain two reasons why 'those communities most at risk of ill health have least access to a range of effective preventive services' (Item A).** (8 marks)

5 **Discuss the sociological evidence that indicates that those social groups most in need of health services are least able to use them effectively.** (20 marks)

6 **Using information from Items A and B and elsewhere, assess the view that inequalities of provision exist within the health service.** (20 marks)

research ideas

- Interview a sample of older people (over the age of 60) and ask them:
  - whether they get their 'flu jab' each autumn and why they do or don't
  - whether they think older people are treated any differently by the NHS than younger people.

  Compare your answers in class.

web.task

Go to the site of the Healthcare Commission at www.chai.org.uk. Find out what the Commission does and look up how well your local health care trust is performing.

- **How does your area compare with others?**

- **Do links appear to exist between the richer areas and 'better performance'?**

- **How useful do you think these tables are?**

Mental health and mental illness

How the pressure to succeed is creating a generation of unruly, depressed teenagers

*By **Sarah Womack**, Social Affairs Correspondent*
The Daily Telegraph (Filed: 14 September 2004)

THE NUMBER of 15 year olds suffering from anxiety and depression has increased by 70 per cent since the mid-1980s, according to a study. (See the graph on the right.)

The mental health of teenagers has sharply declined in the past 25 years while the chances of teenagers lying, stealing or being disobedient – rather than being physically aggressive – have more than doubled.

The research was conducted by the Institute of Psychiatry, King's College London, and the University of Manchester and looked at three generations of 15 year olds, in 1974, 1986 and 1999, based on their parents' assessments.

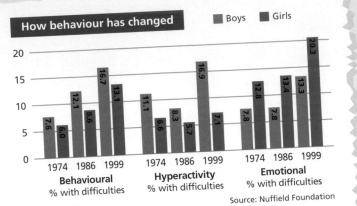

How behaviour has changed — Boys, Girls

Source: Nuffield Foundation

1. **Provide a short summary of what the chart above tells you about young males' and females' mental health over the three periods studied.**

2. **Look at how the research was done – who was asked to decide if the young people had mental health problems?**

3. **What are your views on this research?**

'Normal children given drugs'

*By **David Derbyshire** and **Roger Highfield** at the British Association science festival The Daily Telegraph (filed: 09 September 2004)*

THE RISE OF attention deficit hyperactivity disorder has led to concerns that doctors and drugs companies are turning unpleasant, but essentially normal, human behaviour into medical conditions. Its most serious form, known as hyperkinetic disorder, affects 1.4 per cent of children. Sufferers are unable to concentrate, forgetful, disorganized and easily distracted. At school they are disruptive, find it almost impossible to learn ...

While the most serious cases are generally recognized as psychiatric disorders, diagnosis of milder forms of ADHD, is more controversial. One person's ADHD victim is another's naughty child. Some researchers are concerned that drugs such as Ritalin, the "chemical cosh", are used to suppress essentially normal but disruptive behaviour. In the UK, only 0.3 per cent of all children receive medication for ADHD, compared with six per cent in America.

Teenagers put their finger on the problem, and it's moods ... their parents' moods

*By **Nicole Martin** The Daily Telegraph (Filed: 21 October 2003)*

FORGET moody teenagers. It's moody parents who are disrupting family life, according to one of the largest surveys of British teenagers. When asked to identify their parents' worst trait, four in 10 of the 16,000 teenagers polled said it was their unpredictable moods. But more than half of the teenagers said they were fed up with being compared with "Kevin the Teenager", the monosyllabic and rebellious youth created by the comedian Harry Enfield.

When asked what was the hardest thing about being a teenager, one in five cited negative media coverage and being stereotyped – ahead of exam pressures, mood swings and relationships. Maggie Philbin commented "Whenever I read about them, the headlines shriek about drugs, teenage pregnancy, joyriding and crime. No wonder parents become anxious, but I resent this parental paranoia and the implicit lack of trust."

4. **Do you agree with the findings of the study described above regarding how parents act?**

5. **Look at how the research was done – who was asked about the conduct of parents?**

6. **What are your views on this research?**

7. **Do you think the children described in the article on the left are 'naughty' or 'badly behaved'?**

8. **What conclusions can you draw on how we define mental illness and who decides whether it exists or not?**

Mental illness has been the forgotten twin to physical illness, in terms of the attention paid to it and the funding provided by the NHS. The issue only comes to the fore when a particularly spectacular event hits the headlines. However, mental health is a major problem in society, with about one in seven of the population claiming to have mental health problems at some point in their lives. But mental health is dogged with debates over definitions and over the differences in the extent of mental health problems across different groups in society.

Defining mental illness

Sociology is split between two different approaches regarding how to define mental illness. The two approaches are **social realism** and **social constructionism**

Social realism

Social realism is a general term used to describe the approaches of sociologists who, broadly speaking, accept that there are distinctive sets of abnormal behaviour which cause distress to individuals and to those around them. These forms of abnormal behaviour are classified as mental illness. Social realists such as Pilgrim and Rogers (1999) accept that, at different times and in different cultures, there are variations in what is considered as mental illness. Nevertheless, they argue that, although mental illness may have different names and may or may not be recognized in different cultures, it does actually exist as a real condition.

Social constructionism

Social constructionist perspectives have been very influential in sociological approaches to mental illness and start from the argument that what is considered normal varies over time and from society to society. For example, over the last two hundred years in Britain, alcohol consumption has been seen variously as normal, as morally wrong or even illegal, as a sign of being mentally ill and as a central part of a religious ritual. In fact, most of these different attitudes to alcohol can still be found in Britain today!

Even greater extremes of behaviour have been seen as normal in some societies and as evidence of madness in others. For example, saying that you are possessed by the spirit of your ancestor would suggest madness in contemporary Britain, but for native Americans, or in some West African religions, it would be a perfectly reasonable statement which most people would believe was true.

Mental illness: real or culturally created?

All sociologists agree that there are forms of behaviour that cause considerable stress to the individual involved, and which prevent them from engaging in any meaningful participation in society. They also recognize that how it comes to be defined depends upon cultural differences. Where the difference between realist and constructionist perspectives emerge is more in the stress they place on how far the cultural context determines the levels and types of mental illness.

The best way to understand the sociology of mental health is to see it as a continuum, with those who argue for the overwhelming importance of culture at one extreme and those who argue for the existence of common illnesses (which might go under different names, but are essentially the same) at the other extreme.

Mental illness: the labelling perspective

The degree of flexibility about what constitutes normal and abnormal behaviour has been taken furthest by so-called 'labelling theorists'. Labelling theory (as we saw in Unit 1 Topic 4) examines how labelling occurs in the first place and what effects it has on those who are labelled. Thomas Szasz (1973), for example, argues that the label 'mental illness' is simply a convenient way to deal with behaviour that people find disruptive. Labelling theory rests firmly upon a social constructionist definition of mental illness.

The effects of labelling

According to Scheff (1966), whether someone becomes labelled or not is determined by the benefits that others might gain by labelling the person 'mentally ill'. So, those people who become a nuisance, or who prevent others from doing something they want to do, are far more likely to be defined as being mentally ill than those who pose no threat or inconvenience, and may be ignored.

Once labelled, there are a number of negative consequences for the person, because it is then assumed that all their behaviour is evidence of their mental state. A famous study by Rosenhan (1973) illustrates this. In the early 1970s in the USA, Rosenhan asked eight perfectly 'normal' researchers to enter a number of psychiatric institutions after phoning up and complaining that they were 'hearing voices'. Once the researchers had been admitted into the institutions, doctors and staff regarded them as truly mentally ill and reinterpreted all their behaviour as proof of this. However, the researchers were under strict instructions to behave completely normally at all times.

In a later study, new staff in a psychiatric hospital were told that this experiment was to be repeated in their institution, and they were asked to uncover these researchers who were just pretending to be ill. In this study, staff routinely judged people who were 'genuinely ill' as merely pretending. It would seem, therefore, that there is some confusion as to how even experts can decide who is actually mentally ill.

Erving Goffman (1961) followed the **careers** of people who were genuinely defined as being mentally ill. He suggested that, once in an institution, people are stripped of their

presenting culture – by which he means the image that we all choose to present to the world as 'us'. This may include a style of haircut, make-up, or the requirement that people address us as 'Mr' or 'Mrs' rather than 'Michael' or 'Sarah'. The 'patient' may also lose their right to make decisions about their life and may be required to take medication which can disorientate them.

Quickly, the self-image that a patient has – perhaps of being a respectable, witty, middle-aged person – is stripped away, leaving them bewildered, vulnerable and ready to accept a new role. In this powerless situation, any attempts to reject the label of mental illness can actually be interpreted as further signs of illness, and perhaps as indicating a need for increased medication or counselling. In fact, accepting the role of being mentally ill is seen as the first sign of recovery.

Criticisms of the labelling perspective

The labelling perspective on mental illness has not gone unchallenged. Gove (1982) suggests that the vast majority of people who receive treatment for mental illness actually have serious problems before they are treated and so the argument that the label causes the problem is wrong. Furthermore, he argues that labelling theory provides no adequate explanation for why some people start to show symptoms in the first place.

According to Gove, labelling may help explain some of the responses of others to the mentally ill, but it cannot explain the causes of the illness.

Foucault's perspective on mental illness

A second, very distinctive version of social constructionist theory emerges in the work of the French sociologist, Foucault (1965). He explains the growth in the concept of mental illness by placing it in the context of the changing ways of thinking and acting which developed in the early 18th century. According to Foucault, during the **Enlightenment**, more traditional ways of thinking, based on religious beliefs and on emotions, were gradually replaced by more rational, intellectually disciplined ways of thinking and acting. These eventually led to the significant scientific and engineering developments which formed the basis of the 'industrial revolution'. Foucault argues that as rationality developed into the normal way of thinking, irrationality began to be perceived as deviant.

This shift away from the irrational and towards the rational was illustrated, according to Foucault, by the growth in asylums for those considered mad. Foucault suggests that having mad people in asylums, both symbolically and literally, isolated mad people away from the majority of the population. The asylums symbolized the fact that madness or irrationality was marked out as behaviour that was no longer acceptable.

Although Foucault's writing is very dense and complicated, the essential message is that madness, as we understand it, is a relatively modern invention which emerged from the development of modern 'rational' ways of thinking and acting.

Structuralist perspectives on mental health

Structuralist perspectives on mental health are closely tied to the social realist definition of mental illness. These approaches accept the reality of mental illness and set out to discover what factors in society might cause the illness. As a result of research by sociologists working within this tradition, evidence of clear mental health differences between social groups has emerged. Some of these are discussed next.

Mental illness and ethnicity

Members of ethnic minorities have significantly different chances of mental illness compared to the majority white population. According to Nazroo (2001) people of 'South Asian origin' have very low rates of mental illness, whilst those of African Caribbean origins have particularly high levels of **schizophrenia**, with levels between three and five times higher than the population as a whole. Writers within the structuralist perspective, such as Virdee (1997), explain this by arguing that the sorts of pressures and stresses that can cause people to develop mental illness are more likely to be experienced by members of ethnic minorities because they encounter racism and disadvantage throughout their lives.

However, labelling theorists have argued that some of the behaviour of Afro-Caribbean adults in particular, has been seen as inappropriate in British society, and has therefore been labelled as a symptom of mental illness. Nazroo points out that people of Bangladeshi origin, who are amongst the most deprived groups in the British population and are also recipients of racism, actually have lower levels of mental illness than the general population. They therefore argue that it cannot just be racism and deprivation.

Mental illness and gender

Women are more likely than men to exhibit behaviour defined as mental illness. Overall, women have rates about one third higher than men, but in some specific forms of mental illness, the figures are much higher. For example, women are at least three times more likely to suffer from depression. Structuralists, such as Brown et al. (1995) argue that women are more likely to lead stressful lives – combining careers and the responsibility for childcare, for example, and being more likely to experience poverty and poor housing conditions.

However, labelling theorist and feminist sociologists such as Chesler (1972) go further and argue that the behaviour of women is more likely to be defined as evidence of mental illness because the defining is done by a male-dominated profession. Rather than looking for the real reasons – which are most likely to be stress and poverty – psychiatrists are more interested in defining the problem in terms of an individual's mental state.

Busfield (1988) has suggested that the structuralist position and the labelling approach are not irreconcilable and that women are both under pressure in their lives, which leads to higher levels of mental illness, but are also more likely to have their problems defined as mental illness by psychiatrists.

Inequality, social class and mental illness

Overall, when looking at which group is most likely to suffer from high rates of mental illness, the poorest and most excluded are massively overrepresented.

Link and Phelan (1995) reviewed all the evidence over a period of 40 years between social class and mental illness, concluding that all the research clearly pointed to the close relationship between deprivation and low levels of mental health. A government study (Office for National Statistics Study 2004) found that children from the poorest backgrounds were three times more likely to have conduct disorders than those whose parents were in professional occupations. Structuralist writers, such as Myers (1975), have suggested a '**life-course**' model, which explains the higher levels of mental illness as a result of poorer people consistently encountering higher levels of social problems over their lifetimes, but having limited educational, social and economic resources to continue overcoming the problems. They argue that, eventually, the stress of coping emerges and is expressed through mental illness.

A second form of structuralist explanation is that of **social capital**. The concept of social capital derives from the writings of Putnam (2000) who argues that people who have social networks of friends and relatives are more likely to be happy, to have lower levels of stress and to feel they 'belong' to their local community. The result of this is that they are less likely to suffer from mental illness.

Pilgrim and Rogers (1999), however, point to the arguments of labelling and feminist theorists, who note that within the most deprived groups, there are also higher levels of women suffering from mental illness compared to men and they would suggest that women are more likely to have their problems defined in terms of mental illness.

Mental illness: conclusion

Mental illness is a highly contested issue in sociology. There are arguments over the very definition of the term and how to explain the differences in mental illness rates in the population. However, the approaches are not entirely irreconcilable and Busfield's approach is one that has received much support. She argues that it is probably true that some groups are much more likely to find their behaviour defined as mental illness, compared to the behaviour of other groups. However, it is also true that these very same groups – ethnic minorities, women and the socially excluded – all suffer high levels of stress and so one would expect them to have higher levels of illness. Both processes reinforce each other.

MIND
Mental health and poverty

For a number of years, sociologists had suggested that to see mental health solely as a health problem was to ignore the devastating affect it had on people's lives in general. In particular, it was argued, mental health led people to have high levels of unemployment, homelessness and poverty. In 1998, the mental health pressure group MIND conducted a national survey to find out the extent of poverty amongst people with mental illness. Of those mentally ill people who replied, 98 per cent received some form of state benefit, with 60 per cent entirely dependent on benefits.

They also found that 35 per cent of respondents were too ill to work. However, 38 per cent did some kind of unpaid voluntary work (often because they could not find paid work) and 16 per cent were actively looking for a paid job, but were unable to find one. MIND found that people who had suffered from mental illness and were looking for work, routinely encountered discrimination and stigma.

MIND's research, then, demonstrates that mental illness is more than a health issue, it is a social one too.

MIND (1998) *Mind Disability Benefits Survey*, London: Mind Publications

1 Give examples of the 'devastating effect mental health problems may have on somebody's life'.

2 How representative of people with mental health problems do you think the MIND survey was? Explain your answer.

3 Explain in your own words the problems people suffering from mental illness experienced when looking for employment.

Check your understanding

1. Identify the two sociological approaches to defining mental illness.

2. Explain the key differences between the two approaches you have identified.

3. How does the idea of 'labelling' help us to understand mental illness?

4. What is meant by a structural explanation for mental illness?

5. How does Busfield suggest that the structuralist and labelling approaches can be combined?

6. Why are people from certain ethnic minorities more likely to be defined as suffering from mental illness?

7. What argument do feminist writers use to explain why women are more likely to be defined as suffering from mental illness?

Office of National Statistics

Differences in levels of mental illness

focus on research

1. The table below shows the differences for a range of social groups in their levels of mental illness. What differences in mental illness can you find for the following factors?

(a) social class   (b) ethnicity

(b) employment status   (c) marital status

Mean annual consultation rates per 1000 men at risk for specified psychiatric disorders

SPECIFIED PSYCHIATRIC DISORDER

		Bipolar affective disorders	Schizophrenia	Neurotic disorders	Personality disorders	Alcohol dependence	Drug dependence	Depression
SOCIAL CLASS	I	17.0	1.5	33.2	2.0	8.5	9.6	21.6
	II	13.4	1.4	40.4	1.8	4.9	6.6	32.8
	IIIN	13.1	7.1	55.9	7.4	7.8	15.9	35.0
	IIIM	13.3	4.6	48.2	3.2	8.8	23.6	41.7
	IV	16.3	12.1	58.4	8.1	13.0	25.4	50.9
	V	19.4	25.7	84.8	16.5	23.9	78.5	56.7
ETHNIC GROUP	White	14.5	7.7	49.4	4.6	8.9	20.7	38.5
	Afro-Caribbean	5.7	50.9	21.2	24.1	5.7	7.1	14.2
	Asian	9.1	2.8	39.1	9.8	4.2	0.7	5.6
	Other	7.6	0.0	50.8	5.1	1.3	10.2	25.4
EMPLOYMENT STATUS	Employed full-time	8.6	1.1	37.4	1.6	3.9	5.4	25.0
	Employed part-time	31.7	23.2	51.6	5.7	8.0	22.2	39.7
	Unemployed	24.4	16.0	84.8	15.3	24.3	102.4	66.3
	Student	7.7	4.8	22.2	2.3	0.5	13.4	16.6
	Permanently sick	79.8	102.5	195.7	41.0	66.0	113.4	201.4
	Other	24.8	7.1	58.3	5.8	10.7	17.0	59.3
MARITAL STATUS	Single	13.7	16.2	48.1	8.0	8.5	38.6	27.9
	Married	13.2	1.7	43.8	2.6	4.0	5.2	37.0
	Separated/divorced	26.4	21.1	101.2	11.0	57.7	60.6	101.4
	Widowed	25.9	17.6	97.3	4.1	9.3	70.4	73.5

exploring mental health and mental illness

Item A An Asian woman speaks about her experiences

« It affects your mind. If you feel depressed that you are not treated as other people are, or they look down on you, you will feel mentally ill, won't you? It will depress you that you are not treated well racially, it will affect your health in some way. It will cause you depression, and that depression will cause the illness. »

Quoted in Annandale, F. (1998) *The Sociology of Health and Medicine*, Cambridge: Polity Press, p. 187

Item B Snapshots of race and gender

People of African-Caribbean origin are far more likely to reach the mental health system via the police, the courts and prisons, and to experience the more harsh and invasive forms of treatment (such as electro-convulsive therapy), than other groups.

With regard to mental illness, for all diagnoses combined, women's rate of admission to hospitals in England and Wales was 29 per cent above the rate for men.

Adapted from Annandale, E. (1998) *The Sociology of Health and Medicine*, Cambridge: Polity Press, pp. 143 & 186

Item C Psychiatric diagnoses in Britain and the USA

Katz examined the process of psychiatric diagnosis among both British and American psychiatrists. Groups of British and American psychiatrists were shown films of interviews with patients and asked to note down all the pathological symptoms and make a diagnosis. Marked disagreements in diagnosis between the two groups were found. The British saw less evidence of mental illness generally. For example, one patient was diagnosed as 'schizophrenic' by one-third of the Americans, but by none of the British.

Adapted from Helman, C. (2000) *Culture, Health and Illness*, Oxford: Butterworth/Heinemann, p. 80

1. **Explain what is meant by 'mental health' (Item B).** (2 marks)

2. **Suggest two reasons why members of ethnic minorities might experience depression (Item A).** (4 marks)

3. **Suggest three reasons why the British and American psychiatrists in Item C may have diagnosed the same individual differently.** (6 marks)

4. **Identify and briefly explain two reasons that might explain why women's rate of admission to mental hospitals is higher then men's (Item B).** (8 marks)

5. **Using information from the Items and elsewhere, examine the possible reasons why rates of mental illness vary between different social groups.** (20 marks)

6. **Assess the contribution of labelling theory to an understanding of mental illness.** (20 marks)

research idea

● Watch the film *One Flew Over the Cuckoo's Nest* (or read the original book by Ken Kesey). What perspective on mental illness does this film (or book) illustrate?

web.task

Find the website of the mental health charity MIND at www.mind.org.uk. Use the 'links' section to explore the work of some of the organizations connected with mental health issues. Make a list of all the mental health issues covered. How important an issue is mental health in the UK today?

The medical professions in society

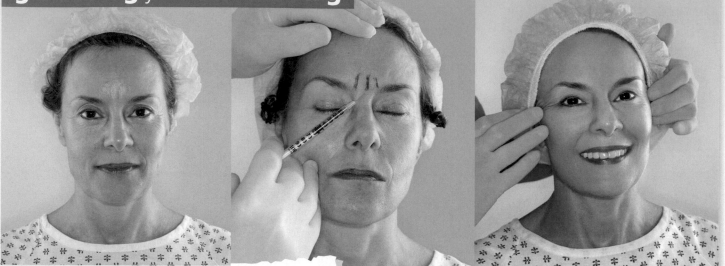

gettingyouthinking

Untrained and out of control: health chiefs target rogue plastic surgeons

By F. Elliot and M. Fitzwilliams
The Independent on Sunday (12 September 2004)

MINISTERS are planning to overhaul Britain's booming cosmetic surgery industry after a review found shocking evidence that vulnerable patients are being exploited by untrained and unscrupulous medics.

Potentially dangerous procedures are being carried out by surgeons with no specific training on patients misled by exaggerated or false claims ... A string of high profile blunders that have left women permanently disfigured has helped to alert the public to the dangers ... Botched tummy tucks, leaking breast implants and bodged botox injections are among a rising number of horror stories emerging ...

1 Would you ever consider plastic surgery or other cosmetic treatment, such as botox injections? Why?

2 Do you think that people should have a right to plastic surgery?

3 Do you think that there are any grounds on which doctors should have the right to refuse to perform some plastic surgery if they think it inappropriate – even if you are willing to pay? If so, what are they?

4 Do you think that tattooists should have similar powers to refuse?

5 Which occupational groups (if any) do you trust more than doctors?

6 Why do you trust doctors?

Members of the medical profession are among the most prestigious and well-paid groups in society. But how did they get this superior status? Was it really through their greater abilities, as they would have us believe? Sociologists are always suspicious of the claims groups make about themselves, and, as you might expect, their views are not always totally supportive of the caring, dedicated image the medical professions like to present. In this topic, we are going to explore the reasons sociologists suggest provide the basis for the power, prestige and affluence of the medical professions. This exploration of the medical professions is useful in its own right, helping us to understand the nature of medical provision in Britain, but it is also a helpful model for understanding how other occupational groups have arrived in their particular position. Some of these, such as the legal profession, have been successful in obtaining prestige and financial rewards, while others, such as the teaching profession, have been much less successful.

There are five main sociological approaches to understanding the position and role of the medical professions. These are:

- *the functionalist argument* – that the medical profession benefits society
- *the Weberian approach* – that the medical profession is just an occupational strategy to get higher income and status
- *the Marxist view* – that the medical profession acts to control the majority of the population and is rewarded for this by the ruling class
- *Foucault's suggestion* – that the power of the medical profession has emerged as a result of their ability to define what is prestigious knowledge
- *the feminist approach* – that the medical profession can best be understood by seeing how it has controlled and marginalized women.

The functionalist approach: professions as a benefit to society

The first approach to understanding the role of the professions developed from the functionalist school of sociology (see Unit 1 Topic 2), associated with the writing of Talcott Parsons, which seeks to show what functions the various parts of society play in helping society to exist.

Barber (1963) argued that professions, especially the medical professions, are very important for society because they deal with people when they are in particularly vulnerable positions. It is, therefore, in the interests of society to have the very best people, who maintain the highest standards, to provide medical care. These people must not only be competent but they must also be totally trustworthy. According to functionalists, true professions can be recognized by the fact that they share a number of 'traits'. These are as follows.

- They have a *theoretical basis* to their knowledge – Doctors have a full understanding of medical theories about the body. This allows them to make independent decisions about the cause of illness and the best cure.

- They are *fully trained* to the highest possible standards – Only the most intelligent can enter and succeed.
- Competence is *tested by examination* – There is no favouritism and doctors are in their position as a result of their ability alone.
- The profession has a *strict code of* '**ethics**' – Doctors deal with people at their most vulnerable and the code of ethics ensures that no patient is exploited.
- They are *regulated and controlled* through an organization (in the case of doctors it is the General Medical Council) which decides who can enter the profession and has the power to punish and exclude for any misconduct.

Critics of the functionalist approach, such as Waitzkin (1979), while agreeing that high standards and trust are all needed, argue that these 'traits' merely justify the high status of doctors. The medical profession simply uses them as barriers to prevent others from entering. This criticism was for a long time supported by the fact that entry to medicine remained largely the preserve of males from higher social-class backgrounds. Only in the last 20 years has there been a significant inflow of women and ethnic minorities into the medical profession. This inflow has largely coincided with an acceptance of the criticisms of the functionalist approach.

The Weberian approach: professionalization as a strategy

The second approach to understanding the power of the medical professions is that, rather than being constructed for the good of the community, they are, in fact, constructed for the good of the medical professions themselves. This argument has developed from the original writings of Max Weber, an early 20th-century sociologist who argued that all occupational groups are constantly vying with one another to improve their prestige and financial bargaining power. There are a number of different techniques used, but the two main ones are the creation of trades unions (which has traditionally been used by the working class) and the construction of professions (which has been used by the middle class).

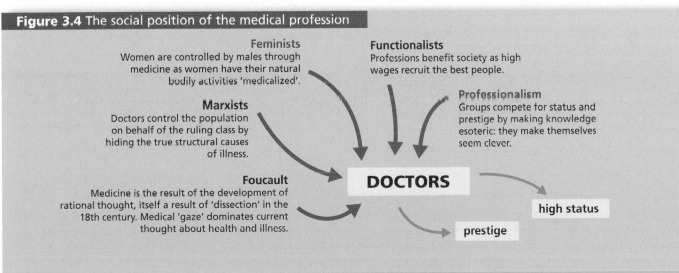

Figure 3.4 The social position of the medical profession

Feminists
Women are controlled by males through medicine as women have their natural bodily activities 'medicalized'.

Functionalists
Professions benefit society as high wages recruit the best people.

Marxists
Doctors control the population on behalf of the ruling class by hiding the true structural causes of illness.

Professionalism
Groups compete for status and prestige by making knowledge esoteric: they make themselves seem clever.

Foucault
Medicine is the result of the development of rational thought, itself a result of 'dissection' in the 18th century. Medical 'gaze' dominates current thought about health and illness.

DOCTORS

high status

prestige

Overall, **professionalization** of an occupational group has actually been a more effective method to gain status and financial rewards. It is for this reason that many other groups, such as teachers and social workers, have tried to gain professional status.

The process of professionalization has four important dimensions:

1 *The production of a body of **esoteric** knowledge* – This means creating an apparently complex body of knowledge which must be placed in the hands of experts.
2 *Educational barriers* – Professionals construct a series of specialist educational courses and qualifications in order to limit the numbers of entrants.
3 *Exclusion of competition* – The profession must wipe out any possible competitors, such as faith healers, homeopaths and herbalists. They do this by claiming that only scientific medicine and surgery are effective.
4 *Maintenance of privilege* – The professional group will fight all attempts to have others impose any control over them. So doctors will demand '**clinical freedom**' – the right to do what they think best – and they will fight any attempts to hand over part of their work to others, such as allowing nurses to prescribe medicines.

These four methods of professionalizing are very similar to the traits suggested by functionalist writers. From a Weberian perspective, therefore, the medical profession is looking after its own interests as well as those of the patients.

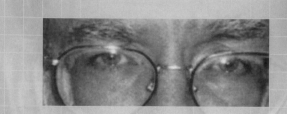

Harold Shipman

It is estimated that the doctor Harold Shipman killed over 250 of his patients. It is thought that he is the most prolific mass murderer in British legal history. He injected elderly patients with too high levels of morphine, thus killing them.

Although he had a much higher number of unexplained deaths than most GPs in Britain and he had one of the highest uses of morphine in Britain, he was able to get away with murdering his patients for almost 30 years.

1 If a relative of yours had died unexpectedly after a visit from a doctor, do you think that you would have questioned it? Please explain your answer.

2 Why do you think Harold Shipman managed to get away with murder for so long?

Marxist approaches

Marxists, such as Navarro (1977), argue that in capitalist societies such as Britain, a small ruling class exploits society for its own benefit. In order to hide this exploitation from people and to maintain its power, the ruling class employs a number of mechanisms, which involve distorting 'reality', so that people come to accept exploitation as 'natural'.

The medical profession plays an important role in this by misleading the population as to the real cause of their illnesses. The medical profession explains health and illness in terms of individuals' actions and genetics – they point the finger away from the poor working conditions, poverty, poor housing and inequalities in society, which are the true, underlying causes of ill health, according to Marxist writers (see Unit 1, pp. 17–18 for more details on Marx). But what doctors do succeed in doing for the health of the population is to keep them fit enough to work.

Marxists also point out that health and illness in a capitalist society are carefully linked to being able to work or not. Doctors play a key role in deciding who is fit to work and who is sick enough to be eligible for state disability and sickness benefits.

Critics have pointed out that this perspective ignores the genuinely beneficial work that doctors do, and that to characterize their work as only misleading and controlling the population is inaccurate. Doctors do work very much within the framework of looking at individual problems, but stress in the

workplace and the role of poverty are well known and recognized by doctors.

Foucault's approach

There is an old saying, 'knowledge is power', and in Foucault's analysis of society this is literally true. According to Foucault (1976), in every society, groups are 'battling' to look after their own interests. The best way of doing this is to get control of what is regarded as 'truth' or 'knowledge'. If other people believe that what you say is 'true' and what others say is 'false', then you have a high chance of getting them to do what you want. So you seek to create an overall framework of thought and ideas, within which all the more specific debates (what Foucault calls '**discourses**') are conducted. This argument is similar in some ways to the Marxist argument we saw earlier.

Foucault argues that, over time, doctors have led the way in helping to construct an idea of 'science', through their activities in dissecting bodies and demonstrating to people the ways in which bodies are constructed in the form of a 'biological machine'. This has resulted in a society where rational scientific thought is prized above all else, where other forms of thought are regarded as inferior, and where doctors have significant prestige and power.

So medicine has played a major part in constructing the way we think and act in contemporary society. In the process, the medical professions have gained considerable benefits in terms of prestige and financial rewards.

Feminist approaches

Feminist sociologists, such as Oakley (1986) and Witz (1992), suggest that the activities of doctors contribute to the social control of women, both as patients and as medical practitioners. They point out that medicine has traditionally been a male occupation, with women excluded or marginalized into junior roles. This simply reinforces the subordinate position of women in society. (However, in the last 15 years, roughly equal numbers of men and women have been training to be doctors.)

Historically, women had always held a key role in healing and traditional health care. For example, the women who we now refer to as 'witches' were very often herbal healers who were eagerly sought out in rural areas. There had always been a degree of competition between male and female health-care practitioners and it was not until 1885 that a law was passed which legally recognized a closed medical profession. Although women were not legally prevented from entering the medical profession, because of the values of Victorian Britain, and because of the nature of the educational system which generally excluded women from higher education, the outcome of the act was that they were effectively prevented from becoming doctors.

Techniques to exclude women from the medical profession

According to Witz, the male-dominated medical profession was successful in excluding females for over half a century by using two techniques – exclusion and demarcation:

- *Exclusion* involves creating barriers so that it is virtually impossible for other groups (in this case females) to enter the profession.
- *Demarcation* involves creating a restricted area of competence and then allowing people to enter this area. At the same time, this area of competence is still controlled by the medical profession. Examples of this include nursing and radiography.

Witz further argues that to combat these techniques, women have used two strategies – inclusion and dual closure:

- *Inclusion* involves using any possible method of gaining entry through, for example, political and legal action.
- The aim of *dual closure* is to accept in part a restricted area of competence, but then to close this off to others and to seek to turn it into a profession. It is exactly this process that is happening to nursing.

The 'medicalization' process

Feminist sociologists, such as Lupton (1994), also claim that the male-dominated profession of medicine has successfully 'medicalized' a number of female problems. By this they mean that normal or natural activities of women (such as childbirth and menopause), or problems faced more often by women (such as depression), have been taken over by the medical profession and turned into medical issues. So, for example, women are expected to give birth in the manner and in the place determined by 'the experts'. For Lupton, this means that male doctors can use this as a means of controlling how women ought to act. According to Lupton, through this process 'women are placed in a position of compliance with expert advice throughout their pregnancy and delivery, and their personal needs and wishes tend to be ignored' (Lupton 1994, p. 148).

When it comes to an 'illness' such as depression – which feminists argue is partly a result of the restricted role of women in society – the medical profession turns it into a medical problem that can be solved by prescribing medicines. This shifts the issue away from the position of women in general, to the particular medical condition of a single woman. One example of the creation of female illness and resulting medical treatment, according to Wertz and Wertz (1981), was the treatment of upper-class women in Victorian Britain. Links were made between the female reproductive and sexual organs and a whole range of illnesses including headaches, sore throats, indigestion and 'inappropriate libido'. This resulted in 'routine' hysterectomies, removals of ovaries and clitorectomies.

The rise of complementary medicine

The traditional male-dominated medical profession's monopoly over health care has been strongly challenged over the last 20 years. Within the profession, there has been an influx of ethnic minorities and women, and from outside the profession the claim to sole expertise on health matters has been challenged by a wide range of groups. Perhaps the biggest external challenge has come from complementary or alternative medicines, which include homeopathy, herbal remedies, acupuncture and a range of other techniques.

Giddens (1991) has argued that this is the result of the development of late modern society. Two particularly relevant characteristics of late modernity are:

1 decline in conformity, with a greater stress on individual desire and choice
2 disillusionment with the claims of professionals and experts in general to have a monopoly of knowledge. The particular result for health care and medicine has been a decline in the acceptance that 'doctor knows best' and an increased demand for choice in what 'cures' and interventions the ill person should undergo.

A third, less significant element of late modernity, which is particularly relevant to mental illness, is that a much wider range of behaviour is tolerated. This makes the distinction between deviant or marginally tolerated behaviour and mental illness far less clear.

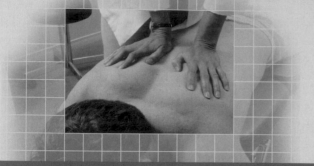

Cant and Sharma
Chiropractic

Cant and Sharma studied the rise in the status of complementary medicine, using chiropractic as an example. (Chiropractic is the manipulation of the spine, joints and muscles in order to realign them.) For over 60 years, chiropractors campaigned to gain legal recognition, which was finally granted in an act of parliament in 1994. Cant and Sharma point out that in order to get this recognition, chiropractors undertook a number of activities.

1 Divisions within the profession were resolved, with the more controversial wing of the profession – who claimed that chiropractic could heal a wide range of non-muscular/skeletal problems – accepting the need to drop their claims, as they were too controversial for the dominant medical profession.

2 They worked hard to gain the approval of the established medical profession, acknowledging its dominant position and dropping any claims to provide an alternative, competing model of health care.

3 The chiropractors had to accept that, within the NHS, they could only see patients if they were referred by doctors. This meant that they became dependent upon the good will of doctors.

4 They had to accept that they had no legal monopoly (as doctors do) to practise their techniques of bone and muscle manipulation. Anyone else can do this, but they cannot call themselves chiropractors.

Cant and Sharma's research is an excellent example of how the medical profession has continued to work to maintain its dominance of health care. Any group offering alternative models, such as chiropractors, has to accept an inferior role if they are to gain any form of legal recognition.

Source: Cant, S. and Sharma, U. (2002) 'The state and complementary medicine: a changing relationship?', in S. Nettleton and U. Gustafsson *The Sociology of Health and Illness Reader,* Cambridge: Polity

1 What compromises did chiropractors have to make in order to gain legal recognition?

2 How did the medical profession ensure that chiropractic had to 'accept an inferior role' in order to be recognized?

Check your understanding

1 Give two examples of the 'traits' of a profession, according to functionalists.

2 According to the 'professionalization' approach, how do professions exclude other competing occupational groups?

3 How do the actions of doctors, in explaining why we are ill and then prescribing medicines, help capitalism?

4 Give one example of how doctors have 'medicalized' a normal activity of women?

5 According to Foucault, what is the relationship between knowledge and power over people?

KEY TERMS

Clinical freedom the right of doctors to do what they think is best without other people having a say.

Discourse a way of thinking about issues.

Esoteric obscure and accessible only to a few.

Ethics a code of behaviour.

Professionalization a tactic used by occupational groups to gain prestige and financial rewards.

web.task

1 Visit the Royal College of Nursing website at www.rcn.org.uk

What aspects of the discussion in this topic are illustrated here?

(You could start with the image on the home page!) It is also useful to look at the section on the RCN's 'mission'.

2 Visit the General Medical Council website at www.gmc-uk.org

What points in this topic does this website illustrate (and also perhaps challenge!).

3 Visit the Institute for Complementary Medicine website at www.icmedicine.co.uk

What ideas about 'the body' and healing lie behind these therapies and treatments?

To what extent are they similar to, or different from, the conventional Western 'biomedical model'?

exploring the medical professions in society

Item A — Nursing and professionalization

« It is commonly held that nursing, since becoming a profession (the first register was set up in 1919), has progressed to become a higher-status, centrally recognized health-care profession. Yet the crucial distinction between nursing and medicine remains: that of curing versus caring. Nursing's professional bodies are caught in a double-bind: in order to be of high status, the profession must lay claim to clinical and curative skills, but in order to remain as 'nursing', the practice must be centred on caring for, not curing, patients.

This dilemma has been addressed in part by the conscious formation of a body of theoretical knowledge, the nursing process, which is particular to nursing and distinct from medicine. To some extent, this has also been the rationale behind the most recent developments in nurse education, for example, the creation of the new Project 2000 and the possibility of a degree in nursing, which superseded the old apprentice-style ward-based training of 'pupil' nurses.»

Marsh, I. (2000) *Sociology: Making Sense of Society*, Harlow: Prentice Hall

Item B — Professionalism

« Professional bodies (such as the General Medical Council) are charged with supervising the profession. But, being members of that profession, they usually whitewash or ignore cases of incompetence, etc. Final sanctions, like striking a doctor off the medical register, are used only rarely and then more often for sexual misconduct than for gross incompetence.»

Trowler, P. (1996) *Investigating Health, Welfare and Poverty*, London: Collins Educational

Item C — The functionalist view

« For functionalist sociologists the higher professions such as medicine are virtually beyond reproach. Professionals are seen as selfless individuals working for the good of the community, often making great personal sacrifices. They need to be of the highest intelligence and skill, have to undergo years of training and in their early careers earn very little. High levels of reward later, then, are necessary to attract, retain and motivate the best people into the professions.»

Trowler, P. (1996) *Investigating Health, Welfare and Poverty*, London: Collins Educational

1 **Explain what is meant by a 'professional body' (Items A and B).** (2 marks)

2 **Identify two ways in which nursing has attempted to improve its status in recent years (Item A).** (4 marks)

3 **Suggest three reasons why professional bodies might 'ignore cases of incompetence' (Item B).** (6 marks)

4 **Identify and briefly explain two reasons why functionalists argue that professionals deserve high rewards (Item C).** (8 marks)

5 **Using information from Item A and elsewhere, examine the possible reasons why nurses have less status and pay than doctors.** (20 marks)

6 **Using information from the Items and elsewhere, assess the view that professionalization is simply a strategy for ensuring high status and rewards.** (20 marks)

research ideas

- Ask a small sample of people to identify five characteristics they associate with doctors. Do your results support the points made in the topic?

- Identify a small sample of people who have actually used some form of 'alternative' healing. Conduct unstructured interviews to uncover their motives in seeking the treatment and the meaning they gave to their experiences.

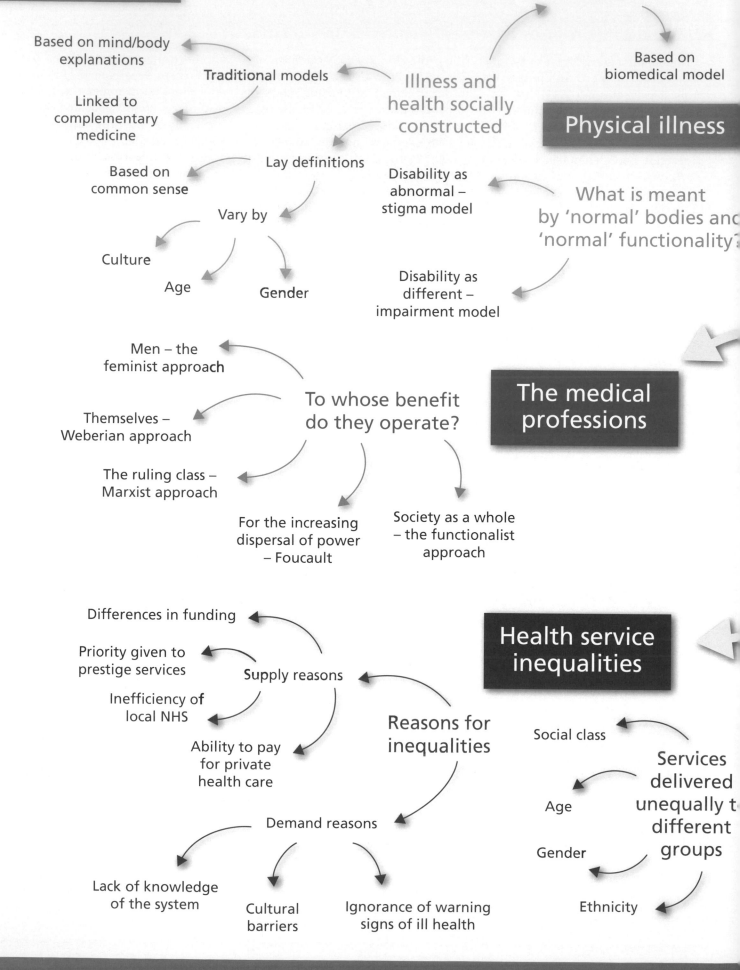

Professional definitions

Based on mind/body explanations

Traditional models

Illness and health socially constructed

Based on biomedical model

Physical illness

Linked to complementary medicine

Based on common sense

Lay definitions

Disability as abnormal – stigma model

What is meant by 'normal' bodies and 'normal' functionality?

Vary by

Culture

Age

Gender

Disability as different – impairment model

Men – the feminist approach

Themselves – Weberian approach

To whose benefit do they operate?

The medical professions

The ruling class – Marxist approach

For the increasing dispersal of power – Foucault

Society as a whole – the functionalist approach

Differences in funding

Priority given to prestige services

Inefficiency of local NHS

Supply reasons

Reasons for inequalities

Health service inequalities

Social class

Services delivered unequally to different groups

Ability to pay for private health care

Age

Gender

Demand reasons

Lack of knowledge of the system

Cultural barriers

Ignorance of warning signs of ill health

Ethnicity

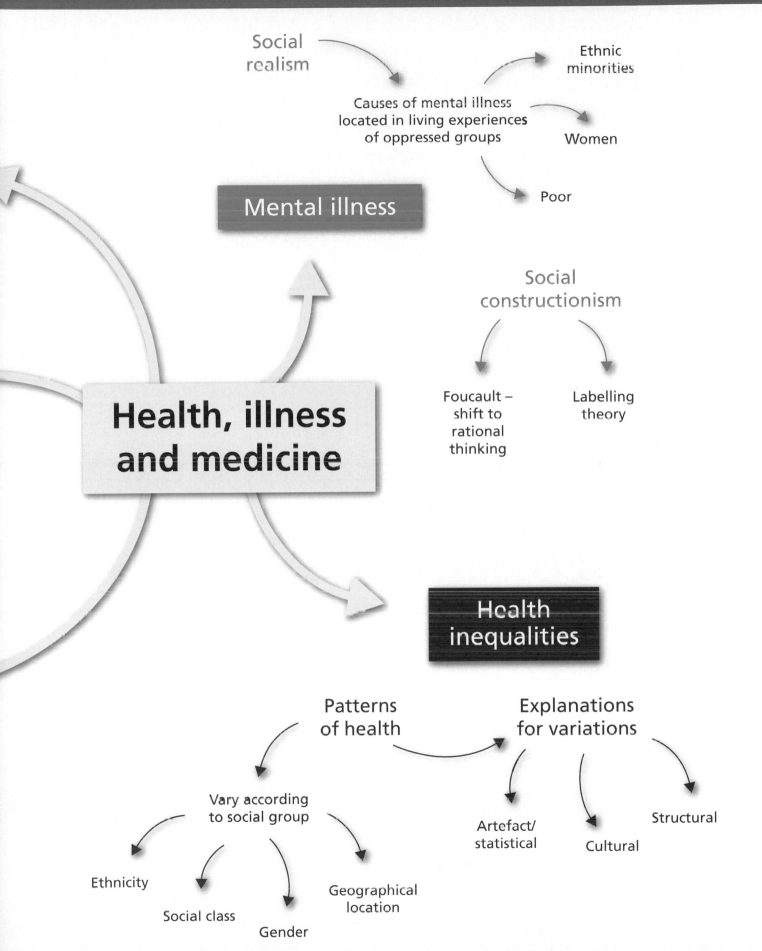

Social
realism

Ethnic
minorities

Causes of mental illness
located in living experiences
of oppressed groups

Women

Poor

Mental illness

Social
constructionism

Foucault –
shift to
rational
thinking

Labelling
theory

Health, illness
and medicine

Health
inequalities

Patterns
of health

Explanations
for variations

Vary according
to social group

Artefact/
statistical

Structural

Cultural

Ethnicity

Social class

Gender

Geographical
location

DEFINING AND ILLUSTRATING WHAT WAS MEANT BY THE MASS MEDIA used to be very simple. 'Mass media' simply referred to channels through which messages are conveyed from a single point to a very large number of other points. A newspaper or a radio broadcast clearly fitted this criterion. The term was also used to describe media which the majority of the population consumed. This latter definition may still apply to newer media forms, but the initial definition may not. New terms have been developed to reflect the changing nature of communication:

- **Interpersonal media** involve messages which are conveyed between single points, such as mobile phones and email.
- **Interactive media** allow a limited degree of communication back from the individual points to the point of origin – examples include digital TV and the internet.
- **Network media** permit messages to be passed between individual, small or large numbers of points in any direction – examples include video conferencing and intranets.

The term 'new media' is used to describe media associated with information and communications technology (ICT). New generation mobile phones, PCs and the internet, computer games consoles and MP3 players are examples of **new media**. Because their consumption can be more individual, they tend to involve smaller audiences. The term 'narrowcasting' is sometimes used to distinguish the new media from the 'broadcasting' of more traditional mass media forms.

The relative ease of access and cheapness of the new media in the affluent nations of the world has enabled its use to spread at a truly dramatic rate. In the first quarter of 2004, 49 per cent of households in the UK (12.1 million) could access the internet from home, compared with just 13 per cent (3.2 million) in the same quarter of 1999.

It's not surprising that the study of the mass media has changed to reflect the changes described above. In this unit, we cover the key debates regarding the ownership, content and consumption of the mass media, and consider their changing patterns and influence.

Mass media

Ownership and control of the mass media

gettingyouthinking

then ...

... now

1 How do the cartoons illustrate changing patterns of ownership of the mass media?

Sociological debates about media ownership have had to change as the nature of that ownership has itself changed. The press barons, film studio magnates and record company bosses of the past were immensely powerful men (and they were invariably men) in their own fields. Their modern-day equivalents can wield power across far wider aspects of human communication.

The low labour costs (increasingly overseas) and lower skill demands involved in assembling modern media hardware have significantly reduced its cost, making ownership ever more widespread. Virtually every household now has at least one TV, which the average person watches for 25 hours each week. Over 20 million people read a daily newspaper; almost 50 per cent of British households have access to a personal computer and it seems almost everyone has a mobile phone, with the latest models providing multimedia capabilities (BFI 2001).

The owners and controllers of the media have potentially more power than ever. In order to examine the possible extent of this power, we need to know a bit more about trends in ownership and consumption.

Trends in ownership

Technological convergence

The ability of digital technology to combine previously separate forms of communication, such as the internet and mobile phones (WAP), has encouraged media companies to merge. The even bigger companies that are created, such as Viacom/CBS and Time Warner/AOL, have more ability to develop a wider range of products and markets.

In the near future, it will be possible for all those who can afford it, or have access to the technology, to conduct all communications via a unified interactive receiver – capable of use as a telephone, computer, wordprocessor, radio, TV and video, from which many interactive commercial, retail, leisure and learning services will be accessible, including pay-per-view TV, video on demand, internet services and home shopping, banking and market research.

Media commentators now talk of **synergy**. This has two aspects:

1 Media products which were once distinct can now be produced as part of a package. For example, products based on the film *Spiderman 2* include a soundtrack CD, computer game, ring tones, action figures, clothing, and so on.
2 The ownership of these different aspects of production and consumption is increasingly in the hands of one massive organization. This means that a range of media products can be promoted together to a global market in a process known as **intracorporate self-promotion** or **cross promotion**.

Transnational ownership

Media companies are no longer restricted by national boundaries, particularly now that ownership rules have been relaxed in the world's richest nations. Media ownership is becoming a global concern with huge media producers combining forces as new technology breaks down old barriers between them. These giant media corporations buy up smaller companies all over the world. There is some concern that this could undermine smaller and more distinctive national and local production.

Media concentration

Media companies are bought and sold at an alarming rate. Over the last 20 or 30 years, the media have become more and more concentrated into fewer and fewer hands. If the American media were owned by separate individuals, there would be 25,000 owners. Instead, only five huge corporations own everything (Bagdikian 2000).

Vertical integration

This refers to the process whereby all the stages in the production, distribution and consumption of a media product are owned by one company. For example, a newspaper owner might own the sawmills that produce the wood, the paper mills that produce the paper, newspaper offices, printing facilities, lorries and newsagents. This cuts costs and increases profits. Vertical integration has been a common feature of some aspects of the media, such as film and the press, for some time. However, the process is spreading to other areas of the media.

Cross-media ownership

This occurs where more than one form of media – say radio and TV stations – come to be owned by the same company, creating what is known as a **media conglomerate**, such as NewsCorp.

Diversification

Many companies move into areas outside the media so that one part of the business can support another until things improve. Granada, for example, owns TV studios, TV and computer rental outlets and motorway service stations. Sony owns film studios and music recording studios although its main source of income is through electronic consumer goods.

Ownership and control

So do the owners of the media actually control its content? Is our information about the world distorted through the eyes of a few, very wealthy, media barons? The extent to which this occurs is an area of intense debate, which centres around the interconnected roles of media proprietors (owners), media professionals (those who work for them) and us, the consumers.

Sociologists have come up with three basic theories to explain the links between ownership and control.

Traditional Marxism

According to this view, the media help maintain the unfair and exploitative capitalist system by 'brainwashing' the public. Media owners are rich and successful people who benefit considerably from capitalism and therefore have a vested interest in ensuring its survival. Because of this, they directly manipulate media output so that it reflects their interests. The media encourage us to support the system and to hold values that enable capitalism to thrive. Marxists call these values capitalist **ideology**.

There is considerable evidence of direct manipulation. Rupert Murdoch, who owns and controls NewsCorp (a huge media corporation which owns, or has a controlling interest in the *Sun*, *The Times*, the *News of the World*, Sky and Fox, as well as over 1000 other media concerns in five continents), has been accused of manipulative practices on many occasions. He allegedly would not allow legitimate coverage of TV reports regarding the Chinese government's suppression of dissidents to be broadcast on Sky News because it might affect business negotiations between Murdoch's companies and the Chinese authorities.

Some commentators suggest that the political power of those who now own most of the media cannot be underestimated. It has been said that the likes of Murdoch and Bill Gates (head of Microsoft) have more global influence than the President of the USA. In the UK, Murdoch has even been dubbed 'the Phantom Prime Minister'.

Critics of the traditional Marxist view highlight the wide range of views which exist in society, which, they claim, would not exist if media manipulation was as powerful as is suggested. Also, they point out, it is impossible for owners to be directly involved in all aspects of their business to the extent that they have any real influence. Their businesses are too immense and they could not possibly find the time. In addition, media owners are not free to act totally as they wish because they are governed by a number of laws and other regulations – for example, the Official Secrets Act and libel laws. Their activities are also monitored by a number of **watchdogs**, such as the Press Complaints Commission.

Because of these criticisms, many Marxists do not agree with the traditional view. They still believe that the media reflect the views of the powerful, but they have a slightly different explanation.

Hegemonic Marxism

This view is similar to the traditional Marxist view in that it believes that the media provide the public with an ideology – views and information that support the capitalist system. However, this group of Marxists does not believe that the content of the media is under the direct control of the owners. Instead, they believe that this ideology is transmitted constantly via institutions such as schools and churches, as well as the media. Eventually, nobody even notices it – the views of the

Sociology AS for AQA

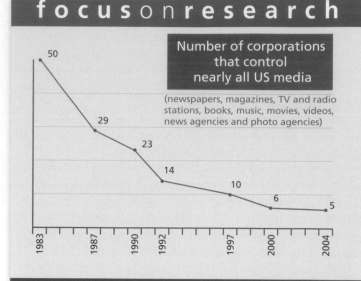

focus on research

Number of corporations that control nearly all US media

(newspapers, magazines, TV and radio stations, books, music, movies, videos, news agencies and photo agencies)

50 — 1983
29 — 1987
23 — 1990
14 — 1992
10 — 1997
6 — 2000
5 — 2004

Ben Bagdikian
The New Media Monopoly (2004)

In 1983, 50 corporations controlled the vast majority of all news media in the USA. At the time, Ben Bagdikian was called 'alarmist' for pointing this out in his book, *The Media Monopoly*. In his 4th edition, published in 1992, he wrote 'in the US, fewer than two dozen of these extraordinary creatures own and operate 90 per cent of the mass media' – controlling almost all of America's newspapers, magazines, TV and radio stations, books, records, movies, videos, news agencies and photo agencies. He predicted then that eventually this number would fall to about half a dozen companies. This was greeted with scepticism at the time. When the 6th edition of *The Media Monopoly* was published in 2000, the number had fallen to six. Since then, there have been more mergers and the scope has expanded to include new media like the internet market. More than 1 in 5 internet users in the USA and 1 in 7 in the UK now log in with AOL Time-Warner, the world's largest media corporation.

In 2004, Bagdikian's revised and expanded book, *The New Media Monopoly*, shows that only five huge corporations – Time Warner, Disney, Murdoch's News Corporation, Bertelsmann of Germany, and Viacom (formerly CBS) – now control most of the media industry in the USA. General Electric's NBC is a close sixth.

Media Reform Information Center 2004
(**www.corporations.org/media/**)

1 Why were Bagdikian's original claims perceived as 'alarmist'?

2 How do Bagdikian's claims illustrate the process of concentration of media ownership?

ruling class have become 'common sense'. Of course, it's always easier to dominate and control people if they are happy to go along with you, and the media have played a key role in bringing about this situation, which is known as **hegemony**.

But why, ask hegemonic Marxists, do the media present views that support the unfair capitalist system? Because of their background, journalists and broadcasters (who tend to be White, middle-class and male) usually subscribe to a 'middle-of-the-road', unthreatening set of viewpoints, which will, they believe, appeal to the majority of readers. Anyone outside the consensus is seen as an extremist. Alternative views are sometimes represented but usually ridiculed.

Agenda-setting

Meetings usually have an agenda – a list of issues to be discussed. The media provide an agenda for discussion in society. How often do you hear people talking about the latest news stories, scandals or soap operas? Hegemonic Marxists argue that the media present us with a fairly narrow agenda for discussion. We talk about the size and shape of a female singer, but don't often discuss the massive inequalities that exist in society. We are more likely to be outraged by the latest events in Albert Square than by the number of people living in poverty. In this way, the public are distracted from really important issues, and the workings of capitalist society are never questioned because its worst points are rarely presented.

But, you may ask, don't we get different political views presented to us so that we can make real choices about how society should be run? In the run-up to the 1997 General Election, only two national newspapers supported the Labour Party, and six supported the Conservatives (although the *Express* and *Sun* switched their allegiance to Labour in the final weeks). People frequently argue that, since New Labour emerged, there has, in any case, been very little difference between the parties, so the agenda for discussion has narrowed even further.

Both of the positions we have looked at argue that the media support the capitalist system by controlling – consciously (traditional Marxism) or unconsciously (hegemonic Marxism) – media output so that it benefits those in power.

The third and final position (**pluralism**) is the one that, unsurprisingly, the media themselves tend to support.

Pluralism

From a pluralist viewpoint, the media are seen as offering a wide selection of the views of the various groups in society. Modern society is democratic and people have freedom of choice. If they did not like the output of the media, they would not buy it or watch it. The media have to give the public what they want – otherwise they would go out of business.

Pluralists raise a number of points in support of their view:

- The media are not all-powerful – governments have tried at various times to legislate against media owners having too much power. For example, **vertical integration** has been considered unfair for two reasons: first, it doesn't allow competition to survive because smaller companies can't compete with the cheaper costs of the conglomerates; and second, it reduces customer choice, because one person's or group's views or products can become too dominant.

- In the USA, the huge film studios have been prevented from owning film production, film distribution and cinemas at the same time. Many countries have **cross-media ownership** rules preventing companies from owning more than one media form in the same area.

- In the UK, however, since the Broadcasting Act of 1996, the rules have been relaxed regarding media and cross-media ownership and Broadcasters are less constrained by rules regarding content. The Communications Act of 2003 has weakened ownership restrictions further, allowing major TV and radio broadcasters to expand their share of the UK media market and this includes non-EU companies or individuals whose potential share was much more restricted previously. Similar restrictions on ownership have been relaxed in the USA and Europe.

The power of the media owner
Rupert Murdoch and News Corporation

Sometimes it is not necessary for powerful media owners to influence the content of the media directly, in order to put their own views across. In the passage below, Richard Searby, Australian chairman of News Corporation (see p. 118), discusses the influence of its owner, Rupert Murdoch.

<< *The management style of News Corporation is one of extreme devolution punctuated by periods of episodic autocracy. Most company boards meet to take decisions. Ours meets to ratify Rupert's. For much of the time, you don't hear from Rupert. Then, all of a sudden, he descends like a thunderbolt from hell to slash and burn all before him. Since nobody is ever sure when the next autocratic intervention will take place (or on what subject), they live in fear of it and try to second guess what he would want, even in the most unimportant of matters. It is a clever way of keeping his executives off balance: they live in a perpetual state of insecurity. Everybody in the company is obsessed with him, he is the main topic of conversation, even among executives who have not heard from him for months; everybody is desperate for any titbit of information about him, especially if it sheds light on what his latest thoughts and movements are.*>>

Richard Searby quoted in Neill, A. (1996) *Full Disclosure*, Basingstoke: Macmillan

1 How does the quotation above provide an example of self-censorship?

- Pluralists also point out that journalists and editors often refuse to go along with what their owners want of them.
- Finally, the media have a strong tradition of **investigative journalism** which has often targeted those in power. For example, two reporters on the Washington Post forced the then President of the USA – Richard Nixon – to stand down after they exposed him for authorizing the bugging of his opponents' offices at Watergate in 1972.

Whether direct manipulation goes on or not, pluralists claim that there is no proof that audiences passively accept what they are fed. Audiences are selective and, at times, critical. To suggest that they can be manipulated is to fail to recognize the diversity of the audience or the ways in which they use the media. This will be considered more fully in later topics.

Check your understanding

1 How have recent developments in media increased the power of media owners?

2 How does traditional Marxism view the influence of media owners on media output?

3 Give an example of the direct manipulation of media output by a media proprietor.

4 How would hegemonic Marxists challenge the view that the media present us with a wide range of opinion?

5 What are the differences between traditional Marxism and hegemonic Marxism?

6 Give examples of three arguments put forward by pluralists to show that the media do not just represent the views of the powerful but cater for everyone in society. To what extent might these views be seen to be out of date?

research ideas

- Conduct a small-scale social survey to discover to what extent people of different ages and/or ethnic and/or class backgrounds believe that the content of the media reflects the wide variety of views present in British society.

web.task

Use the internet to investigate the extent of product synergy in the marketing of the *Harry Potter* stories.

KEY TERMS

Agenda-setting controlling what issues come to public attention.

Cross-media ownership occurs where different types of media – e.g. radio and TV stations – are owned by the same company.

Cross promotion (or **intra-corporate self-promotion**) an aspect of synergy where different areas of a company's business promote other areas owned by the same company.

Diversification the practice of spreading risk by moving into new, unrelated areas of business.

Hegemony domination by consent (used to describe the way in which the ruling class project their view of the world so that it becomes the consensus view).

Ideology the norms and values adopted by a particular group or society.

Investigative journalism journalism that aims to expose the misdeeds of the powerful.

Media concentration the result of smaller media companies merging, or being bought up by larger companies, to form

a small number of very large companies.

Media conglomerate a company that owns various types of media.

New Media digital media offering images, text and sounds plus the capability for the user to interact, such as the internet, 3G mobile phones and digital television.

Pluralism a theory that society is made up of many different groups, all having more or less equal power.

Synergy a mutually advantageous combination of distinct elements, where the

working together of two or more things produces an effect greater than the sum of their individual effects.

Technological convergence the tendency for once diverse media forms to combine as a result of digital technology.

Vertical integration owning all the stages in the production, distribution and consumption of a product.

Watchdog an organization created to keep a check on powerful businesses.

Item A Public hygiene and the media

<< These cost accountants or their near clones are employed by new kinds of media owners who try to gobble up everything in their path. We must protect ourselves and our democracy, first by properly exercising the cross-ownership provisions currently in place, and then by erecting further checks and balances against dangerous concentrations of the media power which plays such a large part in our lives. No individual or company should be allowed to own more than one daily, one evening and one weekly newspaper. No newspaper should be allowed to own a television station and vice versa.

A simple act of public hygiene, containing abuse, widening choice and maybe even returning broadcasting to its makers.>>

Dennis Potter: excerpt from the James MacTaggart Memorial Lecture, Edinburgh Film Festival, 1993 (reproduced in Potter, D. (1994), *Seeing the Blossom: Two interviews and a lecture*, London: Faber and Faber)

Item B All for one

<< When AOL took over Time Warner, it also took over: Warner Brothers Pictures, Morgan Creek, New Regency, Warner Brothers Animation, a partial stake in Savoy Pictures, Little Browne & Co., Bullfinch, Back Bay, Time-Life Books, Oxmoor House, Sunset Books, Warner Books, the Book-of-the-Month Club, Warner/Chappell Music, Atlantic Records, Warner Audio Books, Elektra, Warner Brothers Records, Time-Life Music, Columbia House, a 40-per-cent stake in Seattle's Sub-Pop records, *Time Magazine, Fortune, Life, Sports Illustrated, Vibe, People, Entertainment Weekly, Money, In Style, Martha Stewart Living, Sunset, Asia Week, Parenting,* Weight Watchers, *Cooking Light,* DC Comics, 49 per cent of the Six Flags theme parks, Movie World and Warner Brothers parks, HBO, Cinemax, Warner Brothers Television, partial ownership of Comedy Central, E!, Black Entertainment Television, Court TV, the Sega channel, the Home Shopping Network, Turner Broadcasting, the Atlanta Braves and Atlanta Hawks, World Championship Wrestling, Hanna-Barbera Cartoons, New Line Cinema, Fine Line Cinema, Turner Classic Movies, Turner Pictures, Castle Rock productions, CNN, CNN Headline News, CNN International, CNN/SI, CNN Airport Network, CNNfi, CNN radio, TNT, WTBS, and the Cartoon Network.

The situation is not substantially different at Disney, Viacom, General Electric, or at Murdoch's News Corporation, which is credited with having created the first global media network by investing in both software (movies, TV shows, sports franchises, publishing) and the distribution platforms (the Fox network, cable television and satellite systems) that disseminate the software ...>>

Alterman, E. (2002) *What Liberal Media? The truth about bias and the news,* New York: Basic Books

1 **Explain what is meant by 'cross ownership' in the context of the mass media (Item A).** (2 marks)

2 **Identify two measures to control cross-media ownership that Dennis Potter would like to see (Item A). (4 marks)**

3 **Suggest three reasons why concentrations of media power play such a large part in our lives (Item B). (6 marks)**

4 **Identify and briefly explain two criticisms of the view that media proprietors are in direct control of media output. (8 marks)**

5 **Examine the view that the content of the mass media reflects a wide range of opinions. (20 marks)**

6 **Using information from the Items and elsewhere, assess the view that ownership of the media is becoming increasingly concentrated. (20 marks)**

Public service broadcasting

gettingyouthinking

Annual % share of viewing 1991 to 2003

Year	Channel					
	BBC1	BBC2	ITV (incGMTV)	CH4	CH5	OTHERS (Cable/ Sat/RTE)
1991	34	10	42	10	-	4
1992	34	10	41	10	-	5
1993	33	10	40	11	-	6
1994	32	11	39	11	-	7
1995	32	11	37	11	-	9
1996	33.5	11.5	35.1	10.7	-	10.1
1997	30.8	11.6	32.9	10.6	2.3	11.8
1998	29.5	11.3	31.7	10.3	4.3	12.9
1999	28.4	10.8	31.2	10.3	5.4	14.0
2000	27.2	10.8	29.3	10.5	5.7	16.6
2001	26.9	11.1	26.7	10.0	5.8	19.6
2002	26.2	11.4	24.1	10.0	6.3	22.1
2003	25.6	11.0	23.7	9.6	6.5	23.6

NB: Shares before 1996 have been rounded to nearest whole number

Source: Broadcaster's Audience Research Board, 2003

Qualities of public service broadcasting

● *Quality* – cultural policy (including access to the arts, promotion of domestic and independent film industry) and protection of vulnerable programme types (news, children's programmes, high-cost drama).

● *Accuracy and impartiality* – reliable and credible news, education and information for the public as a contribution to the national political debate.

● *Plurality and diversity* – the allocation of scarce public resources to as wide a range of operators as possible and the promotion of diverse types of content to cater to all segments of society.

● *Access* – universal, affordable access to core services which provide high-quality, accurate news and diverse content.

● *Taste and decency* – consumer protection from an influential medium, including the protection of children from harmful material.

Thomas, A. (1999) *Regulation of Broadcasting in the Digital Age*, Department for Culture, Media and Sport

1 Summarize the trends in the table. What do they tell us about changing patterns in broadcasting?

2 Read the list of qualities of public service broadcasting. To what extent do you think the BBC's current programming meets these requirements. Give examples.

A key strand in the pluralist argument has been that, unlike countries such as the USA, the British media – and broadcasting in particular – are more highly regulated and hence diverse because they are in part publicly owned and controlled.

Public versus private ownership

In the UK, **commercial television** channels, such as ITV1 and Channel 5, are funded mainly through advertising, while **satellite TV** (e.g. Sky/BsB) receives subscriptions from its viewers in addition to advertising revenue. Both types of television, therefore, are concerned with their appeal to advertisers and with profit. However, in the UK, the BBC is a state-owned TV and radio broadcaster. It is controlled by a board of governors appointed by the Home Secretary. The BBC receives its funding from the government via a broadcasting tax known as the **licence fee**. The BBC must, however, satisfy the government that it is providing the service people want in order for this licence fee to be approved. In order to do this, it has to compete with commercial television for viewers/listeners.

All broadcasters have some formal requirements imposed upon them by their **regulators**. There is now a single powerful regulator – the Office for Communications – OFCOM – which has replaced the ITC, Radio Authority, Oftel, Broadcasting Standards Commission and the Radiocommunications Agency.

Public service broadcasting

The BBC and Channel 4 have a much greater obligation to their viewers as particular types of broadcasters. The BBC is expected to provide services of a high standard that inform, educate and entertain. It should offer a wide range of subject matter for local and national audiences, as well as ensuring accuracy and impartiality in its news programming and in coverage of controversial subjects. Channel 4, although funded through advertising, has a remit which centres on complementing ITV through the provision of distinctive output, and is required to show innovation and experiment in the form and content of its programmes.

Some have criticized the values promoted by **public service broadcasting** (PSB) as middle class and patronizing. Many working-class viewers have, until recently, preferred commercial TV since its launch in 1954.

Deregulation

The ITV companies who compete for the right to broadcast in a particular area (Carlton, Granada, Meridian, Grampian, etc.), although regulated and expected to have some PSB remit, have always had greater freedom to pursue profit and mass audiences. However, since the Broadcasting Act was revised in 1990 and 1996, the distinction between state-run PSB and commercial TV has become blurred. Both have had fewer restrictions imposed upon them and, whilst advertising is still not allowed on the BBC, they too have been freer to become more commercial.

The 2003 Communications Act has built upon the **deregulation** introduced by earlier legislation. It has relaxed both ownership and content rules, encouraging greater competition and allowing the free market to play a bigger role in determining content. The 2003 Act, however, was also concerned to preserve PSB in the wake of criticism that it seemed to be under threat.

Many argue that the intentions of the 2003 Act, in part to support all terrestrial broadcasters to deliver PSB, are too little, too late and that public service broadcasting no longer exists. They claim that the public service broadcasters are '**dumbing down**', that BBC1 and C4 increasingly imitate their commercial competitors and are failing in their duty to maintain quality standards for the industry (Liddiment 2001). As the table on the left shows, over the last 15 years an increasingly influential commercial sector has been cable and satellite TV.

Terrestrial TV broadcasters like the BBC and ITV were once the dominant force in Broadcasting. Now they are in direct competition with satellite and cable TV companies, such as

Rupert Murdoch's BSkyB Television, which began to emerge in the late 1980s. Such companies are funded by both advertising and subscriptions, and have the technology to act as global broadcasters. Less bound by regulations over content, they are able to concentrate mainly on popular programming. Therefore, with such large, sometimes **niche audiences** (particular groups of viewers such as 16- to 24-year-old MTV viewers) for certain channels, they can attract massive advertising revenue and so have the capacity to attract viewers away from the terrestrial channels. This increased competition has created a trend towards commercialization for all TV output, giving apparently greater choice, with more and more channels. Terrestrial TV producers have also diversified into cable, satellite and digital TV themselves – for example, with BBC3 and 4, and ITV2. They have also gone into partnership with commercial companies to set up new channels such as UK Gold.

More choice or more of the same?

Since deregulation, there has been the scope for terrestrial TV to bow to pressure to become more commercially successful, in order to compete more effectively with cable and satellite TV. This has meant that quality has been affected as the lowest common denominator among the viewing public has become the main concern.

The aim is to satisfy a mass culture. We don't have more choice, just more of the same thing. There are more repeats and cheap imports, and 50 per cent fewer documentaries, many of which are 'docusoaps' (fly-on-the-wall documentaries such as *Airport* and *Ibiza Uncovered*). There has been a growth of 'infotainment', a mix of news and light entertainment which focuses on personalities and lifestyles of the rich and famous rather than social and political issues. The lifestyles of ordinary people feature more and more with cheap makeover shows of house and garden. Cheap reality TV programmes which make personalities out of unknowns have replaced quality entertainment involving real (and expensive) personalities with genuine talent. Advertising has increased in diversity and influence, with more TV sponsorship and product placement (visible brand identity promoted in mainstream programmes) by advertisers and manufacturers.

On the other hand, popular TV appeals to more people. Who is to say what constitutes good television? The perceived distinction between low culture (or popular culture of the masses) and high culture of the intellectual elite is snobbish and value laden. Popular culture should have equal validity, and may have many equally authentic forms as societies become more fragmented. Besides, PSB is still accessible to everyone, while commercial TV is increasingly becoming a digitized and expensive option for those who can afford it. However, Jackson (2000, 2001) argues that wider social and cultural changes have made the provision of public service broadcasting less necessary, including the view that the concept of minorities is no longer socially meaningful. He concludes that the values of PSB have declining relevance for British society. In any case, as

Cathy Come Home *was an influential TV play about homelessness, first shown in the 1960s.*

Steve Barnett & Emily Weymour
Disneyfication

<<A further critique of television which caught the media's attention in 1999 was the report produced by Steve Barnett and Emily Weymour on behalf of the Campaign for Quality Television. The report entitled 'A Shrinking Iceberg Travelling South: Changing Trends in British Television', compared schedules in 1978, 1988 and 1998, and pointed to a rise in 'quick-fix' TV which is intended to increase ratings. To justify his claim of the 'disneyfication' of British television, Barnett pointed to the fact that the number of single dramas has halved over the last 20 years, while soap operas have increased fivefold, as programmers, pressured to respond to the ratings, are obliged to schedule drama likely to bring the viewers back repeatedly. Barnett quoted from interviews with 30 anonymous programme makers and commissioning editors. These showed, he claimed, increasing disillusionment and a belief that the major ground-breaking dramas tackling social issues, such as *Cathy Come Home,* would not now be funded, as they would be perceived as too risky in the ratings war.

Ultimately, all the problems – centralization, homogeneity, the focus-group mentality – come down to money and ratings in a world of deregulated competition and diminishing budgets. Producers throughout the industry are now expected to perform according to ratings targets and on budgets which are progressively being cut (sometimes even in the middle of filming). In the BBC, the result is a growing culture of self-censorship: 'Every year, they keep cutting. We feel we've become so budget-oriented that we've clipped our own wings – we don't even suggest ideas because we think it will be too expensive'.>>

The Guardian, 25 October 1999

1 Why might ground-breaking dramas which tackle social issues be considered too risky in the ratings war?

2 What sorts of ideas may not be suggested because they may be thought too expensive?

the BBC, its main provider, secures a progressively dwindling viewer base, a licence fee for all may become unjustifiable and PSB may cease to have a coherent provider in the future.

One aspect of PSB which has attracted attention in the wake of increasing competition and commercialization is television news, which is discussed in the next topic.

Check your understanding

1 How does the BBC secure its funding? What might happen if programme ratings are poor?

2 How would you define PSB?

3 Why has the BBC and Channel 4 failed to attract working-class viewers?

4 What impact has deregulation allegedly had on terrestrial television?

5 How does the 2003 Communications Act attempt to support PSB?

6 Why is satellite TV so profitable?

7 Give four criticisms levelled against contemporary TV.

8 How might terrestrial TV broadcasters address these criticisms?

KEY TERMS

Commercial television ITV stations that raise revenues from advertising. TV output that has high ratings.

Deregulation the removal of restrictions on the ownership and content of the media.

'Dumbing down' the accusation that TV output is becoming simpler and easier for all to understand in the quest for ratings.

Licence fee a tax on radio and television paid to the government and then passed on to the BBC provided they fulfil their PSB remit.

Niche audiences special cohorts of viewers with a shared interest, e.g. in sport or music, who are willing to pay for specialist channels.

Public service broadcasting output which is accessible to all, serves a diverse audience, contains quality programming and which educates and informs as well as entertains.

Regulators for broadcasting one body – OFCOM – monitors broadcasting to ensure that its regulations are enforced.

Satellite TV similar to other commercial broadcasters, but also able to raise revenue from subscriptions

Terrestrial TV the main channels still broadcasting in analogue that can be received in principle by everyone. These include BBC 1 and 2, ITV1, Channel 4 and Channel 5 as well as RTE in Wales.

Item A Children and television

<< Whilst the annual percentage share of viewing figures shows a decline nationally in terrestrial TV's audience share against a growth in cable/satellite viewing, the figures mask age-related consumption patterns, especially within 'cable-connected' homes, where cable stations accounted for 54 per cent of total viewing by youngsters under 15 and nearly 64 per cent among those aged under 9. This may be due to the fact that distinctive youth genres are available in constant supply through channels such as Nickelodeon and Cartoon Network. Also, the mode of presentation and material outside of the regular programmes, e.g. advertising, competitions, graphics and use of comedy, has more appeal. Children's channels are becoming highly lucrative for the broadcasters. As an increasingly affluent consumer group, children are being targeted more and more by advertisers willing to pay the huge rates demanded for advertising time. >>

Adapted from: 'Continental Research for the ITC', *The Guardian*, 23 December 1995

Item B Accessibility

<< The problem for the programme makers, with the ratings-chasers on their backs, is that they dare not risk offering any fare that may be too challenging. That means making programmes that are 'accessible'. What is meant by 'accessible' is anything that we can relate to from experience in our own lives, the patronizing assumption being that anything outside our experience will be a turn-off. So out goes much of the difficult stuff and in comes the story to which we can 'relate'. Or the private lives of the famous. Or crime. Or consumer affairs. Or something funny or whimsical. Anything to do with sex, jealousy, conflict, money, power, suffering, anything from which you can elicit an emotional response, is deemed to be 'accessible'. This is where populist television news takes us. >>

Adapted from J. Humphrys, *The Guardian*, 30 August 1999

1 Explain what is meant by 'terrestrial TV' (Item A). (2 marks)

2 Suggest two reasons why cable channels may be more popular than terrestrial channels among the young (Item A). (4 marks)

3 Suggest three reasons why the percentage audience share for terrestrial television may be declining. (6 marks)

4 Identify and briefly explain two problems terrestrial broadcasters might face when in competition with satellite broadcasters. (8 marks)

5 Examine the problems researchers might face in gaining accurate viewing data. (20 marks)

6 Using information from the Items and elsewhere, examine the extent to which PSB can be seen as proof of pluralist theories. (20 marks)

research ideas

- Conduct a survey of TV viewers. Try to find out their favourite programmes. Use a quota sample so that you can see whether there are differences in preferences according to age. Conduct interviews with those choosing PSB-type programmes. Ask whether they feel that TV in general and the BBC in particular has suffered from 'dumbing down'

web.task

Search the BBCs website (www.bbc.co.uk) for information about its purpose, values, charter and regulation. To what extent do these reflect the values of public service broadcasting?

The content of the mass media: making the news

gettingyouthinking

1 Which aspects of the above screen shots suggest that the news:

- is 'up to the minute'?
- comes from around the world?
- employs the latest technology?

2 Think of the music that introduces news broadcasts. What impression does it give?

News: a 'window on the world'?

For most of us, TV news is the most important source of information about what is going on outside our day-to-day experiences. We rely on TV news to help us make sense of a confusing world. As you probably worked out from the questions above, news broadcasts are carefully managed to give an impression of seriousness and credibility. But do they really represent a 'window on the world'? How do TV journalists and editors decide which of the millions of events that occur in the world on any day will become 'news'?

Critics of the media have pointed out that the news is most certainly not a 'window on the world'. Instead, they argue that it is a manufactured and manipulated product involving a high degree of selectivity and bias. What causes this? Three important elements are:

1 institutional factors both inside and outside the newsrooms (such as issues of time and money)
2 the culture of news production and journalism (how news professionals think and operate)
3 the ideological influences on the media (the cause and nature of bias).

Institutional factors

The 'news diary'

Rather than being a spontaneous response to world events, many news reports are planned well in advance. Many newspapers and TV news producers purchase news items from press agencies (companies who sell brief reports of world or national news 24 hours per day). They also receive press releases from pressure groups, government agencies, private companies and individuals, all of whom wish to publicize their activities.

Schlesinger (1978) highlighted the influence of the **news diary**. This is a record of forthcoming social, political and economic events which enables journalists and broadcasters to plan their coverage, and select and book relevant 'experts'. It also allows them to make practical arrangements – which could include anything from liaising with local authorities and the police over outside broadcasts, or organizing satellite link-ups, to sorting out the catering for location staff. Such events might include the Chancellor of the Exchequer's speech on budget day, royal birthdays, the release of a notorious prisoner or the arrival of a famous entertainment personality.

Financial costs

Financial considerations can also influence the news. Sometimes, so much has been spent on covering a world event (sending camera crews, flights, accommodation for journalists, pre-booked satellite links, etc.) that it will continue to get reported on even though very little that is new has happened.

The point at which the news company's financial year-end falls can also affect how, and even whether, costly news items are covered. This is why the BBC was able to cover the pro-democracy demonstrations in Tiananmen square in China, which provided some of the most memorable footage in recent times, and yet was unable, unlike ITN, to give full coverage of the unification of Germany and the demolition of the Berlin wall which occurred later that same year.

Competition

This highlights another factor: competition. News producers are desperate to be the first to 'break the news'. This can cause them to cut corners – for example, accepting 'evidence' from sources without properly checking it, or relying on official sources because they are more easily accessed. This can lead to a biased view in favour of the official side of the argument (see the work of the Glasgow University Media Group, pp. 129–30).

Time or space available

News items have to be selected from the thousands that flood into the newsroom every day, and they then need to be fashioned into a coherent and recognizable product. The average news bulletin contains 15 items which must take exactly the same amount of time to put across each day. Similarly, a newspaper has a fixed amount of space for each news category. Sometimes stories are included or excluded merely because they fit or don't fit the time or space available.

Audience

The time of a news broadcast (and who is perceived to be watching), or the readership profile of a paper, will also influence the selection of news. A lunchtime broadcast is more likely to be viewed by women, and so an item relating to the supermarket price war might receive more coverage than it would in a late-evening news bulletin.

The culture of news production and journalism

News values

Various studies have attempted to identify what makes an item 'newsworthy' for journalists. Galtung and Ruge (1973) identified several key **news values** that might be used to determine the 'newsworthiness' of events. These included:

- extraordinariness: events that are considered 'out of the ordinary'
- events that concern important or elite persons or countries
- events that can be personalized to point up the essentially human characteristics of sadness, humour, sentimentality and so on
- events that are dramatic, clear and negative in their consequences.

Different media have different ways of prioritizing news values. TV news would see picture values as an important consideration, whilst the tabloid press would tend to prioritize stories based on 'human interest' or famous personalities.

Gatekeeping

Journalists thus make decisions about what is and what is not 'newsworthy'. Their work has been referred to as **gatekeeping**:

Figure 4.1 Gatekeeping and news values

Posh & Becks to split?
Soap star attacked
Share prices crash
Mother of 10 wins lottery
England lose again
New figures show gap between rich and poor widening
9/11 hero in wife swap shock
Tragedy of tsunami orphans

Is it extraordinary?
Is it a human interest story?
Is it about a celebrity or rich country?
Is it dramatic?

they only let a tiny minority of events through the 'gate' to the next stage. Gatekeeping is, however, a very hierarchical process, with increasingly powerful gatekeepers at each stage. Only a small proportion of news items passed upwards at stage one make it into the final news product. Further structuring occurs in the final stages when running order or page positions are decided.

Narrativization

A narrative is a story. We are socialized into a culture in which storytelling has an important role. Stories tend to have a beginning, a middle and an end, and we expect this kind of narrative structure. News broadcasts often follow a format in which normality is disturbed by individuals or groups (often 'baddies') who then cause a problem or create a mystery of some sort. Eventually, the intervention of other causal agents (such as brave or heroic figures) ends the story when normality is restored. However, real events do not necessarily follow this **classic realist narrative** and in making them appear to, journalists inevitably distort the truth.

News programmes themselves also have a narrative structure. They place serious political and economic items at the beginning, and perhaps lighter-hearted stories at the end. News media has to also ensure that the composition of the programme or paper conforms to the brand identity of the medium as well as covering a range of news types, such as domestic news, foreign news, sport and business. All of these factors serve to distort the selection and presentation of news.

Bias against understanding

News production works on a 24-hour cycle. News coverage has to fit into the very short period which has developed over the last short period between bulletins. This means that we rarely get an overall picture of events or are allowed to see them in a historical context. This prevents us from ever truly understanding the cause-and-effect relationships involved.

Ideological influences on the media

As we saw in the previous topic, traditional Marxists argue that all of the news selection described above is deliberate and the result of conscious manipulation. News producers have a vested interest in maintaining the capitalist system, and so they help maintain that system by being directly supportive of the ruling class. The news is biased in favour of the powerful in society, and against those who are a threat to that power. While this view may overstate the case, it is certainly true that the ruling classes are appreciative of the role that the media play.

Table 4.1 Influences on media content

Owners and controlling companies	Certain owners directly manipulate the media. Owners and controllers have interests that they wish to promote or defend – Rupert Murdoch made sure that his bid for Manchester United was reported in a positive light in his newspapers.
Media institutions	Media institutions have a public image which they need to maintain. This affects their decisions about what to include and how to present it. The *News of the World*, for example, over-reports sex and scandal as this is what its readers want and expect.
The law	The media are subject to legal controls, such as the Official Secrets Act and the Prevention of Terrorism Act, as well as the laws of libel and contempt of court. Contempt of court means that the media cannot report in a way that might affect the verdict in an ongoing court case.
Constitutional constraints	Media organizations are governed by written 'contracts', such as the BBC Charter, which they agree in order to gain the right to publish or broadcast.
Media regulation and self-regulation	The media have their own standards and regulatory bodies which monitor content. Examples are the Press Complaints Commission and the Broadcasting Standards Council. Professional practices are also an influence. Journalists often censor their own work by taking out what they know will not be published.
Economic factors	The amount of money and resources available will inevitably influence the media, as shown by the example of the coverage of the Gulf War and Tiananmen Square.
Advertisers	Most of the media need advertising to survive. This means that the needs of advertisers will be taken very seriously when decisions are made about the content of the media. For example, there were suspicions that the link between smoking and lung cancer was slow to be reported because of the importance of tobacco companies' advertising.
Audiences	It is assumed that different kinds of people watch, listen and read at different times of the day. A lunchtime TV programme is likely to be aimed at women or pensioners, and early evening programming is likely to be aimed at schoolchildren.
Media personnel (class, race, gender, socialization)	The media may reflect a White, male, middle-class viewpoint, as many people in the media are drawn from these social backgrounds.
Sources	With news coverage in particular, certain groups – such as the government – are believed to be more reliable, honest and objective.

Many newspaper proprietors and TV news producers have received recognition through knighthoods or other honours.

For hegemonic Marxists, the way in which journalists learn what makes a good story is governed by their common White, male, middle-class background. Their lifestyle and standard of living are such that they see little wrong with society and rarely adopt a critical stance. This essentially attunes them to taken-for-granted, common-sense assumptions that maintain the system.

In contrast to these views, pluralists would argue that the news reflects the full diversity of viewpoints in society. Certain views will dominate in each situation, but the direction that the bias takes is not consistent, and so there is no overall slant towards a particular viewpoint.

The Glasgow University Media Group (GUMG)

The GUMG have studied news broadcasts for many years. They use a technique called **content analysis** (see Unit 7, p. 273), which involves detailed analysis of the language and visual images used by the media. They have found that the media consistently reflect the common assumptions of the powerful in society, whilst marginalizing the views of others.

In recent studies, the Group have demonstrated the extent to which the need for TV news to entertain creates a bias against understanding. They use both the reporting of the developing world (GUMG 1999) and the Arab/Israeli conflict (Philo 2004) to illustrate how news, because it now exists in a very commercial market, focuses more and more on exciting events, rather than the historical context and explanation of those events.

The reporting of the Colombian earthquake in January 1999 featured scenes of destruction, chaos, collapsed buildings, frantic rescue efforts and appeals for help. But there was nothing said about the impact of the earthquake on Columbia's coffee-growing region or the long-term economic repercussions on unemployment and investment.

They use coverage of the Israeli/Palestinian conflict to highlight how the agenda for discussion in the news is often framed by ideological influences. Israel is closely allied to the United States and there are very strong pro-Israeli lobbies in the USA and to some extent in the UK. The lack of discussion in the news of the origins of the conflict and the controversial aspects of the occupation of former Palestinian territories by Israel operate in Israel's favour. They go further, suggesting that the style and form of language used further highlight this pro-Israeli stance.

Words such as 'murder', 'atrocity', 'lynching' and 'savage cold-blooded killing' were only used to describe Israeli deaths, but never those of Palestinians. Terrible fates befell both Israelis and Palestinians, but there was a clear difference in the language used to describe them. This was so even when the events described had strong similarities. For example, on 10 October 2000, it was reported that Arab residents of Tel Aviv had been 'chased and stabbed'. The

Greg Philo

Bad news from Israel: media coverage of the Israeli/Palestinian conflict

If you don't understand the Middle East crisis, it might be because you are watching it on TV news. This scores high on images of fighting, violence and drama but is low on explanation. The Glasgow University Media Group interviewed 12 small audience groups (a total of 85 people) with a cross section of ages and backgrounds. They were asked a series of questions about the conflict and what they had understood from TV news. The same questions were then put to 300 young people (aged between 17 and 22) who filled in a questionnaire. We asked what came to their mind when they heard the words 'Israeli/Palestinian conflict' and then what was the source of whatever it was. Most (82 per cent) listed TV news as their source and these replies showed that they had absorbed the 'main' message of the news, of conflict, violence and tragedy, but that many people had little understanding of the reasons for the conflict and its origins. Explanations were rarely given on the news and when they were, journalists often spoke in a form of shorthand which assumed quite detailed knowledge of the origins of the conflict. For example, in a news bulletin which featured the progress of peace talks, a journalist made a series of very brief comments on the issues which underpinned the conflict: Journalist: 'The basic raw disagreements remain – the future, for example, of this city Jerusalem, the future of Jewish settlements and the returning refugees.' (ITN 18.30 16.10.2001)

adapted from the Glasgow University Media Unit website at www.gla.ac.uk/departments/sociology/units/media

1 How did the Glasgow University Media Group try to achieve a representative sample?

2 Why does Greg Philo write that 'if you don't understand the Middle East crisis it might be because you are watching it on TV news'?

reports on television news were extremely brief, but two days later, when two Israeli soldiers were killed by a crowd of Palestinians, there was very extensive coverage and the words 'lynching' and 'lynch mob' were very widely used.

The work of the Glasgow University Media Group shows that the media do not just reflect public opinion, but that they also provide a framework (or agenda) for the public, so that people think about issues in a way that benefits the ruling class. In this respect, the media are a powerful ideological influence. (See also Item A in the 'Exploring' activity on the opposite page.)

Class bias is not the only area of misrepresentation that critics of the pluralist position point to. Women, ethnic minorities, the disabled and the young may also be victims of media bias. The following topics will examine these issues in more detail.

Check your understanding

1 How does the use of a news diary demonstrate that news is not a spontaneous response to world events?

2 Give two examples of the impact of financial factors on news production.

3 Explain in your own words how the format and intended audience for a news programme affect news output.

4 What are 'news values'?

5 Explain in your own words how the process of gatekeeping affects the form that news output eventually takes.

6 Use the work of the Glasgow University Media Group to show how the media influence the way the public thinks about issues.

research ideas

- List the first ten news items from an edition of the BBC evening news. Do the same for ITN news on the same evening. What are the differences? Can they be explained in terms of 'news values'?

- Tape one news programme. Analyse the lead story in terms of the sources that are used, e.g. newscaster's script, live film footage, location report from a reporter at the scene, interview (taped, live or by satellite), archive footage (old film), amateur film, etc.

  Then brainstorm a list of all the people who must have been involved, e.g. reporters, photographers, editors, companies buying and selling satellite time, drivers, outside broadcast crews, film archivists, etc. Discuss how practical problems may have served to structure the story in a particular way.

web.tasks

1 Look at the web pages of the following daily newspapers on the same day: the *Sun*, the *Daily Telegraph* and the *Guardian*. Compare the presentation of their main stories.

  What similarities and differences are there in terms of stories covered and presentation? Why?

2 Search for the home page of the Glasgow University Mass Media Unit. Find out about their latest research.

KEY TERMS

Classic realist narrative a story which begins with normality being threatened by disruptive forces and is resolved when other forces act to restore normality.

Content analysis a detailed analysis of media content.

Gatekeepers people within the media who have the power to let some news stories through and stop others.

Marginalizing making a group appear to be 'at the edge' of society and not very important.

Narrativization the process of turning into a story.

News diary a record of forthcoming events that will need to be covered.

News values assumptions that guide journalists and editors when selecting news items.

Item A Ten conclusions from the Glasgow University Media Group

1 News is reported in a simplified and one-sided way.

2 The effects of events tend to be reported rather than their causes. There is no sense of their development.

3 There is biased use of words in TV news – e.g. 'miners' strike' rather than 'coal dispute'.

4 There is biased use of images in TV news. During the Liverpool council workers' strike, the piles of rubbish and unburied bodies reinforced the effects rather than the causes of the dispute, and put the viewer on the side of the management rather than the strikers.

5 Stories are reported selectively – only certain facts are presented and others are left out.

6 Protesters' tactics are more likely to be reported than their views.

7 There is a hierarchy of access to the media – experts and establishment figures are more likely to get their views heard than ordinary people.

8 There is a hierarchy of credibility whereby only certain groups are asked for their opinion, as they are seen to be more reliable and their remarks more valid.

9 The media have an agenda-setting function. Journalists have a 'middle-of-the-road', consensual outlook informed by their common background and experience. They frame events within a very narrow range, limiting the breadth of possible discussion.

10 Personnel in the media act as 'gatekeepers' – they exclude some stories from the news and include others.

Adapted from GUMG's *Bad News* (1976), *More Bad News* (1980), *Really Bad News* (1982), *War and Peace News* (1985), London: Routledge

Item B Tabloid shift in TV news

Broadcasts today – with the exceptions of the BBC's late evening news and Channel 4 news – have shifted away from political stories and foreign affairs towards a tabloid diet dominated by consumer affairs and crime.

The survey of more than 700 evening news programmes between 1975 and 1999 showed that while the 'dire warnings' of dumbing down have not been borne out, the early evening news programmes on BBC and ITV were pursuing a more tabloid agenda.

By contrast, the BBC's late evening news and Channel 4's news programmes have maintained a broadsheet approach. In the BBC's 6 pm news, tabloid content – such as crime, consumer and showbusiness stories – rose from 18 to 30 per cent. Foreign coverage also rose, but numbers of broadsheet stories, such as politics, wars and social affairs, fell.

On ITV, the trend towards tabloid stories in the early evening news was even more marked, more than doubling from 15 per cent in 1975 to 33 per cent in 1999. Content in the relaunched ITV evening news was broadly the same.

Tabloid stories in the BBC's late evening news fell from 16 per cent in 1975 to 13 per cent in 1999. The proportion of foreign stories increased from 24 to 43 per cent.

Adapted from *The Guardian*, 10 July 2000

1 **Explain what is meant by 'hierarchy of access' (Item A). (2 marks)**

2 **Identify two of the groups who 'are asked for their opinion, as they are seen to be more reliable and their remarks more valid' (Item A). (4 marks)**

3 **Suggest three reasons why the role of 'gatekeeper' is important (Item A). (6 marks)**

4 **Identify and briefly explain two trends in news reporting identified by the research described in Item B. (8 marks)**

5 **Examine the view that the news is biased in favour of the rich and powerful. (20 marks)**

6 **Using information from the Items and elsewhere, assess the view that the news is a 'window on the world'. (20 marks)**

How do the media affect people?

Protesters demonstrate outside the BBC against the showing of the opera Jerry Springer on TV in January 2005

TV and music have a great influence on our students. You only have to hear them sing at a disco to realize they learn lyrics of very sensuous songs off by heart but find it difficult to recite 'Our Father'. It may be useful to discuss, as a class, the frequency of sexual innuendo and references in shows they commonly watch.

What would God say to the following if He appeared before them today?

● Authors of corrupt novels, newspapers, plays, films and indecent styles.
● Those who display eroticism (openly sexual behaviour) in modern music.
● Those who distribute condoms and other contraceptives to the youth of today, knowing full well what behaviour this encourages, and knowing full well that 100 per cent 'safe sex' is a myth.
● Parents who allow their children to watch suggestive and lustful TV shows.

The passage above right is adapted from 'Teachers for Life', an advice leaflet for teachers, produced by a Catholic teachers' group in Western Australia.

1 What is the writer concerned about?

2 What sort of music and TV programmes do you think the writer might object to?

3 What do you think is the writer's view of TV audiences and of young people in particular?

4 To what extent do you agree with the views expressed in the extract? What arguments could be presented against these views?

Groups such as the Christian Right in the extract above, fundamentalist clerics and many Conservative politicians, as well as pressure groups such as Mediawatch (formerly the National Viewers' and Listeners' Association), blame the media for corrupting the morals of society – especially the young. According to such groups, the media are responsible for family breakdown, crime, abortion, underage sex and even homosexuality!

But concern about the media is not just limited to these kinds of groups. Many feminists and Marxists also feel that media messages can be corrupting – for example, by encouraging male violence against women, or by brainwashing viewers into being passive consumers.

Most ideas about media effects start by setting out an overall relationship between the media and their audience. For this reason they are often called 'models of media effects'.

'Hypodermic syringe' model

In 1957, Vance Packard wrote a famous book about advertising called *The Hidden Persuaders*. He described how ordinary people were persuaded to consume goods without being aware of the techniques being used. His view was that the mass media were so powerful that they could directly 'inject' messages into the audience, or that, like a 'magic bullet', the message could be precisely targeted at an audience, who would automatically fall down when hit. This view has become known as the **hypodermic syringe model**. According to this model, the audience is:

● passive – weak and inactive
● homogeneous – all the same
● 'blank pages' to be written on – with the media exerting a powerful influence that provokes an immediate response from the audience.

Sociologists are generally very critical of this model. They believe that it fails to recognize the different social characteristics of audience members. They also believe that people are not as vulnerable as the hypodermic syringe model implies. Nevertheless, it has been very influential in **media regulation** in The UK. The 9 p.m. watershed and age restrictions on video hire, along with a range of other controls, have made censorship of the British media among the most restrictive in the free world.

Cultural effects model

The **cultural effects model** also sees the media as a very powerful influence, but it recognizes that the media audience is very diverse. People have different backgrounds and experiences and this means that they interpret what they see, read and hear in different ways. A programme about life in an inner-London borough, for example, may be interpreted as evidence of racial conflict and deprivation, or as evidence of interesting cultural diversity, depending on who is watching.

However, those who produce the media do expect the audience to respond to their work in a particular way. This anticipated response is known as the **preferred (or dominant) reading**. Those who lack direct experience of the issue presented by the media (in many cases the majority of the audience) are likely to accept this preferred reading.

In the Marxist version of this model, the ideas of the dominant groups in society – i.e. ruling-class ideology (see Unit 1, p. 17) – continually bombard audiences from every direction. It becomes difficult for anyone to retain a critical viewpoint. In the end, most people come to believe that ruling-class ideas are right. They consent to the dominance of the powerful without even realizing it. Many elderly people, for example, are so taken in by the media portrayal of social security claimants as 'scroungers' that they don't even claim the benefits that are rightfully theirs.

Rather than having an immediate, direct effect, as the hypodermic syringe model claims, this model suggests that there is a slow, 'drip-drip' process taking place over a long period of time. Eventually, dominant values come to be shared by most people – values such as 'happiness is about possessions and money', 'you must look like the models in magazines', or 'most asylum seekers are just illegal immigrants'.

Active audience approaches

Other theories of media effects see the media as far less influential. They believe that people have considerable choice in the way they use and interpret the media. There are various versions of this view.

Selective filter model

Think of a sieve: some things pass through while others stay in the sieve. The **selective filter model** holds that media messages are similar: some get through, while others are ignored or rejected by the audience.

Klapper (1960) suggests that, for a media message to have any effect, it must pass through the following three filters:

- **Selective exposure** – A message must first be chosen to be viewed, read or listened to. Media messages can have no effect if no one sees or hears them! Choices depend upon people's interests, education, work commitments and so on.
- **Selective perception** – The messages have to be accepted. For example, some people may take notice of certain TV programmes, but reject or ignore others.
- **Selective retention** – The messages have to 'stick'. People have a tendency to remember only the things they broadly agree with.

Uses and gratifications model

Blumler and McQuail (1968) point out that people get what they want from the media. Old people may watch soaps for companionship or to experience family life, whilst young people may watch soaps for advice on relationships or so that they have something to talk about at school the next day. In other words, the media satisfy a range of social needs, and different people get different pleasures – or gratifications – from the media.

Structured interpretation model

This view suggests that the way people interpret **media texts** differs according to their class, age, gender, ethnic group and other sources of identity. Those who hold this view analyse how and why different groups receive media messages. The methods they use are called **reception analysis**.

This is a more optimistic view than the cultural effects model. Media messages may be interpreted in a variety of ways, and even though one interpretation is dominant (the preferred reading), it is not always accepted.

Morley (1980) argues that people choose to make one of three responses:

- Dominant – they go along with the views expressed in the media text.
- Oppositional – they oppose the views expressed.
- Negotiated – they reinterpret the views to fit in with their own opinions and values.

For example, let's say the news contains a report about the Notting Hill Carnival. The report focuses on 12 arrests for drug dealing. A preferred (or dominant) reading might be that Black people can't enjoy themselves without breaking the law. An **oppositional reading** might be that the police or the media are racist, focusing on drug-related crime unnecessarily. After all, 12 arrests are nothing, considering the millions who attend. A **negotiated reading** might be that there is probably a lot of drug use among Afro-Caribbeans, but that it's mostly cannabis use, which should, in the viewer's opinion, be legalized anyway.

These **active audience approaches** see the audience as interpreting media messages for themselves, and this makes it difficult to generalize about the effects of the media. Some of the most recent postmodern approaches go even further.

Rather than seeing the audience as an undifferentiated mass, or as divided into cultural or other groupings, they argue that generalizations about media effects and audiences are impossible, since the same person may react to the same media message in different ways in different situations. Postmodern thinking on the media will be examined more fully in Topic 7 (see pp. 154–7).

How does this cartoon illustrate the structured interpretation model?

Check your understanding

1 How can the hypodermic syringe model be supported by people of very different views, e.g. Conservative politicians as well as some Marxists and feminists?

2 In what way does the cultural effects model suggest a 'drip drip' approach to media effects?

3 What is the difference between oppositional and negotiated readings?

4 Give two similarities and two differences between the cultural effects model and the hypodermic syringe model.

5 'It is no coincidence that Hollywood films were at their height of popularity during the war years.' How does this statement illustrate the uses and gratifications model?

research ideas

● Complete a media grid for each member of your household, detailing one day's media use. Follow this up by asking each person to state, for each viewing/listening slot, which of the following needs or gratifications it satisfied:

  – diversion (escape from routine)

  – interaction with others (companionship, conversation, etc.)

  – learning (information-seeking, education)

  – advice (personal development, etc.).

Compare their answers.

KEY TERMS

Active audience approaches theories that stress that the effects of the media are limited because people are not easily influenced.

Cultural effects model the view that the media are powerful in so far as they link up with other agents of socialization to encourage particular ways of making sense of the world.

Hypodermic syringe model the view that the media are very powerful and the audience very weak. The media can 'inject' their messages into the audience, who accept them uncritically.

Media regulation control of what we see, hear and read in the media from outside bodies.

Media text any media output, be it written, aural or visual, e.g. magazine article, photo, CD, film, TV or radio programme.

Negotiated reading an interpretation of a media text that modifies the intended (preferred) reading so that it fits with the audience member's own views.

Oppositional reading an interpretation of a media text that rejects its intended (preferred) reading.

Preferred (or **dominant**) **reading** the intended messages contained within the text.

Reception analysis research that focuses on the way individuals make meanings from media messages.

Selective exposure the idea that people only watch, listen or read what they want to.

Selective filter model the view that audience members allow only certain media messages through.

Selective perception the idea that people take notice only of certain media messages.

Selective retention the idea that people remember only certain media messages.

Structured interpretation model the view that people interpret media texts according to their various identities, e.g. class, gender, ethnic group.

Uses and gratifications model the view that people use the media for their own purposes.

Item A The War of the Worlds

A classic example of the powerful influence of the media was the radio broadcast in 1938 of H.G. Wells's book *The War of the Worlds*. The dramatized adaptation of an invasion of Martians into a rural area of New Jersey, USA, was so convincing that it generated mass hysteria in many American states. Significantly, though, not all of the six million listeners responded in the same way.

<< Long before the broadcast had ended, people all over the US were praying, crying, fleeing frantically to escape death from the Martians.>>

Research on the audience response was undertaken by Cantril (1940), who found that several factors affected the extent to which people believed the broadcast to be true. For example, listeners who had not heard the beginning of the programme were more likely to be taken in by it, and those who were not able to check out the story with neighbours, to 'reality test' it, were convinced by the broadcast and reacted accordingly. Radio news was at that time the only source of immediate knowledge about the world at large. As the programme was broadcast in the style of a news programme, listeners were more likely to treat it as real.

Adapted from Haralambos, M. (ed.) (1986) *Sociology: New Directions*, Ormskirk: Causeway Press

Item B Moral issues and bias

The Coal Dispute of 1984 (referred to as the 'miners' strike' by the media) occurred as a result of the decision by the Coal Board to close pits much earlier and in greater number than had been agreed in writing. The police and miners were involved in well-publicized confrontations. The media blamed the miners for both the strike and the resulting violence. They also greatly exaggerated the alleged lack of solidarity among the miners by constantly referring to the 'drift back to work', which, in fact, was the case for only a small minority of miners.

In order to expose the main messages received by the audience, Philo asked audience members, in groups, a year later, to write their own media stories based on photographs. The respondents were shown pictures of violence and asked to put together a news item. Philo found that many of the audience members produced similar stories, focusing on the violence of the picket lines and on the phrase 'drift back to work' (implying that the strike was failing).

Taken at face value this would imply that the audience were all passive victims of the media, as the hypodermic syringe model suggests. However, in follow-up interviews, Philo discovered that the respondents were perfectly able to create stories 'in the style of a biased media', while not actually believing these stories.

While all believed in the media's view that violence is wrong, there was not common agreement on who should be blamed. Working-class trade unionists blamed the police, whilst middle-class professionals were more likely to blame the pickets for starting the trouble.

Adapted from Philo, G. (ed.) (1990) *Seeing and Believing: The Influence of Television*, London: Routledge

1 Explain what is meant by the 'hypodermic syringe' model (Item B). (2 marks)

2 Suggest two ways in which the War of the Worlds example (Item A) appears to support the hypodermic syringe model. (4 marks)

3 Suggest three ways in which the media might have distorted the reality of the strike (Item B). (6 marks)

4 Identify and briefly explain two criticisms of the hypodermic syringe model. (8 marks)

5 Examine sociological criticisms of the cultural effects model. (20 marks)

6 Using material from the Items and elsewhere, assess the view that, rather than having a uniform effect, the media mean different things to different people. (20 marks)

web.tasks

1 There is a great deal of concern about lack of control of the internet. Search the web using the keyword 'censorship' to find out arguments for and against regulation of the internet.

2 Find the website of the Advertising Standards Authority. Look up some of its adjudications (decisions about complaints) and see to what extent you agree with them.

Is there too much violence in the media?

gettingyouthinking

<< Last month, the graphically violent Manhunt game was pulled from the shelves of some retailers, notably Dixons, after parents of a murdered schoolboy claimed his killer was obsessed with the Playstation 2 game. Stefan Pakeerah, 14, was beaten to death with a claw hammer and stabbed by Warren Leblanc, 17, who had lured him to a local park. >>

<< It comes billed as 'the most frightening game ever created', but as Doom 3 went on sale in British stores yesterday, its distributors dismissed accusations that the violence on screen can encourage violence off it.

The sci-fi horror game involves the shooter struggling against zombies, lost souls, demons, maggots and various other monsters unleashed from hell. Along the way, graphics depict exploding heads, chainsaws, axes and decapitations.

It has been granted an 18 rating by the British Board of Film Classification.

The original Doom was linked to the Columbine school massacre, when it was claimed that the teenage killers Eric Harris and Dylan Klebold were influenced by the violent nature of the game. >>

Adapted from *The Guardian*, 14 August 2004

1 Can you think of other examples of violent video games, films and song lyrics?

2 Do you think retailers were justified in removing Manhunt from their shelves?

3 What sorts of people do you think are most vulnerable to screen violence? Why?

4 What arguments could the distributors of Doom use to dismiss accusations that it would cause violence?

In 2003, about 200 million videos were rented and a further 100 million were purchased in the UK. Probably at least twice this number of people watched these videos. Over 30 million video games were sold. Even today, with television audiences increasingly fragmented across multiple channels, a recent broadcast of the 'violent' movie *Die Hard 2* attracted an audience of over 7 million people on just one night. (Broadcast/BARB 2004). The sheer size of these audiences for popular media have long fuelled speculation that they must have some profound impact on society – that out there, in such vast populations, some – perhaps many – disturbed individuals will act out the violence and horror which they have seen on their screens. And perhaps even worse, there must be a 'drip-drip-drip' effect on everyone. Every year, some event makes such speculation newsworthy or some research is produced where scientists are said to have 'proved the link' between video violence and violence in society.

On 12 February 1993, two 10-year-old boys abducted toddler James Bulger from a shopping mall. They tortured and killed him, according to the tabloid press, by mimicking scenes from a video – *Child's Play 3*. Later that year, the judge, in sentencing the boys, speculated on the significant role that the film had played. An obvious example of the dangerous effects of screen violence, you may think. However, things were not quite that simple. The police stated that there was no evidence at all that either of James's killers had seen the video.

This case illustrates the controversy and confusion that surround the 70 years of debate and research about violence and the media. In the main, researchers have fallen into one of two major camps:

1 *the effects approach* – those who think that everyone is affected in much the same way by screen violence
2 *alternative approaches* – those who think that the media's effect depends on who is viewing and the situation in which that viewing takes place.

The effects approach

The main model underpinning the **effects approach** is the hypodermic syringe model (see Topic 4). The audience is seen as a homogeneous (similar) mass who interpret the media in the same uncritical way and are powerless to resist its influence. A direct **correlation** (connection) is believed to exist between screen violence and violence in society. The following are four examples of the possible effects of media violence.

1 'Copycat' violence

In 1963, Bandura *et al.* showed three groups of children real, film and cartoon examples of a self-righting doll ('bobo doll') being attacked with mallets, whilst a fourth group saw no violent activity. After being introduced to a room full of exciting toys, the children in each group were made to feel frustrated by being told that the toys were not for them. They were then led to another room containing a bobo doll, where they were observed through a one-way mirror. The three groups who had

been shown the violent activity – whether real, film or cartoon – all behaved more aggressively than the fourth group. This is the effect known as **copycat violence**.

2 Desensitization

A more subtle approach was adopted by Hilda Himmelweit (1958). She accepted that viewing one programme was not going to affect behaviour in everyone – only in the most disturbed. She suggested, however, that prolonged exposure to programmes portraying violence may have a 'drip-drip' effect, such that individuals are socialized into accepting violent behaviour as normal.

3 Catharsis

Not all effects research focuses on negative effects. Fesbach and Sanger (1971) found that screen violence can actually provide a safe outlet for people's aggressive tendencies (known as **catharsis**). They looked at the effects of violent TV on teenagers. A large sample of boys from both private schools and residential homes were fed a diet of TV for six weeks. Some groups could only watch aggressive programmes, whilst others were made to watch non-aggressive programmes. The observers noted at the end of the study that the groups who had seen only aggressive programmes were actually less aggressive in their behaviour than the others.

4 Sensitization

Some argue that seeing the effects of violence and the pain and suffering that it causes will sensitize viewers – make them more aware of its consequences and so less inclined to commit violent acts. When filmed in a certain way (i.e. ever more graphically), violent scenes can be so shocking as to put people off violence.

Criticisms of the effects approach

- Most effects studies have been conducted using a scientific approach. Some critics say that this makes their findings questionable, as people do not behave as naturally under laboratory conditions as they would in normal life.
- Effects studies often ignore other factors that may be causing violent or antisocial behaviour, such as peer-group influences.
- Effects theorists do not always distinguish between different kinds of screen violence, such as fictional violence and real-life violence in news and current affairs programmes.
- Recent research (see Morrison's work below) shows that the context in which screen violence occurs affects its impact.
- Effects studies often take a patronizing view of children, seeing them as vulnerable to the damaging effects of the media. Recent work, such as that of Buckingham (see below), shows that children are much more **media literate** than researchers have assumed.

Despite these criticisms, the effects approach remains an influence on government policy. A report by Professor Elizabeth Newsom (1994) presented a strong case for greater controls over the renting of videos and, despite a wave of criticism of its use of the effects approach, led directly to the Video Recordings Act, which gave videos certificates and restricted their availability to children. However, the evidence claimed for television's effects is really quite weak. For example, most of the studies which have looked at how children are affected when television first arrives, have found surprisingly little change. The last study was in St Helena, a British colony in the South Atlantic Ocean, which received television for the first time in 1995. Before and after studies showed no change in children's antisocial or prosocial behaviour (Charlton *et al.* 2000).

Alternative approaches

These approaches focus on the audience as a heterogeneous (diverse) and active group, with different social characteristics and different ways of using and interpreting the media. They draw on 'uses and gratifications', 'cultural effects' and other 'active audience' theories (see Topic 4). The following are four examples of recent research using alternative approaches.

1   Buckingham (1993) looked at how children interpret media violence. He criticizes effects research for failing to recognize that gender, class and ethnic identities are crucially important, as is the changing identity of the child as they grow up. Buckingham does not accept that children are especially vulnerable to TV violence. He argues that children are much more sophisticated in their understanding and more media literate than previous researchers have assumed.

2   Julian Wood (1993) conducted a small-scale study of boys' use of video. He attended an after-school showing of a horror video in the home of one of the boys (the boy's parents were away). Wood describes the boys' comments in detail, and is able to demonstrate that, in this situation, the horror film is used almost as a rite of passage. The boys can prove their heterosexuality to each other, behave in a macho way, swear and, above all, demonstrate their fearlessness. Rather than being a corrupting influence, video violence is merely a part of growing up.

3   Morrison (1999) showed a range of clips – including scenes from *Brookside*, news footage and excerpts from violent films – to groups of women, young men and war veterans. All of the interviewees felt that the most disturbing clip was a man beating his wife in *Ladybird, Ladybird* (see left-hand photograph below), a film by Ken Loach. It caused distress because of the realism of the setting, the strong language and the perceived unfairness, and also because viewers were concerned about the effect on the child actors in the scene. By contrast, the clip from *Pulp Fiction* – in which a man is killed out of the blue during an innocent conversation, spraying blood and chunks of brain around a car – was seen as 'humorous' and 'not violent', even by women over the age of 60, because there was lighthearted dialogue. The right-hand photograph below shows a typically 'messy' scene from the film *Pulp Fiction*.

4   Marsha Kinder's (1999) edited collection of essays, *Kid's Media Culture,* features research conducted within different sociological traditions from both macro- and

Scenes from Ladybird, Ladybird *(left) and* Pulp Fiction *(right) – which film do viewers find the more disturbing?*

microsociology. She asserts that the essays situate children's relationships with media products within broader leisure activities, as well as within complex networks of social relations at home, at school and in the broader public sphere (neighbourhood, region, nation). In all of the essays in this volume, then, the kids are not portrayed as timeless, innocent victims who desperately need to be protected from popular culture. Rather, they are seen as historically situated participants who actively collaborate in the production and negotiation of cultural meanings.

A mourner breaks down after the Columbine High School shootings in Denver, USA, in 1999. Thirteen people were killed by two student gunmen Eric Harris and Dylan Klebold

Guy Cumberbatch
The effects of screen violence

Over the years, there have been over 3,500 research studies into the effects of screen violence, encompassing film, TV, video and more recently, computer and video games. This is according to a report commissioned by the Video Standards Council and undertaken by Dr Guy Cumberbatch, Chartered Psychologist and Director of the Communications Research Group, based in Birmingham, who has specialized in the study of media violence for over 25 years.

His Report, published in 2004, concentrated on the more recent epidemic of research, with strong concentration on the most recent, in which computer and video games feature strongly as the subject matter.

Particular reference to computer and video games is made in an oft-quoted USA study by Anderson and Dill (2000), following the Columbine High School massacre. On this infamous study, Dr Cumberbatch concludes:

<< *Anderson and Dill (2000) suggest that violent video games were probably a factor in the massacre at Columbine High School. However, as social scientists,* they should be ashamed of themselves in offering only second-hand hearsay support for this assertion. Such claims are very common, perhaps often made in good faith, and sound very plausible, but they have never stood up to scrutiny. >>

Dr Cumberbatch states that in 1988, Kate Adie researched for BBC's *Panorama* what seemed to be the best-evidenced cases where a crime had been clearly linked to the mass media. In no case was such a link supported by the evidence to a level that would be acceptable to a serious investigative journalist. Every case turned out to be mere speculation – often by reckless journalists. Cumberbatch concludes that the relationship that audiences enjoy with violence in entertainment is a rich and multilayered one, which studies of video violence effects choose to ignore completely. To suggest that these studies are misleading would be too kind. Many appear simply deceitful. However, the absence of convincing research evidence that media violence causes harm does not mean that we should necessarily celebrate it and encourage more. There may be moral, aesthetic, philosophical, religious or humanistic grounds on which we might consider that excessive representations of violence are a matter of some public interest.

In the Conclusions to his Report, Cumberbatch states:

<< *The real puzzle is that anyone looking for research evidence could draw any conclusions about the pattern, let alone argue with such confidence and even passion that it demonstrates the harm of violence on TV, in film/video and in video games. While tests of statistical significance are a vital tool of the social sciences, they seem to have been more often used in this field as instruments of torture on the data until it confesses something that could justify a publication in a scientific journal. If one conclusion is possible, it is that the jury is still not out. It's never been in. Media violence has been subjected to a lynch mob mentality with almost any evidence used to prove guilt.* >>

Adapted from the Video Standards Council website (www.videostandards.org.uk)

---

1 What does Cumberbatch say about the validity of recent research findings on media violence?

2 He concludes that there may be reasons other than alleged causal effects for being concerned about screen violence. What do you think he means by this?

Where are we now?

So, thousands of studies later, we have not really made much progress and many questions remain. Are some people less able to distinguish between artificial and real violence? Is some censorship justified in order to protect us? But would more censorship push violence underground, so that even more disturbing material might become available? Does the way in which violence is depicted make a difference to its impact – for example, if there are differences in power between the participants, or if humour is involved?

The more we seek to find the answers to questions about the effects of media violence, the more questions seem to be generated.

web.tasks

1 **Search the worldwide web to investigate one recent dramatic act of violence that has been linked to the media over the last few years – perhaps the murder of James Bulger or Stefan Pakeerah (see 'Getting you thinking' on p. 136), the Dunblane massacre or the Littleton shootings. To what extent is screen violence blamed? What actual evidence is put forward to link media violence to the murders?**

2 **Go to the page of the American Psychiatric Association's website that covers the effects of media violence at www.psych.org/public_info/media_violence.cfm**

   What does it suggest about the evidence on this issue?

   Compare this page with the view of media sociologist David Gauntlett at www.theory.org.uk/effects.htm

   What criticisms does Gauntlett make of the 'effects model'?

Check your understanding

1 Explain in your own words what is meant by the claim that there is a correlation between screen violence and violence in society.

2 How might the media desensitize their audience to violence?

3 Explain in your own words three limitations of the effects approach.

4 What evidence is there that the effects approach still has its supporters today?

5 Identify and explain three insights into the nature of the audience that critics of effects approaches have put forward.

research ideas

● Investigate what types of violence are considered disturbing by people of different ages, genders, classes or ethnic groups. Present your findings quantitatively.

● Conduct a content analysis of part of one evening's TV programmes on any one channel. Add up the number of times acts of violence are depicted. After noting down each act of violence, explain the type of programme (e.g. news, cartoon, drama) and the type of violence (e.g. real, humorous).

   What do your results indicate about the amount and type of violence on television?

KEY TERMS

Catharsis the process of relieving tensions – for example, violence on screen providing a safe outlet for people's violent tendencies.

Correlation a relationship between two or more things, where one characteristic is directly affected by another.

'Copycat' violence violence that occurs as a result of copying something that is seen in the media.

Desensitization the process by which, through repeated exposure to media violence, people come to accept violent behaviour as normal.

Effects approach an approach based on the hypodermic syringe model (see Topic 4) which believes that the media have direct effects on their audience.

Media literate an intelligent, critical and informed attitude to the media.

exploring violence and the media

Item A The viewing habits of young offenders

A study by Hagell and Newburn for the Policy Studies Institute compared young offenders' viewing habits with those of non-offending teenagers. They found that there were very few differences between the two groups in terms of what they watched, with hardly any having seen the films that were causing concern at the time. Few members of either group had a particular interest in violent output. The young offenders, in fact, generally had had less access to TVs, video, cable or satellite TV. Other factors beyond the media must be causing the differences in behaviour.

Adapted from A. Hagell and T. Newburn (1994) *Young Offenders and the Media: Viewing Habits*, London: PSI

Item B Crime and media violence

Thirty-seven of the top 40 UK software titles listed for 2004 are games. Twenty-three of those titles contain some sort of violence. Fourteen of those titles include graphic violence throughout the duration of the game. Some of the titles in this category include: *Tom Clancy's Splinter Cell: Pandora Tomorrow, Onimusha: Demon Siege, Full Spectrum Warrior, Medal of Honor: Rising Sun, Grand Theft Auto: Vice City, Red Dead Revolver, Hitman: Contracts* and *Soul Calibur II*.

In contrast, a look at the top 40 grossing films over one weekend (16 to 18 July 2004) only reveals 15 movies with any violence. Among those 15 movies, two were documentaries, and many were comedies or children's movies that contained some cartoon-like violence. A comedy about dodgeball, a Harry Potter movie, and *Shrek 2* were included in the list containing violence.

Despite the exposure of young males to an increasing diet of first-person gaming violence, the British Crime Survey of 2000 showed a 20 per cent fall in victims of violence over the previous four years. In the early 1950s, one quarter of all violent crime recorded was 'serious' violent crime. Today it is less than 10 per cent. This is despite the fact that, with the advent of mobile phones, people are more likely to report crime than in the past. Overall, the idea that we now live in a more violent society is very questionable and, certainly, since computer/video games have become prevalent, crime has gone down.

Source: Sims, L. and Myhill, A. (2001) *Policing and the Public, Findings from the British Crime Survey 2000*, London: Home Office

141

Unit 4 Mass media

1 In your own words, explain what is meant by 'desensitization'. (2 marks)

2 Suggest two reasons why the PSI study concludes that 'other factors beyond the media must be causing the differences in behaviour' between the young offenders and the schoolchildren (Item A). (4 marks)

3 Suggests three reasons why it might be said that society is less violent than formerly. (6 marks)

4 Identify and briefly explain two criticisms of the theory that links screen violence and video games with real violence (Item B). (8 marks)

5 Examine the problems with the view that the social situation of audience members affects the way in which media messages are received and understood. (20 marks)

6 Using material from the Items and elsewhere, assess the view that violence in the media should be subject to stricter controls. (20 marks)

gettingyouthinking

Look at these images of women, presented by the media, and then answer the following questions.

1 Which of these women are playing stereotyped female roles? What are these roles?

2 What do these photographs tell us about the way in which women are portrayed in the media?

3 To what extent do you think that images of women in the media are changing?

As women have begun to achieve more visibility outside the home and to compete on a more equal basis with men in the workplace, you might expect this to be reflected in the mass media. Sociological research suggests, however, that, although there is some recent evidence of greater equality, the roles allocated to the sexes across a range of media – such as advertising, television and film – have been restricted in the following ways:

- Women have been allocated a limited range of roles.
- Women are less visible in the media than men.
- Women have been presented as ideals.
- Women have been selected to appeal to men.
- Men have been seen as aggressors, women as victims.

Let's look at these issues in more detail.

A limited range of roles

Women are represented in a narrow range of social roles in the media, whilst men perform the full range of social and occupational roles. Women are especially found in domestic settings – as busy housewives, contented mothers, eager consumers and so on. Tuchman *et al.* (1978) adds sexual and romantic roles to this list.

Women are rarely shown in high-status occupational roles, such as doctors or lawyers. If they are, they are often shown to have problems in dealing with their 'unusual' circumstances. For example, they are portrayed as unfulfilled (motherhood is sometimes offered as the answer to this), as unattractive, as unstable, or as having problems with relationships. If they have children, successful women are sometimes shown as irresponsible, with their children getting into trouble due to their emotional neglect. Men are rarely portrayed in this way.

Whilst these are still the primary representations, there has recently been an increase in the number of 'stronger' roles for women – for example, in TV dramas such as *Sex in the City*, which also have relatively weak 'dorky' men. *Buffy the Vampire Slayer* broke new ground by becoming hugely popular within the typically male-dominated world of science fiction. The lead character is more confident and assertive than many male heroes in contemporary film and TV, such as the Superman character in the *New Adventures of Superman*, who is more caring and sensitive than in earlier versions. Soap operas also tend to promote independent and assertive female characters, whereas male soap characters tend to be weaker. This may be because soaps focus on domestic issues, the only legitimate (accepted) area for female authority.

Visibility

At the beginning of the 1990s, 89 per cent of voice-overs for television commercials were male, probably because the male voice is seen to represent authority. Women were the main stars of only 14 per cent of mid-evening television programmes. Analysis of Hollywood films at that time indicated that few women stars were seen by the major studios as being able to carry a film by themselves, although women were slowly moving into lead roles in traditionally masculine areas, such as science fiction. There are indications that things are improving, with the male-to-female split in speaking parts in prime-time TV now at about 60/40. There are also a growing number of female leads in Hollywood films, such as the *Alien* trilogy and *Tomb Raider*. As Haralambos and Holborn (2004) point out, however, earlier forms of gender representation do not go away. They live on as old programmes recycled on cable and satellite television.

New media also seem to be slow in catching up. A content analysis of 33 popular Nintendo and Sega Genesis video games revealed that there were no female characters in 41 per cent of the games. Females were either absent or cast in the role of victim. In 28 per cent of the games, females were portrayed as sex objects. Almost 80 per cent of the games required violence or aggression as part of the strategy. Almost half of the games included violence directed specifically at other people, with 21 per cent of the games depicting direct violence against women. Most of the game characters were Caucasian (Dietz 1998).

Female issues may still be **marginalized** by the media. Most newspapers have 'women's pages' which focus on women as a special group with special – often emotional – needs. Such pages tend to concentrate on beauty and slimming. Tuchman uses the term '**symbolic annihilation**' to describe the way in which women in the media are absent, condemned or trivialized. Women's sport in particular is underrepresented. Research by Newbold *et al.* (2002) into TV sport presentation shows that what little coverage there is tends to 'sexualize, trivialize and devalue women's sporting accomplishments'. Consider, for example, the way women tennis stars in particular are victims of the male gaze, in a similar way to female characters in many films (see under 'Sex appeal' on p. 144).

Women are also absent from top jobs in the media. An analysis of powerful positions generates the following facts: the majority of media owners are men, as are the higher position holders within media empires. For example, out of 30 top BBC executives in 1996, only four were female. In newspapers, in 1995/96 only 20 per cent of positions of significant decision-making power were held by women. In 2005, fewer than 5 per cent of the chief executives of the largest media companies in Britain and fewer than 10 per cent of editors of national newspapers are female (Equal Opportunities Commission 2005).

Women as ideals

Ferguson (1983) conducted a content analysis of women's magazines between 1949 and 1974, and 1979 and 1980. She notes that such magazines are organized around 'a cult of femininity', which promotes an ideal where excellence is achieved through caring for others, the family, marriage and appearance. Modern female magazines, especially those aimed at teenagers, are moving away from these stereotypes – although Ferguson argues that even these tend to focus on 'him, home and looking good (for him)'. Winship (1987), however, stresses the supportive roles such magazines play in the lives of women, especially as many women are largely excluded from the masculine world of work and leisure. She argues that such magazines present women with a broader range of options than ever before, and that they tackle problems that have been largely ignored by the male-dominated media, such as domestic violence and child abuse. Contemporary women's magazines have moved on a great deal from their historical origins, offering visions of femininity that involve independence and confidence as well as beauty and domestic concerns. However, in magazines like *More*, *Red* and *New Woman* women are still encouraged to look good in order to attract men.

On the other hand, it could be argued that the new crop of men's magazines, such as *Men's Health*, do exactly the same for men. However, the feminist response would be that two wrongs don't make a right; both of these genres are still perpetuating an obsession with appearance that discriminates against women.

It is still the case that most women in films and on television (especially presenters) tend to be under 30. Physical looks, sex appeal and, primarily, youth seem to be necessary attributes for women to be successful in television and in the cinema. The same is not true for men, who are still accepted as sexually appealing until much later in life.

Wolf (1990) points out that the media, especially advertising, present a particular physical image as the 'normal' or 'ideal' body image for women to have, even though this image may be unattainable for the majority of women. Some commentators, such as Orbach (1991), have linked such images to anorexia and bulimia in teenage girls.

Sex appeal

Women are often presented as sexual objects to be enjoyed by men. The most extreme media version of this is pornography and 'Page 3 girls' in newspapers. Mulvey (1975) argues that film-makers employ a 'male gaze', whereby the camera lens essentially 'eyes up' the female characters, providing erotic pleasure for men.

Men's style magazines – such as *FHM*, *Maxim* and *Loaded* – encourage young men to dress, smell and consume in particular ways. There is, however, less of a burden on men to change themselves to conform to this ideal. Whilst women may feel that they need to conform in order to ensure that they are desirable, it is more of an option for men.

Buckingham (1993) argues that many boys and probably most men fear being labelled 'effeminate'. The apparent **feminization of masculinity** has therefore to be offset by more conspicuous and 'macho' behaviour. The 'new lad' that has emerged is supposedly counter-balanced by the 'ladette' (e.g. Sara Cox and Denise Van Outen), who leers at males through an alcoholic haze and is also aggressively sexual. In new magazines for young women, such as *More*, girls are encouraged to be sexual aggressors rather than sex objects. Whilst this may appear to be evidence of equality, some feminist critics argue that the outcome is to make women more available to sexual exploitation by men – which is particularly concerning, given that the rise in binge drinking among young women can make them vulnerable to rape and date rape.

Male aggressor, female victim

Many people are concerned about the media's presentation of sexual violence against women. A Channel 4 series, *Hard News*, analysed more than 600 articles in ten national newspapers in early 1990. They found that, despite the fact that such crime only makes up 2 per cent of all recorded crime, almost 70 per cent of crime stories focused on rape. Such stories were often distorted in their reporting. Rape victims were often stereotyped as either 'good' women (e.g. virgins, mothers) who had been violated, or 'bad' women who led men on. Newspapers often **sensationalized** cases and focused on what they saw as the most 'titillating' aspects – usually the details of the defendant's evidence.

Joan Smith (1989) notes how the female fear of violent assault is used as a basis for many films. These films may add to the stock of fear that already exists in society. They contribute to the notion of women as 'vulnerable and potential victims' of the superior strength of men. Yet women are also presented as needing the protection of males. 'Female fear sells films. It's a box office hit. … Terror, torture, rape, mutilation and murder are handed to actresses by respectable directors as routinely as tickets on a bus. No longer the stock in trade only of pornographers and video-nasty producers, they can be purchased any day at a cinema near you' (Smith 1989).

Changing representations of men in film

During the 1980s, action films such as *Commando*, *Die Hard* and *Predator* paraded the bodies of their male heroes in advanced stages of both muscular development and undress. One film in particular, *Rambo: First Blood Part II*, starring Sylvester Stallone, became a particular focus for concern. The figure of Rambo has been taken to represent the re-emergence of a threatening, physical form of masculinity. In an overview of the period, Jonathan Rutherford (1988) put forward the idea that there existed two key images of masculinity in the late 20th century. He termed these images, 'new man' and 'retributive man'. For Rutherford, images of the new man attempt – partly in a response to feminism – to express men's repressed emotions, revealing a more feminized image. Against this, the face of retributive man represents the struggle to reassert a traditional masculinity; a tough authority.

More recently, male violence in cinema has acquired a glamour and stylishness that seems to celebrate the more traditional **representations** of masculinity. Films like *Lock Stock and Two Smoking Barrels* and *Face Off* present men who gain admiration by solving their problems through violence. These kinds of films are currently outnumbering those that represent alternative views of masculinity, such as *The Full Monty*. However, gratuitous violence is no longer the sole province of the sadistic male, with a growing number of violent films with leading female characters, such as *Kill Bill 1* and *2* and *Crouching Tiger, Hidden Dragon*.

Explanations of gender representations

Feminists have been very critical of the representations of men and women in the media. However, they differ in their emphasis. (See Unit 1, Topic 4, pp. 18–19, for explanations of the different types of feminism.)

- *Liberal feminists* believe that media representations are lagging behind women's achievements in society. However, they also believe that the situation is improving as the number of female journalists, editors and broadcasters increases.
- *Socialist and Marxist feminists* believe that stereotypical images of men and women are a by-product of the need to make a profit. The male-dominated media aim to attract the largest audience possible, and this leads to an emphasis on the traditional roles of men and women.
- *Radical feminists* feel strongly that the media reproduce patriarchy. Traditional images are deliberately transmitted by male-dominated media to keep women oppressed in a narrow range of roles.

Not everyone accepts these kinds of feminist analysis. Critics argue that they underestimate women's ability to see through stereotyping. Pluralists (see Topic 1, p. 119) believe that the media simply reflect social attitudes and public demand. They argue that the media are meeting both men and women's needs – although the question remains: to what extent are the media actually creating those needs in the first place?

David Gauntlett
Men's magazines

There is a generation of younger men who have adapted to the modern world (in a range of ways), who have grown up with women as their equals, and who do not feel threatened by these social changes. These men and their cultures are largely ignored by the problem-centred discourse of masculinity studies.

Because of this, older self-proclaimed gender-aware men and women would almost certainly fail to understand the playful, humorous discourse about gender that circulates in men's magazines. (These magazines are not wholly antisexist, and there is a legitimate concern that dim readers will take 'joke sexism' literally, of course, but the more significant observation should perhaps be that sexism has shifted from being the expression of a meaningful and serious ideology in former times, to being a resource for use in silly jokes today). The magazines are often centred on helping men to be considerate lovers, useful around the home, healthy, fashionable and funny – in particular, being able to laugh at themselves. To be obsessed about the bits which superficially look like 'a reinscription of masculinity' is to miss the point. Men's magazines are not perfect vehicles for the transformation of gender roles, by any means, but they play a more important, complex and broadly positive role than most critics suggest.

Adapted from Gauntlett, D. (2002)
Media, Gender and Identity: An Introduction,
London: Routledge

1 What does the author mean by the 'playful, humorous discourse about gender that circulates in men's magazines'? Give examples.

2 Do you agree that men's and women's lifestyle magazines 'play a more important, complex and broadly positive role than most critics suggest'?

Check your understanding

1. What might be the reason why women often have independent and assertive roles in soap operas?

2. Describe the differences in gender representation in top positions in the media.

3. How does Winship argue that women's magazines can be supportive?

4. What problems are associated with the 'ideal' body image for women?

5. How does Buckingham explain the emergence of the 'new lad'?

6. According to Joan Smith, what are the effects of media representations of women as victims?

7. How do feminists explain the representations of women in the media?

research ideas

- Individually or in groups, conduct a content analysis of a soap opera, a news broadcast, a game show and a TV drama.
  - How many men and women appear?
  - How much time does each gender spend on screen?
  - What roles do they play?
  - How typical is each programme of others of its kind?
  - What conclusions can you draw about men and women in the media?

- Compare the views of young men and young women about the representation of women in the media. You could do this by conducting in-depth interviews or by using a questionnaire. Try showing respondents examples of men's and women's magazines to get them talking.

web.task

David Gauntlett is the author of *Media, Gender and identity: an Introduction*. Go to his book's website at **www.theoryhead.com/gender**

Click on the discussions between him and other writers regarding issues of gender representations.

Read his article about the sexual assertiveness of young women's magazines. What do you think about Gauntlett's view of these magazines? Write a response either agreeing or disagreeing, explaining your reasons and e-mail it to David Gauntlett using the link provided at the end of the article.

KEY TERMS

Feminization of masculinity refers to men adopting behaviour traditionally associated with women, e.g. wearing make-up, showing concern over fashion.

Marginalized forced out of the mainstream.

Representation the way in which people are portrayed by the media.

Sensationalized exaggerated in order to excite an audience.

Symbolic annihilation term used by Tuchman to describe the way in which women in the media are absent, condemned or trivialized.

Item A Women in the press

Item B Women on television

Level of appearance by gender (terrestrial television)

Level of appearance	Male no.	(%)	Female no.	(%)	Total no.	(%)
Major role	1,482	16	1,080	23	2,562	18
Minor role	1,475	16	693	15	2,168	16
Incidental/interviewer	6,217	68	2,922	62	9,139	66
Total	9,174	100	4,695	100	13,869	100

Source: Broadcasting Standards Commission Report 1999, p. 100

Item C Women in the media

<< The presentation of women in the media is biased because it emphasizes women's domestic, sexual, consumer and marital activities to the exclusion of all else. Women are depicted as busy housewives, as contented mothers, as eager consumers and as sex objects. This does indeed indicate bias because, although similar numbers of men are fathers and husbands, the media has much less to say about these male roles; men are seldom presented nude, nor is their marital or family status continually quoted in irrelevant contexts. Just as men's domestic and marital roles are ignored, the media also ignore that well over half of British adult women go out to paid employment, and that many of both their interests and problems are employment related.>>

Tunstall, J. (1983) *The Media in Britain*,
London: Constable

1 Explain what is meant by the term 'presentation of women in the media' (Item C). (2 marks)

2 Compare the covers of the magazines in Item A. Identify two assumptions that they make about the interests of young men or young women. (4 marks)

3 Identify three patterns in the data in Item B. (6 marks)

4 Identify and briefly explain two reasons why more men appear on TV than women. (8 marks)

5 '... the media has much less to say about ... male roles; men are seldom presented nude, nor is their marital or family status continually quoted in irrelevant contexts' (Item C). Discuss how helpful this statement is in understanding the representation of men in the media. (20 marks)

6 Using material from the Items and elsewhere, assess the view that women's representation in the media is distorted and limited. (20 marks)

Media representations

gettingyouthinking

1 How do you think most people would interpret what is happening in this photograph?

2 Why will they think this?

3 What other possible interpretations can you think of?

In the photograph above, a Black, plain-clothes police officer leads some of his uniformed colleagues in chasing a suspect. However, many people are likely to interpret the photograph differently, believing that the Black man is being chased by the police. This mistake should come as no surprise, as many people do associate young Black men with criminality. Why is this? Perhaps the explanation lies with the **representation** of ethnic minorities in the media. Ethnic minorities tend to be either ignored by the media or, when they do actually appear, portrayed in distorted ways that owe more to **stereotypes** than to reality. But ethnic minorities are not the only groups who have reason to be concerned about their portrayal in the media. This topic will look at media representations of various groups.

Ethnic minorities

Old films, comics and adventure stories that portrayed Black people as happy, dancing savages with a brutal streak have,

thankfully, largely disappeared from modern television and films. However, the media still have a tendency to associate Black people with physical rather than intellectual activities, and to view them in stereotypical ways. The findings of recent research generally make for depressing reading:

- underrepresentation and stereotypical characterization in entertainment genres
- negative, problem-oriented portrayal in factual and news forms
- a tendency to ignore inequality and racism.

Black people are portrayed in the media in the following ways:

- *As criminal* – van Dijk (1991) conducted a content analysis of tens of thousands of news items across the world over several decades. He found that Black crime and violence are one of the most frequent issues in ethnic coverage. Black people, particularly African-Caribbeans, tend to be portrayed, especially in the tabloid press, as criminals – and more recently as members of organized criminal gangs. The word 'Black' is often used as a prefix if an offender is a member of an ethnic minority, e.g. 'a Black youth'. The word 'White' is rarely used in the same way. In a now famous study by Stuart Hall, *Policing the Crisis* (Hall *et al.* 1978), the alleged crime wave of Black muggers was cited as a moral panic (see p. 151) created by the establishment through the media to justify more repressive social control measures at a time when capitalism was in crisis. The truth is that a Black person is 36 times more likely to be the victim of a violent attack than a White person.

- *As a threat* – Tabloid newspapers are prone to panic about the numbers of ethnic minorities in the UK. It is often suggested that immigrants are a threat in terms of their 'numbers', because of the impact they might have on the supply of jobs, housing and other facilities. The same newspapers are also concerned about refugees and asylum seekers, who are allegedly coming to the UK to abuse the welfare state and take advantage of a more successful economy than their own.

- *As abnormal* – Some sections of the media are guilty of creating false cultural stereotypes around the value systems and norms of other cultures. For example, tabloid newspapers have run stories that suggest that Muslims have negative attitudes towards women. They claim that they 'force' daughters into arranged marriages against their will. The distinction between 'forced' marriage – an extremely rare occurrence, strongly disapproved of by Asian communities – and arranged marriage, which is based on mutual consent, is rarely made. A survey of Asian viewers, by the market research company Ethnic Focus (2003), cited the most common complaint, which was 'that the media divided Asians into two camps; either miserable folk being forced into loveless marriages or billionaires who had come to the UK with nothing and had now made a fortune.'

- *As unimportant* – Some sections of the media imply that the lives of White people are somehow more important than the lives of non-White people. News items about disasters in other countries are often restricted to a few lines or words, especially if the population is non-White. The misfortunes of one British person tend to be prioritized over the sufferings of thousands of foreigners.

- *As dependent* – As the government report *Viewing the World* (2000) points out, stories about less developed countries tend to focus on the 'coup–war–famine– starvation syndrome'. The implication of such stories, both in newspapers and on television, is that the problems of developing countries are the result of stupidity, tribal conflict, too many babies, laziness, corruption and unstable political regimes. It is implied that the governments of these countries are somehow inadequate because they cannot solve these problems. Such countries are portrayed as coming to the West for help time and time again. The idea that the poverty of developing countries may be due to their exploitation by the West is often ignored and neglected.

'One Britain was killed in a plane crash in South Africa today. The Kenyan airlines Airbus was carrying 320 passengers from Nairobi to Johannesburg. No one survived.'

Underrepresentation

Surveys of television, advertising and films indicate that Black people are underrepresented. When they do appear, the range of roles they play is very limited. Black people are rarely shown as ordinary citizens who just happen to be Black. More often they play 'Black' roles, their attitudes and behaviour being heavily determined by their ethnic identity. Some soaps, such as *Eastenders,* have, in fact, included Black and Asian characters as ordinary members of the community. However, its main rival on ITV, *Coronation Street*, has only recently begun to include Black characters despite its 40-year history and despite being set in what would long have been a multicultural area of Manchester.

Ghettoization

Some critics have commented on the recent tendency for ethnic issues and interests to be covered by specialized programming and channels. This, they claim, isolates mainstream audiences from minority cultures and further inhibits their understanding and tolerance. Also, the main channels may decide not to cover minority issues as they consider them to be well catered for elsewhere.

On a more positive note, the media have been very positive in their exposure of problems such as racism. The murder of the Black teenager Stephen Lawrence by White racists in 1993 received high-profile coverage, both on television and in the press. Even the *Daily Mail* presented a front-page story highlighting police racism, and attempted to 'name and shame' the racists who committed the murder.

The cast of BBC TV soap EastEnders at an awards ceremony

BBC research into race
Representation of ethnic minorities on TV

In a recent survey by the BBC in answer to the question 'Are ethnic minorities better represented on TV than they were 10 years ago?', the answers were as follows:

	Total	White	Black	Asian
Yes	78%	80%	73%	67%
No	8%	7%	12%	16%
Don't know	13%	12%	15%	17%

Source: BBC News Online special report: Race UK, 20–31 May 2002, conducted by ICM research for the BBC

1 **How might you criticize the phrasing of this question?**

Table 4.2 Attitudes shown towards characters in TV drama		
	Able-bodied characters (%)	Disabled characters (%)
Sympathy	7	34
Pity	2	12
Patronizing	14	30
Sadness	3	16
Fear	7	16
Avoidance	3	9
Attraction	43	33
Respect	51	39
Mocking	8	10
Abuse	13	15

Source: Cumberbatch, G. and Negrine, R. (1992) *Images of Disability on Television*, London: Routledge

An interesting recent development is media recognition of the influence of ethnic cultures on White culture. Comedy shows such as the *Ali G* show and *Goodness Gracious Me* highlight, albeit in a comic way, how Black youth subcultural styles have infiltrated the styles of both White and Asian youth.

The disabled

Ten per cent of the UK population are disabled, yet disabled people make up only 1.5 per cent of the characters we see on television. Table 4.2 above right shows that disabled characters who do appear tend to be subjected to negative emotional responses.

There have, however, been recent improvements, particularly in the cinema. Films such as *The Piano* (1992) and *Four Weddings and a Funeral* (1997) had disabled characters – with conditions as diverse as cerebral palsy, deafness, dumbness and blindness – leading fulfilling and independent lives.

The elderly

Whilst old age is generally represented as undesirable in the media, significant numbers of older middle-class males are portrayed in prominent social positions. In films and television, older men such as Michael Douglas are still seen as sexual partners to young women. Females, however, must match up to a youthful ideal all their lives. Even in non-fiction programming, such as news broadcasts, younger women tend to complement older men.

Soap operas often feature older people, but this reflects the perceived market for such programmes. Sitcoms tend to show the elderly as feeble, vague or cantankerous – just think of Victor Meldrew in *One Foot in the Grave*. The very old are underrepresented in all aspects of the media, and the problems of ageing, such as decline and dependency, are generally ignored.

Class

The upper classes are often seen in nostalgic representations which paint a rosy picture of a time when Britain was great, and honour, culture and good breeding prevailed. Wealth and social inequality are rarely critically examined. Examples of this type of representation include TV costume dramas such as *Pride and Prejudice*, and films such as *A Room With a View*.

The middle classes are over-represented in the media, possibly because most of the creative personnel in the media are themselves middle class. In news and current affairs, the middle classes dominate in positions of authority – the 'expert' is invariably middle class.

Jhally and Lewis (1992) found that, on American TV between 1971 and 1989, 90 per cent of characters were middle class, whilst the percentage of working-class characters over the period fell from 4 per cent to only 1 per cent. In the

UK, members of the working class tend to appear as criminals, single parents, 'welfare scroungers' or delinquent children. Soaps have tended to show working-class life in a more positive, if unrealistic, light – presenting an ideal of a tight-knit community with a shared history and mutual obligations. British cinema has tried to portray working-class life more realistically. In the 1960s, films such as *A Taste of Honey*, and *Saturday Night, Sunday Morning* examined the realities of domestic life. More recently, *Secrets and Lies* and *The Full Monty* have shown working-class problems in a sensitive way, challenging social inequality, racial intolerance and class conflict. Some TV comedy and drama, such as *The Royle Family*, has also begun to adopt a more naturalistic approach to working-class family life.

Gay men and lesbians

Until recently, gay people have generally been either invisible in the media or represented in a negative light – being stereotyped as either 'camp' gay men or 'butch' lesbian women.

Gay men were heavily stigmatized in the wake of the initial Aids reporting, but, since then, sexuality has been more openly discussed. Several celebrities have recently 'come out' (declared their sexual orientation publicly). These include Elton John,

George Michael, Stephen Gateley and Will Young. Lesbian sexual orientation has been embraced by mainstream female performers such as Madonna, Britney Spears and Christina Aguilera through stage shows in which the female performers have stunned audiences with open-mouth on-stage kisses.

It appears that homosexuality is now much more acceptable within the popular media. Graham Norton, the openly gay presenter of a popular TV chat show, has a huge following of mainly heterosexual viewers. Two of the last three winners of the *Big Brother* reality game show have been gay. Mainstream television dramas now explore the lives of gay people, while *Coronation Street*, the longest-running soap, has had two main storylines featuring a gay character and a transsexual character, both of whom have been sympathetically portrayed. Such acceptance may be less evident in the news media.

Youth and 'moral panics'

Young people are often presented as a problem by the media. By identifying groups of young people as 'football hooligans' and 'ravers', the media can create a **moral panic** – in which the behaviour of such groups is seen as a threat to the moral order and stability of society. The media play a key role in

Table 4.3 Moral panics and 'folk devils' – some examples

Dates	Moral panic – the perceived problem	'Folk devil' – the group to blame	Potential victims
Late 1940s–1980s	Violent youth – civil unrest: threat to public order/decency/safety	Most youth subcultures, such as 'mods and rockers'	Ordinary citizens and their property
Every decade	Football hooliganism – street violence; vandalism, damage to life/property	Organized, 'mindless' hooligans who are not 'real' fans	Innocent bystanders; 'real' football fans
Late 1960s	Hippies – a threat due to their alternative lifestyle, drug-taking and sexual freedom	Long-haired, young middle classes	All decent, hardworking people
1960s and 70s	Sex on screen – corruption of children and offence to the unwitting viewer	Irresponsible film and TV producers	The impressionable young, decent folk
1970s	Mugging – threat to peace in the streets and personal security	Black youths	The vulnerable on the street
Mid 1970s	'Scroungers' – social security fraud	Undeserving, fraudulent claimants (often non-White)	Everyone who pays taxes
Early 1980s	Aids – death through 'deviant' sexual practices	Mainly gay men	The sexually active, above all young, single people
1980s, 90s	Glue-sniffing, out-of-control youth; premature death	Youth underclass	All lower working-class youth
Late 1980s–1990s	Club culture – ecstasy – drug deaths; threats to public order	Clubbers; ravers	All young people; the general public
Mid 1990s	Satanic ritual abuse – widespread sexual abuse of children by parents	Mostly incestuous fathers and overzealous social workers	Children and the family unit
Mid 1990s	Children, violence and the family (plus video nasties) – moral decline; family breakdown; corruption of young	Children of 'underclass' families; irresponsible parents	Toddlers; small children
Late 1990s	Paedophilia, child pornography	Middle-aged men, organized through the internet	Every child
2000s	Gun culture	Black drug criminals	All innocent bystanders; corrupted youth
2000s	Overwhelming immigration	Asylum seekers	All decent, tax-paying citizens

creating moral panics by sensationalizing and grossly exaggerating the threat that these groups pose. They soon become 'folk devils' – evil people who are threatening our ordinary, everyday lives.

Ironically, the media's desire to produce sensational stories about youth, sometimes out of nothing, can help create the very behaviour they are attacking. For example, many young people are actually attracted by sensational coverage of youth groups (which they otherwise might not have heard about or recognized). They begin to conform to media stereotypes in order to acquire status and recognition in the eyes of their peers, and some notoriety in the wider society. The prejudiced attitude of the general public and the police drives them further towards deviance (a process known as **deviance amplification**). Thus a real problem is created out of something that would probably have remained fairly small scale had it not been for the media's sensational coverage.

KEY TERMS

Deviance amplification the reinforcing of a person's or a group's deviant identity as a result of condemnation by agencies of social control such as the media.

Folk devils – groups seen by the media as evil and a threat to the moral well-being of society.

Moral panic public concern, created by the media, about the behaviour of certain groups of people who are seen as a threat to the moral order and stability of society.

Representation manner in which the media present an individual, group or event.

Stereotype a typical or 'shorthand' picture of a certain group.

Check your understanding

1. What does van Dijk's study tell us about media representations of ethnic minorities?

2. What do the media suggest is the main motivation for refugees and asylum seekers in coming to the UK?

3. How is the relationship between developing countries and the West portrayed in the media?

4. How have representations of the disabled improved recently?

5. Compare media representations of the upper, middle and working classes.

6. How is the popular media's attitude to gay people changing?

7. Explain in your own words the terms 'moral panic' and 'folk devils'.

8. How can media coverage of deviant youth groups actually make the 'problem' worse?

web.task

1. Go to the website of the Refugee Council at www.refugeecouncil.org.uk. What do they have to say about media coverage of refugees and asylum seekers?

2. Go to the website of the Campaign against Racism and Fascism at www.carf.demon.co.uk and select 'Features'. Scroll through the articles to find those that are concerned with media coverage of minority groups such as ethnic groups and asylum seekers.

3. Find the report, Viewing the World, at the website of the Department for International Development. This can be accessed from the main government website www.open.gov.uk

What methods does the study use and what are its key conclusions about media coverage of development issues?

research ideas

- Watch a range of television programmes one evening. Conduct a content analysis by counting the numbers and types of roles taken by older and younger people. What conclusions can you reach about media representations of age?

Item A Press coverage of immigration

In February 2004, there was extensive coverage of the enlargement of the European Union in the national newspapers, centring on the free movement of workers in the new Member States.

Mass-circulation tabloid headlines included the following:

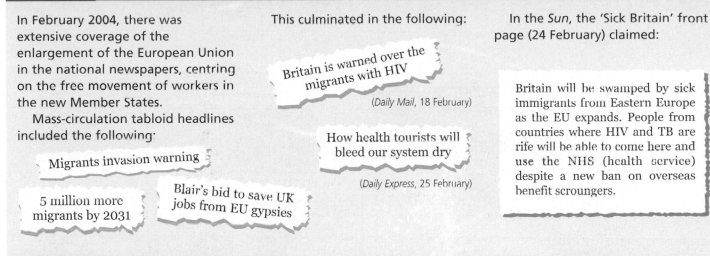

Migrants invasion warning

5 million more migrants by 2031

Blair's bid to save UK jobs from EU gypsies

This culminated in the following:

Britain is warned over the migrants with HIV

(*Daily Mail*, 18 February)

How health tourists will bleed our system dry

(*Daily Express*, 25 February)

In the *Sun*, the 'Sick Britain' front page (24 February) claimed:

Britain will be swamped by sick immigrants from Eastern Europe as the EU expands. People from countries where HIV and TB are rife will be able to come here and use the NHS (health service) despite a new ban on overseas benefit scroungers.

Item B Over-50s rail at TV stereotyping

<< Just days after Victor Meldrew was killed off and Inspector Morse had a fatal heart attack, a new survey has found that older people resent being stereotyped as either grumpy or sweet in TV comedy and drama. The study of the over-50s also found a lack of interest among older audiences in programmes specifically aimed at them, and it found that older viewers believe that over-50s are underrepresented on TV programmes aimed at mass audiences.

The advertising industry in particular is criticized by 50-somethings for portraying a narrow, idealized version of consumers. People in the 50-to-60 age group felt strongly that advertisers should change their attitudes and the images they use during the next five to ten years, to reflect the profile of their changing market.

The survey, *Age in the Frame*, which was drawn from the results of focus group sessions, is published today by the Independent Television Commission and Age Concern England.

While many over-50s enjoyed *One Foot in the Grave*, they found it unfortunate that Victor Meldrew's grumpy character was the best-known old person on TV. *Last of the Summer Wine* also came in for criticism, though again some older people said they still found it funny. But one focus group participant described the long-running sitcom as 'patronizing'. He said: 'It's just a bunch of daft old gits running around and fancying a woman with wrinkled stockings around her ankles.'

The report found that older viewers resent being pigeon-holed as the *Songs of Praise* generation, when they have a wide range of interests and viewing habits.

One respondent said: 'We like the same things we liked when we were younger. I like *The Royle Family* and *Have I Got News For You,* just like my grandson.' A lady in her 60s added that she liked 'a good violent American thriller – the type of thing with Al Pacino in it.' Over half of over-65s, and 40 per cent of over-50s, thought there should be more older people on TV, and that older women are particularly underrepresented.>>

Guardian, 27 November 2000

---

1 Explain what is meant by the term 'underrepresented' (Item B). (2 marks)

2 Suggest two ways that the headlines in Item A may be seen as evidence of a moral panic. (4 marks)

3 Identify three stereotypes associated with older people (Item B). (6 marks)

4 Identify and briefly explain two possible effects of the headlines described in Item A. (8 marks)

5 Discuss the role of the mass media in creating moral panics. (20 marks)

6 Using material from the Items and elsewhere, assess the view that stereotyping in the media is declining. (20 marks)

Postmodernism and the media

Family viewing in the 1950s

Media in the home today

Look at the cartoons above.

1 In what ways do they show that our use of the media is changing?

2 How do they show that the media themselves have changed?

3 What effect might these changes have on family life?

4 To what extent may changes in the media have reduced social interaction?

5 To what extent may changes in the media have increased social interaction?

6 'Media output was once highly structured for us – now we structure it to suit ourselves.'
How far do you consider this statement to be true?

People – at least those who can afford the technology – are now exposed to an ever-increasing range of media. Once part of a whole family experience, **media consumption** has become a more individual affair (just look at the cartoons above). But it can also involve a worldwide community, through technology such as the internet. Viewers take in a much wider range of programming and images, often flicking from channel to channel and producing their own viewing schedules through the use of video, DVD and other emerging technologies. They may take digital photos or videos on their phones, e-mail them instantly or edit them before sending them across the world wide web. How has this all come about and what are the implications for societies and their cultures?

Postmodernism and the media

As we saw in Unit 1, Topic 6, it has been suggested that societies have entered a new stage of development known as postmodernism. In economic life, information technology is increasingly becoming more important than manufacturing technology. White-collar workers, who specialize in the production of information and knowledge, now outnumber industrial workers. The globalization of mass media, information technology and electronic communication, such as e-mail and the internet, has led to the decline of national cultures and the growing importance of cultural diversity in our lifestyles.

Dominic Strinati (1995) argues that the mass media are centrally important in the development of postmodern society, for the following reasons:

- The part people played in the manufacture of goods once determined their social, national and local identities. These identities were further structured by factors such as social class, gender and ethnicity. In postmodern society, however, identities are increasingly being structured through consumption patterns. Now, the media provide most of our experience of social reality. What we take as 'real' is to a great extent what the media tell us is real. Our lifestyles and identity are defined for us by the media. For example, TV programmes and lifestyle magazines tell us what our homes and gardens should look like. Advertising tells us what products we need to buy to improve the quality of our lives. Magazines tell us how we can make ourselves attractive to potential partners. The news tells us what issues we should be thinking about. Fly-on-the-wall documentaries reassure us that other people share our anxieties, and so on.

- Image and style have more significance than form or content. In the postmodern world, we learn through the media that the consumption of images and signs for their own sake is more important than the consumption of the goods they represent. We buy the labels and packaging rather than the clothes or goods themselves. People are judged negatively for wearing the wrong trainers, rather than because of some fault in their character or lack of ability.

- In the past, a **cultural hierarchy** existed. Classical music, for example, was considered to be more 'serious' and 'important' than pop music. But in the postmodern world, there are constant crossovers between '**high culture**' and '**popular culture**'. The classical musicians Luciano Pavarotti, Vanessa Mae and Nigel Kennedy have all attempted pop music projects, whilst pop artists such as Paul McCartney have experimented with classical music. Time and place have also become confused and **decontextualized**. For example, Fatboy Slim sampled a few lines from a protest song of the American Civil Rights Movement of the 1960s, 'Praise you', and turned them into a number one record (the result was brilliant dance music devoid of political meaning). Shakespeare's *Romeo and Juliet* was re-presented as a teen movie set in late 20th-century Los Angeles.

The popular media themselves have become the subject of heated intellectual debate. For instance, you can now study towards an honours degree in Star Trek. The 'cultural expert', whose views have more weight than those of ordinary consumers, no longer exists. Now we are all experts.

According to postmodernists, it is the constant bombardment of media imagery in this **media-saturated society** that has caused all of this, transforming not only individual societies but even national identities – to the extent that, as some claim, we now live in a '**global village**'. People all over the world share many of the same consumption patterns and the same image-conscious outlook. Companies such as Disney, Levi Strauss, McDonald's, Sony and Coca-Cola target their products at a global audience. People across the world have real-time access to world news from CNN, while their kids argue about switching over to MTV.

Nawal El Saadawi
War, Lies and Videotape

In *War, Lies and Videotape*, media critics and activists examine the newly-emerging global media systems. The following extract is adapted from a contribution by Nawal El Saadawi, a world-renowned Egyptian feminist:

<< Never before in history has there been such domination of people's minds by the mass media ... such a concentration and centralization of media, capital and military power in the hands of so few people. The richest seven countries control almost all the technological, economic, media, information and military power in the world.

To expand the global market, the media plays its role in developing certain values, patterns of behavior and perceptions of beauty, femininity, masculinity, success, love and sex. The media creates a global consumer with an increasing desire to buy what the transnational capitalists (TNCs) produce, thereby maximizing their profits.

In spite of all these obstacles, we have to continue the struggle locally and globally. Globalization from above by the TNCs and their media should be challenged by globalization from below by women and men who are the majority of the world. We have to create our own media and communicate with each other through the internet, e-mail and other electronic devices. With the continuous advance in communication technology, we will be able to reach each other with less money and less time. The decentralization of the media and communication technology is inevitable, and it can be turned to our favor. The unveiling of the mind is our goal, to be accomplished by exercising political power through local and global organizations. >>

Aristide *et al.* (eds) (2000) *War, Lies and Videotape*, New York: International Action Center,

1 What role has the media played in promoting globalization?

2 How and why should globalization be resisted?

Criticisms of the postmodern view of the media

Postmodernists are criticized for exaggerating the extent to which wider social influences have subsided. Their critics argue that they underplay the continuing importance of class, gender and ethnicity in our lives, and that they exaggerate the changes that the media have brought about. Inequality remains a key issue, as access to the internet, digital television and so on is denied to many millions of poorer people worldwide. How can a 'global village' exist when so many cannot enter it?

Resistance to global media

The growing influence of the global corporations and media giants has not gone unnoticed. They are often accused of eroding national cultures or even undermining them. Islamic countries denounce the Western media for using degrading images of women. Eastern political regimes (e.g. China, Malaysia), fearing undesirable political and moral messages, have boycotted Western-owned satellite broadcasters. Even Rupert Murdoch has realized that, by promoting local culture through the Star satellite that he owns (which broadcasts to Asia), he will gain more government approval – and ultimately bigger audiences – than he would by imposing Western programmes on Eastern audiences.

In parts of Europe, resistance to 'McDonaldization' (the American take-over of culture) has had a reverse effect. New broadcasting technology is being used for the development of more local and regional programming, aimed at preserving distinctive European cultural traditions and outlooks.

The explosion of satellite, digital and internet technologies has transformed the way in which most of us organize our lives. Families, communities, and national life have all been affected. There is no doubt that – whatever the exact nature of their influence – the media have had an immense impact on modern societies throughout the world, and that, in the process, the world has become a smaller place.

web.task

Visit the website of Globalise Resistance which brings together groups and individuals opposed to the global growth of corporate power at www.resist.org.uk

Check your understanding

1. **Identify three changes associated with the shift towards a postmodern society.**

2. **What is the relationship between consumption and identity? Give an example of your own.**

3. **What is meant by the phrase 'style is more important than substance'?**

4. **Why might postmodernists argue that Fatboy Slim's version of 'Praise you' is just as valid as the original?**

5. **Explain in your own words the term 'globalization'.**

6. **Give examples of two positive and two negative outcomes of globalization.**

research ideas

- Design a questionnaire and conduct a survey within your school or college to assess the differences in access to and consumption of the new media, in relation to class, gender, ethnicity and age. Consider both household ownership and personal consumption of the following media forms: PCs, web TV, cable TV, games consoles, WAP phones, DVD players, videos, MP3 players, digital cameras.

- Draw up a list of the top five terrestrial TV programmes amongst your peer group. What proportion show signs of American influence? How many are reflective of British culture? Do the same for cable/satellite TV.

KEY TERMS

Cultural hierarchy term used to describe how opinions and tastes of particular individuals and groups, who are seen to have more cultural expertise, are valued above the tastes of others.

Decontextualized used to describe something that has been taken out of the situation in which it arose.

'Global village' the idea that the world has become much smaller as the media allow us all to communicate easily with each other and to share ideas and lifestyles.

High culture cultural forms, such as opera, that are associated with high-status or elite sections of society and considered 'superior' to other forms of culture.

McDonaldization the idea that American culture has overwhelmed other national cultures – literally that McDonald's has taken over the world.

Media consumption use of the media.

Media-saturated society a society in which every aspect of social life is influenced by the media.

Popular culture cultural forms, such as soap operas, that are preferred by the majority of the population.

exploring postmodernism and the media

Item A Use of new technology in the UK 1997 to 2004

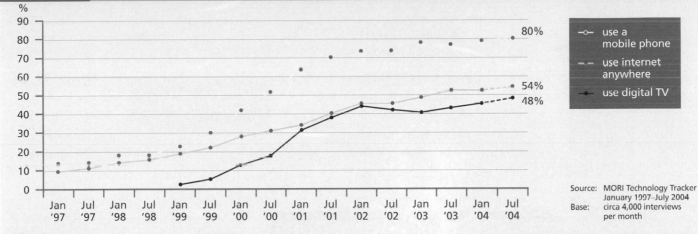

Source: MORI Technology Tracker
January 1997–July 2004
Base: circa 4,000 interviews per month

- use a mobile phone — 80%
- use internet anywhere — 54%
- use digital TV — 48%

Item B Class differences in the use of new technology

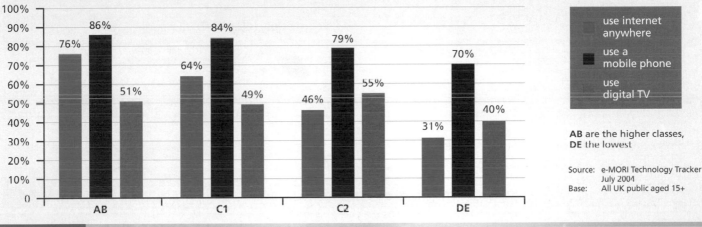

- use internet anywhere
- use a mobile phone
- use digital TV

AB are the higher classes, **DE** the lowest

Source: e-MORI Technology Tracker
July 2004
Base: All UK public aged 15+

Item C Cultural imperialism

In 1981, American films accounted for 94 per cent of foreign films broadcast on British TV, 80 per cent of those broadcast on French TV and 54 per cent on West German TV. In Western Europe as a whole, American imports represented 75 per cent of all imports. The share represented by US-originated programmes in other parts of the world is even greater. These media products depict Western (often idealized) lifestyles. This cultural imperialism is transnational. More recently, there has been some debate as to whether the US dominance is slipping, with increased competition at regional, national and local levels. However, what has happened to replace American programming is in many cases a local adaptation of American television formats. Local cultures are re-presented in an Americanized form.

Adapted from Taylor, S. (2001) *Sociology: Issues and Debates*, London: Routledge

1 Explain what is meant by the term 'cultural imperialism' (Item C). (2 marks)

2 Suggest two reasons why the use of new technology is increasing (Item A). (4 marks)

3 Identify three patterns in the relationship between class differences and the use of new technology (Item B). (6 marks)

4 Identify and briefly explain two possible consequences of inequality of access to the media. (8 marks)

5 Examine the postmodernist view of the media. (20 marks)

6 Using information from the Items and elsewhere, discuss the effects of new media technologies on societies. (20 marks)

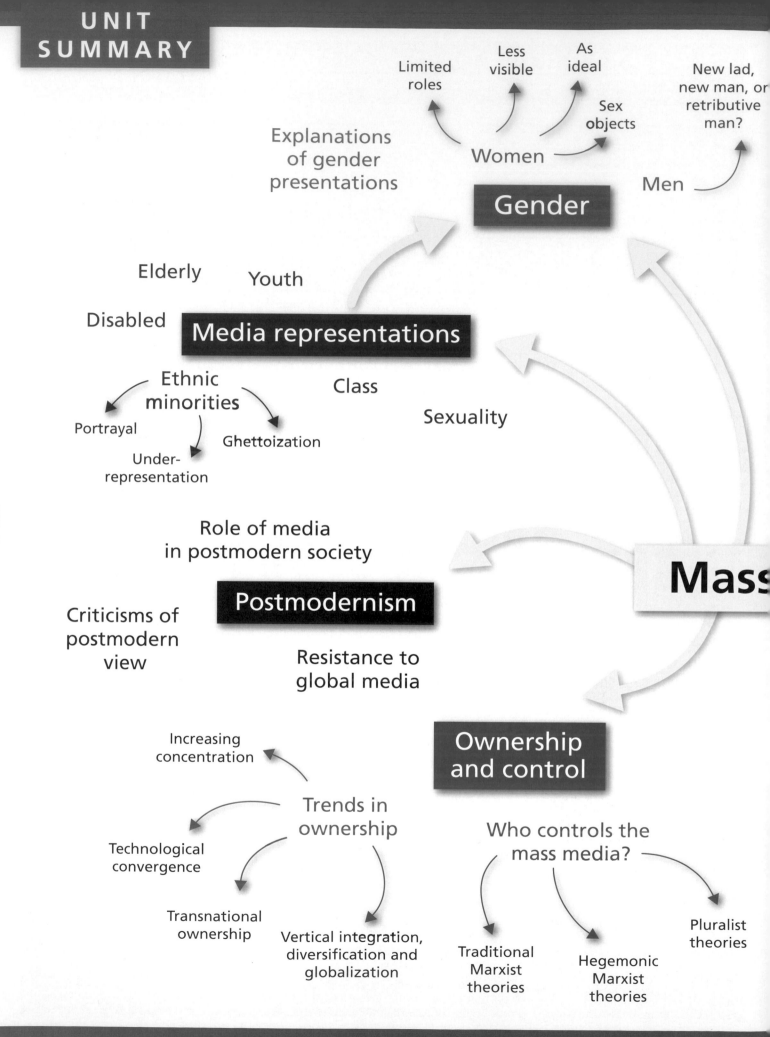

Less
visible

Limited
roles

As
ideal

New lad,
new man, or
retributive
man?

Sex
objects

Explanations
of gender
presentations

Women

Men

Gender

Elderly

Youth

Disabled

Media representations

Class

Ethnic
minorities

Sexuality

Portrayal

Ghettoization

Under-
representation

Role of media
in postmodern society

Mass

Criticisms of
postmodern
view

Postmodernism

Resistance to
global media

Increasing
concentration

**Ownership
and control**

Technological
convergence

Trends in
ownership

Who controls the
mass media?

Transnational
ownership

Vertical integration,
diversification and
globalization

Traditional
Marxist
theories

Hegemonic
Marxist
theories

Pluralist
theories

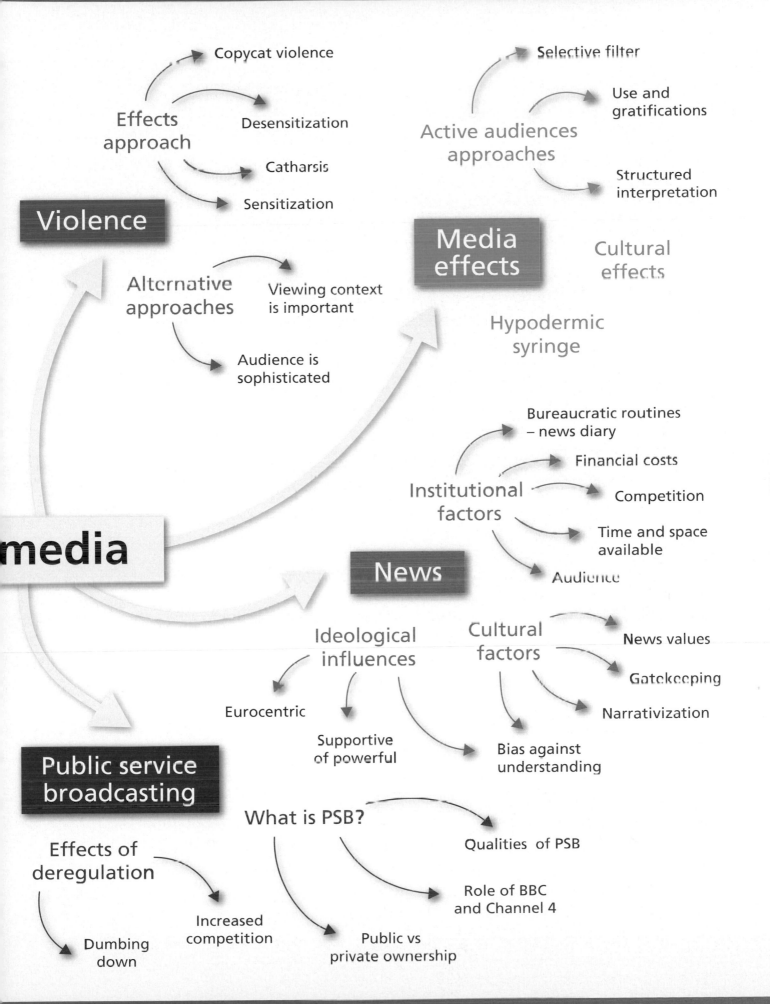

Copycat violence

Desensitization

Effects approach

Catharsis

Sensitization

Violence

Alternative approaches

Viewing context is important

Audience is sophisticated

Selective filter

Use and gratifications

Active audiences approaches

Structured interpretation

Media effects

Cultural effects

Hypodermic syringe

media

Bureaucratic routines – news diary

Financial costs

Institutional factors

Competition

Time and space available

Audience

News

Ideological influences

Cultural factors

News values

Eurocentric

Gatekeeping

Supportive of powerful

Bias against understanding

Narrativization

Public service broadcasting

What is PSB?

Qualities of PSB

Effects of deregulation

Role of BBC and Channel 4

Increased competition

Dumbing down

Public vs private ownership

EDUCATION IN THE UK IS A FASCINATING AREA FOR STUDY. On the one hand, it provides a fertile ground for the application of sociological theories in practical and tangible ways; on the other, it gives a real insight into the impact political decisions have on society. The different educational sectors which have been chopped and changed over the last 60 years also provide further insights into the impact of social class, gender and ethnicity on social mobility in UK society.

Schools for which parents pay fees are known as 'private' or 'independent' schools. The top independent schools (e.g. Eton, Harrow, Roedean) are also called 'public schools'. About 7.5 per cent of the school population attend such schools, yet about 75 per cent of the top jobs in the UK, such as top politicians, judges and senior civil servants, are held by ex-independent school pupils. In the state sector, schools cater for children of different ages through infant schools (aged 5 to 7), junior schools (7 to 11) and secondary (11 to 16). The equivalent in independent schools are pre-preparatory (aged 5 to 7), preparatory (8 to 11/13), private/public school (11/13 to 18). Independent schools usually have sixth forms. A growing number of state schools have given up running a sixth form because small class sizes made them uneconomic. They either join into consortia (sharing arrangements) with other schools or their pupils stay on in education post-16 (over half of all pupils) by going to FE Colleges (all age groups) or Sixth Form centres (16 to 19).

A wide variety of schools and educational institutions exist today following the policies of various governments which have enabled different areas to continue to offer different provision. The key area of disagreement between the main parties has been over 'selection', where a school can choose whom to allow in on the basis of ability. Conservatives have tended to favour selection, whilst the Labour party in principle oppose it. Parents choosing secondary schools for their children today often face a bewildering range of options, including single-sex or co-educational comprehensive schools, city academies, specialist sports colleges, foundation schools (which are not controlled by the local authority but by central government and which may select on the basis of ability), voluntary schools (those emphasizing a particular faith) and, for those who can afford it, the various private schools.

This unit will examine not only the educational policies which have led to this state of affairs , but will also try to explain what goes on and why within this myriad of institutions.

AQA specification	topics	pages
Candidates should examine:		
Different explanations of the role of the education system.	Topic 1 covers the key theoretical perspectives on the role of education.	162–167
Different explanations of the different educational achievement of social groups by social class, gender and ethnicity.	These are covered at length in Topics 3, 4 and 5.	174–191
Relationships and processes within schools, with particular reference to teacher/pupil relationships, pupil subcultures, the hidden curriculum and the organization of teaching and learning.	Topic 6 focuses on pupil responses to education, including subcultures. Topics 3, 4 and 5 also contain material relating to teacher/pupil relationships, the hidden curriculum and teaching and learning.	174–197
The significance of state policies for an understanding of the role, impact and experience of education.	Topic 2 traces the development of the education system. Topic 7 analyses state responses to education and the economic system.	168–173 198–201

UNIT 5

Education

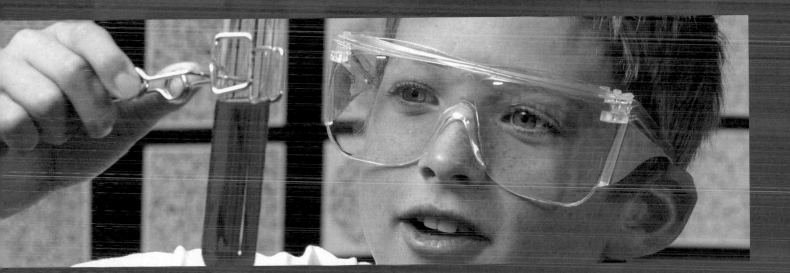

The role of education in society

1 Look at the photographs above. Using these and any other ideas you may have, make a list of the purposes of school for:

(a) individuals

(b) society as a whole.

2 Is there anything that occurs in schools that you feel has no purpose? If so, what?

3 What have you really learned at school/college this week? Who will gain from your acquiring this knowledge, set of attitudes or skills?

4 Could you learn effectively without school?

5 Would society suffer if schools did not exist? Explain your answer.

The education system is one of the most influential institutions in society. It takes individuals from the age of 4 or 5, for six or so hours per day, over a period of at least 11 years. It bombards them with a vast amount of knowledge, attitudes and skills. These are acquired either formally through set lessons or informally through what is known as the **hidden curriculum** – the processes involved in being 'schooled' and the various interactions that take place whilst in school. By the time they finish compulsory education, most pupils will have spent over 15 000 hours in lessons.

So why do modern societies invest so much in **schooling** the next generation? Some of the answers can be found by looking at the introduction of compulsory education over 100 years ago.

The introduction of compulsory education

Children of the upper and middle classes have always had the option of private schooling, but **state education** for all has only been available in Britain since 1880, when it was made compulsory for children up to the age of 10. There were a number of possible reasons for the introduction of compulsory education:

● To create a more skilled workforce – Britain had been 'the workshop of the world' but other countries were catching up. Many employers believed that, in order to remain competitive, the new industrial society required a numerate, literate workforce able to cope with the complexities of modern industrial production.

● To improve the effectiveness of our armies – The high casualties of the Crimean War (1854–6) were seen as partly due to inexperience and poor tactics. Better-trained, fitter soldiers (who could read, write and count) might have given Britain a better showing.

● To re-socialize the feckless (aimless or wasteful) poor – Many Victorians felt that the working classes were poor through their own fault – spending unwisely, drinking too much and living immorally. They needed to be taught to lead a more responsible and respectable life.

● To reduce the level of street crime – Remember Oliver Twist? Many felt that compulsory schooling would get young pickpockets 'off the streets', thus reducing the high levels of petty theft.

● To ward off the threat of revolution – The upper classes feared the 'tide of socialism' that was 'sweeping' through Europe. (After all, Marx himself was writing throughout the period leading up to the introduction of compulsory education.) Free education, on the one hand, could make the ruling classes appear generous, while on the other, giving them **ideological control** over the masses. The working class would learn to respect authority, follow instructions and conform to rules.

● To provide a 'human right' – Many **liberal** thinkers felt that education could improve the life experience of all citizens, including the working class.

Many of the above influences are still shaping the modern education system. The introduction of **Key Skills**, numeracy and literacy in primary schools, and all the developments in **vocational education** (discussed in Topic 7), reflect continuing concern about the skills levels of the workforce. Similarly, the importance of discipline and rules in schools indicates that the social control of young people is still a priority.

Most sociologists agree that education is important, both in teaching skills and in encouraging certain attitudes and values, but they disagree about why this occurs and who benefits from it.

What does the picture below tell us about the reasons for the introduction of compulsory education during the 19th century?

Functionalist approach

Functionalists argue that education has three broad functions:

1 *Socialization* – Education helps to maintain society by socializing young people into key cultural values, such as achievement, individualism, competition, **equality of opportunity**, social solidarity, democracy and religious morality.

2 *Skills provision* – Education teaches the skills required by a modern industrial society. These may be general skills that everyone needs, such as literacy and numeracy, or the specific skills needed for particular occupations.

3 *Role allocation* – Education allocates people to the most appropriate job for their talents, using examinations and qualifications. This is seen to be fair because there is equality of opportunity – everyone has the chance to achieve success in society on the basis of their ability.

Marxist approach

Marxists challenge the functionalist approach. Althusser (1971) disagrees that the main function of education is the transmission of common values. Rather, he argues that education is an ideological state apparatus (see Unit 2, Topic 2, p. 42). Its main function is to maintain, legitimate (justify) and reproduce, generation by generation, class inequalities in wealth and power, by transmitting ruling-class or capitalist values disguised as common values. Althusser argues that this is done through the hidden curriculum: the way that schools are organized and the way that knowledge is taught means that working-class people are encouraged to conform to the capitalist system, and accept failure and inequality.

Bowles and Gintis (1976) argue that education serves to reproduce directly the **capitalist relations of production** – the hierarchy of workers from the boss down – with the appropriate skills and attitudes. Education ensures that workers will unquestioningly adapt to the needs of the system, without criticism.

Bowles and Gintis suggest that what goes on in school corresponds directly to the world of work. Teachers are like the bosses, and pupils are like the workers, who work for rewards (wages or exam success). The higher up the system the individual progresses, however, the more personal freedom they have to control their own educational or working experiences, and the more responsibility they have for the outcomes.

Bowles and Gintis point out, however, that success is not entirely related to intellectual ability. Those pupils who fit in and conform rise above those who challenge the system. This explains why White middle-class pupils tend to do better. Schools therefore reproduce sets of workers with the appropriate outlook for the position that they come to occupy.

Functionalists see education as turning pupils into model citizens, whilst Marxists argue that it merely turns working-class kids into conformist workers. However, despite their differences, functionalist and Marxist accounts of education do share some similarities – for example, they are both structuralist theories (see Unit 1, Topic 3, p. 12) in that they see social institutions as more important than individuals. Consequently, they do not pay much attention to what actually goes on in classrooms or to the views and feelings of teachers and pupils.

How would Marxists and functionalists differ in their interpretation of a school assembly?

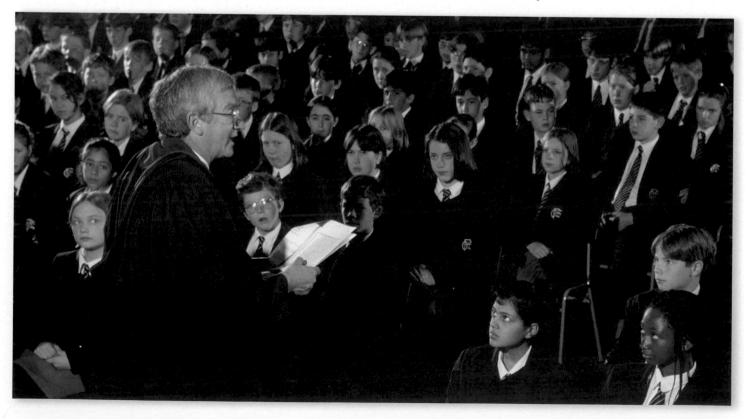

An alternative view: Paul Willis

Paul Willis (1977) provides a major critique of both perspectives when he points out that both theories are **deterministic**. This means that they both see pupils as passive products of the educational system. Both theories, argues Willis, fail to take into account the tendency of many pupils to resist these processes. (After all, are most kids in your experience docile 'teacher's pets'?)

Willis's study identified proschool and antischool subcultures (see Unit 1, Topic 4) which were nicknamed the 'earoles' and the 'lads' respectively. 'Earoles' did what teachers expected of them, whereas the 'lads' took little notice of school rules, teachers and work – they substituted their own definitions of what school was about, based on 'having a laff'. However, in developing these strategies to cope with the boredom of school, the 'lads' were also developing a way of coping with the boring and routine type of job that they would ultimately end up in. Even rebellion, says Willis, is reproducing the right type of workforce needed for the capitalist system – a workforce who are uncritical and 'just get on with it'.

Willis's study is a good example of an **eclectic** approach to sociology. He uses an ethnographic, interactionist approach to understand the meanings pupils give to their schooling, and then applies a Marxist perspective to explain them. Recent writers have applied some of Willis's ideas to present-day anti-school subcultures (see Topic 6), seeking to address a common criticism of Willis's work (now a quarter of a century old) – that is, that he concentrated solely on White working-class males, neglecting 'the potential of female, Black and disabled students as significant agents of resistance' (Rikowski 2001).

Approaches such as Marxism and functionalism, which relate educational experiences to wider society, as well as **interactionism**, which focuses more on the actual workings of the school, feature throughout the sociology of education, so it is important to have a basic grasp of these theories. Check Unit 1, Topics 3 to 5, to remind yourself if you are unsure of them.

How do these cartoons illustrate Willis's view of education?

Check your understanding

1 Give three of the main reasons why education was made compulsory in 1880.

2 According to functionalists, what are the main functions of schools?

3 What does Althusser consider to be the main purpose of education, and how is it achieved?

4 Why do you think the theory of Bowles and Gintis is sometimes called 'correspondence' theory? Give examples.

5 Why, according to Bowles and Gintis, do White, middle-class pupils do better?

6 Who were the 'earoles' and the 'lads'?

7 How does Paul Willis challenge the traditional functionalist and Marxist accounts?

research ideas

- Interview a range of your teachers. Ask them to explain the values which they consider are encouraged by the following aspects of school organization and routine: assemblies, speech days, sports days, school uniform, registration, house competitions, school rules, prefects, detention.

  Evaluate the extent to which their responses subscribe to functionalist, Marxist or liberal views of education.

- Organize a small research project to discover what people consider to be the primary purpose of education. Compare class, gender and age patterns in terms of the extent to which the wider social purposes are recognized. Which groups see school as most individually beneficial – for example, as helping someone to get a better job?

KEY TERMS

Capitalist relations of production how members of the workforce are organized in relation to each other under capitalism. (In capitalist industrial societies, this is usually hierarchical, with a few at the top making all the decisions and giving out orders, whilst the majority do what they are told.)

Deterministic the view that a particular outcome is inevitable.

Eclectic borrowing freely from various sources; in this context, mixing a range of explanatory approaches.

Equality of opportunity every person having the same chances.

Hidden curriculum the informal learning of particular values and attitudes in schools.

Ideological control getting people to behave in a desired way by convincing them that it is in their interests to behave in that way.

Interactionism a sociological perspective that takes a small-scale approach to the study of society, focusing particularly on how individuals react to each other in specific social situations.

Key Skills competence in communication, application of number and information technology as applied to post-16 study, assessed through portfolio evidence and external written tests.

Liberals open-minded people who believe in personal freedom, democracy (the involvement of everyone in decision-making) and the rights of others.

Schooling the process of compulsory education.

State education education provided by local and central governments.

Vocational education education designed to teach the skills needed for particular occupations.

web.task

Search for government educational policy documents and statements at www.dfes.gov.uk. What are the government's stated aims? How do these aims relate to the sociological views you have been introduced to in this unit?

Item A Traditional standards

If Britain is ever to achieve industrial and economic prosperity again, schools should encourage competition, discipline, decency, self-reliance and eventually prosperity, through a return to hard work, selection, higher standards and biblical morality. We must make it clear to children that there is a distinction between work and play. The playground is the playground, available in short doses for the release of high spirits and horseplay. The classroom, where such are still to be found, is a place where the dominant value is work, labelled as such, and not disguised as anything else. It should be a place where results are expected against a certain time schedule; a place where children should learn, as early and as frequently as possible, the satisfaction, joy and legitimate pride of being stretched to the very limit of their capacity and thereby turning in as faultless a piece of work as they can manage; a place where the teacher gets it across that our second best is not good enough; a place where the shortcomings of even the worst homes are to some extent rectified and not used as a constant excuse for inaction. Schools should get a hard grip on the surly, deceptive and uncooperative, at the earliest possible moment. It is imperative to support the hard-working, the inventive and the original. This means selection, ideally as sophisticated and even-handed as possible. We must toughen up the educational process so that everything else – learning, creativity, technical skills, wealth-creating potential – can flourish properly. Children must learn biblical stories such as the Good Samaritan because the stories will speak for themselves.

Adapted from a speech made in 1984 by Tom Howarth, Senior Tutor, Cambridge University, quoted in R. Burgess (ed.) (1986) *Education, Schools and Schooling*, Walton-on-Thames: Thomas Nelson

Item B The 'lads'

Extract 1

The space won from the school and its rules by the 'lads' is used for the shaping and development of particular cultural skills principally devoted to 'having a laff'. The 'laff' is of particular importance to the 'lads' – 'We can make them laff, they can't make us laff.' It is used in many contexts – to defeat boredom and fear, to overcome hardship and problems – as a way out of almost anything. The school is generally a fertile ground for the 'laff'. Specific themes of authority are explored, played with and used in their humour ... When a teacher comes into the classroom he is told 'It's alright, Sir, the deputy's taking us, you can go. He said you can have the period off.' The 'lads' stop second and third years around the school and say 'Mr Argyle wants to see you.' Argyle's room is soon choked with worried kids.

Extract 2

Joey: On a Monday afternoon, we'd have nothing right? Nothing hardly relating to schoolwork, Tuesday afternoon we have swimming and they stick you in a classroom for the rest of the afternoon, Wednesday afternoon you have games and there's only Thursday and Friday afternoon that you work, if you call that work. The last lesson Friday afternoon we used to go and doss, half of us wagged out of lessons and the other half go into the classroom, sit down and just go to sleep ...

Spanksy: Skive this lesson, just go up on the bank, have a smoke, and the next lesson go to a teacher who, you know, will call the register ...

Bill: It's easy to go home as well. Last Wednesday, Eddie got his mark and went home…

Eddie: I ain't supposed to be in school this afternoon, I'm supposed to be at college on a link course.

Paul Willis: What's the last time you did some writing?

Fuzz: Last time was in careers, 'cos I writ 'yes' on a piece of paper, that broke me heart 'cos I was going to try and go through the term without writing anything. 'Cos since we've come back, I ain't dun nothing [it was halfway through term].

Willis, P. (1977) *Learning to Labour*, Aldershot: Ashgate

1 Explain what is meant by the 'hidden curriculum'. (2 marks)

2 Suggest two ways in which the writer of Item A might like to see schools 'toughened up'. (4 marks)

3 Suggest three ways in which the 'lads' described in Item B might 'have a laff' at school. (6 marks)

4 Identify and briefly explain two reasons why the 'lads' (Item B) may have rejected the values of the school. (8 marks)

5 Examine the functionalist argument that schools serve the interests of both the individual and society. (20 marks)

6 Using information from the Items and elsewhere, assess the Marxist view that education benefits the ruling class. (20 marks)

How has education changed?

SECONDARY SCHOOL PERFORMAN

BOLTON	KEY STAGE 3 RESULTS				GCSE/GNVQ RESULTS		
	PUPILS AGED 14	(% achieving level 5 or above in test)			PUPILS AGED 15	5 or more Grades A*-C	5 or more Grades
		ENGLISH	MATHS	SCIENCE			
Al Jamiah Al Islamiyyah	22	55%	59%	36%	23	0%	22%
Bolton Muslim Girls' School	65	95%	71%	54%	61	54%	97%
Bolton School Boys' Division	-	-	-	-	139	96%	96%
Bolton School Girls' Division	-	-	-	-	120	99%	99%
Canon Slade CofE School	270	90%	90%	88%	246	81%	98%
The Deane School	154	46%	53%	47%	175	27%	80%
George Tomlinson School	123	41%	42%	42%	85	22%	91%
Harper Green School	288	68%	59%	59%	258	36%	92%
Hayward School	260	63%	58%	56%	232	31%	91%
Little Lever School Specialist Language College	210	64%	70%	63%	231	47%	97%
Lord's College	-	-	-	-	9	44%	89%
Mount St Joseph RC High School, Bolton	183	63%	67%	69%	205	42%	92%
Rivington and Blackrod High School	310	70%	71%	69%	303	52%	94%
St James's Church of England Secondary School	200	80%	83%	84%	178	56%	99%
St Joseph's RC High School and Sports College	174	73%	85%	78%	154	69%	
Sharples School	214	48%	56%	66%	203	42%	
Smithills School	328	65%	58%	62%	278	45%	

1 **Why do so many schools produce glossy brochures? Where does the money to produce these come from? What else could it be spent on?**

2 **Why have recent governments been keen to produce education 'league tables'?**

3 **Apart from improving quality, what can schools do to improve their position in league tables?**

4 **Why do you think the developments discussed here are sometimes referred to as the 'marketization' of education?**

5 **What arguments can be put forward:**
   (a) in favour of marketization?
   (b) against marketization?

This topic will examine some of the major changes in the organization of the education system in England and Wales, and, in particular, the role played by central government.

1944 to 1965

Until the Second World War (1939–45), children of the working classes attended elementary school up to the age of 14. The school-leaving age was then raised to 15 in 1947. Since its introduction in 1880, compulsory state education had been a fairly haphazard affair, controlled by local administrators who oversaw the provision of basic skills plus religious and moral instruction, with boys and girls often taught separately – girls were usually trained in domestic competence, and boys in technical skills. A small proportion of bright working-class children won scholarships to continue with free education in otherwise fee-paying schools that were mainly attended by the middle classes.

The tripartite system

As part of the aim to create a 'land fit for heroes' after the Second World War, Butler's Education Act of 1944 introduced '**secondary education** for all'. The upper classes continued to be educated in the **public schools** and top universities. The Act had no effect upon their education, but it did aim to abolish class-based inequalities within education. A tripartite system was to be introduced, providing three types of school, each suited to one of three types of ability:

● grammar schools for the academic
● secondary technical schools for the artistic/creative
● secondary modern schools for everyone else.

The basic principle underlying this system was 'equality of opportunity for all'. All children would take an **IQ test** at 11 in order to allocate them to a school suited to their abilities. Only those who 'passed' the **11+** test went to grammar or technical schools. However, schools were supposed to have similar standards of provision, and **parity of esteem**, as each school aimed to provide the most suitable education for the development of each type of learner.

Problems of the tripartite system

- Middle-class children were disproportionately 'selected' for grammar schools, and working-class children for the secondary moderns. Many middle-class children who failed the 11+ were sent into private education by their parents.
- Working-class self-esteem was further damaged by the poor image secondary moderns had. 'Parity of esteem' did not happen, and employers, parents and children themselves generally viewed secondary moderns as inferior to grammar schools, which were also able to recruit better-qualified teachers and had better resources.
- The impact that labels have upon pupils' self-concept and motivation was becoming more widely recognized. Sociological research indicated that being labelled a failure created a self-fulfilling prophecy, as secondary modern pupils were not expected to achieve by their teachers and did not bother trying (see *Focus on research*).
- It was felt by some that the IQ tests were culturally biased against working-class children.
- Very few technical schools were built, due to the greater cost of equipping them.
- Many people were critical of the system because of the unfair way in which it operated. Girls were often sent to secondary moderns even though they had passed the 11+, because schools then were more commonly single sex and there were fewer girls' grammar schools. Girls' marks were also adjusted downwards because it was assumed that boys matured later.
- There were also regional variations. It was twice as easy to get into a grammar school in some parts of the country, compared with others, because the percentage of available places varied.

By the mid-1950s, it was generally agreed that the tripartite system had failed in its aims. Educational attainment was overwhelmingly class based – most working-class children left school at 15 and entered work, while middle-class children continued into further and higher education. Twenty per cent of the school population went to grammar schools, 5 per cent to technical schools and 75 per cent to secondary moderns. A system that failed three-quarters of all schoolchildren was seen as a great waste of talent – although many middle-class parents wanted to retain it. In an attempt to apply the principle of 'equality of opportunity for all' genuinely, the tripartite system was abolished (although some areas resisted and continue the system until this day).

1965 to 1979

Comprehensive schools

In 1965, the Labour government instructed all local authorities to submit plans for comprehensive reorganization. Comprehensive schools educated all children – regardless of class, gender, ethnicity and ability – under one roof. The aim was to promote both social justice and tolerance. A great deal of money was spent on upgrading facilities and on teacher training, so that these schools could not only maintain the standards of the grammar schools, but also provide a broader curriculum and greater sporting and recreational opportunities.

The Labour government also embarked on a rapid expansion of higher education, creating more universities, the polytechnics and the **Open University**. All of these innovations were aimed at increasing working-class access to higher education. However, the public school system and its disproportionate access to **Oxbridge** remained intact.

In 1967, the Labour government set up six Educational Priority Areas (EPAs) in poverty-stricken areas of the UK, which received more cash and more teachers for primary schools. This was known as **compensatory education** (see Topic 3). The scheme was eventually abandoned in the 1970s having shown little sign of success.

'Progressive education' and mixed-ability teaching

The school-leaving age was raised to 16 in 1972, forcing all pupils to sit exams. Teachers had to find new ways of engaging this sometimes reluctant extra year-group. More significantly, many teachers had seen the damage caused by the labelling of pupils according to ability (both in the tripartite system and by **streaming** in comprehensive schools). Teachers began to experiment with **mixed-ability teaching**. They wanted to enable all pupils to achieve their maximum potential and, rather than teach all of the class the same thing at the same time, they believed that learning should be child-centred and a process of guided discovery.

By the late 1960s, critics were claiming that **progressive education** was neglecting the '3 Rs' (**R**eading, w**R**iting, a**R**ithmetic), and that standards had fallen. Conservative opposition to what was seen as Labour's educational initiative grew throughout the 1970s.

Comprehensives, especially in the inner cities, were frequently attacked for lack of discipline, poor results, truancy and large class sizes. The opposition education minister, Margaret Thatcher, eventually became prime minister in 1979, and teachers were never to have the freedom to exercise their professional autonomy again.

1979 to 1988

Conservative education policy in the 1980s was characterized by the following initiatives:

- An emphasis on preparing young people for work and industry – A number of measures such as the introduction of Youth Training Schemes and work experience in schools became known as the '**new vocationalism**' (see Topic 7 for more details).
- A renewed focus on selection – In 1980, the **Assisted Places Scheme** was introduced, giving bright working-class pupils free places in public schools if they passed the school's entrance exam.
- Centralization and a rejection of localized policy and provision – Local funding that reflected social deprivation was felt to have been excessive and wasteful, especially where Labour-controlled local authorities were involved. Other ways of funding schools were introduced, invariably at the expense of poorer areas, but good for the government in terms of middle-class votes.

1988 to 1997

The most influential legislation since 1944 was introduced with the 1988 Education Reform Act:

- The Assisted Places Scheme was expanded.
- All pupils would study the **National Curriculum** – this would involve the same subject content at various key stages from the age of 7 to 16, in Maths, English, Science, History, Geography, Technology, Music, Art, physical education (PE) and a modern language. It would include only 10 to 20 per cent of optional subjects, with more options allowed at GCSE (the new exam standard to replace CSE and O-level).
- Pupils would sit national tests (**SATs**) at 7, 11 and 14. These would be used to draw up **league tables** which would inform parents of each school's performance.
- Schools could decide how to manage their budgets or, if they wished, opt out of local authority control altogether, and become grant maintained schools, which could make their own decisions about how to recruit pupils. They could select on the basis of ability if they wished.
- **Marketization** – parents would be allowed to choose which school to send their children to. The restrictions on entry were removed, allowing popular schools to expand, whilst unpopular schools might be closed. Increased competition between schools for pupils would, it was hoped, drive standards up further.
- A new inspection system was proposed (introduced in 1992) for all schools, to be overseen by a new body called OFSTED. Inspections were to be more rigorous and inspection reports published, providing a further source of information about schools for prospective parents.
- **City Technology Colleges** were to be introduced, co-funded by industry, to provide special opportunities for pupils in inner-city areas.

Many critics felt that the Act was actually concerned with reducing the power of the Labour-controlled local authorities. Concerns were also expressed over the damaging, stressful effects of testing on pupils. **Parental choice** was largely a

focus on research

Rosenthal and Jacobson
'Pygmalion in the classroom'

Rosenthal and Jacobson noted that Mexican children, a traditionally low-achieving group, also suffered from low teacher expectations. They devised an experiment to test the hypothesis that teachers' expectations in themselves affected their pupils' educational attainment.

They were able involve a suitable sample of teachers in their research by posing as educational psychologists. They claimed that a sophisticated IQ test, which they had devised, could identify children who could be predicted to display 'dramatic intellectual growth' in the future. They administered the test to pupils and told the teachers which pupils had scored highly and which had not. However, no real testing took place. 'High-flying' and 'non-achieving' pupils had, in fact, simply been labelled at random.

A few months later, they administered a real intelligence test and found that the so-called 'high flyers' achieved significantly higher scores than the so-called 'underachievers'. The teachers also perceived the former to be happier, better-adjusted and more interesting than the rest. Fascinatingly, those pupils who were not labelled as high flyers, but who performed well, against expectations, were described as showing 'undesirable' behaviour.

As pupils were not told of their initial 'assessment' outcome, Rosenthal and Jacobson concluded that their research demonstrated that the expectations held by teachers about their pupils' ability were a significant influence upon pupils' intellectual development.

Rosenthal, R., and Jacobson, L. (1968) *Pygmalion in the Classroom*, New York: Holt, Rinehart & Winston

1 How might this research be criticized as unethical?

2 How does this research serve to justify the phasing out of the tripartite system?

3 Several attempts to replicate this research have failed to find a similar correlation between teachers' expectations and pupil achievement. How else might pupils in this subsequent research have responded to low teacher expectations?

myth, as few extra places were available in the most popular schools. League tables were felt to be counterproductive by

For sale:
within catchment area of
sinking comprehensive
school – £200,000

For sale:
within catchment area of
desirable specialist school
– £300,000

many, as low achievers and difficult pupils were less likely to be entered for examinations than before, because schools did not want their results affected. The National Curriculum has since been slimmed down, while the extent of testing was reduced after protests from overburdened teachers.

New Labour: 1997 onwards

New Labour inherited many of these new initiatives and took forward most of them to introduce **Curriculum 2000**. Post-16 students had long been criticized for being too narrowly specialized in their studies and lacking essential skills for higher education and employment. Also, the vocational/academic divide (the lack of parity of esteem between vocational students studying on BTEC, GNVQ and NVQ courses and students studying A-levels) was seen to be depriving industry of the brightest students.

With the introduction of Curriculum 2000, more mixing of academic and vocational studies became possible, and the number of courses increased. Rather than just three A-levels, students could now study four or five courses including AS-levels (a level between GCSE and A-level), or vocational subjects (BTECs, GNVQs), plus a Key Skills qualification. In the second year, they would then continue either with the vocational subjects they wished to specialize in or with the full A-level (A2). However, integrated vocational and academic programmes have largely failed to materialize, proving unpopular with both pupils and their parents.

New Labour also introduced many initiatives of their own, including the abolition of higher education grants and the extension of student loans. They tried to tackle **social exclusion** by improving educational opportunities for the long-term unemployed and single mothers. Grant maintained schools were renamed '**foundation schools**'. They no longer receive grants from central government, but still retain special status and therefore have a great deal of control over how they recruit

pupils. Extra funding has been poured into the inner cities, and pupils in lower-income families can now apply for Educational Maintenance Allowances.

Diversity and parity of esteem revisited

Under the Conservatives, the general thrust of change had been towards a system that was standardized, measurable, accountable and cost-effective. However, recent developments are emphasizing more diversity. **Specialist schools** have been encouraged and 10 per cent of their pupils can be selected according to ability. By 2003, over 1000 comprehensive schools nationally (23 per cent) had top-up funding to help them develop their specialism. The government intends to extend the specialist school programme to at least half of all comprehensives by 2006.

In 2001, it was proposed that **City academies** should be established to provide high-quality education for all age groups in deprived areas of the inner city. Academies are now being extended to deprived rural areas.

New Labour have also encouraged differentiation within the system to develop the potential of the most able. There is a growing tendency to teach pupils according to their individual needs and aptitudes. This has led to abler primary school children being taught alongside older age groups, increased use of banding and setting, and the introduction of more tiers within GCSE specifications.

The recent emphasis is on a coherent system of 14-to-19 education and a unified qualifications framework which finally removes the barriers between vocational and academic courses (see panel below).

Despite greater variety of provision since the introduction of the National Curriculum, the overall emphasis remains on measurement, accountability and cost effectiveness. However, there is a growing recognition that the education system needs to deliver success for all, whatever their background.

Key points of the Tomlinson Enquiry into 14–19

- A single, overarching diploma framework, with four levels of qualification (Entry, Foundation, Intermediate and Advanced)

- Increased stretch for the best (raising standards), participation for all

- Less (but more rigorous) assessment

- Aspiration to parity between vocational and academic programmes

- Learning at your own pace – levels will be divorced from age

- Work experience will be a key component

- More detail will be available to HE/employers on learning outcomes

Do you feel these proposals would have benefited your and your friends' education?

Sociological thinking has either informed change or been critical of it at various points in the process. This is especially apparent in sociological explanations of differential educational attainment – that is, why some social groups do better or worse than others – as the following topics will show.

Check your understanding

1 How was the education system organized prior to 1944?

2 Why was Butler's Education Act introduced?

3 Why did the idea of 'parity of esteem' not work?

4 What were the aims of progressive education?

5 How did the 1988 Education Reform Act seek to create a uniform and more efficient system?

6 Why would critics argue that the Act was more concerned with curbing the influence of Labour-controlled local authorities?

7 Why was post-16 education reformed?

8 How has secondary educational provision become more diverse in recent years?

research ideas

- Conduct a survey on a sample of adults over the age of 45, including ex-grammar and ex-secondary modern school pupils. Compare their experiences in terms of teacher expectations, personal feelings, attitudes to school, the curriculum, examination success, age at leaving education, final job/career.

- Interview an experienced member of your school or college staff. Ask them to describe the impact that the following changes had upon their educational career and experiences:
  (a) the introduction of the National Curriculum, school/college inspections, league tables, competition between schools/colleges, parental choice
  (b) the introduction of Curriculum 2000, including new AS-levels and Key Skills
  (c) the introduction of Citizenship and work-related learning.

KEY TERMS

11+ IQ test taken at the age of 11 to determine what sort of school you would attend under the tripartite system.

Academies (previously called **City academies** but now being opened in deprived rural areas) all-ability schools established by sponsors from business, faith or voluntary groups working in partnerships with central government and local education.

Assisted Places Scheme a scheme whereby the government funds bright students from the state sector to attend public schools.

City academies see **Academies**

City Technology Colleges schools funded partly by industry, aimed at giving extra opportunities to inner-city pupils.

Compensatory education making more resources available to schools in poorer areas in order to compensate (make up) for deprivation.

Curriculum 2000 a complete revision of post-16 education, whereby students in their first year take more subjects at a level between GCSE and A-level. They then specialize in fewer subjects at full A-level in the second year.

Foundation schools schools funded directly by central government rather than local authority. They do not have to conform to local authority guidelines, e.g. on selection (known as 'grant maintained schools' before 1998).

IQ tests supposedly objective tests that establish a person's 'intelligence quotient' (how clever they are).

League tables rank ordering of schools according to their test and examination results.

Marketization the move towards educational provision being determined by market forces.

Mixed-ability teaching teaching pupils together, regardless of their ability.

National Curriculum what every pupil in every state school must learn, decided by the government.

New vocationalism a series of measures in the 1980s that re-emphasized the importance of work-related education.

Open University university set up to provide a means of acquiring degree-level education by distance learning, via correspondence, video and TV.

Oxbridge the collection of colleges forming Oxford and Cambridge universities.

Parental choice ability of parents to choose which schools to send their children to.

Parity of esteem equal status, equally valued.

Progressive education child-centred approaches to teaching and learning.

Public schools the top private fee-paying schools, e.g. Eton, Harrow, Roedean.

SATs (Standard Attainment Tests) tests for 7, 11 and 14 year olds in English, maths and science. Used to compare school performance.

Secondary education education between ages 11 and 16.

Social exclusion the situation where people are unable to achieve a quality of life that would be regarded as acceptable by most people.

Specialist schools schools which have a particular focus within their curriculum and links to specialist areas of work, e.g. arts and media, business, languages, health care and medicine. They can select 10 per cent of their intake on the basis of ability.

Streaming where pupils are taught in groups according to their perceived ability.

Vocational work-related.

Item A The A-to-C economy

Those who get Grade C at GCSE boost their school's league table position. Those who get a D or less don't score at all. Gillborn and Youdell in their research *Rationing Education* (Open University Press, Buckingham 1999) have noted that a new ethos has emerged in schools which they call the 'A-to-C economy'. They found schools were having to prioritize particular groups in order to survive and that everything in the three schools they studied (two in London, one in the Midlands) was being judged in proportion to the percentage of A to Cs the school was likely to get. They were constantly promoting any innovation that would make their league table figures look good, such as a move away from mixed-ability teaching towards setting, as in some subjects the syllabus is different for the different tiers. Other strategies include encouraging lower-ability pupils to opt for non-examined subjects, entering pupils for the lower tier (grades C to G) because there is more chance of them achieving a C grade than risking them taking the higher tier papers even though they may have the chance to achieve an A or B grade. Their research showed that the students who were disadvantaged by the system were mainly Black, White working-class, or had special needs.

Adapted from Smithers, R. and Berliner, W. *The Guardian*, 19 March 2002; Ahmed, K. *The Observer*, 24 February 2002

Item B The old boy network

Ex-private [fee-paying] school students hold upwards of 75 per cent of the top jobs in British institutions, including the government, the civil service, the church, the legal system, the armed forces and the financial system in the City. Yet, they make up only about 7 per cent of the school population. Furthermore, those who control these institutions come overwhelmingly from a few exclusive schools – for example, Eton, Harrow, Winchester and Westminster – and have attended Oxford or Cambridge universities (the so-called 'Oxbridge connection'). Those who occupy the top jobs perpetuate these inequalities in two ways:

- by sending their own sons and daughters to these same schools
- by appointing new recruits to top jobs from these schools.

This restrictive elite self-recruitment is known as the 'old boy' (or 'school tie') network. (Public schools don't have to follow the National Curriculum, nor are their teachers inspected by central government officers.)

Adapted from Denscombe, M. (1993) *Sociology Update*, Leicester: Olympus Books

1 Explain what is meant by 'league tables' (Item A). (2 marks)

2 Identify two reasons why many schools have moved away from mixed-ability teaching (Item A). (4 marks)

3 Suggest three ways in which someone in a 'top job' can attempt to ensure that their sons and daughters attain a position of similar status (Item B). (6 marks)

4 Identify and briefly explain two reasons why it is more likely that middle-class parents will get their children into their first-choice school (Item B). (8 marks)

5 Examine the sociological arguments and evidence in favour of the view that changes to the education system have resulted in greater equality of opportunity for all pupils. (20 marks)

6 Using material from the Items and elsewhere, assess the view that the main thrust of educational reform has been to increase the control of education by those outside the education system. (20 marks)

web.tasks

1 Visit the site www.eng.umu.se/education/ which provides an excellent history of British education in words, pictures and contemporary documents.

2 Visit the Standards site www.standards.dfes.gov.uk and find information on different types of schools and key educational initiatives.

Class and educational achievement

getting you **thinking**

- 30 000 children left school in 2001 without a GCSE grade A to G. These children were overwhelmingly from unskilled and semi-skilled social backgrounds.

- In 2002, just one in five of the top performing comprehensives were in inner-city areas.

- In 2002, in the 100 schools with the highest percentage of pupils on free school meals, only 29 per cent of pupils gained five A* to C grades at GCSE. Those schools with the smallest proportion of pupils on free school meals achieve twice the national average in GCSE results with 93 per cent of students achieving five A* to C grades.

In addition, children from working-class backgrounds:

- are less likely to be found in nursery schools or pre-school playgroups

- are more likely to start school unable to read

- are more likely to fall behind in reading, writing and number skills

- are more likely to be placed in lower sets or streams

- are more likely to leave school at the age of 16

- are less likely to go on into the sixth form and on to university.

1 **Make a list of possible explanations for the points in the list on the right. Use the photographs to help you.**

2 **Compare your list with those of others. Rank the explanations you have identified in order, with the most important first.**

3 **Explain why you have ranked some explanations higher than others.**

It seems obvious: our educational success or failure is simply the result of our ability and motivation. When sociologists look at educational achievement, however, they find that there are distinct patterns. It seems that ability and motivation are closely linked to membership of certain social groups.

Class: patterns of achievement

Differential educational attainment refers to the tendency for some groups to do better or worse than others in terms of educational success. The issue was initially considered by sociologists solely in terms of class as they attempted to explain the huge class differences that existed between schools within the tripartite system (see previous topic). Differences between boys and girls and between different ethnic groups are a more recent focus, which will be explored in later topics.

Explanations of class differences in educational attainment

Differential educational attainment has been explained in a number of ways:

- **material deprivation**
- **cultural disadvantages**
- cultural capital.

Material deprivation

Certain groups have less money than others and so are not able to make the most of their educational opportunities.
For example:

- They may not have the time and space at home to do schoolwork.
- They may not be able to raise money for educational trips.
- They may not have access to educational materials such as books, computers and the internet.
- They may experience ill health, have to work part-time to support their studies, or have to care for younger siblings.

Governments have attempted to reduce the material disadvantages faced by working-class pupils through **positive discrimination**. This takes the form of programmes of compensatory education (see previous topic) which plough more resources into poorer areas. The Conservative government in the 1990s allocated up to 25 per cent more money to local authorities in poor areas; and the introduction of Educational Action Zones by the Labour government in the late 1990s was also an attempt to raise standards by compensating for deprivation. Schools in deprived areas were given extra funding and allowed more independence than other state schools. However, the scheme was not extended beyond its initial five-year term. Excellence in Cities is a recent initiative which aims to improve the education of children in the inner cities (see panel above right).

Excellence in Cities (EiC)

This government programme to develop new strategies to raise performance was set up in March 1999 to improve the education of inner-city children; the aim was to drive up standards to match those found in the best schools. The following five items comprise the main policy strands.

- **Specialist Schools** (see main text)
- **Learning Mentors** – 800 were appointed in July 2000 – the plan is to recruit 3000 by 2004 in an attempt to reduce the numbers of pupils excluded each year, currently 12 000.
- **Learning Support Units** – 450 have been established to tackle problems of disruptive pupils without excluding them; the target is 1000 including 360 outside the EiC programme; the number of exclusions was cut by 15 per cent from 1997 to 99.
- **Gifted and Talented Children** – part of a national strategy for educationally gifted and talented pupils – includes summer schools at universities for those pupils whose families have not themselves been to university.
- **Beacon Schools** – one of the main strands of the EiC initiative, established to help raise standards in schools through the sharing and spreading of good practice through mentoring, work shadowing, in-service training and consultancy.

The recent introduction of Educational Maintenance Allowances for post-16 students has two main aims.

1 to offset the need for older students to work part time, often for long hours, to support their studies
2 to support parents by removing the need for them to pay for their child's travel, equipment and food costs whilst they remain in schooling.

In terms of university education, recent changes have been less favourable to poorer groups. Forsythe and Furlong (2003) found that the costs of higher education and the prospect of debt were putting bright working-class students off higher education, despite higher achievement post-16 for pupils of lower social classes. At the same time, those working-class students who did enter higher education often had to juggle academic commitments with part-time work. The decision to introduce £3000 top-up fees in 2003 has also been controversial. Research by the Centre for the Economics of Education (Forsyth and Furlong 2003) suggests that the expansion of university places planned for 2010 will lead to a sharp rise in less-able children from wealthy families going to university and a decline in working-class students of all abilities.

Cultural disadvantages

The education system is mostly controlled by middle-class people, many of whom are White. Those who share these characteristics may well be viewed more positively and be more likely to succeed in the tests and exams created to assess their abilities. The 11+ test (see Topic 2) was criticized for middle-class bias. Being able to unscramble an anagram (a jumbled-up word) such as 'ZOMRAT' to form the name of a famous composer (MOZART) is much easier for a child familiar with anagrams (because their parents do crosswords) and classical composers (because they have seen their names on CD covers in their parents' music collection).

Much (now dated) research into language has identified class differences in spoken and written language which disadvantage working-class children. The middle classes succeed not because of greater intelligence but merely because they use the preferred way of communicating.

Cultural capital

The idea of cultural capital (see Unit 1, Topic 2, p. 8) is used by Marxists to explain cultural influences on educational success. Bourdieu and Passeron (1977) suggested that middle-class culture (cultural capital) is as valuable in educational terms as material wealth (economic capital). Schools are middle-class institutions run by the middle class. The forms of knowledge, values, ways of interacting and communicating ideas that middle-class children possess are developed further and rewarded by the education system. Working-class and ethnic-minority children may lack these qualities and so do not have the same chances to succeed.

Ball *et al.* (1994) showed how middle-class parents are able to use their cultural capital to play the system so as to ensure that their children are accepted into the schools of their choice. The strategies they use include attempting to make an

impression with the headteacher on open day, and knowing how to mount an appeal if their child is unsuccessful in their application to a particular school. West and Hind (2003) found that interviews were also often used to exclude certain types of families, particularly working-class and poor families, whereas middle-class parents often had the cultural capital to negotiate such interviews successfully. The government plans to ban such interviews in 2005.

In *Education and the Middle Class* (2003), Power *et al.* note that, once middle-class parents had secured a place in the school of their choice, 'travelling time, homework and the schools' perceived exclusiveness made it difficult for children to maintain an 'external' social life, thus focusing peer group activity within the school territories and in the company of academically able and often ambitious students like themselves'. They conclude that an important aspect of cultural capital is the pursuit of 'conspicuous academic achievement' by both middle-class parents and children.

The influence of the school: interactionist explanations

Interactionist explanations of differential educational achievement – based on 'labelling theory' (see Unit 1, Topic 5, p. 22) – look at what goes on in schools themselves, and, in particular, teacher–pupil relationships. These theories had a major impact on the development of both the comprehensive system and the idea of 'progressive' education. Labelling theories suggest that teachers judge pupils not by their ability or intelligence, but by characteristics that relate to class, gender and ethnicity, such as attitude, appearance and behaviour. Becker (1971) showed how teachers perceive the 'ideal pupil' to be one who conforms to middle-class standards of behaviour. We also saw in the study by Rosenthal and Jacobson (see previous topic) how teachers' expectations can impact on pupil

Cultural capital in action

Leech and Campos
Selection by mortgage

Research at Warwick University in 2001 found that middle-class parents were willing to pay a premium of almost 20 per cent on house prices in order to get their children places at good comprehensives. Their study of two areas of Coventry found that house prices within the catchment areas of two popular schools were between 15 per cent and 19 per cent higher than similar homes lying just outside these areas. Top of the league for higher house prices near desirable schools is Ashover school in Derbyshire, which has an average house price in its catchment area of £275 000. That's £200 000 higher than the norm for houses in the area.

The research found that middle-class parents are very adept at playing the system which allows parents to state a school preference and which permits popular schools to expand. This 'selection or admission by mortgage' reinforces social-class disparities in education, because suburban schools which serve affluent areas cannot expand sufficiently to include all who want to go there. This has resulted in the shrinking of catchment areas and consequently the social-class make-up of schools. League tables distort these trends further as middle-class parents consult them and make financial decisions about home-buying which benefit their children.

Leech, D. and Campos, E. (2000) *Is Comprehensive Education Really Free? A study of the effects of secondary school admissions policies on house prices*, University of Warwick Economic Research Paper 581

1 **What stops working-class children from gaining access to schools in 'good areas'?**

2 **Why is this phenomenon called 'selection by mortgage'?**

motivation. Middle-class teachers are more likely to perceive middle-class behaviour as evidence of commitment to study, and working-class cultural demeanour as evidence of indiscipline, lower ability or motivation. They may hold different expectations of eventual achievement, which in turn can affect pupils' progress according to the ways in which they are labelled and sorted into ability groups. Stephen Ball (2002) goes so far as to suggest that setting is 'social barbarism', because it allows well-off children to be separated from 'others' whom their parents may consider socially and intellectually inferior. He points out that research evidence shows that grouping by ability leads to greater social-class inequalities between children. Studies show that pupils in bottom sets are often taught by the youngest and least experienced teachers with the highest rates of staff turnover. Also, there is less interaction between pupils in lower sets compared with higher sets. Pupils in lower sets experience lower self-esteem because they are both dispirited and demeaned by the experience. They are more likely to be alienated from school, apathetic about education and consequently disruptive.

The curriculum

Some sociologists have argued that what is taught in schools – the curriculum – actually disadvantages the working class. The knowledge that they encounter at school does not connect with their own cultural experience. Working-class experience is almost invisible in the school curriculum. History, for example, tends to deal with the ruling classes – such as kings, queens and politicians – rather than with the vast majority of ordinary people.

Recent government policies have emphasized the importance of differentiating between pupils. One the one hand, this promotes the idea that pupils need to be taught in different ways depending upon factors such as their ability and their learning styles. On the other hand, differentiation between pupils also now takes place through the creation of different types of school – some of these emphasize an academic curriculum, some specialize in particular subject areas that have currency in the local job market and some emphasize work related learning and vocational studies. The encouragement of differing curriculum models in schools means that, increasingly, a less comprehensive intake will be attracted. Academically focused schools, high in the league tables, are more populated by middle-class, able pupils. Specialist and foundation schools are allowed to continue to select 10 per cent of their pupils on the basis of aptitude. The remaining comprehensive schools will have an ability range skewed towards the lower end and populated by a higher proportion of working-class pupils. Research by the Education Network in 2002 found that Specialist and foundation schools (see Topic 2) have an advantaged intake compared with their comprehensive school neighbours, and less than half the number of deprived children, as measured by the number of free school meals.

Class is still considered by far the most significant factor influencing educational attainment – thought to have three times the effect on educational achievement of ethnicity and five times the impact of gender (Drew 1995). However, these other dimensions are still important and will be explored in the following two topics.

Why might the most successful comprehensive schools be keen to attract middle-class pupils?

Sociology AS for AQA

KEY TERMS

Cultural disadvantage this term has been used in two ways: 'cultural deprivation' theory suggests that some pupils' backgrounds are in some way deficient or inferior (e.g. in not placing sufficient emphasis on the importance of education); 'cultural difference' explanations suggest that pupils' backgrounds are simply different, and that the mismatch with the culture of the school places them at a disadvantage.

Differential educational attainment the extent to which educational achievement differs between social groups.

Educational Maintenance Allowance (EMA) a means-tested sum of up to £30 per week given to post-16 students to support them in meeting the daily costs of coming to school. The payments are paid only if the student proves they are attending regularly.

Material deprivation lack of money leading to disadvantages such as an unhealthy diet and unsatisfactory housing.

Positive discrimination treating certain groups more favourably than others, usually to help overcome disadvantages.

Check your understanding

1 Outline in your own words the meaning of the phrase 'differential educational attainment'.

2 How has recent government policy attempted to address material deprivation?

3 How do material factors influence working-class students' experience of higher education?

4 Give three examples of ways in which differences in class culture might affect achievement in education.

5 How does Ball argue that cultural capital helps middle-class children to gain a place in the school of their choice?

6 Using examples, explain how labelling can affect educational success.

7 What does Ball mean by the term 'social barbarism' in relation to setting?

8 How does the recent development of differentiation within and between schools impact on class and educational achievement?

web.task

Use the UCAS website at **www.ucas.ac.uk** to investigate class differences in higher education applications. What patterns can you find and how do they appear to be changing? Has the reduction in government financial support for students in the last few years had any effect on applications?

research ideas

● Interview other people in your class to find out their experiences of setting and banding. Compare their experiences with Ball's views on p. 177.

Item A Children still class-bound

Children from working-class homes are no more likely to get educational qualifications than they were 20 years ago, writes Geraldine Hackett. Research from the Institute of Education's centre for longitudinal studies suggests that social class remains a major factor in determining life chances. According to the early study, 'Obstacles and Opportunities on the Route to Adulthood', for those born into poverty, there remains persistent underachievement. The report says that education provides an avenue for children from disadvantaged backgrounds, but their peers from advantaged families gain even more from school.

The report says: 'Class of origin and childhood poverty make educational attainment more difficult for children of similar test scores.' For children from disadvantaged backgrounds, the die is cast by the time they reach the third year of secondary schools, when they may have already started to truant.

Times Educational Supplement,
23 December 2000

Item B A class apart?

Despite efforts from many sides, social class still dictates educational prospects.

Student applicants from the upper social classes are more likely to be admitted to the London School of Economics than any other university, the latest official statistics reveal. The LSE leads a batch of elite London academic institutions, including King's College and University College London, where a much larger proportion of students from posh backgrounds have successful applications than students from poorer backgrounds.

The figures have emerged as two Oxford academics reiterate their calls to abolish the interview system at the Oxbridge universities, after research showed that half of all independent school students attaining three A grades at A-level ended up at Oxbridge universities, compared to just under a third of those with the same grades from state schools.

Adapted from *Times Educational Supplement,* 16 November 1999

Item C Educational achievement and class

social-class grouping		% with higher education	% attended private school	% with no qualifications	% with literacy and numeracy below level 1
middle class	1 Professional	78	26	3	6
	2 Employers/Managers	35	12	17	8
	3a Intermediate non-manual	30	6	19	12
working class	3b Skilled manual	9	1	40	21
	4 Semiskilled manual	5	1	56	31
	5 Unskilled manual	1	1	74	37

Source: Adapted from DFES *Skills for Life Survey*, October 2003, HMSO, and HEFCE Survey 2004

Note: Level 1 means foundation level GCSE grade D to G equivalent; 'below level 1' therefore means below the level of a GCSE pass.

1 Explain what is meant by the term 'underachievement' (Item A). (2 marks)

2 Suggest two possible reasons why 'half of all independent school students attaining three A grades at A-level ended up at Oxbridge universities, compared to just under a third of those with the same grades from state schools' (Item B). (4 marks)

3 Identify three patterns in the data in Item C. (6 marks)

4 Identify and briefly explain two possible reasons why there is greater participation in higher education for members of higher social classes (Item C). (8 marks)

5 Examine the ways in which material factors affect the educational achievement of different social classes. (20 marks)

6 Using information from the Items and elsewhere, assess the view that factors within schools are the greatest influence on social-class differences in educational achievement. (20 marks)

Ethnicity and educational achievement

Read the information below and then answer the questions that follow.

Drawing on the best evidence ever assembled on race and achievement in England, David Gillborn and Heidi Safia Mirza found that, while all the principal minority groups now achieve higher results than ever, White pupils have improved more than most (Gillborn and Mirza 2000). As a result, some minorities are even further behind the majority than they were a decade ago. The situation is especially serious for Black, Pakistani and Bangladeshi pupils. These are some of the report's key findings:

- Black pupils often enter school better prepared than any other group but fall behind as they move through the system.

- The achievement gap between 16-year-old White pupils and their classmates of Pakistani and

African-Caribbean origin has roughly doubled since the late 1980s.

- The gender gap is now present in every ethnic group. Girls are more likely to achieve five higher grade GCSEs in all the principal minority groups.

- The gender gap is beginning to make good some ethnic inequalities. Girls of Bangladeshi, Pakistani and African origin now outstrip White boys, but girls of African-Caribbean origin (38 per cent) are less likely to achieve five higher grade passes than White boys (45 per cent), Bangladeshi boys (40 per cent) and Indian boys (58 per cent).

- Too few local education authorities (LEAs) take race seriously. Around one in three do not monitor exam results for differences between ethnic groups.

1 What evidence is there that the educational achievement of some ethnic groups has shown less improvement than that of others?

2 What do you understand by the phrase 'The gender gap is beginning to make good some ethnic inequalities'?

3 What do you think needs to be done to address the underachievement of some ethnic groups?

Material and cultural explanations of educational disadvantage referred to in the previous topic also apply to the experience of ethnic minorities, because many tend also to be working class. In every ethnic group, middle-class pupils achieve higher average results than working-class pupils from the same ethnic group. However, middle-class Black pupils are the lowest attaining middle-class group. Their chances of five higher-grade GCSEs (38 per cent in the most recent figures) are less than working-class Indians (43 per cent), and only a little better than working-class Whites (34 per cent) (DfES 2002).

Bangladeshi, Pakistani and Black children are more likely to be brought up in low-income families and subsequently suffer educational disadvantages in line with or worse than those of working-class Whites.

Drew (1995) examined the relative impact of class, gender and ethnicity on educational attainment. Whilst class was clearly the most important factor, African-Caribbean males were still at the bottom of each class group in terms of attainment. However, African-Caribbean females, although they suffer from initial disadvantages in school, tend to do significantly better than working-class White pupils by the time they take their GCSEs. Fuller (1984) suggests that they may appear 'cool' in order to present a positive self-image to boys and teachers, but that they recognize the importance of getting good qualifications (see Topic 6).

Children of Indian, Chinese and African-Asian origin also do very well within the education system. There is a strong emphasis on self-improvement through education in these cultures, and many of the children come from professional backgrounds, providing support, appropriate role models and material advantages. Their culture is perceived more positively by teachers than that of African-Caribbean males. In addition to all of the points listed in the previous topic (for children from working-class backgrounds), African-Caribbean males:

- tend to get fewer GCSEs and poorer grades than any other group
- are overrepresented in special schools for children with behavioural or learning difficulties
- tend to get expelled or suspended up to four times more often than their White counterparts.

Whilst some Pakistani and Bangladeshi children do relatively badly in school, recent research has shown these groups to be catching up. The length of time Asian immigrant groups have lived in Britain varies. Those who have been here longer achieve more highly in the education system, because older siblings, educated here, are able to help their younger brothers and sisters. Also, reflecting changes within the White community, females generally tend to perform better than males within each ethnic group (see Topic 5).

Material and cultural factors

Many working-class and ethnic minority pupils may feel undervalued and demotivated by an educational system that does not recognize their qualities, which are based on their class and ethnic culture.

African-Caribbean underachievement has been blamed on the high numbers of one-parent families in African-Caribbean communities. Some politicians have suggested that, because many of these families are female-headed, African-Caribbean boys, in particular, lack the discipline of a father-figure, and this, they suggest, may account for the high percentage of African-Caribbeans in special schools. For girls, on the other hand, the role model provided by a strong, independent single mother is a motivating influence, and this helps to explain their relative success in education. However, although a slightly higher number of African-Caribbeans do live in one-parent families, it should be noted that most children of African-Caribbean origin live in nuclear families.

A recent study showed that recent arrival into UK had a significant negative effect on performance (by the equivalent of more than one level in each core subject). Like social class and recent arrival, the level of mother's education was also a significant factor (Haque and Bell 2001).

Language has also been seen as a problem for children of African-Caribbean origin, who may speak different dialects of English; and for children from other ethnic groups who come from homes where a language other than English is spoken. This language difference may cause problems in doing schoolwork and communicating with teachers, leading to disadvantage at school.

Ball (2002) shows how ethnic-minority parents are at a disadvantage when trying to get their children into the better schools. The parents, especially if born abroad, may not have much experience of the British education system and may not be able to negotiate the system. This may be compounded by a lack of confidence in their English-language skills.

Issues such as uniform (which markets a school well and fosters an impression of discipline) may disrupt teacher–pupil relationships, particularly between teachers and ethnic minority pupils whose cultural influences may exert more pressure on them to subvert the formal dress codes of the school, e.g. by refusing to remove baseball caps. This may provoke more antischool behaviour, truancy and the constructive exclusion of 'problem children'. Gewirtz (2002) identifies further socially exclusive practices, such as the creation of complex application forms requiring high levels of literacy and often available only in English.

Labelling and racism in schools

Boys of African-Caribbean origin often have the label 'unruly', 'disrespectful' and 'difficult to control' applied to them. Gillborn (1990) found that African-Caribbean pupils were more likely to be given detentions than other pupils. The teachers interpreted (or misinterpreted) the dress and manner of speech of African-Caribbean pupils as representing a challenge to their authority. In perceiving their treatment to be unfair, the pupils responded, understandably, in accordance with their labels. Tony Sewell (1996) claimed that many teachers were fearful of Black boys in school, the result of socialization into stereotypical assumptions (see Focus on research, Topic 6, p. 195). Jasper (2002) goes further to suggest that the expectations that White female

Look at the graph and table below, and then answer the question that follows.

Figure 5.1 Ethnicity, gender, social class and educational achievement

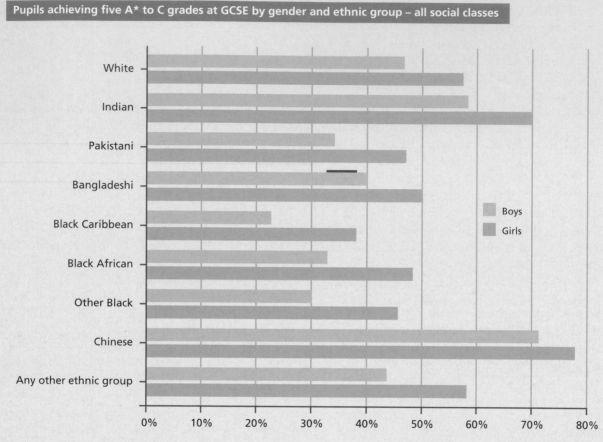

Pupils achieving five A* to C grades at GCSE by gender and ethnic group – all social classes

Source: National Statistics Online, January 2004

Table 5.1 Achievements at GCSE/GNVQ in 2003, by ethnicity, free school-meal provision and gender

| GCSE or GNVQ 5 or more A* to C | Non-free school meals | | | | | | Free school meals | | | | | |
| | 15 year olds | | | % achieving | | | 15 year olds | | | % achieving | | |
	Boys	Girls	Total	Boys	Girls	Total	Boys	Girls	Total	Boys	Girls	Total
White	210,995	204,442	415,437	50.2	61.1	55.6	28,036	27,507	55,543	17.1	24.2	20.6
Mixed	3,680	4,013	7,693	49.3	62.6	56.3	1,160	1,295	2,455	22.7	33.4	28.4
Asian	12,631	11,779	24,410	53.9	65.5	59.5	5,949	5,607	11,556	32.9	45.5	39.0
Black	6,154	6,543	12,697	33.1	48.7	41.1	3,003	3,175	6,178	21.5	31.7	26.8
Chinese	953	850	1,803	72.1	79.8	75.7	128	116	244	62.5	75.9	68.9

Source: DfES 2003

The entitlement to free school meals is often used as an indicator of low income. What do the figures above tell us about:

1 educational achievement (as measured by GCSE performance) and gender

2 educational achievement and ethnicity

3 educational achievement and social class (as measured by entitlement or not to free school meals)

4 the relationship between class, gender and ethnicity in relation to GCSE attainment?

teachers have of Black boys' behaviour dictate the form and style of the teaching that they offer them, a style less conducive to learning than they offer to other groups. However, Sewell has recently been attacked by many in the Black community for suggesting that Black culture and peer pressure are as detrimental to the achievement of Black children as racism. Sewell argues that an anti-intellectual culture and knowledge of sport and popular music give Black children status in the eyes of White students, but harm their own chances of success in education.

While few would argue that teachers display overt racism, Wright (1992) found considerable discrimination in the classroom. She observed Asian and African-Caribbean children in primary schools and found that teachers paid Asian pupils, especially girls, less attention. They involved them less in discussion and used simplistic language, assuming that they had a poor command of English. Teachers also lacked sensitivity towards aspects of their culture and displayed open disapproval of their customs and traditions. This had the effect of making the girls feel less positive towards the school. It also attracted hostility from other pupils, who picked up on the teachers' comments and attitude towards the Asian pupils. Despite this, teachers did have high expectations of Asian pupils with regard

to academic success. Connolly (1998) has conducted similar research and confirmed her findings (See Topic 6).

The same was not true of African-Caribbean pupils, who were expected to misbehave and who were more harshly treated than White pupils who exhibited similar 'bad' behaviour. Teachers also made little effort to ensure that they pronounced names correctly, causing embarrassment and unnecessary ridicule. Finally, pupils of both Asian and African-Caribbean origin were victims of racism from White pupils.

The curriculum

Some sociologists have argued that the curriculum – what is taught in schools – actually disadvantages ethnic minorities. The knowledge that they encounter at school may not connect with their own cultural experience, while **ethnocentrism**, resulting from the use of out-of-date material, could be potentially offensive by reflecting old colonial values and racial stereotypes. Coard (1971) showed how the content of education also ignored Black people. The people who are acclaimed tend to be White, whilst Black culture, music and art are largely ignored. Coard argued that

focus on research

David Gillborn & Deborah Youdell
Rationing education

Gillborn and Youdell (1999) studied two London comprehensive schools over a two-year period using lesson observation, analysis of documents, and interviews with pupils and teachers. In both schools, approximately twice as many White as Black pupils were achieving five or more higher grade GCSE passes.

Although Gillborn and Youdell found that 'openly racist teachers and consciously discriminatory practices were rare', they did find that 'widespread inequalities of opportunity are endured by Black children'. Teachers had an expectation that 'Black pupils will generally present disciplinary problems and they therefore tended to feel that 'control and punishment' had to be given higher priority than 'academic concerns'. They also expected Black pupils, on average, to do less well than their White peers.

In their turn, most Black pupils felt they were disadvantaged. By and large, the Black pupils expected to be blamed for disciplinary problems and they expected that teachers would underestimate their future achievements. In these circumstances, it was hardly surprising that they ended up doing, on average, less well than the White pupils attending the same schools.

Adapted from Haralambos, H. and Holborn, M. (2004)
Sociology: Themes and Perspectives (6th edn),
London: Collins Education

1 What problems are there in researching racism among teachers?

2 Why might teachers have expected Black pupils to present discipline problems?

this led to low self-esteem among Black pupils. However, this assertion was refuted by both the Swann Report (1985) and Stone (1981), who noted that, despite feeling discriminated against by some teachers, African-Caribbean children had been able to maintain an extremely positive self-image.

Since the 1970s, some effort has been made to address the neglect of other cultures in the curriculum. **Multicultural education**, which acknowledges the contribution of all of the world's cultures, has become more common, although it has been criticized for focusing only on external factors ('saris and samosas') and failing to address the real problem of racism. Ethnic-minority languages still do not have the same status as European languages, and schools are still required to hold Christian assemblies. The National Curriculum itself has also been criticized for being ethnocentric – especially in its focus on British history and literature. Geography also emphasizes Britain's positive contribution to the rest of the world, rather that the negative consequences of unfair trade and employment practices.

Problems of categorization

Classifying according to ethnic origin is by no means simple. The term 'ethnic minorities', for example, includes many different groups and does not take account of class and gender differences within those groups. Gillborn and Gipps (1996) argue that terms such as 'White', 'Black', 'Asian' and 'other' actually prevent any real understanding of differences in achievement. Postmodernists go further: they argue that the increasingly diverse nature of contemporary societies makes it impossible to explain educational achievement (or anything else) in terms of broad categories such as class or ethnicity, and that the generalizations that are made actually do more harm than good. They suggest that a conscious attempt needs to be made to understand the complexities of cultural difference and identity in modern society.

Check your understanding

1. Briefly describe some of the material disadvantages that might be faced by ethnic minorities from working-class backgrounds (see also previous topic).

2. What are the possible reasons for differences in educational achievement between Asian groups?

3. Suggest two reasons why some ethnic minorities do well within the education system.

4. Give three examples of ways in which cultural differences may affect ethnic achievement in education.

5. How may the labelling of Black boys have a negative impact upon their achievement?

6. How, despite generally high expectations, does the behaviour of teachers towards Asian children impede their success?

7. How might the curriculum itself disadvantage ethnic minority pupils?

8. What barriers to understanding underachievement are caused by placing pupils into broad ethnic categories?

KEY TERMS

Ethnocentric emphasizing White middle-class culture at the expense of other cultures.

Multicultural education education that recognizes cultural diversity.

research ideas

- Analyse the content of a sample of text books at your school or college. Focus on visual images, examples and case studies. To what extent do they recognize the variety of ethnic groups in contemporary Britain?

web.tasks

1. Search for statistics about ethnic groups and education at the Department for Education and Employment website at **www.dfee.gov.uk/statistics/**

   What statistics and reports are available? Do they tell us anything about the government's priorities?

2. Use the UCAS website at **www.ucas.ac.uk** to investigate class and ethnic differences in higher education applications. Select 'Statistics' and then choose from the menu.

   What patterns can you find and how do they appear to be changing? Has the reduction in government financial support for students in the last few years had any effect on applications?

exploring ethnicity and educational achievement

Item A Low expectations of pupils

The evidence that many teachers continue to have low expectations of pupils from some ethnic and linguistic minorities can be found in the impact of largely hidden, day-to-day decisions about such issues as placement in streamed classes. Evidence from school inspectors suggests that in schools that emphasize tight setting, some groups learning English as an additional language are likely to be placed disproportionately in low sets, especially in English (Ofsted 1999).

The introduction of tiered GCSE examinations has added new risks of discriminatory decision-making at that stage. Gillborn and Youdell (1999) have shown that Black children are markedly less likely to be entered for higher-tier examinations, depriving them of the opportunity to win higher grades.

Adapted from Cline, T. and Shamsi, T. (2000) *Language Needs or Special Needs? The assessment of learning difficulties in literacy among children learning English as an additional language: a literature review,* London: DfEE

Item B Ethnically excluded?

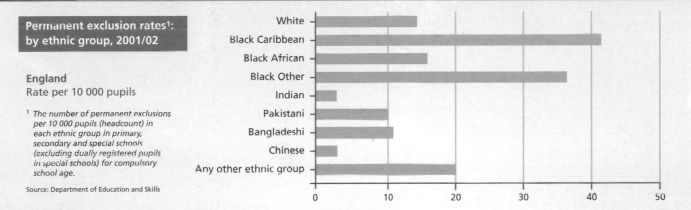

Permanent exclusion rates[1]: by ethnic group, 2001/02

England
Rate per 10 000 pupils

[1] The number of permanent exclusions per 10 000 pupils (headcount) in each ethnic group in primary, secondary and special schools (excluding dually registered pupils in special schools) for compulsory school age.

Source: Department of Education and Skills

Item C A-level attainment and ethnic origin

Source: Adapted from Trowler, P. (1995) *Investigating Education and Training,* London: Collins Educational, p. 113; and Haralambos, M. and Holborn, M. (2000) *Sociology: Themes and Perspectives* (5th edn), London: Collins Educational, pp. 869–70

Percentage of those reaching A-level/vocational equivalent standard, by ethnic group	1988	1997
● All ethnic minorities	31%	39%
● White	38%	46%
16 to 19 year olds in full-time education		
● All ethnic minorities	56%	63%
● White	37%	50%

---

1 Explain what is meant by linguistic minority (Item A). (2 marks)

2 Suggest two reasons why permanent exclusion rates are higher for Black pupils (Item B). (4 marks)

3 Identify three patterns in the data in Item B. (6 marks)

4 Identify and briefly explain two possible reasons why, despite greater staying-on rates than Whites, ethnic minorities still achieve fewer post-16 qualifications than Whites (Item C). (8 marks)

5 Examine the view that differences in educational achievement between ethnic groups are the result of material factors alone. (20 marks)

6 Using information from the Items and elsewhere, assess the view that it is schools themselves that are the cause of differences in achievement amongst ethnic groups. (20 marks)

Gender and educational achievement

getting you thinking

1 What do the pictures suggest are the key differences in the socialization of boys and girls?

2 What features of schooling might seem more in line with girls' experiences outside school?

3 What features of schooling might seem to conflict with boys' experiences outside school?

4 What, according to Ray O'Neil, has increased the mismatch between boys' socialization and schooling?

<< It is my view that boys are simply not socialized in a way that suits the process of being educated. The overstimulating, action-packed and exciting world they are now able to choose to belong to outside, more than ever conflicts with the relatively confined and passive nature of the classroom environment. >>

Ray O'Neil, deputy headteacher of a primary school in Gravesend, Kent

Until the late 1980s, there was much concern about the underachievement of girls. They did not do quite as well as boys in exams, and were also less likely to take A-levels and enter higher education. However, since the early 1990s, girls have begun to outperform boys at most levels of the education system. For example, they do better at every stage of the National Curriculum SAT results in English, Maths and Science, and in all subjects at GCSE and A-level. However, there are still concerns about the subject choices made by girls. For example, they are still less likely than boys to apply for degree courses in the 'hard' sciences (chemistry and physics) and information technology. This may impact negatively on their post-educational opportunities in terms of training and jobs.

Why has girls' achievement improved?

The job market

There are increasing job opportunities for women in the **service sector** of the economy. Many girls have mothers in paid employment providing positive role models. As a result, girls recognize that the future offers them more choices – economic independence and careers are now a real possibility.

Female expectations

Many women are now looking well beyond the mother–housewife role. In a 1976 survey, Sue Sharpe discovered that girls' priorities were 'love, marriage, husbands, children, jobs and careers, more or less in that order'. When the research was repeated in 1994, she found that the priorities had changed to 'job, career and being able to support themselves' above all other priorities.

Feminism

The work of feminist sociologists in the 1970s and 1980s led to a greater emphasis on equal opportunities in schools. Teaching approaches and resources were monitored for sex bias to ensure more 'girl-friendly schooling', especially in the sciences. Consequently, teachers are now more sensitive about avoiding gender stereotyping in the classroom. Various antisexist initiatives have raised both teachers' and girls' consciousness. Single-sex classes in some subjects, projects such as **Girls into Science and Technology**, and the exploration of sexism through **PSE** and citizenship classes have all made a difference. However, recent analysis of primary and secondary school text books (Best 1993, Abraham 1996) found that women continue to be presented as passive or in a narrow range of often domestic jobs (shopping or buying domestic appliances), whilst men are shown as active, running a business or investing.

Behaviour

There is mounting evidence that girls work harder and are more motivated than boys. On average, girls put more effort into their work and spend more time on homework. They take more care with presentation of their work, are better organized and, consequently, meet deadlines more successfully than boys. Research shows that:

- on average, girls read three times as much as boys
- while the average Year 7 girl will spend 40 minutes on a homework task, the average boy will spend 12 minutes
- the concentration span of girls is four times greater than that of boys.

Many boys believe school work should be done at school, and are not prepared to draft and redraft assignments (Burns and Bracey 2001).

Changes in the organization of education

The National Curriculum emphasis on science means that girls cannot avoid doing some 'hard' science. Also, the coursework involved in GCSE and some A-levels requires organizational skills and sustained motivation – skills that girls seem to be better at than boys. However, Debra Myhill (1999) points out that recent shifts to increase the proportion of unseen examinations in English have actually been paralleled by an increase in the outperformance of boys by girls in that subject.

Better socialization for schooling

Research shows that girls spend their leisure time differently from boys. Whereas boys relate to their peers by *doing* (i.e. being active in a range of ways), girls relate to one another by talking. This puts girls at an advantage, because school is essentially a language experience – most subjects require good levels of comprehension and writing skills. Among boys, peer group pressure is often very strong. It is noticeable from research that boys who do well at school are often helped at home, away from the view of the peer group. Boys often consider it weak to request help from a teacher and it is also especially difficult for a boy to accept help from another boy. Girls, on the other hand, are happy to help each other. It is an acceptable part of being female.

What are the concerns about boys' achievement?

- Boys are behind girls by the age of 6. Patterns of underachievement of reading and writing are set very early.
- The average girl is outperforming the average boy by 10 per cent across Key Stages 3 and 4 and A-level.
- At age 11, the average boy is nine months behind the average girl in development of speaking skills, 12 months behind in literacy and six months behind in numeracy.

- In English at GCSE, 64.4 per cent of girls achieve a high grade, compared with 46.9 per cent of boys. Traditionally, boys have matured later than girls, who have always been ahead in language at primary level.
- Less-able boys are virtually unemployable because they lack interest, drive, enthusiasm and social skills (Burns and Bracey 2001).
- Young men are much more likely than young women to be excluded from school (DfES 2003).
- 'Many boys talk of being bored and said that education has little relevance to them ... Boys and young men want a varied curriculum to combat boredom for those who are less academic' (*Listen Up*, Home Office, consultation with young people carried out by National Youth Agency and Youth Net 1999).

Why are boys underachieving?

Changes in the job market/status frustration

Some commentators, notably Mac an Ghaill (1994), suggest that working-class boys are experiencing a 'crisis of masculinity' (see Unit 2, pp. 55 and 62). They are socialized into seeing their future male identity and role in terms of having a job and being a 'breadwinner'. However, the decline of **manufacturing industry** and the rise in long-term unemployment make it increasingly unlikely that males will occupy these roles.

Moreover, new jobs in the service sector are often part-time, desk-based, and suited to the skills and lifestyles of women. In some families, females may be the primary breadwinners. Consequently, traditional masculine roles are under threat. Working-class boys' perception of this may influence their motivation and ambition. They may feel that qualifications are a waste of time because there are only limited opportunities in the job market. They may see their future as bleak and without purpose. Consequently, they don't see any point in working hard at school.

Peer group status

Some boys may gain 'street cred' and **peer group status** from not working. These boys may create subcultures in some schools, which are both antieducation and antilearning. These subcultures are explored in more depth in Topic 6. Their members may well see schoolwork as 'uncool' and unmasculine. In particular, reading may be regarded as boring, feminine and to be avoided at all costs. This may explain why boys are less conscientious and lack the application for coursework skills. The following quote from a headteacher illustrates this well:

<< *It is better to be famous for being a clown or a toughie than working hard and being a failure.*>>

Bob Perris, headteacher,
Hedworthfield Primary School, Jarrow

Ann Phoenix
Proper men?

Ann Phoenix of Birkbeck College said, 'We found 11 to 14 year olds believed you could not be masculine and be seen to be working hard at school. It is the same whether the boys are White, Black, Asian, working class or middle class. They think that to be properly masculine, you have to be good at sport, particularly football ... you need to be seen not to work. Those who are clever – swots, stiffs, boffs or whatever you want to call them – are unpopular and seen as not male.'

Daily Telegraph, 10 November 1998

1 What evidence is there that gender differences cut across class and ethnic differences?

2 How does Phoenix suggest boys' peer groups control the ways boys display their masculinity?

Social control differences

There is also some evidence that teachers are not as critical with boys as with girls. They may have lower expectations of boys, expecting work to be late, rushed and untidy, and expecting boys to be disruptive. Some research suggests that boys are less positively influenced than girls, or even turned off, by primary-school environments which are female dominated and may have an emphasis on neatness and tidiness.

Unrealistic attitudes

There are signs that boys' overconfidence may blind them to what is actually required for educational success. Research

Confident femininity?

Uncertain masculinity?

indicates that they are surprised when they fail exams and tend to put their failure down to bad luck rather than lack of effort. On the other hand, girls are more realistic, even self-doubting, and try that much harder in order to ensure success.

What about the future?

Some feminist researchers are concerned that girls are still underachieving because of disruptive boys. Teachers may be so tied up with controlling boys that girls don't get the attention they deserve. Recent research shows that girls' educational achievement has improved despite continuing male dominance of the classroom, curriculum content (for example History's focus on the lives of men) and greater demands on teacher time (Francis 1998).

Feminists are also still concerned about the narrow subject choices that females are making at further and higher education level. Females are still more likely to take arts subjects, and males are more likely to take scientific and technological subjects. Such gender stereotyping may be the result of gender socialization in early childhood (e.g. different toys and activities around the home), teacher advice on subject choice, and a continuing perception that the sciences are masculine subjects.

The debate may be influenced by social class and gender. Although middle-class girls outperform all other groups, working-class girls constitute a significant number of underachievers in the school system, and should not be neglected. Moreover, girls from some ethnic backgrounds perform significantly worse than many other groups.

Many feminists believe that the current concern about boys and achievement is simply a 'moral panic' which reflects antifemale sentiments and a patriarchal society. (Why, instead, aren't girls praised for their improvements?)

Gender and subject choice

- While girls are now achieving better academic results than boys at age 16, relatively few young women are choosing science or science-related subjects for further study.

- Boys dominate in maths, science and technology at A-level and far more men than women study these subjects in higher education. This has significant implications for men's and women's career choices and future earnings: 60 per cent of working women are clustered in only 10 per cent of occupations; and men are also under-represented in a number of occupations.

- Pupils' subject and course choices are influenced by a range of factors: their own views and expectations, those of their peers, parents and teachers, and the media.

From the Standards Site at www.standards.dfes.gov.uk/genderandachievement/understanding/subjects

1 What impact might this pattern of subject choice have on the future earnings of men and women?

Check your understanding

1 What have been the overall trends in male and female achievement in the last 20 years?

2 How might changes in the economy affect both female and male attitudes towards education?

3 How may changes in both the organization of the education system and classroom practices have benefited the education of females?

4 How may aspects of boys' socialization explain why they underachieve at school?

5 What characteristics do male antischool cultures possess that undermine educational success for boys?

6 Explain how class and ethnicity may be just as important as gender in explaining the current achievement patterns of boys.

KEY TERMS

Girls into Science and Technology a pre-National Curriculum initiative designed to encourage females to opt for science and technology.

Manufacturing industry industries that actually make goods. Most of the work in such industries is manual and based in factories.

Peer group status being seen as 'big' or important in the eyes of friends and other people around you.

PSE Personal and Social Education. Sometimes known as PSHE (including Health Education) or PSME (including Moral Education).

Service sector a group of economic activities loosely organized around finance, retail and personal care.

research ideas

- Conduct a content analysis of two science and technology textbooks used at your school or college. One should be significantly older than the other, if possible. Count the number of times that males and females appear in diagrams, photographs, etc., and record how they are shown. Find examples that are gender specific. What roles do they suggest as typical for each gender? Is there a change over time?

- Interview a sample of boys and girls. Try to find out if they have different expectations about future success. Are there differences in the amount of time they spend on homework?

web.task

The government's concern about gender and achievement is demonstrated by their creation of a website devoted to the issue. Visit it at www.standards.dfee.gov.uk/genderandachievement for statistical data and summaries of research.

exploring gender & educational achievement

Item A Poor boys

Debates about boys and schooling take three main forms. There are stories about 'poor boys', who are victims of feminism or teachers, about schools which fail them and about their laddishness. 'Poor boys' stories call for alterations to the curriculum and teaching to favour boys. 'Failing schools' stories lead to punitive inspection processes, hit squads and action zones. Like 'poor boys' the 'boys will be boys' stories call for alterations to teaching to favour boys and, in addition, seek to use girls to police, teach, control and civilize boys. But these responses are based on oversimplified explanations of what is happening in schools. Not all boys are doing worse than girls. The picture is far from simple. Rather than spending our time in handwringing, we must try to understand the complexity of the situation. If we ask 'Which boys, in which areas, are doing badly?', we find that the impact of class and ethnicity on achievement is greater than that of gender.

Adapted from Epstein, D. *et al.* (eds) (1999) *Gender and Achievement*, Milton Keynes: Open University Press

Item B Forget gender, class is still the real divide

'Reports of girls' GCSE success obscure the true picture,' says Gillian Plummer. Yet another simplistic, statistical interpretation of gender differences in examination results makes the national news: 'Boys are outperformed by girls in GCSEs.' As a result, the government wants all education authorities to take action in raising the academic performance of boys.

But beware: simplistic statistical analyses are dangerously misleading. We do not have a hierarchy in which girls are positioned in the top 50 per cent and boys in the bottom 50 per cent at GCSE. It is social class, not gender or race differences, which continues to have the single most important influence on educational attainment in Britain.

The majority of boys and girls from socially advantaged families do much better in all subjects at GCSE than the majority of girls from socially disadvantaged families.

While, overall, girls do outperform boys at GCSE, working-class girls do only marginally better than working-class boys in public examinations.

The desperate need for detailed research on the educational failure of the majority of working class girls has been hidden by:

- statistics recording the admirable rise in the achievements of middle-class girls, who are taken to represent 'all girls'
- serious concerns about the deviant behaviour and particularly poor exam performance of working-class boys.

It is dangerous and inaccurate to imply that all boys underperform and that all girls do well.

The real question is: what action is being taken to raise the academic performance of working-class girls (as well as other underachievers)?

Adapted from *Times Educational Supplement*, 23 January 1998

---

1 **Explain what is meant by the word 'laddishness' (Item A).** (2 marks)

2 **Identify two explanations for the underachievement of boys (Item A).** (4 marks)

3 **Suggest three ways in which teaching might be altered to favour boys.** (6 marks)

4 **Identify and briefly explain two reasons why the writer of Item B believes that social-class differences are more significant than gender differences.** (8 marks)

5 **Discuss explanations of the recent improvements in the educational attainment of girls.** (20 marks)

6 **Using information from the Items and elsewhere, assess sociological explanations of boys' underachievement in education.** (20 marks)

How do pupils respond to education?

getting you thinking

Sociology AS for AQA

1 Look at the photographs. Compare the pupils in the two photographs in terms of their likely:

(a) attitudes to education

(b) home background

(c) educational achievement.

2 Identify one occasion from your own education where most pupils seemed positive about their school experience.

3 What was it about the school, teachers or pupils that contributed to these feelings?

4 Identify one occasion from your own education where most pupils seemed negative about their school experience.

5 What factors do you think caused this? Was the negativity confined to particular pupil groupings, such as specific class, gender or ethnic groups?

6 Why do you think that some groups are proschool (in favour of school) whilst others are antischool (against it)?

Pupils respond to their schooling in different ways. Some groups accept the rules and the authority of teachers without question, while others may devote all their attention to rule-breaking and avoiding work. You have probably encountered examples of both during your compulsory education. Sociologists are interested in these subcultures. Why do they form, and what effect do they have on their members, other pupils, teachers and schools?

In the 1970s, a great deal of media concern was directed at inner-city comprehensives and the alleged misbehaviour of their pupils. This prompted sociologists such as Paul Willis (see p. 165) to examine the possible reasons for the development of these mainly male, working-class groups of 'undisciplined' school pupils, or antischool subcultures. As we saw in Topic 1, Willis identified a group of 'lads' – whose main aim at school was to have a 'laff' by rejecting the values of the school – and a more conformist group, referred to by the 'lads' as 'earoles'.

On a general level, all subcultures have things in common: their members gain status, mutual support and a sense of belonging from the subculture. According to Hargreaves (1967), antischool working-class subcultures are predominantly found in the bottom streams of secondary schools. In fact, he argued, they are caused by the labelling of some pupils as 'low-stream failures'. Unable to achieve status in terms of the mainstream values of the school, these pupils substitute their own set of delinquent values by which they can achieve success in the eyes of their peers. They do this by, for example, not respecting teachers, messing about, arriving late, having fights, building up a reputation with the opposite sex, and so on.

Writers such as Hargreaves and Willis refer to the pro- and antischool cultures as **homogeneous**, coherent groups, sharing their own uniform sets of values. Peter Woods (1983), however, argues that this is too simplistic. He argues that pupils use a variety of **adaptations**, depending upon the ways in which the values of the school are accepted or rejected. Some pupils may partially accept aspects of the school's values but reject others. It is now recognized that responses will also differ within and between the different categories of pupils, and in different school situations. The study of school subcultures is, therefore, a lot more complex than it used to be.

Male subcultures

The anti-school male subcultures of the early 1970s made a degree of sense in that their members nearly all got jobs, despite their lack of qualifications. Their **coping strategies** – what the 'lads' in Willis's study called 'having a laff' – also equipped them for the monotony of the work they were destined for.

The economy has changed, however, and very few working-class jobs remain in manufacturing. Has this changed the antischool subculture of the 'lads'? There is concern that some working-class boys are stuck in a time warp. That is, they imagine that work will be available whatever happens to them in school, and so they make little effort. In a sense the 'laff' is on them when they find that this is not the case and they are forced to join training schemes. Riseborough (1993) describes how boys on **YTS schemes** show some awareness and resentment of their predicament. They quickly realize that there is little likelihood of a job at the end of the scheme, and that they are being exploited.

Mac an Ghaill (1994) illustrates the complexity of subcultural responses by examining the relationship between schooling, work, masculinity and sexuality. He identifies a range of school subcultures, as follows.

The 'macho lads'

This group was hostile to school authority and learning, not unlike the lads in Willis's study. Willis had argued that work – especially physical work – was essential to the development of a sense of identity. By the mid-1980s much of this kind of work was gone. Instead, a spell in youth training, followed very often by unemployment, became the norm for many working-class boys.

The academic achievers

This group, who were from mostly skilled manual working-class backgrounds, adopted a more traditional upwardly mobile route via academic success. However, they had to develop ways of coping with the stereotyping and accusations of effeminacy from the 'macho lads'. They would do this either by confusing those who bullied them, by deliberately behaving in an effeminate way, or simply by having the confidence to cope with the jibes.

The 'new enterprisers'

This group was identified as a new successful proschool subculture, who embraced the 'new vocationalism' of the

The Bash Street Kids – an example of antischool subculture?

1980s and 1990s (see Topic 7). They rejected the traditional academic curriculum, which they saw as a waste of time, but accepted the new vocational ethos, with the help and support of the new breed of teachers and their industrial contacts. In studying subjects such as business studies and computing, they were able to achieve upward mobility and employment by exploiting school–industry links to their advantage.

'Real Englishmen'

These were a small group of middle-class pupils, usually from a **liberal professional** background (their parents were typically university lecturers, or writers, or they had jobs in the media). They rejected what teachers had to offer, seeing their own culture and knowledge as superior. They also saw the motivations of the 'achievers' and 'enterprisers' as shallow. Whilst their own values did not fit with doing well at school, they did, however, aspire to university and a professional career. They resolved this dilemma by achieving academic success in a way that appeared effortless (whether it was or not).

Gay students

Finally, Mac an Ghaill looked at the experience of a group neglected entirely by most writers – gay students. These students commented on the **heterosexist** and **homophobic** nature of schools, which took for granted the naturalness of heterosexual relationships and the two-parent nuclear family.

Female subcultures

Mac an Ghaill refers to the remasculinization of the vocational curriculum. By this he means the higher-status subjects such as Business Studies, Technology and Computing, which have come to be dominated by males. Girls are more often on lower-level courses – doing stereotypical work experience in retail or community placements, for example. In Mac an Ghaill's study, although girls disliked the masculinity of the 'macho males', most sought boyfriends. Lower-class girls, in particular, even saw work as a potential marriage market. More upwardly mobile girls saw careers more in terms of independence and achievement.

Griffin (1985) studied young White working-class women during their first two years in employment. Rather than forming a large anti-authority grouping, they created small friendship groups. Their deviance was defined by their sexual behaviour rather than 'trouble-making'. Most importantly, there was not the same continuity between the school's culture and that of their future workplace as there had been for the lads in Willis's study. Instead there were three possible routes for the girls, which they could follow all at the same time:

- the labour market – securing a job
- the marriage market – acquiring a permanent male partner
- the sexual market – having sexual relationships, while at the same time maintaining their reputation so as to not damage marriage prospects.

Ethnic subcultures

O'Donnell (1991) showed how the various ethnic subcultures have distinctive reactions to racism, prejudice and discrimination, which may have different effects on educational performance. Males of African-Caribbean origin often react angrily to and reject the White-dominated education system, gaining status and recognition through other means. Males of Indian origin show their anger, but do not tend to reject the education system. Instead, they succeed because they use the education system to their advantage. We saw in Topic 4 that Black boys underachieve within the education system, whether because of institutional racism, teacher stereotyping or the anti-educational influences of their culture and peer group. For Sewell (2000), the culture of the streets is anti-educational. It is a culture that puts style and **instant gratification** ahead of the values of school and college. Males of African-Caribbean origin see educational success as a feminine thing. The way for them to get respect is through the credibility of the street. In Sewell's terminology, the young man wants to be a 'street hood'. Success in the school room marks the Black boy out from his peers or classmates and is likely to make him the target of ridicule or bullying. According to Sewell, educational failure becomes a badge to wear with pride.

Connolly (1998) found in his recent investigation of three classes of 5 to 6 year olds in a multi-ethnic inner-city primary school that some negative stereotypes are not just confined to boys. Like Black boys, girls were perceived by teachers as potentially disruptive but likely to be good at sports. The teachers in one school tended to 'underplay the Black girls' educational achievements and focus on their social behaviour'. Like their male counterparts, they were quite likely to be disciplined and punished, even though their behaviour did not always seem to justify it.

Other studies point out that African-Caribbean females resent negative labelling and racism in schools. They particularly resent the fact that many teachers expect them to fail. Like males, they develop resistance to schooling. However, they do not form totally antischool subcultures – they realize that these lead to educational failure. Instead, they adopt strategies that enable them to get what they need from the system, that allow them to maintain a positive self-image, obtain the qualifications they desire, and above all prove their teachers wrong.

Mirza (1992) found that the Black girls in her study, while rarely encountering open racism, were held back by the well-meaning but misguided behaviour of most of the teachers. The teachers' 'help' was often patronizing and counter-productive, curtailing both career and educational opportunities that should have been available to the Black girls. For example, the girls were entered for fewer subjects to 'take the pressure off', or they were given ill-informed, often stereotypical, careers advice. The girls, therefore, had to look for alternative strategies to get by, some of which hindered their progress – such as not asking for help. Alternatively, they helped each other out with academic work, but were seen to resist the school's values by refusing to conform through their dress, appearance and behaviour. Connolly (1998) also examined the treatment in school of boys and girls of South Asian origin. He found that teachers tended to see South Asian boys as immature rather than as seriously deviant. Much of their bad behaviour went unnoticed by teachers and was not punished to the same extent as that of Black boys. The South Asian boys, therefore, had difficulty in gaining status as males, which made it more difficult for them to enjoy school and feel confident. However, teachers did have high expectations of their academic potential and they were often praised and encouraged. South Asian girls were seen as even more obedient than the South Asian boys, even though in reality their behaviour showed a similar mix of

work, avoidance of work and disruption, which was largely indistinguishable from their male peers. Expectations regarding their academic potential were high and it was felt that they needed little help when compared with other groups. These judgements were more likely to be related to the perception that they were largely quiet, passive, obedient and helpful, rather than to academic outcomes.

It is clearly the case that the actual or perceived membership of subcultures in school has an impact on pupils' experience of schooling and their achievement, in a variety of ways. But the situation can be highly complex and it is difficult to generalize about the nature of school subcultures and their impact on educational experience.

focus on research

Tony Sewell

Black masculinities and schooling

How Black boys survive modern schooling

Sewell (1996) found that Black pupils belonged to a range of both pro- and antischool subcultures as a result of the lack of positive recognition of their culture and stereotyped views held by many teachers. He found that Black pupils were disciplined excessively by teachers who were socialized into racist attitudes and

who were scared of these students' masculinity, sexuality and physical skills. The Black boys adapted in various ways, some of which reinforced these stereotyped views, and behaved in ways that could be interpreted as violent and disruptive. Sewell adapts Merton's typology of deviance in describing the subcultural responses that emerged:

1 *Conformists* – Black boys who were often praised for their positive behaviour and attitude who were said to be adopting White values at the expense of losing their African-Caribbean identities – the largest group though still less than half the cohort

2 *Innovators* – accepted the goals of the school, but maintained a rebellious and antischool posture, while avoiding trouble through their adoption of 'intelligent strategies'

3 *Retreatists* – a small group of loners who kept themselves to themselves

4 *Rebels* – who adopted the signs and signals of aggressive African-Caribbean masculinity and rejected the school. Their behaviour was aggressively masculine and they perceived masculinity in terms of sex and money. Their favoured term of abuse was 'pussy', which they used to imply homosexuality or femininity and low status. Other pupils perceived them to be bullies.

Adapted from Blundell, J. and Griffiths J. (2002)
Sociology since 1995, Lewes: Connect Publications

1 What, according to Sewell, is the cost of Black boys' lack of acceptance by the school?

2 What is the difference between 'innovators' and 'rebels'?

3 What do you think Sewell might mean by the 'intelligent strategies' adopted by innovators?

4 How does each subculture's behaviour relate to the traditional goals of education (academic success and progression to further education) and the accepted means of achieving them (hard work, cooperation and intellectual development)?

Check your understanding

1 How, according to Hargreaves, did 'low stream failures' respond to their label?

2 Explain in your own words why the work of early writers on pupil cultures has been criticized.

3 How has the economic situation for working-class males changed since the 1970s?

4 Which of Mac an Ghaill's male subcultures were proschool, and which antischool? What were the reasons for this?

5 Give three examples of the ways in which the experience of female subcultures is said to be different from that of male subcultures.

6 Why, despite their generally positive identification with school, do Black girls remain disadvantaged in the education system?

7 According to Connolly, how do teachers' perceptions of South Asian pupil subcultures affect their experience of schooling?

KEY TERMS

Adaptations refers here to different ways of responding to compulsory schooling (e.g. by being a teacher's pet, by going through the motions but not trying to achieve anything, or by doing your own thing).

Coping strategies ways of 'getting by' in an unpleasant situation.

Heterosexist biased against homosexuals.

Homogeneous the same throughout, undifferentiated.

Homophobic fearing that homosexuals pose a threat of some kind.

Instant gratification seeking pleasure straight away rather than being prepared to put off immediate pleasure for future reward.

Liberal professional university-educated (usually in the arts/humanities) people who tend to be open-minded and encourage personal freedom and self-expression, and who tend to work in areas that enable this outlook to thrive.

YTS Youth Training Scheme (see Topic 7).

research ideas

- Conduct a participant observational survey of your school or college to identify pro- and antischool subcultures. (Use Mac an Ghaill's categories as well as some of your own.)

- Design a questionnaire to examine the relationships between class, ethnicity and gender and subcultural membership.

web.task

Go to www.chavscum.co.uk – this a humorous site that claims to have identified a subculture called 'chavs' (there are various other names for this group – go to the site to find the full list). Look around the site.

To what extent do you think this group actually exists? And, if they do exist, what attitudes towards education are they likely to have?

exploring how pupils respond to education

Despite being fresh out of Torquay Boys' Grammar, Adrian Bougourd, 18, Will Rushmer, 19, and Ryan Hayward, 18, beat the other five teams on the Channel 4 fantasy share game show, *Show Me The Money*, at the end of the ten-week series. The youngest contestants [on the show] have made a profit of over £55,000 on an imaginary £100,000 lump sum in only eight weeks.

The teenagers, who have all recently started university, with 11 A-level A grades between them, are not new to stocks and shares. They started taking an interest in the stock market last year when their school entered the ProShare national investment programme. That competition for school pupils ended in May, and was won by a group of girls from Haberdashers' Aske's School, who were still doing GCSEs at the time.

Both Will, who is studying economics at Warwick, and Ryan are hoping for a career in the City in either fund management or investment banking once they have finished their degrees. Adrian, who is studying finance, accounting and management at Nottingham University, is toying with the idea of financial journalism. The Three Freshers, as they called themselves for the show, are just one of thousands of investment clubs in the UK.

The Times, 11 November 2000

Item B Gang culture

Gang culture in the north east of England means teenagers deliberately fail exams to stay cool, a study says. A poll of 4,000 Tyneside teenagers says peer pressure stops many pupils from studying or taking part in lessons.

Researchers say an antischool subculture known as 'charvers' reject school as uncool and refuse to do GCSE course work, meaning they fail their exams. They say the situation could be the same across other UK cities, although the groups might have different names. The charvers typically wear fake designer and sports gear and are usually from poor backgrounds.

Researchers questioned teenagers aged between 15 and 17. They found the charvers' attitude was that school was uncool but college was OK, and that most expected to resit their GCSEs at FE colleges.

The research was by Lynne Howe, director of the South Tyneside Excellence in Cities programme.

She said: 'For some youngsters – those known as charvers – being cool and well thought of among their peers is the most important thing.

'These youngsters were largely from a deprived population but they didn't lack confidence or self-esteem. They deliberately fail their GCSEs because their social standing outside school is more important than any qualification.

'They were scared of being called names, physical threats and damage to the family home and property if they were seen doing homework or answering questions in class, but they consider college cool.'

The former teacher said the teenagers identified five different groups in school, including charvers, radgys (more aggressive than charvers), divvies (impressionable hangers-on to the charvers), goths (wear dark clothes but often work hard) and freaks, who work hard and are considered 'normal' by teachers.

Nearly a third of the 15 year olds said they had been picked on for doing well at school, while the same proportion admitted teasing others who participated in lessons. More than 90 per cent of bright pupils said they wanted to go to university but only one in four said they were doing their best at school.

Some said they would rather fail their GCSEs and take resits at college, hoping to get into higher education later, than risk being targeted by bullies while still at school.

Source: BBC Online News, September 2004

1 **Explain in your own words what is meant by 'antischool subcultures' (Item B).** (2 marks)

2 **Suggest two ways in which the writer of Item B considers educational achievement to be affected by peer group membership.** (4 marks)

3 **Identify three reasons 'charvers' give for deliberately underperforming at school (Item B).** (6 marks)

4 **Identify and briefly explain two ways in which the proschool subculture described in Item A differs from the antischool subcultures referred to in Item B.** (8 marks)

5 **Examine the view that school subcultures merely reflect the social background of their student members.** (20 marks)

6 **Using information from the Items and elsewhere, assess sociological explanations of subcultures as a source of educational failure.** (20 marks)

TOPIC 7

Education, work and the economy

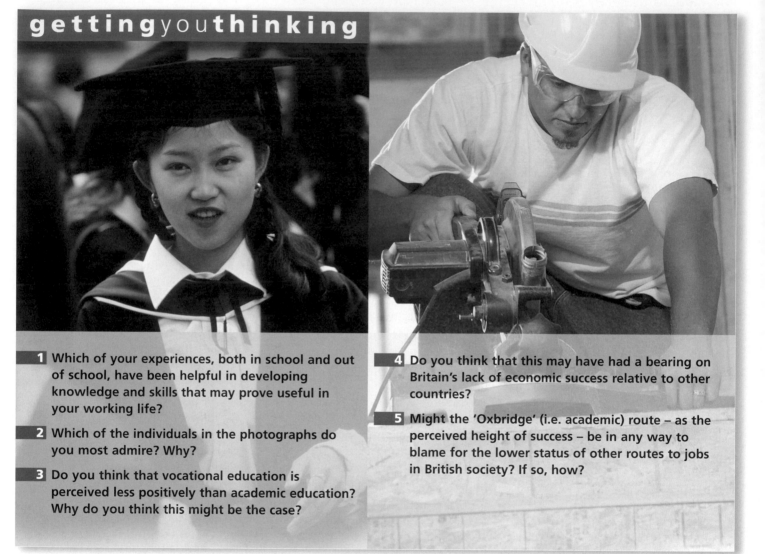

gettingyouthinking

1. **Which of your experiences, both in school and out of school, have been helpful in developing knowledge and skills that may prove useful in your working life?**

2. **Which of the individuals in the photographs do you most admire? Why?**

3. **Do you think that vocational education is perceived less positively than academic education? Why do you think this might be the case?**

4. **Do you think that this may have had a bearing on Britain's lack of economic success relative to other countries?**

5. **Might the 'Oxbridge' (i.e. academic) route – as the perceived height of success – be in any way to blame for the lower status of other routes to jobs in British society? If so, how?**

The 'new vocationalism'

Ever since the introduction of compulsory education, successive governments have recognized that the low status of work-related (or vocational) education is a problem. In Topic 1, we saw how these concerns helped to justify the introduction of compulsory state education in the first place. These arguments reappeared in the 1980s. It was claimed that the British workforce lacked appropriate technical skills because schools had lost touch with the needs of industry. Individuals who left school at 16 or 18 were ill equipped for work. Even those with higher qualifications tended to enter professions such as law or medicine rather than engineering or manufacturing. Consequently, Britain was viewed as being at a disadvantage in relation to international competition, and it was suggested that

this 'skills crisis' was a significant factor in Britain's industrial decline.

It was felt that education had been dominated for too long by the liberal humanist tradition and the academic concerns of the universities, which emphasized a critical appreciation of subject knowledge for its own sake. This was fine for developing a nation of critics, but no help in developing the economy – in fact, it was a barrier, according to the New Right.

Although people interested in industry have for a long time studied vocational courses – such as City and Guilds qualifications or BTECs in colleges of further education – these were mostly post-school courses. It was felt that school pupils had not got enough experience of industry to make proper decisions about what jobs they wanted to do. Whilst the more able school leavers may have been denied an industrial future due to lack of awareness, the less able needed the proper knowledge and skills to make them more employable. So a number of schemes were developed, which were grouped together under the title the 'new vocationalism'.

These training and education schemes aimed to make young people more familiar with the world of work. They included courses such as General National Vocational Qualifications (GNVQs which developed skills and knowledge related to broad occupational areas) and National Vocational Qualifications (NVQs – job-specific qualifications which demonstrate 'on the job' competencies such as 'production machine sewing'), which are often studied part time in college in the evening, or on day release, alongside full-time work.

Vocational education involves industry-related studies, mainly based in school or college. **Vocational training**, on the other hand, is designed to develop job-specific knowledge and skills in mainly work-like situations. Key developments in vocational training are outlined in the table on p. 201.

Criticisms of the 'new vocationalism'

Vocational education and training have had many critics. Finn (1987) argues that there is a hidden political agenda to vocational training. It provides cheap labour for employers, keeps the pay rates of young workers low, undermines the bargaining power of the unions (because only permanent workers can be members) and reduces politically embarrassing unemployment statistics. It may also be intended to reduce crime by removing young people from the streets.

Critics such as Phil Cohen (1984) argue that the real purpose of vocational training is to create 'good' attitudes and work discipline rather than actual job skills. In this way, young people come to accept a likely future of low-paid and unskilled work. Those young unemployed who view training schemes as cheap labour, and refuse to join them, are defined as irresponsible and idle, and are 'punished' by the withdrawal of benefits.

It is not proven that young people lack job skills. Many have already gained a lot of work experience from part-time jobs.

Youth unemployment is the result not of a shortage of skills, but of a shortage of jobs.

Critics also point out that the sorts of skills taught to YTS trainees are only appropriate for jobs in the secondary labour market. This consists of jobs that are unskilled, insecure, and pay low wages – such jobs offer little chance of training or promotion, employer investment is very low, and labour turnover is consequently very high.

In practice, it is lower-ability students who tend to be channelled into vocational courses. The new vocationalism thus introduces another form of selection, with working-class and ethnic minority students being disproportionately represented on these courses.

Training schemes do not appear to be breaking down traditional patterns of sex stereotyping found in employment and education; nor are they encouraging girls to move into nontraditional areas. In fact, they are structured so as to reproduce gender inequality. Buswell (1987) points out that the types of schemes into which girls are channelled, such as retail work, lead to occupations where they are low paid when young, and work part time when older, reflecting women's position in the labour market.

Many sociologists are sceptical about the claims for vocationalism. They argue that the central aim of giving students skills is fine in theory, but has been difficult to achieve in practice. **Competence-based learning** and assessment often become more about getting the right boxes ticked, rather than developing real skills. However, there have been some benefits arising from the new vocationalism – although it may be that these are simply the result of the extra resources being pumped into education to support all of the initiatives.

Bridging the vocational/academic divide?

Recent initiatives have aimed to start vocational education and training much earlier by bringing it into the compulsory phase of education in schools. All schools have now been encouraged to participate more fully in work-related learning and it has become a part of the National Curriculum. Since September

1998, schools have had the flexibility to ignore aspects of the Key Stage 4 National Curriculum to arrange extended work-related learning for those students who want it, or would benefit from it.

The changes brought about in post-16 education and training by Curriculum 2000 should, in theory, have enabled students to mix and match vocational and academic qualifications. Vocational A-levels can be studied alongside traditional subjects, and all students have been encouraged to achieve 'Key Skills' qualifications. However, there is, as yet, little evidence of this happening. Most middle-class White students are still opting for the traditional academic curriculum as before, while vocational courses continue to be dominated by working-class and ethnic-minority students. Partly as a result, the government set up the Tomlinson review of 14–19 education (Working Group on 14–19 Reform 2004) to try to end the vocational/academic divide for good. The division between compulsory and post-16 education, which has divided curriculum provision in the past, is to be overcome by the development of 'seamless' provision between the ages of 14 and 19 through an overarching diploma framework.

Pre-16 learners would continue to follow the statutory curriculum, gaining recognition towards the award of a diploma where appropriate. They would be able to opt for a substantial element of vocational learning, but would not be able to specialize in specific occupational areas. Post-16 learners would have greater choice to select between:

- a range of **specialized diploma** lines, designed to provide a basis for progression within lines of learning covering the range of vocational and academic options
- **open diplomas** which enable the learner to select a mixed pattern of subjects or lines of learning.

All diplomas would have the same basic structure of a core – including numeracy, communication and computer literacy – combined with the opportunity for specialization in particular areas. The New Labour government is aiming to make the world of work more familiar to all pupils as they progress through school, to inform their future choices better and, it is hoped, to provide employers with sufficiently skilled workers in the future. Whether these aims cut across class, ethnic and gender lines remains to be seen.

Check your understanding

1 In your own words explain why Britain was seen to be at a disadvantage in terms of equipping people for industry.

2 What was the 'new vocationalism'? Give examples.

3 What is the difference between vocational education and vocational training?

4 What do you consider to be the three most serious criticisms of vocational training?

5 What is meant by the vocational/academic divide, and how has the government tried to remove this divide?

6 How has focus on work-related learning recently shifted from post-16 to 14-to-19?

research ideas

- Survey a group of post-16 students at your school or college. Choose a sample that includes students following both academic and vocational courses. Why did they stay on at the age of 16? What is motivating them, and what do they hope to achieve from their qualifications? Are there differences in the motivations of students following academic and vocational courses?

- Conduct interviews with students who have undertaken work experience. Find out about their experiences and whether they feel that these have made them better equipped for a future job.

web.tasks

1 Find out about government policies on training at the Department for Education and Skills website at www.dfes.gov.uk

Do you think that these will be successful? Do they represent real opportunities for young people, or might there be other motives behind the policies?

2 Look into the proposed reforms of 14 to 19 education at www.14-19reform.gov.uk

Do you think you would benefit from the proposals?

KEY TERMS

Competence-based learning type of learning where the aim is to demonstrate that a particular skill has been acquired.

Vocational education work-related courses offered in schools and colleges (usually with a small amount of work experience).

Vocational training work-related courses offered through work experience (usually with a small amount of time in college).

Item A What kind of education?

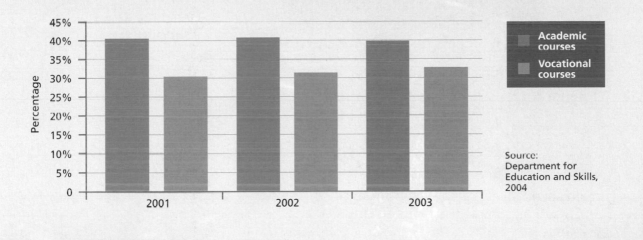

Percentage of 16 year olds in full-time education by type of course, England, 2001 to 2003

Source: Department for Education and Skills, 2004

Item B The image and the reality of youth training

There is often a gap between the image promoted of youth training and its reality. The literature of YT often suggested that it could open up exciting and creative opportunities for young people regardless of social background. However, youth trainees have long complained that they are being trained for 'Noddy jobs'. Certainly, there is evidence that the majority of YT places are provided by the big retailers – e.g. supermarkets and department stores, such as BHS and Marks and Spencer. Consequently, YT trainees have generally found themselves trained in a narrow range of skills, such as working on the till, shelf-filling and stocktaking, which are common to most retail jobs. One study found that 80 per cent of the jobs that YTS trainees went into required no entry qualification. There is also evidence that some employers are using YT as a screening device. If the trainee is uncomplaining, docile and flexible about the mundane tasks they are allocated, there is a good chance that they will be offered a post. Finally, whilst YT schemes emphasize equal opportunities for females and ethnic minorities, there is evidence that female training places reinforce traditional gender roles, whilst in some areas youth training places with major employers have been monopolized by White youth.

Adapted from Maguire, S. (September 1993) 'Training for a living? The 1990s youth labour market', *Sociology Review*, 3(1)

1 Explain what is meant by the term 'youth training' (Item B). (2 marks)

2 Identify two trends in the table in Item A. (4 marks)

3 Identify three examples of the gap between the image promoted of youth training and its reality (Item B). (6 marks)

4 Identify and explain two possible reasons why the percentage of 16-year-olds studying vocational courses increased between 2001 and 2003 (Item A). (8 marks)

5 Examine the ways in which the 'new vocationalism' reinforces inequalities. (20 marks)

6 Using information from the Items and elsewhere, assess the view that 'new vocationalism' was necessary and has been a success. (20 marks)

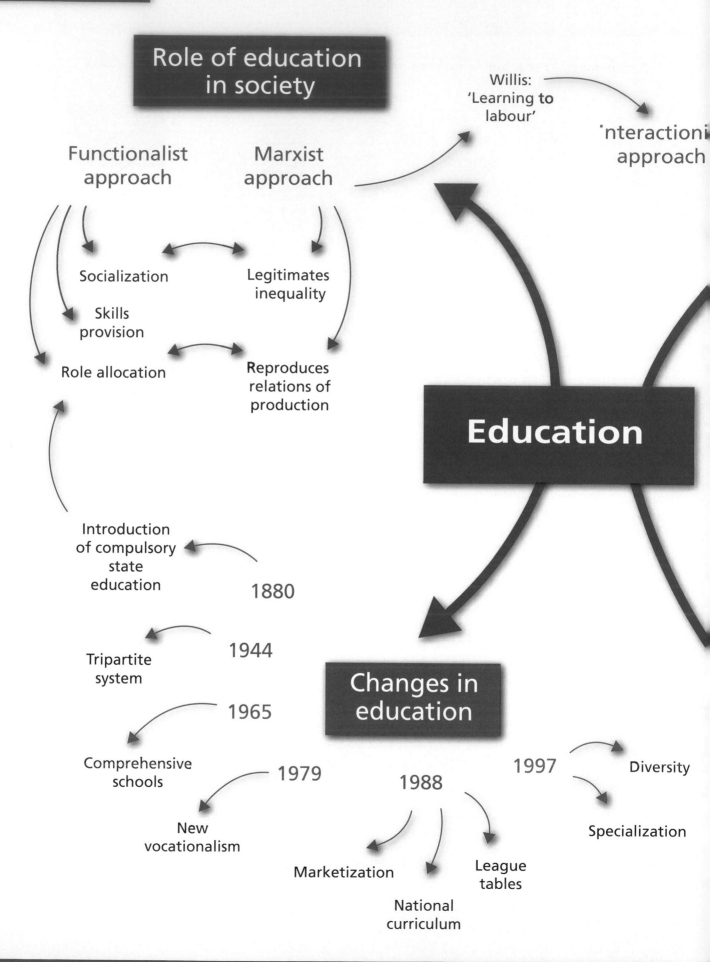

Role of education in society

Willis: 'Learning **to** labour'

'nteractioni approach

Functionalist approach

Marxist approach

Socialization

Legitimates inequality

Skills provision

Role allocation

Reproduces relations of production

Education

Introduction of compulsory state education

1880

1944

Tripartite system

1965

Changes in education

Comprehensive schools

1979

1988

1997

Diversity

New vocationalism

Marketization

League tables

Specialization

National curriculum

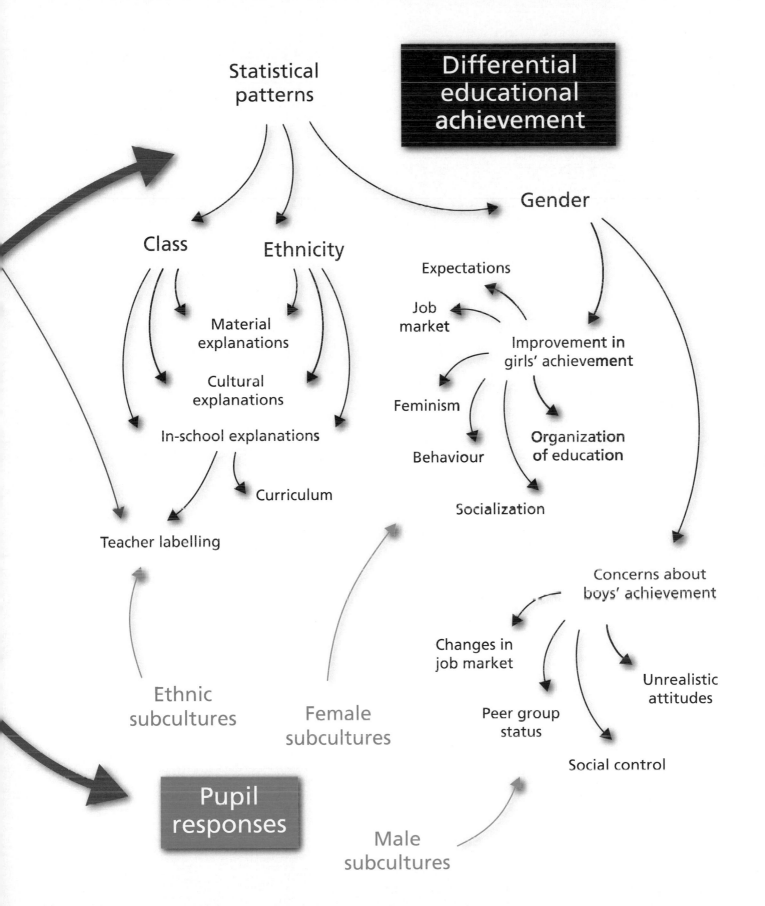

Statistical patterns

Differential educational achievement

Class

Ethnicity

Material explanations

Cultural explanations

In-school explanations

Curriculum

Teacher labelling

Ethnic subcultures

Female subcultures

Gender

Expectations

Job market

Improvement in girls' achievement

Feminism

Behaviour

Organization of education

Socialization

Concerns about boys' achievement

Changes in job market

Peer group status

Unrealistic attitudes

Social control

Male subcultures

Pupil responses

EVERY YEAR, NEWSPAPERS PUBLISH LISTS OF BRITAIN'S WEALTHIEST INDIVIDUALS; these lists provide some astonishing facts – for example, the richest person in the UK is the Duke of Westminster, who is worth £4.4 billion (though this is nothing compared to Microsoft owner, Bill Gates, who is worth £37.5 billion). What the list fails to point out is that a tiny proportion of the British population owns the vast majority of the wealth. Furthermore, a disproportionately small section of the population, partially overlapping with the most wealthy, earns a very high share of the income. At the other extreme, it is claimed that, according to one definition, as many as 12.5 million people are living in poverty.

How can this inequality and poverty still exist in a society which taxes people more heavily the more they earn, and a society which has a huge welfare state? In this unit, we explore the sociological and social policy issues arising from these questions. In Topic 1, we begin by clarifying exactly what we mean by the terms 'wealth' and 'income'. We then move on to look at the different ownership and earning patterns in contemporary Britain, before examining the reasons for the continuation of such inequality.

Topics 2, 3 and 4 carry out a similar analysis with regard to the subject of poverty. We begin with definitions and measurement in Topic 2, before examining the extent and causes of poverty in Topic 3. Topic 4 then moves on to discuss the explanations for the continuation of poverty today.

Topic 5 provides a slightly different perspective by considering how it might be possible to eradicate poverty through social policy initiatives. We identify and explore a range of sociological and ideological programmes which provide very different policies to combat poverty.

Topic 6 is very closely related to Topic 5, in that it takes these ideological approaches to eradicating poverty and examines what impact these have in practice.

AQAspecification	topics	pages
Candidates should examine:		
Different definitions of poverty and wealth and income	Definitions of income and wealth are covered in Topic 1, poverty in Topic 2.	206–17
Different explanations of the distribution of poverty, wealth and income between different social groups	Explanations of the distribution of income and wealth are covered in Topic 1. Topic 2 discusses the distribution of poverty.	206–17
Different explanations of the existence and persistence of poverty	Topic 3 investigates the groups most at risk of poverty. Topic 4 covers sociological explanations of poverty.	218–23
Different solutions to poverty, with particular reference to the role of social policy	Topic 5 looks at possible solutions to poverty.	230–35
The nature and role of public, private, voluntary and informal welfare provision	Topic 6 focuses on welfare provision.	236–41

UNIT 6

Wealth, poverty and welfare

Wealth and income

gettingyouthinking

*A retired couple on a 'SKI' holiday
(SKI = 'Spending the Kids' Inheritance')*

≪ Most people were keen to use up their financial assets during their retirement and were not planning to leave substantial amounts as bequests. But those who owned homes hoped to pass these on to their children.

The distribution of wealth is highly unequal – much more so than the distribution of income ... income and wealth are very closely related – those with a gross annual income of less than £5000 had median total wealth (including state pension wealth) of only about £3000 (median = the middle group of wealth owners). Those on incomes of over £35 000 a year had median total wealth of about £110 000. ≫

Rowlinson, K., Whyley, C. and Warren, T. (1999)
Wealth in Britain: A Lifecycle Perspective,
London: Policy Studies Institute

1 Do you think that people should have a right to pass wealth on to their children, or does it give some people an unfair advantage in life?

2 Do you think that we ought to have much higher rates of tax for the better off, to ensure that there is less inequality in society?

3 In your opinion should we have inequalities in income, or do you think that everyone should have the same wage? Give the reasons for your answer.

Wealth

Problems of definition

Wealth is defined as the ownership of property, shares, savings and other assets. However, within that overall definition, there is some debate about exactly what we should include as property and 'assets'. For example, does a person's house constitute wealth? Yes, of course, if they sold it, then they would receive a very large amount of money – but where would they live? But even that is too simple. Some people live in houses which are enormous and far exceed what they need – so does the excess beyond their needs count as wealth?

A similar debate surrounds **pensions** – some argue that pensions must be defined as wealth, because they are savings, while others argue that pensions are essential and so they do not actually constitute wealth.

So how we define wealth is not as easy as first appears. The answer to the problem of definition faced by sociologists is that we normally talk about **marketable wealth**. By this, we mean the range of assets that a person is reasonably able to dispose of, if they should so wish. Marketable wealth, therefore, is generally taken to exclude house and pension.

Problems of measurement

A further problem with wealth is actually measuring it. Unlike income, which we discuss later, the **Inland Revenue** does not conduct a yearly assessment of wealth. So, researchers obtain their information in one of the following two ways:

1 looking at the assessment of wealth made for tax purposes when someone dies
2 asking a sample of rich people the extent of their wealth.

Problems arise with both methods.

Inland Revenue statistics based on inheritance tax

Using information obtained from wills usually only provides us with out-of-date figures. What is more, wealthy people will attempt to limit the amount of wealth that they declare for tax purposes. Charitable trusts, early distribution of wealth to younger family members before death and financial holdings abroad are all common ways to avoid tax. All of this means that the wealth of the rich may be underestimated. On the other hand, poorer people who do not pay **inheritance tax** are excluded from Inland Revenue statistics, so their wealth may be underestimated too.

Surveys

Because of these problems, sociologists turn to surveys, but rich people are extremely reluctant to divulge their true wealth. Either way, the figures will probably be inaccurate.

Changes in wealth distribution over time

We have just seen some of the difficulties of trying to define wealth. However, even bearing in mind the differences that occur if we include such things as house values and occupational pensions, we can still make the simple, clear statement that wealth is distributed very unequally in British society.

In the 1920s, one per cent of the population owned over 60 per cent of all marketable wealth. A further 9 per cent owned 29 per cent, leaving 90 per cent of the population with about 11 per cent of marketable wealth. By the 1970s, however, the share of the top one per cent had halved to about 30 per cent, while the wealthiest 10 per cent (including the top one per cent) owned about 50 per cent of wealth. However, after 20 years in which this pattern of inequality stabilized, inequality began growing again during the 1990s.

Patterns of wealth today

If we include houses and pensions in the definition of wealth, then **personal wealth** more than doubled in the period between 1980 and the early part of the 21st century. This reflects the growth in home ownership. As house prices have increased faster than inflation, those who own homes (over 70 per cent of householders) have become 'richer'. However, for those who do not own their homes or have no pension, their personal wealth declined. In fact, during the period 1980 to 2000, the number of people without any assets (and therefore no wealth) increased from 5 per cent to 10 per cent of the population.

However, if we look only at personal marketable wealth – which consists largely of property, shares and other savings/investments – the situation is very different. Shares in companies are now held by a relatively high proportion of the population, as a result of the 1980s government sell-off of public utilities such as water, electricity and gas – and more recently as a result of some building societies 'giving' shares to their account holders, when they became banks.

Despite this increase in share ownership, a very large proportion of shares and other assets are owned by very few people. The wealthiest one per cent of the population own about 23 per cent of total marketable wealth (see Table 6.1), and the wealthiest 10 per cent own 56 per cent of all marketable wealth – mainly in the form of company shares. If we compare the total wealth of the richest one thousand families with the total wealth of the least wealthy half of the population – about 28 million people, then the richest one thousand had 15 000 times more total wealth!

Income

Defining income

Like wealth, income is difficult to measure. Once again, those with large amounts of income (who are of course often 'the wealthy') will seek to minimize their income levels on their income tax returns, and will employ accountants and tax experts to do just that.

But there are also methodological problems that sociologists face in trying to measure income levels. They have to decide whether to calculate income by household or by individual (poverty statistics, for example, are increasingly based on

Table 6.1 Marketable wealth, 1979 to 2001								
	1979	1983	1987	1992	1996	1997	2000	2001
Percentage of marketable wealth owned by:								
Most wealthy 1%	20	20	18	18	20	22	22	23
Most wealthy 10%	50	50	51	50	52	55	55	56
Least wealthy 50%	8	9	9	7	7	7	6	5

Source: Inland Revenue statistics, *Personal Wealth*, Table 13.5

households). They must decide which is more important, income before tax, or income after tax? And what about people who work for 'cash in hand'? Finally, many people receive state benefits, but also receive some services free (bus passes, for example) which others have to pay for – is this income?

Income distribution

Overall, income is more evenly distributed than wealth, but that does not mean there is any great amount of equality. The income of the highest-earning 20 per cent of households is four times higher than the lowest-earning 20 per cent – even after tax and including benefits for the lowest income earners. Furthermore, it appears that income inequalities are actually increasing, as Figure 6.1 below shows. This illustrates the growth in inequality between 1979 and 2002, using the Gini coefficient, a statistical measure of income inequality. The nearer the number 0, the greater the degree of income equality, and the nearer the number 1, the greater the income inequality.

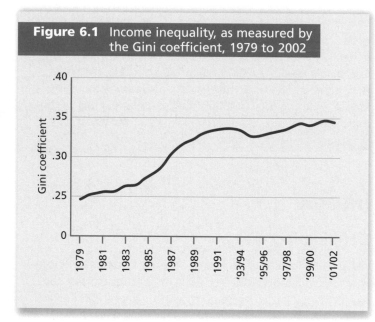

Figure 6.1 Income inequality, as measured by the Gini coefficient, 1979 to 2002

Changes over time

Income inequality is actually increasing, and has been doing so since the early 1980s. On average, income has risen by 44 per cent since 1979, with the wealthiest 10 per cent of the population experiencing an increase of 70 per cent in real terms. On the other hand, the poorest 10 per cent have had an income decrease of 9 per cent.

Income and the life cycle

Income inequality needs to be seen as a dynamic, changing concept. It is not that the same people are necessarily in the lowest (or highest) wage earners for their entire lives. The research suggests that income is closely related to the **life cycle** – people's earnings gradually rise over their lifetime and when

focus on research

Kawachi, Kennedy & Wilkinson
Crime and inequality

In 1996, Wilkinson published a famous study which linked income inequalities with high mortality and morbidity among poorer people. In a later study, Kawachi, Kennedy and Wilkinson wanted to see if inequality levels could also explain higher crime rates. They compared statistics on crime levels in different areas in the USA with various levels of income inequality. This, then, was a comparative study using official statistics on crime and income inequality. They found that *in general*, crime rates were highest when levels of inequality were at their highest and, conversely, where inequality was lowest, so too were crime rates – but this was not always the case.

The key factor which influenced the outcome of the relationship was the degree of *social capital*. This term describes the sense individuals have of belonging to a network of people living in a particular neighbourhood. Crime rates were a direct outcome of the two linked factors of inequality and social capital. The higher the level of inequality and the lower the degree of social capital, the higher the crime rate. They concluded that focusing solely on levels of inequality in income and wealth in understanding social problems ignored the key factor of social capital.

Kawachi, I., Kennedy, B.P. and Wilkinson, R.G. (1999) 'Crime, social disorganisation and relative deprivation', *Social Science and Medicine*, 48, pp. 719–31

1 In what way was the study 'comparative'?

2 What is meant by the term 'social capital'?

3 What did the study find about the relationship between inequality, social capital and crime?

their children leave home, but when they reach pensionable age, income declines sharply again.

Redistribution and the impact of taxation

We have seen that income and wealth are unequally distributed in the UK. However, as people pay higher rates of tax the more they earn, and as the lowest income groups receive a range of state benefits, the outcome should be that the levels of inequality are much lower. The evidence suggests that this is partly true, in that tax and benefits do redistribute, but not as much as might be expected.

Redistribution in the UK is based upon a mixture of taxes and benefits. These include the following:

- *Direct taxes* – These are taken straight out of a person's wage. These tend to be 'progressive', in that the more a person earns, the more they must pay in tax. Over the last 20 years, direct taxes have been reduced.
- *Indirect taxes* – These include taxes (such as **VAT**) which are added to purchases. Indirect taxes tend to be 'regressive' in that they hit poorer people harder, as they spend a higher proportion of their incomes on necessities. People with higher incomes can choose to save money if they wish. Indirect taxes have increased over the last 20 years.
- *Cash benefits* – These include payments by the government to lower earners and unemployed people. Depending upon how high these benefits are, they can significantly redistribute income or not. Since 1997, there has been a real increase in cash benefits, so that it has had a redistributive effect. The bottom 30 per cent of households have received about £20 a week more because of an increase and restructuring in benefits.
- *Benefits in kind* – These are services provided by the state which are freely available, such as education and health services. Currently, the lowest earning 20 per cent of households receive on average about £5200 worth of benefits per year.

What effects do these taxes and benefits have on the redistribution of income?

If we start by looking at incomes before tax, then the richest 20 per cent earn about 18 times more than the poorest 20 per cent. After income tax and the addition of various benefits, the ratio drops to 4 to 1. However, there are still some adjustments to be made. Most goods have VAT (value-added tax) charged on them, and this has a greater proportional impact on poorer families (because more of their income is spent, and less is saved). As a result, the actual ratio of incomes between the richest and poorest is about 6 to 1.

The tax and social security systems, therefore, do have an impact – they reduce inequalities by about two-thirds – but this still leaves considerable inequality.

Explanations for inequalities of wealth and income

Explanations for the continuing existence of – and indeed growth in – inequalities in income and wealth can be divided into two main categories: specific explanations and theoretical explanations.

Specific explanations for increases in income inequality

Government policy

Changes in taxation and state benefits have actually lowered taxes on the rich in real terms, while state benefits have declined relative to the increase in average earnings for those employed.

Two-earner households

Pahl (1988) has pointed out that there is an increasing division between households. On the one side, there are households in which there is no adult worker at all; on the other side, the number of two-earner households is rising. The divide is increasing because there is a decline in single-earner households, while the other two household types are growing – and as they do so, the differences in earnings are also growing.

Growth of lone-parent families

This links to the point above. The fastest growing type of family is the one-parent family. Because of childcare responsibilities, the parent (usually a woman) is more likely to work part-time or to have no employment.

Job insecurity

Employment patterns are changing, and the prospect of a job for life is gradually being replaced by job insecurity. People are now expected to perform a range of jobs in their working careers. A Joseph Rowntree Foundation survey in 1999, for example, found that 40 per cent of people who had lost their jobs in the previous six months had been unemployed in the previous two years – showing that unemployment is now a normal expectation for some employees, as employers demand more 'flexible' labour. The impact on income is that those with more reliable work can expect a regular income, while the increasing numbers in 'flexible' employment often experience peaks and troughs of income.

Specific explanations for the retention of wealth

Globalization

Most economies in the world are now linked in a **global economy**. If a democratically elected government were to seek to take wealth away from the very richest, the rich would move their money out of the country. This would have a huge impact on the British economy. Governments are therefore very cautious about upsetting the very rich.

The nature of the taxation system

The tax system in the UK allows a substantial proportion of wealth to be passed from one generation to another. This maintains wealth within the same small group.

Political decisions

If governments wanted to reform the tax system, increase benefits for lower-income families or raise the minimum wage, they could do so. Therefore, a key factor in maintaining inequalities of wealth and income is the choices made by politicians.

Entrepreneurial talent

It is possible for very clever (and possibly fortunate) people, from relatively humble backgrounds, to become rich – although, in practice, very few do so.

Theoretical explanations for income and wealth inequalities

There are three broad types of explanation for inequalities in wealth and income: functionalist (see pp. 12–15), Marxist (see pp. 17–19) and Weberian (see p. 18).

Functionalist-based theoretical explanations

These argue that society needs inequality in order to reward the more able, who undertake the most important social and economic positions. Critics have pointed out that this is more of a justification than an explanation. For example, it could be argued that nurses or social workers contribute more to society than advertising executives, yet they earn far less.

Marxist–based theories

Marxist theories claim that capitalism is based upon inequality, with the rich actively seeking to exploit the rest of society. Inequality is, therefore, inevitable in capitalism.

Weberian-based explanations

These suggest that society is best seen as various interest groups competing among themselves to ensure that they benefit the most. Weber argues that this results in more powerful groups finding ways to obtain the highest incomes and maintain their wealth.

Check your understanding

1 Explain why it is difficult to define 'wealth'.

2 Why might the statistics we have on wealth be inaccurate?

3 What changes in wealth distribution have taken place since the 1970s?

4 Which is less unevenly distributed across the nation, income or wealth?

5 In your own words, describe any one specific and one theoretical reason for the continuing inequalities in income and wealth.

6 How does the 'global economy' have an impact on wealth distribution within the UK?

research ideas

- Ask a sample of people to estimate the amount of wealth owned by the richest one per cent and the richest 10 per cent of people in the UK. Compare their responses with the actual figures. What do the results tell you about people's perceptions of wealth?

- Organize a small focus group (perhaps from another student group not studying sociology). Show them the figures on the differences in wealth and income. Ask them to discuss the reasons for such differences. Compare their views with the theoretical explanations in this topic. Which theory comes closest to their views?

KEY TERMS

Global economy refers to the way in which investment and trading now span the entire world. This hinders individual governments' control of the economy, because companies can simply move to other countries.

Inheritance tax tax on wealth when a person dies.

Inland Revenue the government department responsible for taxes on earnings and wealth.

Life cycle refers to the changes in a person's economic and social situation over their lifetime.

Marketable wealth all a person possesses (does not include their pension or house).

Pension a regular payment made to someone when they retire from paid employment.

Personal wealth wealth owned by individuals. This can be compared with institutional wealth, which is wealth owned by companies.

Redistribution the transfer of wealth from the rich to the poor. In theory, the taxes the rich pay are used to fund services for the poor.

VAT (value-added tax) a tax charged on most goods and services. It is an indirect tax because it is not taken directly from people's wages.

Wealth the ownership of property, shares, savings and other assets.

web.tasks

1 Search the site of the Joseph Rowntree Foundation at www.jrf.org.uk for their latest research on income and wealth. What does it tell us about the changing distribution of income and wealth?

2 The House of Commons Library produced a detailed research report on income and wealth in 2004. It can be found at www.parliament.uk/commons/lib/research/rp2004/rp04-070.pdf

Look at page 39. Find out which countries in Europe had the highest and lowest levels of income inequality – you may have to remind yourself about 'The Gini coefficient' (see p. 208).

exploring wealth and income

Item A The distribution of income

Distribution of real[1] household disposable income[2] (see p. 222) UNITED KINGDOM

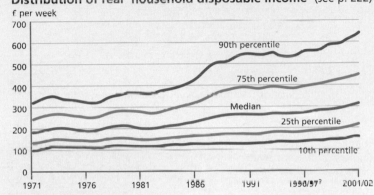

£ per week

90th percentile
75th percentile
Median
25th percentile
10th percentile

1971 1976 1981 1986 1991 1996/97[3] 2001/02

1 Data adjusted to 2001/02 prices using the retail prices index less local taxes.

2 Equivalized household disposable income before housing costs.
See Appendix, Part 5: Households Below Average Income, and Equivalization scales.

3 Data from 1993/94 onwards are for financial years. Data for 1994/95 onwards exclude Northern Ireland.

● Median refers to the level of income of the middle range of people in the UK.

● The 90th percentile refers to the richest 10 per cent and the 10th percentile refers to the poorest 10 per cent.

Source: *Social Trends* 34, London: Office for National Statistics, 2004

Item B Explanations of increases in inequality

<< Several explanations have been put forward to account for both shifts in individual earnings and the overall growth in inequality of earnings since the mid-1980s. The growth of unemployment, changing forms of work, the decline of the male 'breadwinner' and the increase in women's labour-force participation, the decline of trade-union influence and national collective bargaining structures, and changes in the taxation and benefit systems are among the factors that have influenced the rapid growth of income inequality in the UK.>>

Abercrombie, N. and Warde, A (2000) *Contemporary British Society* (3rd edn), Cambridge: Polity Press, p. 119

Item C Wealth accumulation

<< Among the factors found to affect wealth accumulation, the most important was ability to accumulate wealth – those with higher incomes and lower outgoings were most likely to put money into financial savings, mortgages and occupational or personal pension schemes. Attitudes towards saving and knowledge about different schemes also had an effect on wealth accumulation. Finally, the availability of suitable savings and investment schemes was also a key factor.>>

Joseph Rowntree Foundation, *Findings*, July 1999

1 Explain what is meant by 'distribution of income'. (2 marks)

2 Identify two trends in the graph in Item A. (4 marks)

3 Identify three sources of wealth (Item C). (6 marks)

4 Identify and briefly explain two reasons why income inequality in the UK has increased (Item B). (8 marks)

5 Examine the view that statistics on income and wealth are always inaccurate. (20 marks)

6 Using material from Item C and elsewhere, assess explanations of the distribution of wealth and income. (20 marks)

Defining and measuring poverty

Public definitions of poverty	
Someone in the UK was in poverty if ...	*% agreeing*
...they had enough to buy things they really needed, but not enough to buy the things that most people take for granted	28%
...they had enough to eat and live, but not enough to buy other things they needed	60%
...they had not got enough to eat and live without getting into debt	90%

Source: Jowell, R., Witherspoon, S. and Brook, L. (eds) (1995) *British Social Attitudes Survey*, Aldershot: Gower

A national survey was carried out in order to find out how 'ordinary people' defined poverty.

The respondents were offered the three definitions shown in the table above and asked which one(s) they agreed with (they could agree with more than one). The (cumulative) percentage agreeing with each definition is shown in the table.

1 If someone could not afford to buy the items pictured, which of the definitions of poverty in the table (if any) would you consider applied to them? Look at each item separately.

2 Which definition of poverty do you agree with? Explain your answer.

3 According to the figures above, to what extent does the public agree with your definition?

4 Break into small groups. Suggest four important reasons for poverty in the UK today.

5 Do you think it is possible to talk about poverty in the UK when we can see such extreme deprivation in other parts of the world?

Each time there is an election, the political party in government will announce all that they have achieved in combating poverty. They will manage to produce convincing statistics to show that poverty has decreased under their government. The opposition parties will angrily denounce these statistics as biased, and produce a completely different set, which show, quite clearly, that poverty has *increased* during the governing party's time in office. How do we make sense of this? The answer lies, quite simply, in the different definitions and measurements that can be used.

Sociologists have defined poverty in two different ways:

1 **absolute poverty**
2 **relative poverty**.

Absolute poverty

This definition is usually traced back to the 19th-century antipoverty campaigner Seebohm Rowntree. Rowntree was concerned that politicians refused to recognize the sheer extent of poverty in the UK. Therefore, in the 1890s, he conducted a 'scientific' survey to discover the real extent of poverty. Part of this survey involved constructing a clear definition that distinguished the poor from the non-poor. The definition was based on deciding what resources were needed for a person to be able to live healthily and work efficiently.

To find the amount of income a person needed, Rowntree added together:

- the costs of a very basic diet
- the costs of purchasing a minimum amount of clothes of minimum quality
- the rent for a basic level of housing.

The 'poverty line' was then drawn at the income needed to cover these three costs.

Advantages of an absolute definition of poverty

An absolute definition provides us with a clear measure of who is in poverty at any one time. It also provides us with a tool to compare the extent of poverty in different societies, and in the same society at different periods of time.

Disadvantages of an absolute definition

An absolute definition fails to take into account the fact that what is regarded as poverty changes over time. What is a luxury today may be a necessity tomorrow, as fashion, acceptable standards of housing and general standards of living change. This makes it very hard to decide exactly what constitutes a 'minimum' standard of clothes or an 'acceptable' diet. The absolute definition of poverty is, in fact, a measure of destitution – that is, the failure to obtain the absolute necessities to keep life going. But poverty is not actually **destitution** – someone can be poor, but still be able to struggle on.

The 'budget standard measure'

A contemporary version of the absolute definition is the 'budget standard measure', which is a rather more sophisticated version of Rowntree's original work. One version of this was developed by the Family Budget Unit, led by Bradshaw (1990). Bradshaw used detailed research information on the spending patterns of the poorest to construct an income that would provide a 'modest but adequate budget'. According to this measure, any family living below this income would be regarded as poor by any reasonable person.

Relative poverty

An alternative way of looking at poverty is to see it in terms of the normal expectations of any society. As societies change and become more (or less) affluent, so the idea of what is poverty will change too. Central heating and colour televisions were at one time luxuries – yet today the majority of homes have them. More recently, mobile phones and home computers have become part of a 'normal' standard of living for a very large section of the British population.

Relative poverty places poverty in relationship to the 'normal' expectations of society. If a person, or family, is unable to achieve a moderate standard of living, then they are poor.

Advantages of the relative definition of poverty

The relative definition links poverty to the expectations of society – reflecting the fact that people do measure their own quality of life against that of other people. It also broadens the idea of what poverty is – from lacking basic necessities to lacking a range of other 'needs', such as adequate leisure.

Disadvantages of the relative definition

The relative definition does have a number of disadvantages, however:

- It can only be used within any one society; it does not help with cross-cultural comparisons. (You are measuring poverty by asking people what is acceptable within their society – not across the world.)
- There is the difficulty of deciding what is or is not a 'normal' standard of living.
- It also has the rather absurd implication that, no matter how rich people become, there will always be poverty, as long as not everybody is equally rich. This is because relative poverty is as much a measure of inequality as poverty. As long as there is inequality, it could be argued, there is poverty.

Measuring relative poverty

There are two ways of **operationalizing** (measuring) the concept of poverty within the relative approach:

1 the **relative income measure**
2 the **consensual measure**.

The relative income measure (HBAI)

This approach measures income as a proportion of typical household income – the idea being that, if a family has a lower-than-average income, they cannot afford an acceptable standard of living. The most commonly used measure is that a household is in poverty if it receives less than 60 per cent of the **median** British income. This approach is now used by the British government and the European Union as the threshold measure of poverty. It is called **Households Below Average Income** or **HBAI** approach.

A consensual measure of poverty

A second approach is to measure the extent of poverty in terms of what possessions and services the majority of people think are necessary in a society. The measure is constructed by asking people to rank in order a list of possessions and services which they consider to be necessities. The resulting list is used as the basis to work out what most people regard as an unacceptable level of deprivation. This approach was used originally by Mack and Lansley in *Breadline Britain* (1993), and developed later by Gordon *et al.* in *Poverty and Social Exclusion in Britain* (2000).

Poverty and social exclusion

The concept of poverty is closely linked to that of **social exclusion**, and there is some debate over whether the term social exclusion should replace 'poverty'.

Poverty is usually seen as lack of income to purchase the goods and services that allow people to participate fully in society. In many ways, it is a 'static' concept, based on inability to purchase a socially accepted standard of living. Social exclusion, on the other hand, widens the horizon of analysis and looks at a range of interconnecting disadvantages from which certain groups in society suffer. These groups have the worst housing, health, education and job prospects in society, while suffering from the highest levels of stress, crime victimization and unemployment.

The idea of social exclusion comes from two sources. In the UK, it was originally developed by Townsend (1979), the very person who first introduced the notion of relative poverty. Townsend amended his definition of poverty to argue that poverty turned into social exclusion when it denied people full membership of society. This also coincided with the European Commission rejecting the idea that poverty in any meaningful financial sense (such as exists in developing countries or was experienced in Europe in the 1920s and 1930s) continued to exist. Instead, the Commission saw a wide range of extreme

inequalities in European societies which could not be remedied solely by increasing the income of the poor.

This is the crucial distinction between the ideas of poverty and of social exclusion. For poverty campaigners, if low incomes can be eradicated, then the problem of poverty will disappear. For campaigners who wish to eradicate social exclusion, extreme inequalities in health, housing, environment, crime victimization and education would all have to be tackled. Finally, social exclusion is seen as a problem that continues across generations, so that patterns of poor health, low educational attainment and high levels of victimization continue within the same families and neighbourhoods. Social exclusion is, therefore, a much wider and more complex issue.

Measuring social exclusion

According to the government's Social Exclusion Unit:

>> *Social exclusion is a shorthand term for what can happen when people or areas suffer from a combination of linked problems such as unemployment, poor skills, low incomes, poor housing, high crime environments, bad health and family breakdown.* >>

Because social exclusion is something which is manifested in virtually every aspect of life, actually measuring it is difficult. As a result, various 'indices' or measures have been developed which try to capture a snapshot of a wide range of disadvantages that the socially excluded face in life. The New Policy Institute, for example has developed 50 indicators which measure levels of:

- income
- employment
- educational attainment
- mental and physical health
- housing and homelessness
- living in a disadvantaged neighbourhood.

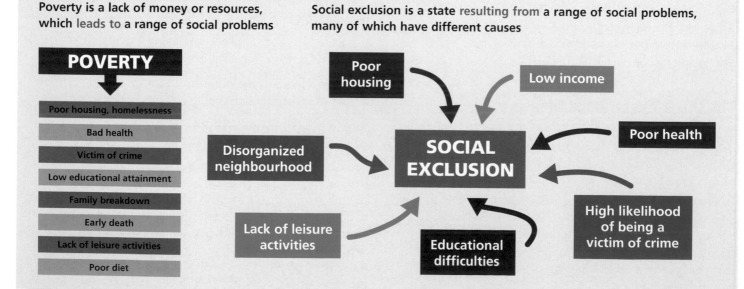

Figure 6.2 The differences between poverty and social exclusion

Poverty is a lack of money or resources, which leads to a range of social problems

POVERTY

- Poor housing, homelessness
- Bad health
- Victim of crime
- Low educational attainment
- Family breakdown
- Early death
- Lack of leisure activities
- Poor diet

Social exclusion is a state resulting from a range of social problems, many of which have different causes

Poor housing
Low income
Poor health
SOCIAL EXCLUSION
Disorganized neighbourhood
Lack of leisure activities
Educational difficulties
High likelihood of being a victim of crime

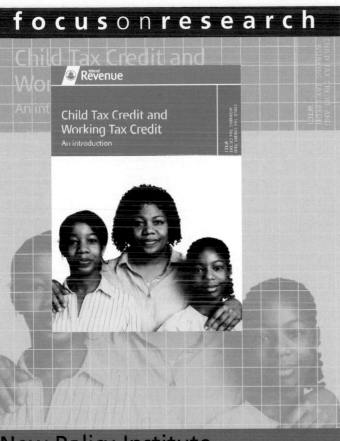

New Policy Institute

Monitoring poverty and social exclusion

The New Policy Institute has been undertaking a series of annual reports monitoring the latest changes in poverty levels. This is the sixth in the series, which began in 1997, the year that New Labour were elected. The researchers reanalysed a wide range of official statistics from government departments in order to see exactly what was happening. The Institute concluded that overall poverty was decreasing, influenced by the growing numbers of people in employment. This was strengthened by the introduction of a system of *tax credits,* which provided additional income for low-earning households. However, in terms of wider social exclusion, educational inequalities remained static, health inequalities were still high and certain parts of the country, particularly the North East, had a noticeably higher range of social problems than elsewhere.

> Palmer, G., North, J., Carr, J. and Kenway, P. (2003)
> *Monitoring Poverty and Social Exclusion 2003*,
> York: Joseph Rowntree Foundation

1 What reasons did the report identify for the decrease in poverty?

2 What did the report find out about the level of social exclusion?

Check your understanding

1 Explain the difference between an absolute and a relative measure of poverty.

2 What criticisms have been made of absolute definitions of poverty?

3 Relative definitions of poverty have been criticized by campaigners against poverty in developing countries – why might this be?

4 Give two examples of how researchers have actually 'operationalized' the relative poverty concept.

5 Why has there been criticism of the concept of poverty and a move towards the use of the term 'social exclusion'?

researchideas

- Draw up your own list of ten essential items for an AS-level student today. Ask a representative sample of students which items they agree are necessary: 'which all [AS-level students] should be able to afford, and which they should not have to do without' (see Item A on p. 217).

- At the time of writing, the government guarantees all people over retirement age a minimum income of £105 per week. Check for update at **www.thepensionservice.gov.uk/pensioncredit/**. Now work out (a) your weekly income (b) how much you spend per week *including* (if you are living with parents) an estimate of the cost of your food, travel, heating and lighting and council tax. What are your views on the incomes of retired people on minimum income?

web.tasks

1 Find out what the British government is doing about social exclusion – this is on the Social Exclusion Unit website at **www.socialexclusion.gov.uk**

2 Find detailed information on poverty and further research at the poverty site of the New Policy Institute at **www.poverty.org.uk/income/income_choices.htm**

Table 6.2 Summary of the poverty and social exclusion indicators

Indicator	Change over time		Indicator	Change over time	
	Over the last 5 to 6 years	Over the latest year of available data		Over the last 5 to 6 years	Over the latest year of available data
Income			*Adults aged 25 to retirement*		
1 Individuals with low income	Improved	Improved	24 Individuals wanting paid work	Improved	Improved
4 Low income by economic status	Steady	Steady	26 Low pay	Improved	Improved
6 Persistent low income	Steady	Steady	28 Insecure at work	Improved	Steady
8 Material deprivation	Improved	Improved	29 Access to training	Improved	Steady
Children			30 Premature death	Improved	Steady
9 Low birthweight babies	Worsened	Worsened	31 Obesity	Worsened	Worsened
10 Infant mortality	Steady	Steady	32 Limiting longstanding illness or disability	Steady	Steady
11 Births to girls conceiving under age 16	Improved	Improved	33 Mental health	Improved	Improved
12 Low attainment at school (16 year olds)	Improved	Improved	*Older people*		
13 Low attainment at school (11 year olds)	Improved	Steady	34 No private income	Steady	Steady
14 School exclusions	Improved	Worsened	35 Benefit take-up	Worsened	Steady
15 Children in workless households	Improved	Improved	36 Excess winter deaths	Steady	Steady
16 Concentration of poor children	Steady	Steady	37 Limiting longstanding illness or disability	Steady	Steady
17 In young offender institutions	Worsened	Steady	38 Anxiety	Steady	Steady
Young adults			39 Help from social services to live at home	Worsened	Worsened
18 Unemployment	Improved	Worsened	*Communities*		
19 Low pay	Improved	Improved	41 Concentration of poverty	Steady	Steady
20 Destination of school leavers	Improved	Steady	42 Transport	Improved	Improved
21 Problem drug use	Worsened	Steady	43 Without a bank or building society account	Steady	Improved
22 Without a basic qualification	Steady	Steady	44 Burglaries	Improved	Steady
23 With a criminal record	Steady	Steady	45 Without household insurance	Improved	Improved
			46 Dissatisfaction with local area	Steady	Steady
			47 Without central heating	Improved	Improved
			48 Overcrowding	Steady	Steady
			49 Homelessness	Worsened	Worsened
			50 Mortgage arrears	Improved	Improved

Note: Where there are gaps in the numbering, that is because no information is available for those indicators.

Source: New Policy Institute (2003) Monitoring Poverty and Social Exclusion 2003, York: Joseph Rowntree Foundation www.poverty.org.uk/reports/mpse%202003%20findings.pdf

KEY TERMS

Absolute definition of poverty a person is in poverty if they are unable to afford the most basic necessities of life. Poverty is seen as destitution.

Consensual measure (of poverty) a form of the relative definition of poverty, based on a lack of the goods and services deemed necessary by most people in society.

Destitution failure to obtain the absolute necessities to keep life going.

Households Below Average Income (HBAI) the measure used by the British government which puts the poverty threshold at 60 per cent of median income.

Median income the middle band of income.

Operationalize how sociologists go about finding a way to measure a concept (e.g. poverty).

Relative definition of poverty a person is in poverty if they are unable to afford the standard of living considered acceptable by the majority of people.

Relative income measure (of poverty) a form of the relative definition of poverty, based on having only a certain proportion of the average income in a society.

Social exclusion when people suffer a series of linked problems, such as unemployment, poor skills, low incomes, poor housing and high crime, which prevent them from enjoying full membership of society.

Item A Measuring poverty by consensus

David Gordon and colleagues used a consensual definition of poverty, using earlier work by Mack and Lansley (1993).

They used the following methods to define poverty. (Please note that the table shown on the right is a much shortened version of the full table used in the research and referred to in the following extract.)

<< The table ranks the percentage of respondents identifying different adult items as 'necessary, which all adults should be able to afford and which they should not have to do without'. People of all ages and walks of life do not restrict their interpretation of 'necessities' to the basic material needs of a subsistence diet, shelter, clothing and fuel. There are social customs, obligations and activities that substantial majorities of the population also identify as among the top necessities of life.>>

Gordon, D. et al. (2000) Poverty and Social Exclusion in Britain, York: Joseph Rowntree Foundation

Essential requirements (1999)	Necessary	Not necessary
Bed and bedding for everyone	95	4
Heating to warm living areas of the home	94	5
Damp-free home	93	6
Visiting friends or family in hospital	92	7
Two meals a day	91	9
Medicines prescribed by doctor	90	9
Refrigerator	89	11
Fresh fruit and vegetables daily	86	13
Warm waterproof coat	85	14
Replacement or repair of broken electrical goods	85	14
Visits to friends or family	84	15
Celebrations on special days such as Christmas	83	16

Item B Absolute poverty

<< So, for example, a widely accepted indicator of third world poverty is the numbers of people living on less than $1 per day, on the grounds that people on such incomes are literally in danger of starving to death. This threshold is often termed 'absolute income poverty'. But the use of such a threshold in the UK would obviously be completely inappropriate.>>

New Policy Institute/Joseph Rowntree Foundation Measuring Poverty and Social Exclusion www.poverty.org.uk/income/income_choices.htm

Item C Social exclusion

<< The main causes and consequences of social exclusion are: poverty and low income; unemployment; poor educational attainment; poor mental or physical health; family breakdown and poor parenting; poor housing and homelessness; discrimination; crime; and living in a disadvantaged area. The risk factors for social exclusion tend to cluster in certain neighbourhoods, but not everybody at risk lives in a deprived area. Poverty and social exclusion can also pass from one generation to the next. >>

Social Exclusion Unit (2004) Breaking the Cycle London: HMSO (p. 7)

1 Explain what is meant by the phrase 'subsistence' when referring to diet, shelter, clothing and fuel (Item A). (2 marks)

2 Suggest two other items that might be added to the list in Item A. (4 marks)

3 Item A refers to necessities such as 'social customs, obligations and activities'. Suggest one example of each of these. (6 marks)

4 Identify and briefly explain two criticisms of an absolute definition of poverty being used to measure poverty in the UK today (Item B). (8 marks)

5 Examine the difficulties faced by sociologists in operationalizing a relative definition of poverty. (20 marks)

6 Using material from the Items and elsewhere, assess the argument that 'social exclusion' is a more useful term than that of 'poverty'. (20 marks)

The extent of poverty

gettingyouthinking

≪ We tend to think that poverty hits family members equally, yet research indicates that this is not the case. There can be affluence for some and poverty for others, within the same household. A household with a high income could, in fact, contain a number of poor people, because the main income earner might not want to share 'his' (it is usually the male) wages.

Studies have shown that income is not shared equally within families, with men having greater 'personal spending money' than women and more control over financial decisions. Bringing money into the household seems to bring a sense of entitlement as to how it is spent, with the man generally as the higher earner being the one with greater control over family expenditure.≫

Flaherty, J., Veit-Wilson, J. and Dornan, P. (2004)
Poverty: the facts (5th edn) London: CPAG

1 In your opinion, does the person who earns the highest income in the family have the greatest right to say how it is spent if there is a dispute?

2 Should both earners in a marriage/partnership keep their own money and only pool their earnings to pay for 'family' expenses?

3 What rights should the children have to decide how the money is spent?

4 If the parents have low incomes, should the children take on a part-time job?

5 If they do, should the children keep the money they earn?

6 How might the results of the study mentioned above help us to appreciate the complexity of understanding who is in poverty?

As we saw in Topic 2, the numbers of people living in poverty will vary according to which definition and measurement are used. But if we take the measure most commonly used by the government – that is, the number of households with incomes below 60 per cent of median income after housing costs – then the figures indicate that about 22 per cent of the population are in poverty. In total, there are about 12.5 million people living in poverty.

Poverty, then, is very widespread in Britain and not just restricted to a few 'unfortunates'.

Who are the poor?

The answer to this is a lot more complicated and confusing than simply identifying a particular group of the population. It depends first upon:

● how you wish to *classify* people,

and then once you have done this:

● whether you wish to know the *composition* of the poor by percentages

● whether you wish to know the *risk* of being in poverty according to membership of a group.

Classifying by family type or economic status

Sociologists have chosen two ways of classifying people when they wish to measure the extent of poverty. These involve viewing the poor through the lens of **family** or **household status** on the one hand (for example 'lone parent family') or by **economic status** on the other (for example 'unemployed'). These are complementary methods which simply involve the sociologist shifting their gaze at poverty from one angle to another. So we are looking at the same 'panorama', but seeing it from different directions.

The composition of the poor

The first piece of information sociologists want is the **composition of the poor**, that is what percentage of all poor people are formed by particular categories of households or economic status groups. The pie charts in Figure 6.3 illustrate the composition of the poor.

When we classify the poor by family (household) status, the single largest category in poverty is composed of couples with children, followed by single people and third, lone parents. When, instead, we break down the groups of people living in poverty by using the classification 'economic status', then the largest group consists of the long-term **sick, disabled people** and lone parents unable to work (classified as 'other inactive' in Figure 6.3 below). The next largest group is composed of retired people.

If you look at the pie charts in Figure 6.3, you will see that 30 per cent of all poor people are couples with children, when classified by household, and 32 per cent of all poor people are 'economically inactive', when classified by economic status.

These two different ways of classifying and counting the composition of the poor are very useful, but it should be remembered that these are largely the same people, but just looked at from a different perspective.

Measuring poverty by risk groups

An alternative method of measuring poverty is by **risk** groups. By this, we mean looking at the poor once again in terms of both household composition and economic status, but this time instead of dividing them according to what percentage of all poor people these groups provide, we look at what proportion of each group are in poverty.

Table 6.3 below illustrates this. It shows that 51 per cent of all lone parents live in poverty, and 'only' 11 per cent of couples without children do.

If we look at risk by income group (see Table 6.4 on p. 220), then 75 per cent of 'unemployed people' live in poverty, compared to only 4 per cent of 'singles or couples all in full-time work'.

Table 6.3 Risk of poverty by family status in 2002/3

Proportion living in poverty*

Family status	Percentage
Pensioner couple	23%
Single pensioner	20%
Couple with children	19%
Couple without children	11%
Lone parent	51%
Single without children	24%

defined as living in households with below 60% of median income after housing costs

Source: Dept for Work and Pensions (2004) *Households below Average Income 1994/5 to 2002/3*, Corporate Document Services

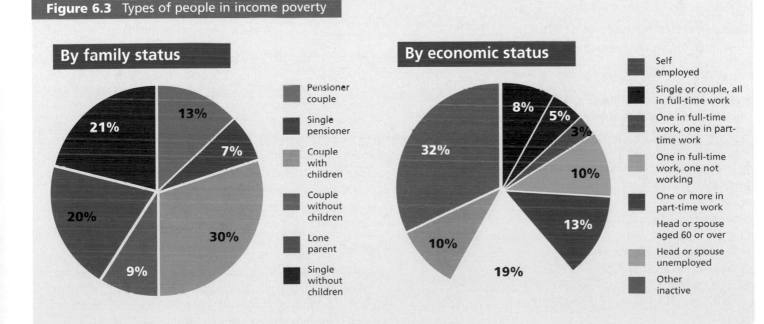

Figure 6.3 Types of people in income poverty

By family status
- 13%
- 7%
- 21%
- 20%
- 30%
- 9%

Legend:
- Pensioner couple
- Single pensioner
- Couple with children
- Couple without children
- Lone parent
- Single without children

By economic status
- 8%
- 5%
- 3%
- 32%
- 10%
- 13%
- 19%
- 10%

Legend:
- Self employed
- Single or couple, all in full-time work
- One in full-time work, one in part-time work
- One in full-time work, one not working
- One or more in part-time work
- Head or spouse aged 60 or over
- Head or spouse unemployed
- Other inactive

Table 6.4 Risk of income poverty by economic status

Proportion living in poverty*

Economic status	Percentage
Self-employed	21%
Single or couple, all in full-time work	4%
One in full-time work, one in part-time work	5%
One in full-time work, one not working	18%
One or more in part-time work	30%
Head or spouse aged 60 or over	25%
Head or spouse unemployed	75%
Other inactive**	64%

* defined as living in households with below 60 per cent of median income after housing costs (figures are for 2002/3)

** all those not included in previous groups (includes the long-term sick, disabled people and non-working lone parents)

Source: Dept for Work and Pensions (2004) *Households below Average Income 1994/5 to 2002/3*, Corporate Document Services

'Composition of the poor' or 'risk of poverty' – which is the better measure?

The answer is that neither is better (or worse), just different. We can see the composition of the poor in terms of absolute numbers or we can see how different groups run higher or lower risks of being in poverty. Both of these approaches help understand poverty and allow policymakers to develop ways of combating poverty.

Extending the range of risk groups

In recent years, the concept of risk groups has been extended beyond economic or household groups to include such things as gender, disability, age and ethnicity. Increasingly, sociological research has sought to find out what specific risks of being in poverty are associated with these categories.

What complicates matters, however, is that all of these groups overlap. For example, disabled people are more likely to be unemployed than the population average, while older people are more likely to be disabled.

Because of the history of immigration to the UK and birth patterns, ethnic minority families are heavily overrepresented among couples with children, but are also more likely to be unemployed. However, it is important to remember that although there are numerous overlaps, each way of classifying is simply looking at that same 22 per cent of the population but from different angles. Also, none of this alters the fact that whichever classification you use, there are about 12.5 million people in the UK who are living in households with incomes below 60 per cent of the median.

High risk groups and poverty

Below, we look at a 'snapshot' of groups who have a high risk of living in poverty – drawing examples from all of the classifications above.

Lone-parent families

The number of lone parents – the overwhelming majority of whom are women – has grown from just over half a million at the beginning of the 1970s, to about 1.75 million in 2001. Over 50 per cent of lone parents in the UK live in poverty.

Lone-parent families are more likely to be poor for two, possibly overlapping, reasons:

1 Women from poorer backgrounds have a higher risk of becoming lone parents in the first place. So they are already more likely to be at risk of poverty before having children.
2 Any lone parent is likely to be poorer because they have to combine childcare with employment. This means that they are more likely to work part time, so their incomes on average will be lower.

It is important to remember, however, that not all lone mothers are poor – it is just that they are more at risk of poverty.

Children

Some 30 per cent of children are living in low-income families. In 2001/2, there were 3.8 million children living in poverty. This is a decline of almost three-quarters of a million since 1998, but an increase of 1.9 million compared to 1979.

Approximately 75 per cent of all children living in households where the parent or parents are unemployed live in poverty. However, because there are high levels of employment, it is still true to say that over half of all children in poverty are living in households with at least one parent working, and just under half are living in households with no employed parent.

The unemployed

About 1.8 million children come from households with no parent in employment. But it is not just children who are hit by unemployment. About 75 per cent of unemployed people now live in poverty.

Those who are unemployed for a long time face much greater problems than those who are out of work for a short period. These problems include a lower level of income, the gradual exhaustion of savings, and deterioration in the condition of clothing, furniture and general possessions. After three months of unemployment, the average **disposable income** of a family drops by as much as 59 per cent. It is not just financial losses that occur as a result of long-term unemployment – there are psychological effects too, such as lack of confidence, stress and depression. These further undermine people's ability to obtain work.

The low paid

Thirty-one per cent of all poor people are in full- or part-time employment, but simply do not earn enough to live on. People who are low paid tend to be those with fewer skills, and they often live in areas where there are relatively few jobs, so competition keeps wages low. As we have seen, there is a link between **low pay** and lone parenthood, in that lone parents usually have to take part-time jobs because of childcare responsibilities – and approximately 70 per cent of part-time work is low paid according to the Low Pay Commission (2003).

Sick and disabled people

According to government statistics, there are approximately 6.2 million adults (14 per cent of all adults) and 36,000 children (3 per cent of all children) who suffer from one or more disabilities. Of these, 34 per cent are living in poverty. The average income for a disabled adult, under pensionable age, is 72 per cent of that for non-disabled people. The impact of disability also goes beyond the individual person concerned, with 52 per cent of working-age adults with a disabled child themselves living in poverty.

There are several reasons for the poverty of long-term sick and disabled people, and their carers. They may be unable to work, or the work they can do may be limited to particular kinds of low-paid employment. At the same time, people with disabilities often have higher outgoings, such as having to pay for a special diet or having to pay for heating to be on all day.

Older people

About 18 per cent of the population – over 11 million people – are over retirement age, and over 65 per cent of **older people** are women. With the gradual rise in life expectancy, the number of older people in the population is likely to continue to increase.

Because of government policies since 2000, the numbers of older people in poverty has declined, from about 33 per cent of older people in 2000 to 22 per cent in 2003.

Being old does not necessarily make people poor – it is just that the risk increases. Those people who are poor in old age are most likely to be those who have earned least in their working lives.

Ethnic minorities

People from ethnic minority backgrounds run a substantially higher risk than the majority population of living in poverty – 69 per cent of people of Pakistani and Bangladeshi origin, 46 per cent of people of African origin and 32 per cent of people of African-Caribbean origin are poor.

Ethnic minority groups have substantially higher rates of unemployment than the majority of the population. This holds true even if the person has the same educational qualifications as the majority population. Those of African-Caribbean origin and a majority of those of Asian origin have a greater chance of earning lower wages than the majority population, and they are more likely to work in the types of employment where wages are generally low.

Women

The majority of the poor in the UK are women – most of the groups we have discussed above are likely to have a majority of women members. Lone parents are overwhelmingly women who are more likely to be in part-

Blanden et al. (2002)
Poverty and social mobility

Blanden and colleagues were interested in finding out whether poverty persisted over generations and to what extent the increased levels of social mobility experienced in the UK had helped eliminate poverty. In order to do this, they reanalysed two well-known longitudinal studies – the 1958 National Child Cohort Study and the 1970 British Cohort Study (both of which had been used for a range of purposes including medical and educational studies). The researchers concluded that the chance of being better off than one's parents had reduced for those who grew up in the 1970s and 1980s, compared to the earlier cohort. More of the 1970s cohort were in poor families at the age of 16 than the older cohort. In the majority of cases, children remained in the same quarter of the income distribution as their parents. In the 1958 cohort, almost 20 per cent of males and females rose from the lowest earning quarter of families to the top. But in the 1970s cohort, the figures had fallen to 15 per cent. The increase in educational opportunities in the last 30 years has been more likely to benefit the children of the more affluent, rather than the poor.

Blanden, J., Goodman, A., Gregg, P. and Machin, S. (2002) *Changes in Intergenerational Mobility in Britain*, Royal Economic Society

1 What is meant by the term 'social mobility'?

2 What did the researchers conclude about the relationship between increased social mobility and poverty?

time work, to be in low-paid work, or to be unemployed, leading to the situation where 51 per cent of lone families are poor. Single female pensioners are also slightly more likely to be poor (21 per cent) than single male pensioners (17 per cent). This is because they are less likely to have savings, as a result of low earnings throughout their lives.

Risk of poverty and region

The chances of living in poverty vary considerably across the country and within cities. Indeed, in relative terms, the UK lies only second to Mexico in the industrialized world for the extent of regional inequalities in living standards.

People living in Wales, the North East, Inner London and Yorkshire are most likely to be poor, and those living in outer London and the South East are least likely to be poor. These largely reflect differences in rates of pay and in levels of unemployment.

Poverty: a risk not a state

When we talk about poor people, it is rather misleading, because it gives the impression that there is a group of people who live in poverty all their lives. This is true for some people, but the majority of the poor are people who live on the margins of poverty, moving into poverty and out again, depending upon a range of economic factors, government decisions, family responsibilities and their earning possibilities.

Check your understanding

1 According to the text, how many people in the UK are living in poverty?

2 What percentage of the population is this?

3 Identify the different ways of classifying and measuring those who are in poverty

4 What are the implications of the fact that these classifications overlap?

5 Why is long-term unemployment so much worse a problem than shorter-term unemployment?

6 Are all old people poor? What does poverty in old age reflect?

7 Poverty is 'a risk not a state'. Explain what this means in your own words.

research ideas

● Go through job adverts in your local papers. Compare the salaries on offer and identify the lowest- and highest-paid jobs? What weekly wages before tax do they offer? What is the median pay rate in your area?

● Ask a sample of people to estimate the proportions of the various groups shown in the graph in Item A who are actually living in poverty. Then show them the actual percentages. How closely do their estimates match the figures? Are they surprised at the figures?

web.tasks

1 **Find out the latest figures on 'households below average income', and the latest figures for the 'poverty line'. Search the website of the Child Poverty Action Group at www.cpag.org.uk to find this and much more information.**

2 **What particular problems are faced by groups who run a high risk of poverty? Why do they often find it hard to break out of poverty?**

Search the world wide web to find out more about the disabled, single-parent families, child poverty, ethnic minorities, the unemployed, older people and the low paid.

3 **The BBC News website gives a simple summary of some of the facts on the extent of poverty:**

http://news.bbc.co.uk/1/shared/spl/hi/pop_ups/ 03/uk_poverty_and_social_exclusion/html/1.stm

KEY TERMS

Composition (of the poor) refers to a way of analysing poverty figures by illustrating which groups provide the largest proportions of people living in poverty.

Disposable income how much people actually have left to spend after paying fixed bills (such as council tax or housing costs).

Economic status refers to a way of classifying poor people by how they obtain their income.

Family status refers to a way of classifying poor people by the sorts of family types they belong to. Used interchangeably with 'household status'.

Household status used interchangeably with 'family status'.

Low pay defined as earning less than half the average male wage (women's average wages are lower than men's).

Older people refers to people of pensionable age, currently 60 for women and 65 for men.

Risk of poverty refers to a way of analysing poverty figures by classifying groups by their chance of being in poverty.

Sick and disabled people 'sick' refers to chronic illness, where people are unwell on a long-term basis. 'Disabled' refers to people officially classified by the government (on the basis of a medical report) as suffering from some form of disability.

exploring the extent of poverty

Item A Lone-parent families

Lone-parent families are more than twice as likely to be on low incomes as couples without children, and three times as likely as adults without children.

Source: Department for Work and Pensions (2002) *Households below Average Income series 1994/5 to 2000/1*, Corporate Document Services, reproduced in Joseph Rowntree Foundation (2002) *Monitoring Poverty and Social Exclusion*

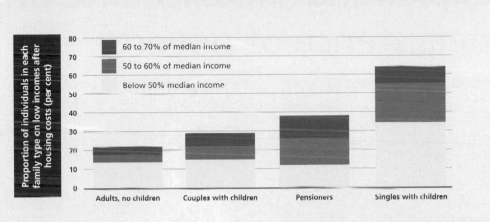

Item B The risk of poverty

<< Poverty in the UK is largely determined by three factors – access to the labour market, extra costs, and the failure of policies to deal with them. Poverty is caused by not having access to decently paid employment. It is also the result of the extra costs of having a child or a disability. Poverty is particularly acute when these two factors combine. Moreover the social security system often fails to meet adequately the needs generated by unemployment, low pay, having a child or ... being disabled. Thus poverty is also caused by policies – i.e. it is avoidable, not just the consequence of random misfortune. The risk of poverty is not shared out evenly – it depends upon social class, on gender and on race.>>

Oppenheim and Harker, quoted in Beresford, P., Green , D., Lister, R. and Woodward, K. (1999) *Poverty First Hand* London: CPAG

Item C Low income

Nearly a fifth of the population – around 10 million people – continues to experience low income at least two years in three.

Source: British Household Panel Survey, Waves 1 to 9, analysis by J. Rigg and S. Jenkins, Institute for Social and Economic Research, University of Essex, reproduced in Joseph Rowntree Foundation (2002) *Monitoring Poverty and Social Exclusion*

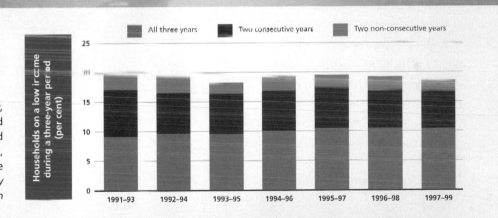

---

1 Explain what is meant by the term 'risk of poverty' (Item B). (2 marks)

2 Identify two causes of poverty suggested in Item B. (4 marks)

3 Suggest three reasons why a high proportion of the 'singles with children' group are in poverty (Item A). (6 marks)

4 Identify and briefly explain two reasons why government benefits have not eliminated poverty. (8 marks)

5 Examine the view that poverty is a risk not a state. (20 marks)

6 Using information from the Items and elsewhere, assess the factors that cause women and ethnic minorities to have a higher risk of poverty than some other groups. (20 marks)

Explaining the existence and persistence of poverty

1 Write down the first four words that come into your head when you look at the photo above.

2 If a homeless person were to ask you for money, what would you reply?

3 Compare your responses to questions 1 and 2 with those of with people sitting around you. Discuss with them the reasons for your replies.

4 Why do you think people like the man shown in the photo live the way they do? Is it their own fault? Bad luck? The fault of an unjust society?

5 How would you resolve their problems?

Arguments about the causes of poverty can be traced back as far as we have written records. Intriguingly, it seems that, although the terminology has changed, the actual explanations for the existence of poverty have not changed over the centuries. On the one side, there are those who claim that affluence is a combination of natural ability and hard work; on the other side, there are those who argue that the poor are unfortunate, or that the 'system' is against them. So one argument lays the blame at the feet of the poor themselves, while the other blames the society that condemns some people to poverty:

● **Dependency**-based explanations argue that poverty is the result of individual or cultural deficiency. Such explanations include the belief that there is a specific section of the working class that does not want to work, called the **underclass**.

● **Exclusion**-based explanations focus on the way in which some people are 'made to be poor' by the economic and political system.

Dependency-based explanations

These sorts of explanations argue that the poor are, in some way, the cause of their own poverty. At their most extreme, they suggest that the welfare system in the UK actually makes people dependent on it by providing an attractive alternative to work.

Three different approaches exist, based on:

- **individual deficiency**
- the **culture of poverty**
- the underclass.

Individual deficiency

Explanations that centre on the concept of dependency stress that people who are poor are in that state because of some personal or cultural deficiency. Essentially, it is their fault if they are poor.

The individual as scapegoat

This is the approach that many 19th-century writers took, and it remains, to some extent, in the idea of the '**scrounger**'. There is little evidence that this could explain any more than a tiny proportion of poverty. However, the myth of the scrounger was used powerfully in the 1980s as a justification for cutbacks in welfare.

The dependent individual

This idea was developed by Marsland (1996) who argued that the individual's will to work was undermined by excessively generous state welfare benefits, and that the need to look after other family members was weakened by the extensive provision of state services. The result was a high level of dependence on the state.

The culture of poverty

This idea was originally suggested by Oscar Lewis (1966) in his study of poor people in Mexico. Lewis argued that poor people in a 'class-stratified and highly individualistic society' were likely to develop a set of cultural values that trapped them in their poverty. It is important to stress the ideas of class and **individualism**, for Lewis is not arguing that these people are necessarily deficient. He believes that they are caught in a society that really does put barriers in their path – but that the poor themselves help ensure that they are trapped by developing a set of values that prevent them from breaking out of poverty. These cultural values include:

- a sense of **fatalism** and acceptance of their poverty
- an inability to think for the long term
- a desire for immediate enjoyment.

Critics of this approach argue that there is no such thing as a culture of poverty – rather, such cultural values are a perfectly rational reaction to conditions of hopelessness. In the USA, the poorest groups really are excluded, and they are unlikely to be allowed to break out of their poverty. In such a situation, the poor may feel that there is no point in long-term planning.

The underclass

The underclass approach is a development of the cultural explanations for poverty, but it extends the analysis much further and introduces a very radical critique of the American and British welfare systems. In the culture of poverty thesis (see above), the 'cause' of poverty lies in a cultural adaptation to a highly class-stratified society; in the underclass approach, on the other hand, poverty is a response to cultural, economic and welfare changes.

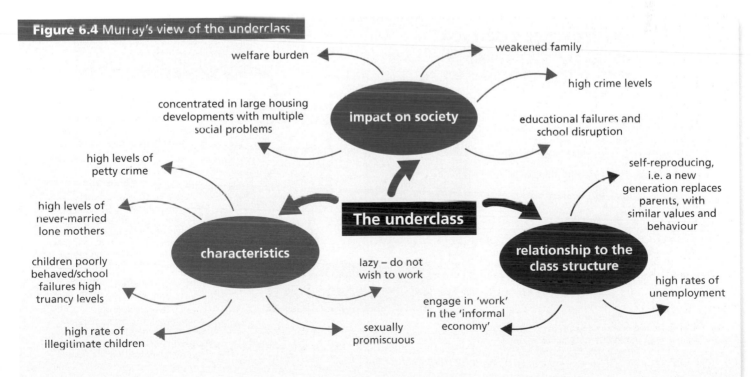

Figure 6.4 Murray's view of the underclass

The argument, first developed by an American writer, Charles Murray, is that an underclass (see Unit 1, p. 8) exists, consisting of people who are lazy and make no effort to work or look after themselves (see Figure 6.4). These people prefer to live off the state rather than work. By underclass, Murray means a significant and self-reproducing group who form a distinctive bottom element of the class structure in British and American societies.

Murray accepts that there are poor people who are poor through no fault of their own. Nevertheless, he believes that the bulk of poverty is caused by those who do not make the effort to earn a living, and/or waste what they do have. Murray's analysis (1994) is slightly different for the USA and the UK. His analysis of the USA focuses heavily on 'American Blacks' as the source of the underclass; in the UK, his analysis is not race-based.

Murray argues that a clear segment of the working class distinguishes itself through the following factors:

- *Crime* – Murray points out that a very high proportion of violent and property crime is carried out by a small proportion of the population.
- *Illegitimacy* – There are very high levels of children born outside marriage (and in particular to never-married women). These children are the outcome of casual sex, and the fathers have no interest in supporting the child or mother.
- *Economic inactivity* – Here, Murray is referring to the high levels of long-term unemployment that characterize the same relatively small group of people. Murray argues that it is not that they are unemployed in any traditional sense, but that they prefer to collect state benefit and to work in the **'hidden' economy**. Poverty is a way of life and is chosen by members of the underclass.

Murray's work has been fiercely attacked by a wide range of writers. The consensus among critics is that Murray is, quite simply, factually wrong. There is no evidence from social surveys that a group exists that rejects the work ethic. Research shows that the majority of lone parents would like a stable relationship. There is also no evidence of an automatic overlap between lone-parent families and crime.

Exclusion-based explanations

Exclusion-based explanations argue that the poor are poor because they are prevented from achieving a reasonable standard of living by the actions of the more powerful in society.

This approach stresses differences in power between the various groups in society. Those who have least power – the disabled, older people, women, ethnic minorities and, of course, children – have significantly higher chances of living in poverty. Within this approach we can distinguish three strands:

1 poverty, powerlessness and the **labour market**
2 **citizenship** and exclusion
3 poverty and capitalism: the economic-system approach.

Poverty, powerlessness and the labour market

In all societies, the least powerful groups are the most likely to lose out economically and socially, and they will form the bulk of the poor. Indeed, poverty and powerlessness go hand in hand. The powerless include women, lone parents (usually women), the very young and the very old, as well as those with

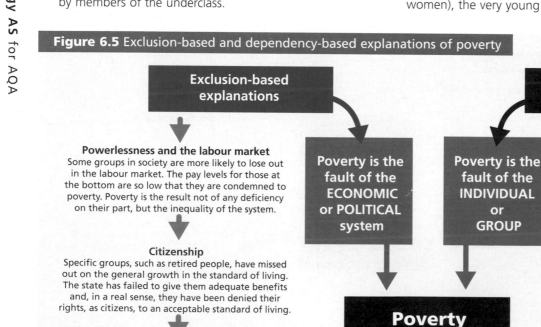

Figure 6.5 Exclusion-based and dependency-based explanations of poverty

Exclusion-based explanations

Powerlessness and the labour market
Some groups in society are more likely to lose out in the labour market. The pay levels for those at the bottom are so low that they are condemned to poverty. Poverty is the result not of any deficiency on their part, but the inequality of the system.

Citizenship
Specific groups, such as retired people, have missed out on the general growth in the standard of living. The state has failed to give them adequate benefits and, in a real sense, they have been denied their rights, as citizens, to an acceptable standard of living.

Marxism
The political and economic system is designed to keep a large proportion of the population in poverty – so that a few may remain rich.

Poverty is the fault of the ECONOMIC or POLITICAL system

Poverty is the fault of the INDIVIDUAL or GROUP

Poverty

Dependency-based explanations

The deficient individual
Some people are lazy or less able – with effort, they could escape from poverty.

The culture of poverty
Some groups have developed a set of values that trap them in poverty. The members of the group or subculture believe there is no chance to escape from their situation. This brings about a self-fulfilling prophesy.

The underclass
A significant proportion of poorer people have developed a lifestyle based on not working. They live by (petty) crime and benefit fraud.

disabilities. When these powerless groups do get employment, it is likely to be in short-term, low-paid, temporary and possibly 'unofficial' work. For many supporters of the welfare state, it is these groups who deserve help, because they are blameless 'victims' of the economic system.

Citizenship and exclusion

Field (1989) has developed this argument, and linked it to the idea of 'citizenship'. Field argues that three groups in society have, over the last 20 years, been excluded from the rights that citizens should enjoy, including the right to a decent standard of living. These are:

- the long-term unemployed
- lone-parent families
- those on state retirement pensions.

Together these groups comprise what he calls (rather confusingly) the 'underclass'. Field argues that these groups have been particularly hit by several factors:

- government policies, which have increased the gap between rich and poor
- increases in the core number of long-term unemployed
- an increasing tendency to **stigmatize** and blame the poor for their poverty, rather than look at wider economic and social factors.

Once again, the answer to the problem of poverty lies in a better-organized and comprehensive welfare state.

Poverty and capitalism: the economic-system approach

The final, and most radical, explanation for poverty is provided by those in the Marxist tradition (see Unit 1 Topic 4, p. 17). They see poverty as an inevitable outcome of the capitalist system. According to Marxist theory, the economy is owned and run by a small ruling class, who exploit the majority of the population who work for them. Poverty emerges from three main causes:

1 The wealth of the ruling class is created from paying the lowest possible wages to people – because it is the profits that produce the wealth.
2 The poor act as a warning – having a group in poverty provides a direct warning to the rest of the workforce of what could happen to them if they didn't work hard.
3 Poor people provide a 'starting point' against which other workers can measure their own income (rather than against the income of members of the ruling class).

For Marxists, the welfare state is a means of hiding exploitation, and it is used by the rich and powerful to provide just enough in the way of health care and income support benefits to prevent a serious challenge to their authority.

Beresford et al. (1999)
Poverty first hand

Beresford and his colleagues pointed out that most research undertaken on poverty had been by 'experts' and pressure groups. Typically, they collected statistics on poverty and then worked out the numbers of people in that situation. Even the definition of poverty was provided by these experts. Beresford and colleagues wanted to find out the views and attitudes of poor people themselves. In order to do so, they approached a wide variety of local groups across the country, mainly composed of people on low income, and then interviewed representatives from each. In all, 137 people were interviewed.

The results showed that living in poverty was a difficult and demoralizing situation, in which they felt stigmatized by the attitudes of others. The majority of the people believed that the causes of poverty were in the way society was organized, rather than in individual failings. They vehemently rejected the notion of the underclass. They would like to find work if they could or, if they were already in employment, in better-paid work.

Beresford, P., Green, D., Lister, R. and Woodard, K. (1999) *Poverty First Hand*, London: CPAG

1 Typically, who does most research on poverty?
2 How representative of the poor do you think the sample was likely to be?
3 What were the views of the sample on the causes of poverty?

Causes of poverty

<< What thoughtful rich people call the problem of poverty, thinking poor people call, with equal justice, the problem of riches. >>

R.H. Tawney

1 Explain what the quote above tells us about the causes of poverty.

research ideas

- Carry out a 'content analysis' of newspapers to see what approach they take in their stories to the issue of poverty (or people in poverty, the homeless, etc). Do they blame the victims or other factors?

  You should do this by finding newspaper sites on the web and then searching them for the stories.

- Conduct a series of in-depth interviews, or design a questionnaire, to find out what the public think are the main causes of poverty.

  Compare their views with the sociological explanations. Which explanation has most public support? Why might this be the case?

Check your understanding

1 Explain how, according to some writers, the welfare state can actually be the cause of poverty?

2 What is the 'culture of poverty'? Give two examples of the values of the 'culture'.

3 According to Charles Murray, what is the 'underclass'?

4 What do sociologists mean by 'exclusion-based approaches'?

5 What three groups have been excluded from the rights of citizenship, according to Field?

6 From a Marxist perspective, how does capitalism cause poverty?

web.tasks

1 Search the web for the 'underclass'.

To what extent do you think American ideas of the underclass apply in the UK?

2 Go to the British government website www.direct.gov.uk/Homepage/fs/en and search it using the terms 'social exclusion' and 'social inclusion'.

Which of the explanations of poverty discussed above do you think underlie government policies?

KEY TERMS

Citizenship refers (in this particular case) to the belief that people living in British society have certain 'rights', including the right to have a decent standard of living.

Culture of poverty a set of values that some poorer people in society share, which they pass on to their children. The result is that they get trapped in poverty.

Dependency the state of being dependent. It is used to refer to the idea that some people live off the hard work of others.

Exclusion the idea that some people are prevented from being able to get on in life and enjoy the benefits of an affluent society.

Fatalism acceptance that what happens is the result of luck or 'fate'.

'Hidden' economy all the 'cash-in-hand' and casual work that is never reported to authorities such as the Inland Revenue.

Individual deficiency refers to a person's specific faults or weaknesses which make them unable to get on in society and be successful.

Individualism the belief that individuals are far more important than social groups.

Labour market refers to the sorts of jobs and employment conditions that people have.

'Scrounger' someone who claims welfare benefits they are not entitled to, and/or who manipulates the benefits system to their own advantage.

Stigmatize to mark something out as bad.

Underclass a term first used by Charles Murray to describe those people whom he claims have developed a lifestyle which depends upon state support and who have no desire to seek employment.

Item A The undeserving poor

<< So, let us get it straight from the outset: the underclass does not refer to a degree of poverty, but to a type of poverty.

It is not a new concept. I grew up knowing what the underclass was; we just didn't call it that in those days. One class of poor people was never even called poor – they simply lived with low incomes. Then there was another set of poor people ... these poor people didn't lack just money. They were defined by their behaviour. Their homes were littered and unkempt. The men in the family were unable to hold a job for more than a few weeks at a time. Drunkenness was common.

The children grew up ill-schooled and ill-behaved and contributed a disproportionate share of the local juvenile delinquents.>>

Murray, C. (1990) *The Emerging British Underclass*, London: IEA (Health and Welfare Series), p. 1

Item B Look after yourself

The British labour market has many of the worst features of the USA – ranging from high turnover of staff to inequality of income – but without the compensating virtues of mobility and managerial dynamism. In the UK, the search for maximum and immediate profit to meet the demands of shareholders, means that firms are less willing to offer lifetime employment and less willing to undertake training, as both of these are costly. The result is that employees are paid the lowest possible wages, while the social benefits of pensions, health care, holidays and a general sense of caring for workers, both as employees and citizens, are largely absent. The underlying belief is that, in this kind of market economy, everybody looks after themselves.

Adapted from Hutton, W. (1995) *The State We're In*, London: Vintage, pp. 281–4

Item C From disadvantage to social exclusion

The problems of social exclusion are often linked and mutually reinforcing. The risk of social exclusion is highest for those with multiple disadvantages. The figure on the right illustrates this, showing that the likelihood of being out of work increases with the number of disadvantages experienced by an individual. For example, more than 50 per cent of those with three or more labour-market disadvantages are nonemployed, compared with 3 per cent without any of these characteristics.

Likelihood of non-employment amongst multiple disadvantaged groups

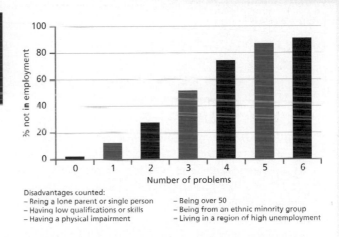

Source: Berthoud, 2003

Non-employment is defined as being either not working at least 16 hours a week or not in full-time education, and not having a working partner.

Disadvantages counted:
– Being a lone parent or single person
– Having low qualifications or skills
– Having a physical impairment
– Being over 50
– Being from an ethnic minority group
– Living in a region of high unemployment

Source: Social Exclusion Unit (2004) *Tackling Social Exclusion: Taking stock and looking to the future* , London: Office of the Deputy Prime Minister

---

1 Explain what is meant by an 'underclass' (Item A). (2 marks)

2 Suggest two characteristics that Murray might associate with the underclass. (4 marks)

3 Identify three ways in which 'the search for maximum and immediate profit' may help harm the workforce (Item B). (6 marks)

4 Identify and briefly explain two reasons why there is a relationship between multiple disadvantage and unemployment (Item C). (8 marks)

5 Examine the view represented by the statement: 'What thoughtful rich people call the problem of poverty, thinking poor people call, with equal justice, the problem of riches'. (20 marks)

6 Using material from the Items and elsewhere, assess the extent to which the existence of an underclass is a key cause of poverty. (20 marks)

Competing approaches to poverty and the welfare state

gettingyou**thinking**

Look at each of the photographs.

1 **What is causing the people above to be in poverty?**

2 **Suggest different ways in which the people in each situation might be taken out of poverty.**

3 **What are the advantages and disadvantages of these approaches? Which do you favour, if any? Explain your answer.**

We have seen in earlier topics that there is considerable debate over the definitions, causes and even the extent of poverty in the UK. Clearly, if there is no agreement on any of these, then finding one programme to eradicate poverty that is acceptable to all is, to say the least, difficult. This topic explores the various solutions to poverty that have been put forward, and gives some examples of actual policies that have been tried. It looks at the four main approaches to solving the problem of poverty:

● the New Right approach
● the social democratic approach
● the 'Third Way'
● the Marxist approach.

The New Right approach

The New Right have developed a series of arguments which attack the welfare state and see it, both directly and indirectly, as one of the main causes of poverty. New Right theorists, such as Marsland (1996) argue that, in a democratic, capitalist society, wealth is created by those people who successfully run companies, and by others who innovate, have entrepreneurial ideas and start new companies. Everyone else relies upon these people for jobs, and therefore incomes. These **entrepreneurs**

are motivated by money, and it is therefore up to government to encourage entrepreneurs and owners of successful companies to flourish. This is best done where there is a 'free market' – that is, an economic system where there are a number of competing firms seeking to offer their services, and where the government does not interfere.

Welfare as an indirect cause of poverty

In order to ensure that entrepreneurs are well rewarded, taxation must be kept as low as possible. This is done by minimizing the size of the government and by keeping expenditure as low as possible. The **welfare state** – including provision of **state benefits** for those without employment – is the largest area of government spending, employing a massive array of people to deliver benefits and services. Without the costs of employing the staff and the expenditure on welfare payments, taxes could be much lower. The welfare state is, therefore, an indirect cause of poverty, because:

● it discourages the efforts of entrepreneurs to start new companies which would create new jobs
● it hinders successful, established companies by burdening them with taxes.

Welfare as a direct cause of poverty

Welfare also has a direct role in causing poverty. This is because the welfare state actually undermines the will to work. It does this by providing free health and care services, plus financial support for those who do not want to work. So, those who prefer to live on state benefits can do so, thus placing a huge burden in the form of increased taxes and lost productivity on the rest of the population. Murray (1990) coined the term 'the underclass' to describe this group (see Topic 4, pp. 225–6).

Poverty and inequality

According to the New Right approach, there must always be inequality, because only a few can be successful. Competition in the free market will ensure that the best people get to the top. However, their success can generate the employment and the taxation to eliminate poverty. By encouraging some to be successful, therefore, the majority will not live in poverty. New Right writers, such as Pryke (2000), dismiss the relative definition of poverty, which they see as an ideological attack on inequality (see Topic 2, p. 213).

Criticisms of the New Right approach

The New Right approach has been heavily criticized on a number of grounds. The first of these is that poverty would actually increase if the welfare state were abolished. The welfare state and the **minimum wage** help to protect workers from exploitative employers. If there were no welfare state, society would be split between a wealthy minority, and a mass of the poor who would have little stake in society.

The New Right approach has been very influential in the USA, where a law was introduced in 1996 (known as PRWORA – Personal Responsibility and Work Opportunity Reconciliation Act). This Act means that nobody can receive more than five years of total state assistance over their lifetime. After this time, they may receive no state cash payments of any kind. Supporters of the Act, such as Clark and Hein (2000), claim that it has been a great success because it has helped slash payments on welfare, and it is true that employment levels have risen. Critics say the Act bears out all their fears and has simply forced people into jobs paying only minimum wage rates, which still leaves them in dire poverty.

The social democratic approach

This approach to combating poverty underpins the type of welfare state which existed from the late 1940s until the 1980s. It has since been moving towards a late modernity/Third Way model. Social democrats, such as Crosland (1956), argued that in any society, there will be some groups who are in poverty through no fault of their own. Some people may be disabled or retired, others may be unable to work because of childcare responsibilities – or the economy may be passing through a crisis and there may not be enough jobs. The role of the welfare state is to ensure that these people are cared for and are guaranteed a decent standard of living.

Although this approach seems quite uncontroversial nowadays, the idea of a welfare state that guaranteed health care, pensions and financial benefits for the unemployed was very radical in the 1940s, when it was first introduced. Before that time, those in need had to rely on charity for health care, while the unemployment benefits that were available were extremely basic. The social democratic model moved beyond the debate over who 'deserved' help and who did not, and treated everyone in poverty as someone in need. It was not really concerned about whether the person asking for help was actually deserving or not.

In this model of welfare, then, poverty is eliminated by means of **welfare benefits** provided by the state and paid for out of general taxation.

Criticisms of the social democratic approach

The social democratic approach has been strongly criticized by supporters of the Third Way, such as Giddens (1999), who suggests that it has failed to respond to the social, political and economic changes which have occurred since the 1980s in the UK. According to these critics, the welfare state has remained wedded to the model of society in the 1940s. In particular, it has failed to respond to the growth in single parenthood and the changing position of women in society. Traditionally, benefits had gone to families, with the assumption that there was a working husband/father (or a husband/father who wanted work). By the 1990s, this was no longer typical of families in poverty. There were large numbers of single mothers who wanted to work, but who were caught in a **poverty trap** – where the state benefits they lost when they began to work outweighed the income they received. As a result, there was an incentive not to work.

At the same time, the costs of the welfare state were becoming too great for the government to bear, as expectations of health care, housing and standards of living grew. The original welfare state had been based on the costs of providing a very basic living standard. As the relative definition of poverty became more widely accepted, so this basic living standard seemed increasingly out of touch with what people expected.

The 'Third Way' – the theory of late modernity

From the 1940s until the 1980s, the social democratic approach, with its emphasis on a comprehensive welfare state, was seen as the only way to combat poverty. But there were many criticisms of the system. On the political right, there were those who said that it was not only too expensive, but that it also undermined self-help. On the left, there were those who argued that the system was not generous enough, and that the levels of state benefit simply maintained people in poverty without actually doing anything radical to eliminate poverty.

Table 6.5 Solutions to poverty – summary of different approaches

Approach	View of welfare state	View of poor people	Strategy to eliminate poverty	Role of government
New Right	BAD – wasteful and inefficient; undermines the will to work	Lazy or less able than successful people	To let entrepreneurs create wealth for themselves and, therefore, jobs for others	To create the conditions for successful commerce, e.g. low taxes, few regulations
Social democratic	GOOD – role is to ensure a fair society	Unfortunate people	An all-encompassing welfare state paid for through tax	To organize, provide and fund a 'free' welfare state
Third way	Essentially good, but too expensive and inefficient	Most poor people could work but they either can't (the majority) or don't want to (the minority)	Make a society in which all people can get employment with adequate income to live on	To overcome the barriers that prevent people working
Marxist	Hides the true exploitation of the majority of the population by the few rich	Exploited by the ruling class	REVOLUTION! – Take over control of the economy and the state	Governments in capitalist societies are just there to represent the interests of the ruling class
Outsider critique	Ineffective, out of touch with cultural realities for groups such as women, ethnic minorities & disabled	Excluded and stigmatized	Citizenship and equal rights	To ensure that all groups have access to employment and services

cultural and family differences of some ethnic minorities. We have just commented on the difficulties faced by lone-parent families headed by women; women of African-Caribbean origins have high rates of lone parenthood. Those of Bangladeshi and Pakistani origins have much lower rates of employment, and therefore the new tax credit system which rewards women for going out to work does not help them. The issue for writers such as Modood is not so much direct racism, as a lack of flexibility and response to different cultural circumstances by the welfare state.

Disability, welfare and poverty

Disabled people might well claim to be the most marginalized of all groups when it comes to welfare and poverty. Disabled people are heavily overrepresented among the poor. It is difficult to find employment and even more difficult to find adequately paid employment. According to Oliver (1996), this is because society stigmatizes disabled people by seeing them as less able, which makes it difficult for them to obtain decent employment. Oliver also argues that assumptions about what is 'normal' means that workplaces, leisure facilities and public transport are organized on the basis of able-bodied people. In the last 10 years, legislation has been introduced to bring about a degree of equality and there is now a Disability Rights Commission to enforce the law.

Check your understanding

1 According to the New Right:

(a) How do entrepreneurs help to solve the problem of poverty?

(b) How can the welfare state undermine the 'will to work'?

2 Which approach is associated with the introduction of the welfare state?

3 What is the role of the welfare state, according to social democrats?

4 What is the role of the welfare state, according to Marxists?

5 Explain in your own words what the term 'disciplinary tendency' means, and give one example.

KEY TERMS

Child tax credits give wage earners (up to a certain level of salary) additional payments for each child they have.

Disciplinary tendency where people are forced into certain patterns of behaviour, e.g. the unemployed are forced to undertake skills training or lose their rights to state benefits.

Entrepreneur person who takes risks in order to make a profit

Minimum wage the lowest legal wage an employer can pay.

Poverty trap where a person who gets a job experiences a drop in income, because their wages are lower than the welfare benefits they were receiving when unemployed.

Tax credits (see also **Child tax credits**) a way of helping people in low-wage jobs or part-time employment. People in work have their tax adjusted so that the government will add money to their salary, rather than take it away.

Tax incentives encouraging a particular course of action by rewarding people with tax relief or extra tax benefits.

Welfare benefits/state benefits the financial support that the government gives people as part of the welfare state, e.g. disability benefits and pensions.

Welfare state a system of welfare benefits and services provided by central or local government.

Item A | Welfare to work

From 1997, the Labour government effectively placed work at the centre of its social policies, with initiatives aimed not merely at increasing employment or reducing unemployment, but also at using work to tackle social exclusion.

The government wanted to devise a system that was more 'active',

offering claimants a 'hand up, not a hand-out'. In practice, this meant making benefit payments more conditional on undertaking activities geared to labour market (re-)entry. The government has introduced a minimum wage and a series of tax credits to help those in low pay with families ... all this based on the belief

in making work pay, because benefit claimants would only take work if there was sufficient financial incentive to do so. Supporting people in work costs a lot less than paying social security benefits.

Adapted from Bochel, H., Bochel, C., Page, R. and Sykes, R. (2004) *Social Policy: Issues and Developments,* Harlow: Pearson (pp. 67 & 76)

Item B | A New Right view of the welfare state

<< The monopolistic position of the welfare services prevents them from learning from competition and experience. The bureaucratic structure prevents them from operating with the flexibility and

attention to changing circumstances that we take for granted from the private sector. Their colossal scale inhibits innovation and encourages depersonalized routinization. The commitment of their managers at all

levels to centralized planning stands in the way of local and individual initiative and enterprise.>>

Marsland, D. (1996) *Welfare or Welfare State?* Basingstoke: Macmillan

Item C | A Marxist view of the welfare state

Thus, in contrast to the social democratic view, it is insisted that, under capitalism, the functioning and management of state welfare remain part of a capitalist state. The benefits of the welfare state to the working class are not generally

denied, but they are seen to be largely the by-product of securing the interests of [the ruling class]. The role of the welfare state is not to eliminate poverty, but to maintain a basic standard of living to ensure the continuation of capitalism.

Furthermore, by paying benefits to the poor, capitalism gives the appearance of being 'caring'.

Adapted from Pierson, C. (1991) *Beyond the Welfare State?* Cambridge: Polity Press, p. 53

1 Explain what is meant by the term 'minimum wage' (Item A). (2 marks)

2 Identify two policies the government has introduced to help people in low-paid families (Item A). (4 marks)

3 Identify three reasons why the author of Item B believes that the welfare state is in need of reform. (6 marks)

4 Identify and briefly explain two purposes of the welfare state according to the Marxist view (Item C). (8 marks)

5 Examine the New Right view that the welfare state actually causes poverty. (20 marks)

6 Using material from the Items and elsewhere, assess the effectiveness of the welfare state in eliminating poverty. (20 marks)

research ideas

- Interview a small sample of people to discover their opinions on eliminating poverty.
  - Do they think it can be achieved, and, if so, how?
  - What are their different views?
  - How do these link to sociological views and the policies of the different political parties?

web.task

Use the websites of the main political parties to compare their approaches to welfare and poverty (and remember that each party is going to be biased in the information it gives you).

Conservative Party	**www.conservatives.com**
Labour Party	**www.labour.org.uk**
Liberal Democrats	**www.libdems.org.uk**

Welfare provision

Does an elderly man in a home have a right to pay for sex?

The tale is told by James Barrett, consultant psychiatrist at the Charing Cross Hospital, London, who was called to see 'Mr Cooper' (not his real name) after staff at the old people's home where he lived complained that he had been pestering them for sex. Mr Cooper, who was in his 80s, had been paying an elderly woman to visit him to provide sexual services. When she stopped visiting, he asked staff to arrange another prostitute, difficult for him as his eyesight and hearing were failing.

The staff demurred and Mr Cooper made advances to female carers. Dr Barrett suggested the simplest way of resolving the matter would be to comply with Mr Cooper's wishes but staff thought it illegal and didn't want 'someone like that' at the home. 'They seemed disappointed I was not going to prescribe a drug to lower Mr Cooper's libido,' Dr Barrett writes in the *British Medical Journal*.

The matter was referred to the head of social services for the elderly in the borough, who took legal advice. This suggested 'the crime of procurement would not have been committed' were staff to call prostitutes. Managers now found a new worry – that once his modest savings ran out, they might have to pay for the visits, if the encounters proved to control his advances towards staff.

Matters got worse and the old people's home had to hire a male member of staff to follow Mr Cooper's 'every tottering step'. Eventually it relented and arranged for Mr Cooper to meet a prostitute at a neutral venue.

The cab was called and Mr Cooper was 'tremulous with anticipation', when it was called off. Managers had decided the arrangement could only be justified if it could be shown to have 'a beneficial effect on his behaviour in an NHS setting'.

The case was passed to the local NHS hospital, which reluctantly accepted there was no other solution. A room was allocated and staff told a special 'therapist' would call the day after Mr Cooper was transferred to the hospital. But before he could be admitted to enjoy the liaison he had long sought, he developed pneumonia and died.

The British Medical Association said: 'It is not an appropriate use of NHS facilities. Seeing a prostitute is not about improving people's health.'

Source: *The Independent*, 23 October 2004, p. 27

The advertisement on the right seeks to persuade people to take out insurance to cover themselves for private health care.

1 If you had to choose just one of the following statements as the nearer to what you believe, which would it be?

(a) Health care should be available solely on the basis of a person's need.

(b) A person has the right to buy private health care if that is how they decide to spend their money.

2 Make a list of reasons for your choice.

3 Make a list of reasons why the other view is mistaken.

4 Now discuss the two statements with others and see what agreement or disagreement there is. You could take a vote at the end.

5 Read the article above. Do you think that the gentleman should have had sex paid for by the state? Do you think his 'needs' were just as legitimate as the need for health care discussed earlier? What are the limits to a welfare state?

Don't just get better
Get the best
Private medical cover from an
award-winning insurer*

* Winner of the Your Money Direct Award for Best Private Medical Insurance Provider for four years running

AXA PPP healthcare
Be Life Confident

The development of welfare

The situation before the welfare state

Before the introduction of the welfare state, there had been a variety of forms of welfare provision, most of them based on charity, though the state did intervene over some issues.

Combating poverty

Measures to combat poverty date back as far as 1601, when the government introduced what we might now call a 'minimum wage'. In 1834, the Poor Law (Amendment) Act introduced the workhouse system: the poor and the old had to go and live in workhouses if they were destitute. In order to ensure that people did not 'abuse' the system, the conditions inside the workhouses were deliberately made worse than the conditions outside – on the principle of 'less eligibility', which assumes that people will always take from the state unless they find conditions would be worse than those they already had.

The conditions in which the poor lived in the 19th century were appalling, so it is difficult for us to imagine just how bad workhouse standards were. Indeed, for a very large number of people, entry to the workhouse was a death sentence.

Workhouses remained in various forms until 1928, although in 1908 and 1912 the Liberal governments introduced sickness benefits (for males only) and old age pensions, which meant that the workhouses were no longer needed.

Health care was largely based on charity or payment until the Second World War (1939), with poorer people having no access to doctors at all, apart from the charitable clinics. In the 1920s and 1930s, working-class people took out insurance with local doctors, paying a small amount each week to have the right to call out a doctor.

Housing

Housing conditions were appalling in 19th-century Britain and a number of **philanthropists** raised funds and built housing projects (many still existing in the old ex-industrial cities) for the poor. However, only the 'respectable' poor were allowed to rent these properties. By the 1920s, the demand for housing was so great that local authorities were given power to build social-housing projects, although it was still necessary to prove respectability to get a property.

The welfare state

The coming of the welfare state dramatically changed all this. A 'system' of welfare based on charity was seen as demeaning and was replaced with one based on the right to welfare, where the only criterion for help was that of being in need.

The welfare state followed the **Beveridge Report** of 1942, which analysed the flaws of the previous system based on a mixture of charity, local authority intervention and private provision by the more affluent.

Beveridge identified what he called the five 'evils' which he felt the government needed to wipe out (see Table 6.6). These were: want (poverty), ignorance, disease, squalor and idleness. The resulting policies introduced between 1944 and 1948, brought about the NHS, the extension of schooling, the social

Table 6.6 Tackling social evils: the welfare state

Social evil	Welfare state
Want (poverty)	Poverty was to be tackled by payment of unemployment and sickness benefits, and a 'safety net' benefit that would cover everyone not covered by these other benefits. Today, this safety-net benefit is known as 'income support'.
Ignorance	Free schooling was to be extended (to age 15), and new schools were to be built.
Disease	A National Health Service (NHS) was to be set up, whereby everyone would have a right to free health care. Before this, people either paid for their health care, or applied to charitable hospitals.
Squalor (poor housing)	A massive programme of house-building was to be undertaken to get rid of poor-quality housing ('slums').
Idleness (unemployment)	The government was to commit itself to ensuring that never again would there be a return to mass unemployment.

security system, an increase in social housing and a commitment to full employment. This system became known as the 'welfare state'.

Explanations for the introduction of the welfare state

The question that many academics have asked is: why was the welfare state introduced in the 1940s and not before, as the 'evils' identified by Beveridge were not new?

The most common explanation is that a general consensus was reached during the Second World War that it would be impossible to ask the people who were suffering so greatly to return to a society of high unemployment and poverty – a situation which had characterized the 20th century up to that time. The major political parties agreed that an organized system of welfare needed to be introduced which provided a safety net for ordinary people, but did not disturb the unequal nature of British society. This is a **pluralist** explanation, which sees the various power groups in society vying with each other and arriving at an agreement.

A more radical view of the situation has been suggested by Marxist-influenced writers such as Ginsberg (1998). They argue that the welfare state can best be understood in a more complex, 'two-sided' way. On the one hand, the welfare state was a true advance for the working class, emerging from the class conflict as a concession wrestled from capitalism. However, it was also a way for the ruling class to control the mass of the population by giving them a safety net which would prevent them falling into extreme poverty. It would provide them with housing and give health care (and so maintain a healthy working population). At the same time, education would provide a better disciplined workforce and full employment was not a problem in the years following the Second World War. However, the most important thing was that the welfare state maintained the capitalist system with its inequalities of income and wealth intact.

The welfare state in context

During the early to mid 20th century, other countries also began to introduce welfare systems. However, their answers to the problems of poverty, education, housing and so on were quite different. In fact, a wide variety of different systems of welfare have developed across the world. In a famous study, Esping-Anderson (1990) has suggested that all capitalist **welfare regimes** can be divided into three main types:

1 Liberal welfare states

These provide only a minimum level of services and cash benefits. In these societies, the poor, sick and disabled are helped by their families, by charitable organizations and religious groups. Those people in employment usually pay into insurance schemes to ensure that they receive health, pensions and unemployment benefits. The state provides services for those most in need but these are 'means tested' – that is, people have to prove that they are in real need before they can receive help, and their situation (their 'means') is thoroughly examined to decide whether or not they should receive help. Examples of this type of welfare regime include the USA, Portugal and Spain.

2 Corporatist welfare states

These systems have high-quality health, education and welfare services organized by the state, but are funded by a mixture of state support and insurance schemes. Other non-government organizations, such as churches, trades unions and employers' organizations, are heavily involved in providing services. Corporatist welfare states are usually conservative in their views on society. They tend to fund people in conventional families and provide less support for lone parents and women (who are expected to obtain help through their husbands and/or family). These services are means tested, as in the liberal welfare regimes. Examples of this sort of regime include France, Belgium and Germany.

3 Social democratic welfare states

Social democratic welfare states place considerable emphasis on equality. There is a high level of taxation and a very high-quality, extensive set of welfare services. Because the state-provided services are so high, there is very little private provision of welfare. There is great emphasis on full employment, so that the costs of the system can be supported, because relatively few people are out of work and because most of those in work are also paying taxes. People have a right to state services and these are 'universal', in the sense that anyone has access to them. Examples of this regime can mainly be found in Scandinavia, with Sweden most commonly being given as the prime example.

Welfare regime debates

We have just seen how the welfare state emerged in the UK. In other countries, different forms of welfare regime were adopted. The different regimes reflect different decisions as to how to resolve the problems of:

- who should receive services and cash benefits
- what agencies should provide the services – the state, or a mixture of private companies and charities.

Who should receive benefits?

Philosophical arguments

One debate that has dogged the provision of welfare has been the question of who should receive state benefits. Those who support the idea of universal benefits (**universalism**) argue that state benefits – such as free health care, pensions and child allowances – should be given to all those who need them, irrespective of their income. The thinking behind this is that it helps to draw society together and promotes social harmony.

Those who support the targeting of benefits (**selectivism**) argue that universalism simply wastes resources on those who have no need of them. It also undermines people's desire to look after themselves, their family and other members of the community. Universalism thus weakens rather than strengthens social harmony and any sense of community.

Practical arguments

The debate between those who support the universal provision of welfare and those who support selective provision also involves arguments about practicality.

It is true that universalism does provide help to those who have no need of it. However, because everyone gets the same benefits, and there is no complex bureaucratic mechanism to assess who is eligible, the costs of providing the benefits are actually quite low. Furthermore, universal provision ensures that everyone who needs help gets it (because everyone does), and it also eliminates the stigma attached to claiming state benefits.

Selectivists point out that universal benefits are wasteful. By targeting the more needy, the levels of benefit could be higher and the quality of services could be better. It is true that, for some benefits, the administrative costs of targeting are expensive, but, despite this, overall, money would be saved on most benefits.

The state or the mixed economy of welfare?

The **'mixed economy' of welfare** refers to the move away from a state monopoly of health and care provision, to having a number of different providers, including:

- **for-profit/private organizations**
- **voluntary (charitable) organizations**
- **informal care** provided by family and friends.

Before the introduction of the welfare state, many services we now associate with it, such as health care, were provided either

Karen Rowlingson

Pension planning

The mixed economy of welfare is based on the idea that people make rational choices about spending their money and, if they had less tax, they would spend their money on the most sensible services they need. Perhaps the most important welfare service that most people need after health is pension planning – yet relatively few people save for a pension from an early age. Rowlingson decided to interview a small cross section of people of different ages, sexes and incomes, to find out why so few people who do not have compulsory occupational pension schemes actually save for their pensions. Rowlingson was interested in attitudes and so undertook a series of in-depth, qualitative interviews. In all, she questioned 41 people. After the interview, each person was given a £10 voucher as a token of appreciation. Interviews took place in the respondents' homes and lasted between 45 minutes and three hours. She found that people did not save for a number of reasons, which included the following:

- It is difficult to imagine growing old (when you are young) and having need of a pension.
- Financial constraints mean that people have to spend the money even if they wish to save.
- It 'tempts fate' to plan ahead (if you save a lot, you tempt fate that you will die early).

Rowlingson therefore concluded that it is mistaken to rely on voluntary pension plans if society is not to face major problems in the future.

Rowlingson, K. (2002) 'Private pension planning: the rhetoric of responsibility, the reality of insecurity', *Journal of Social Policy*, 32(4)

1 Suggest reasons why Rowlingson used in-depth interviews for this research.

2 To what extent do you think the sample used was representative of the British population?

3 Why does the researcher conclude that it is wrong for society to rely on voluntary pension plans?

by profit-making organizations or by charities. In the last 20 years, there has been a resurgence of both private companies and charitable (or non-profit-making) organizations. The main reason for this has been the influence of the New Right on Conservative governments during the 1980s and 1990s, and the subsequent acceptance of many of their arguments by succeeding Labour governments, which have incorporated these ideas into their 'Third Way' ideology (see Topic 5).

The New Right has argued that the state provision of welfare is both inefficient and of a poor standard, because there is no incentive for the providers of welfare either to attract 'customers' or to save money. The employees of the NHS, for example, continue to receive their salaries no matter how inefficient the system or how rude they are to the people who use their services. This is because the NHS has been, until recently, a **monopoly** – that is, the only provider of health services. Supporters of the New Right argue that, if the NHS had to make a profit, its employees would certainly have to act differently. The term used to describe this is the 'discipline of the market'.

Since the 1980s, governments have partially accepted these arguments, and a number of reforms have been introduced that attempt to bring the discipline of the market into the provision of health and welfare. These changes include:

- handing over some areas of welfare and health-care provision (e.g. housing and the care of older people) to private or charitable organizations
- encouraging the NHS to subcontract certain activities to private organizations (e.g. private hospitals may undertake routine operations such as removal of cataracts and hip replacements)
- the building of new NHS hospitals that are shared with private health-care organizations.
- grants to voluntary organizations to help support their activities
- requiring local health-care trusts to operate to stringent financial and customer-care standards.

Another area of this 'mixed economy' of welfare is the growing emphasis on informal care by family members. The government strongly supports this form of care, primarily because it is cheap. For example, grants are available to enable family carers to stay at home to look after family members with disabilities.

Criticisms of the mixed economy of welfare

Critics of the mixed economy of welfare argue that the state is abandoning its responsibilities, and that it is a step back to the time before the welfare state. The main criticisms are these:

- The growth of private health care and its funding by government means that a two-tier system has developed, in which the more affluent are able to buy better health care, while the majority of the population have to make do with second-class services.
- Charitable organizations, which are often staffed by volunteers, may have less expertise than professionals.
- Feminist sociologists, in particular, have pointed out that the burden of informal care usually falls upon the women in families.

Who has benefited from the welfare state?

The main aim of the welfare state has been to ensure a certain minimum quality of life for all citizens of the UK. For many commentators, this suggests that the welfare state is a mechanism for redistributing wealth from the better off to the less well off. It does this by taxing the affluent at a higher rate and then using the surplus taxes to pay for welfare services, which are more likely to be used by the poorer groups in society. But does it actually do this?

To answer this question we need to look at the different services provided by the state. In the 1990s, Hills (1998) undertook a massive overview of the state of the welfare services and, although there have been changes since then, the overall conclusions he reached are still accepted as largely accurate today.

Education

Hills concluded that this favoured the middle-income groups overall. The most affluent pay both taxes and fees for private schools, so do not benefit, while the poorer groups tend to have the worse-quality schools and the lowest educational outcomes. In terms of value, therefore, the middle class benefit.

Health

According to Le Grand (1982), cited in Hills (1998), the middle class benefited more from the health service. According to Le Grand, this was because they ask for more services, are more knowledgeable about the system and have greater awareness of possible health risks. Le Grand called this the 'inverse care law'. However Hills' research found no evidence to support this 'law' and points out that, in fact, the health service is highly beneficial to poorer groups in society and widely used by them.

Social security and tax credit payments

Hills suggests that households earning below the median income do actually benefit more from the social-security and tax-credit system, while those in the top half pay more in tax and receive less in benefits.

It appears therefore that the welfare state does redistribute income and wealth. However, the next question is: by how much does it redistribute? According to the Office for National Statistics – the government's own statistical department – the overall degree of redistribution is fairly small. Before tax and redistribution via the welfare state, the highest-earning 20 per cent of households receive over 50 per cent of all income, while the lowest-earning households receive 2 per cent of income. After tax and taking into account the redistribution which occurs, the highest-earning 20 per cent receive 44 per cent of income and the lowest-earning 20 per cent receive 7 per cent of all income (ONS statistics cited in Palmer et al. 2004).

Hills also points out the importance of seeing the redistributive effects of the welfare state over a person's lifetime. He argues that, although over a full lifetime the poorest are likely to benefit from the welfare state, the majority of the population actually finance themselves over their lifetime. This is because people pay higher taxes during their adulthood when their demands upon the welfare state are relatively low. In old age, they then return to take from the welfare state through demands upon health services and pensions. However, as lower-paid people are more likely to die younger, although they will have paid less into the system, proportionately they will take less out.

Check your understanding

1. **What three types of welfare regimes are there?**

2. **What are the advantages of:**
   (a) **the universal provision of benefits?**
   (b) **the selective provision of benefits?**

3. **Why has there been a resurgence in the provision of welfare services by private companies and voluntary organizations?**

4. **How has the New Right attacked the welfare state?**

5. **Which members of the family are most likely to provide 'informal care'?**

KEY TERMS

Beveridge Report introduced the welfare state in the UK.

For-profit/private organizations organizations that provide services in order to make a profit.

Informal care care provided by family or friends.

'Mixed economy' of welfare refers to the fact that welfare is provided not just by the state, but also by private and voluntary organizations.

Monopoly a situation in which there is only one provider of goods or services and, therefore, no competition.

Philanthropy another term for charity, usually used when rich people give large amounts to charity.

Pluralism a theoretical position in sociology which sees society consisting of competing groups seeking to get the best for themselves. Society is the result of this managed competition.

Selectivism/targeting the belief that only those with limited financial resources should receive welfare services and benefits.

Universalism the belief that everyone should be entitled to free welfare services and benefits.

Voluntary (charitable) organizations independent organizations that provide health or welfare services, but do not seek to make any profit.

Welfare regime 'ideal type' term used to categorize similar sorts of welfare provision in different countries.

exploring welfare provision

Item A The British welfare regime

<< Britain's history of welfare development has shown that, along with Sweden, the UK led Europe in introducing a comprehensive and universal welfare system. In that sense, the early emphasis on equality and citizenship, rights to a wide range of benefits, and 'free' health care, all point to the UK being a prototype of the social democratic model. However, over time, the UK developed a welfare system that was founded on liberal rather than social democratic principles and a rather basic or minimal idea of how much help people should receive in times of need.

Britain's welfare system today represents an interesting mix of principles and influences from the past. There is still a relatively strong commitment to welfare state principles and a high proportion of the nation's wealth is spent on welfare. However, the recent revival of the concept of the mixed economy of welfare emphasizes the role of private and voluntary organizations. For all these reasons, therefore, the British model combines elements of the liberal type of welfare system and remnants of a social democratic approach.>>

Source: Blakemore, K. (2003) *Social Policy. An Introduction*, Buckingham: Open University Press, p. 57

Item B A critical perspective on the welfare state

<< The welfare state functions in various ways to bolster and renew capitalism.

First, its existence makes capitalism seem more humane and acceptable, disguising its underlying brutality.

Second, the welfare state ensures that a sufficiently educated, healthy and securely housed working population is available in the labour market.

Third, the welfare state contributes directly to capital accumulation through its investment in infrastructure, such as hospitals, schools, etc. (thereby making profit for capitalists).>>

Ginsberg, N. (1998) 'The socialist perspective', in P. Alcock, A. Erskine and M. May *The Student's Companion to Social Policy*, Oxford: Blackwell

1. Explain the meaning of the term 'mixed economy of welfare' (Item A). (2 marks)

2. Suggest two reasons for the introduction of a welfare state in a capitalist society (Item B). (4 marks)

3. Give three examples why the early British welfare state could be seen as an example of a social democratic model of welfare (Item A). (6 marks)

4. Identify and explain two reasons why some people may believe that it is better to use a mixture of private and voluntary organizations to deliver welfare rather than the state. (8 marks)

5. Examine the view that welfare provision should be universal. (20 marks)

6. Using information from the Items and elsewhere, assess the view that it is the responsibility of the government to provide a 'welfare state'. (20 marks)

research ideas

- Research the debate about universal and selective benefits. All parents, no matter what their income, receive child benefits for children and young people up to the age of 18 (or 16, if not in full-time education). Ask a small sample of parents whether they think this is a good idea, or whether the benefits should only go to the poorer parents.

- Conduct an opinion survey to find out what the public think of the welfare state in general. Do the public support the welfare state?

web.tasks

1. Find the websites of three local charitable organizations. What sorts of work do they do?

2. Go to the NCVO website at www.ncvo-vol.org.uk

What is the NCVO? What does it do? Go to the 'press briefing' section and see what information you can find about the importance of voluntary organizations. Should we need so much voluntary provision when the welfare state exists?

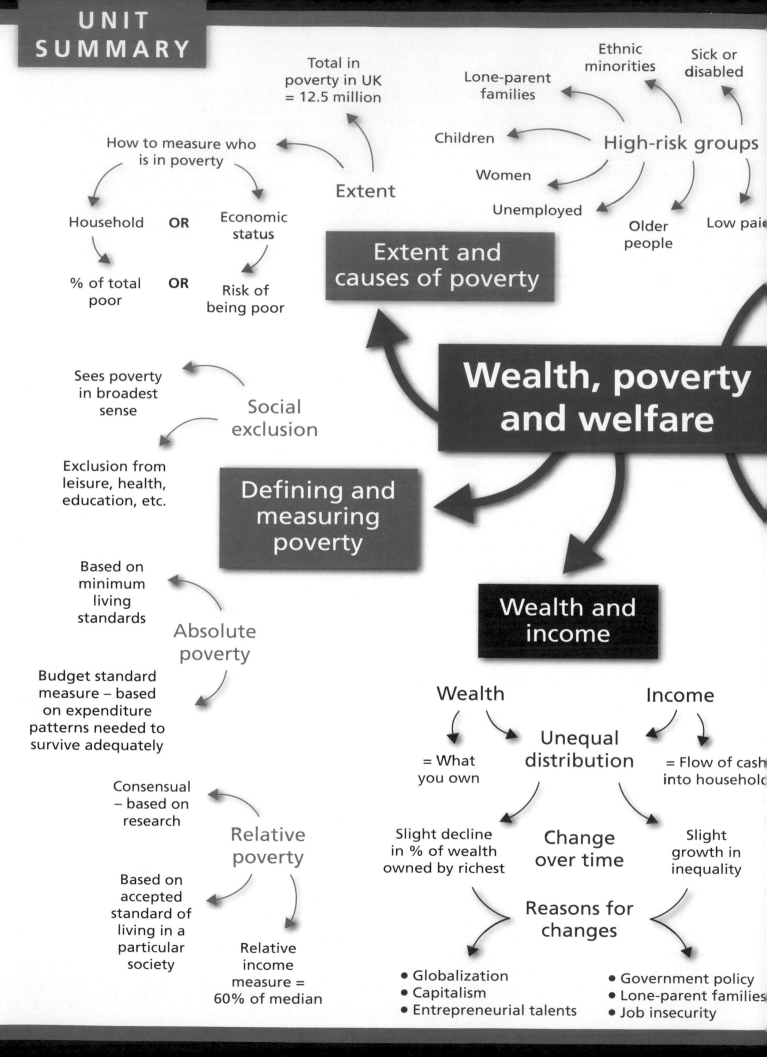

Total in poverty in UK = 12.5 million

How to measure who is in poverty

Household **OR** Economic status

% of total poor **OR** Risk of being poor

Extent

Ethnic minorities

Lone-parent families

Sick or disabled

Children

Women

High-risk groups

Unemployed

Older people

Low paid

Extent and causes of poverty

Sees poverty in broadest sense

Social exclusion

Exclusion from leisure, health, education, etc.

Wealth, poverty and welfare

Defining and measuring poverty

Based on minimum living standards

Absolute poverty

Budget standard measure – based on expenditure patterns needed to survive adequately

Wealth and income

Wealth

Income

= What you own

Unequal distribution

= Flow of cash into household

Consensual – based on research

Relative poverty

Based on accepted standard of living in a particular society

Relative income measure = 60% of median

Slight decline in % of wealth owned by richest

Change over time

Slight growth in inequality

Reasons for changes

- Globalization
- Capitalism
- Entrepreneurial talents

- Government policy
- Lone-parent families
- Job insecurity

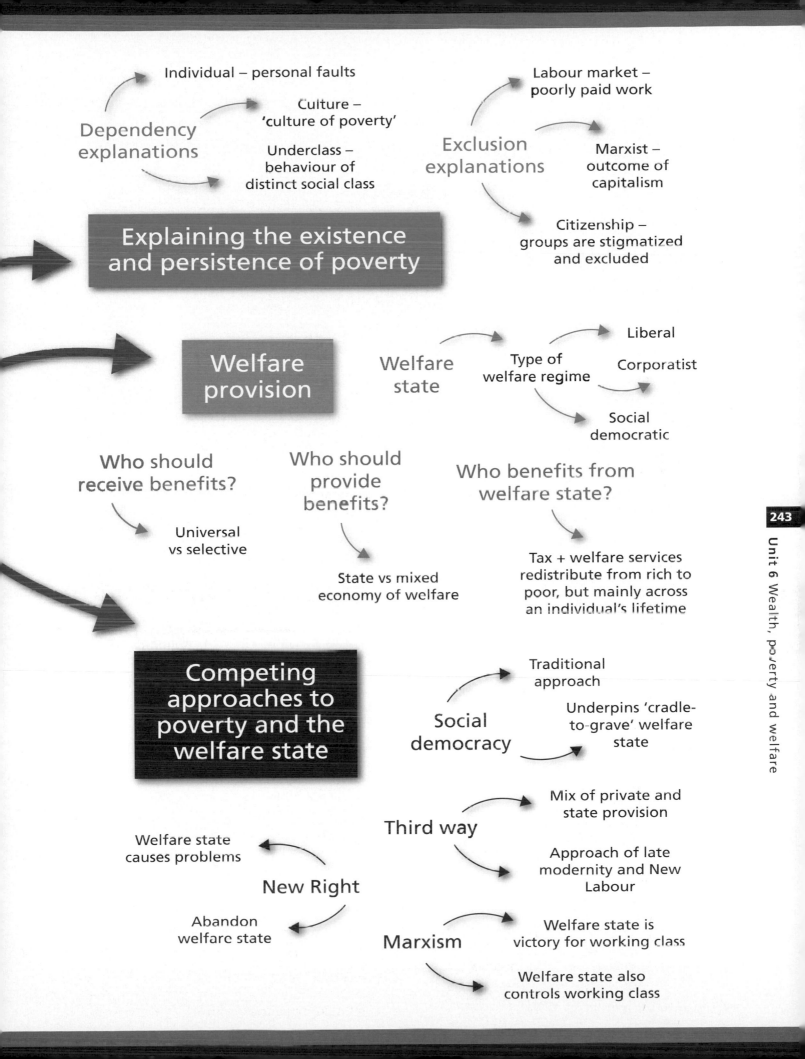

Individual – personal faults

Culture – 'culture of poverty'

Dependency explanations

Underclass – behaviour of distinct social class

Labour market – poorly paid work

Exclusion explanations

Marxist – outcome of capitalism

Citizenship – groups are stigmatized and excluded

Explaining the existence and persistence of poverty

Welfare provision

Welfare state

Type of welfare regime

Liberal

Corporatist

Social democratic

Who should **receive** benefits?

Universal vs selective

Who should **provide** benefits?

State vs mixed economy of welfare

Who benefits from welfare state?

Tax + welfare services redistribute from rich to poor, but mainly across an individual's lifetime

Competing approaches to poverty and the welfare state

Social democracy

Traditional approach

Underpins 'cradle-to-grave' welfare state

Third way

Mix of private and state provision

Approach of late modernity and New Labour

Welfare state causes problems

New Right

Abandon welfare state

Marxism

Welfare state is victory for working class

Welfare state also controls working class

TURN TO ANY PAGE IN THIS BOOK and you'll find claims and debates about the nature of society. There are arguments about the rights and wrongs of family life, the fairness of the education system and the influence of the media to name just three. But how do we know that the contents of the book are accurate? What distinguishes the statements that sociologists make from those of your friends, parents, journalists or people on radio phone-ins?

The answer is that sociology is based on research. And without research, sociologists cannot make any greater claim to explaining the world than anyone else. That means it is vital that all research is of the highest standard – if not, then we cannot rely on it.

Anyone studying sociology must also study the methods sociologists use. Armed with this knowledge, they will be able to carry out their own research and to critically examine existing sociological studies. If the research methods in a study are found to be flawed, then the claims made by that sociologist cannot be completely accepted.

In this unit we cover the main methods used by sociologists, and give a wide range of examples of research studies using each method.

AQA specification	topics	pages
Candidates should examine:		
The different quantitative and qualitative methods and sources of data including questionnaires, interviews, observation techniques and experiments, and documents and official statistics	Discussion of questionnaires and interviews primarily in Topic 4, experiments in Topic 1, observation in Topic 2 and documents and official statistics in Topic 5.	246–57 264–75
The distinctions between primary and secondary data, and between quantitative and qualitative data	Primary methods of data collection are those covered in Topics 2 to 4. Secondary data is the focus of Topic 5. Quantitative data is explained in Topic 2 and qualitative in Topic 3.	252–75
The relationship between positivism, interpretivism and sociological methods	Topic 1 includes a section on 'The relationship between theories and methods'.	246–51
The theoretical, practical and ethical considerations influencing the choice of topic, choice of method(s) and the conduct of research	The key factors affecting choices in research are covered in Topic 1.	246–51
The nature of social facts and the strengths and limitations of different sources of data and methods of research	Different sources of data are evaluated as they occur throughout the Unit.	whole unit

Sociological methods

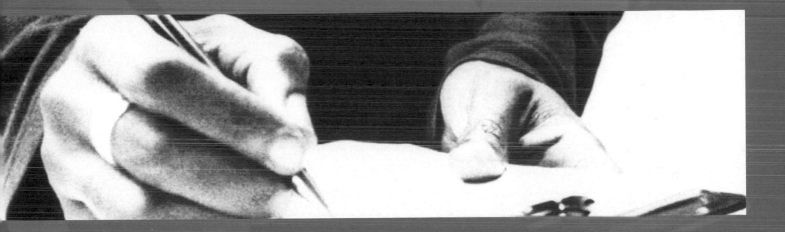

Methods, theories and ethics

gettingyouthinking

Karen Sharpe studied the lives of prostitutes by acting as a 'secretary' for them. Read the passage (right) about the aims of her research and then answer the questions that follow.

<< The central objective of my research was to understand why and how women entered the world of prostitution: to discover the motivating factors, the dynamics of the introductory process, and how they learnt the skills, values and codes of conduct of the business. I wanted to explore the importance and impact of prostitution on their lifestyles and to put the 'deviance' of prostitution into context with other aspects of their criminality. I also wanted to discover how the women themselves and their families and friends, subjectively defined, perceived and rationalized their activities.>>

1 What methods would it have been possible to use in this research? What are their advantages and disadvantages?

2 This research was conducted by a woman. What problems would have been faced by a male researcher?

3 Do you think that this research is justifiable? Explain your answer.

Sharpe, K. (2000) 'Sad, bad and (sometimes) dangerous to know: street corner research with prostitutes, punters and the police' in R.D. King and E. Wincup (eds), *Doing Research on Crime and Justice*, Oxford: Oxford University Press, p. 364

Sociologists generally try to take a 'sideways' look at social life – seeking to provide insights into the social world that the ordinary person would never normally have. In some ways, this interest in society is shared by journalists and other 'interested observers' of the world, but whereas these people tend to rely heavily on their *common sense* or *personal experience* in exploring society, sociologists reject these as adequate ways of explaining society. Instead, they argue that the best way to study society is to conduct research which uncovers patterns that would normally remain hidden. But the activities of sociologists do not stop there – once they have uncovered these patterns, they then seek explanations for the relationships between them. This process of constructing explanations for the social patterns is known as 'theorizing'.

So, research leads – eventually – to theories.

Even that is not the end of it. For once theories exist, other sociologists are influenced by them and will use them as the starting point for their research.

So, research leads to theories, which lead to more research and – yes, you've guessed it – more theories!

But the process is even more complicated than this. We need to know why some areas of social life are chosen and not

others. Are they more interesting? Are they more important? Is someone paying for the research?

And we need to think very carefully about the moral or ethical issues involved in choosing what to study, in doing research itself and, finally, in interpreting and publicizing the findings.

What does sociological research set out to do?

- *Gather data* – the first task of research is simply to gather information about the social world. This very basic function is the starting point for any kind of sociological understanding. Knowledge can take the form of statistical information, such as the numbers of marriages and divorces, and sociological 'facts', such as the attitudes of people in society towards marriage as an institution. However, we need to be wary about accepting these 'facts' at face value. As we shall see later, what is a 'fact' for one person may not be for others, as they may use different theories and methods to interpret the facts. A famous example of this is research on suicide by Durkheim (1897/1952). He collected a large number of statistics, on which he then based his theory on the causes of suicide. However, much later, other sociologists suggested a very different interpretation of these same 'facts' (see Item A on p. 251).

- *Make correlations* – Research can go further than just gathering information; it can help us explore relationships between different elements of society. This can be in the form of **correlations** (showing that two things are linked in some way), such as the fact that there is a statistical relationship between drug use and crime. Statistics show that those who commit burglary are also likely to be heavy users of drugs. At this point all we know is that there is a link between burglary and drug-consumption.

- *Develop theories* – The final role of research is to support or disprove a **sociological theory**. (A theory is simply an explanation of social events.) Researchers gather information and statistics that help sociologists to explain why certain social events occur. Often this involves providing an explanation for correlations. So, if a correlation exists between drug use and crime, various theories can be developed. One theory is that drug users are more likely to commit burglary because they need money to pay for their drug habit. An alternative is that burglars have a high income and so are more likely to have a pleasurable lifestyle that involves using drugs.

The relationship between research and ethics

Research can have a powerful impact on people's lives. It can do so in both harmful and beneficial ways. Therefore, researchers must always think very carefully about the impact of the research and how they ought to behave, so that no harm comes to the subjects of the research or to society in general. These sorts of concerns are generally discussed under the umbrella term **ethical issues**.

Most sociological researchers would agree that there are five areas of ethical concern:

- choice of topic
- choice of group to be studied
- effects on the people being studied
- effects on the wider society
- issues of legality and immorality.

Choice of topic

The first ethical issue relates to the decision about what to study. Merely by choosing an area, the researcher might be confirming some people's prejudices about a particular issue. For example, many sociologists are concerned about the extent of research into the 'negative' side of African–Caribbean life, with studies on school failure, lower levels of job success and even the claimed higher rate of criminality. Critics argue that merely by studying this, a continued association is made between race and criminality or race and failure.

Choice of group to be studied

One of the trickiest problems that sociologists face is gaining access to study particular groups. The more powerful the group, the less likely it is that the sociologist will manage to obtain agreement to study its members. The result, as you will see, is that the groups most commonly studied by sociologists are the least powerful – so students, petty criminals and less-skilled workers are the staple diet of sociological research. The really powerful evade study. Does sociology have a duty to explore the lives of the powerful?

Effects on the people being studied

Research can often have an effect on the people being studied. So, before setting out to do research, sociologists must think carefully about what these effects will be, although it is not

focus on research

Amia Lieblich
Effects on people being studied

Lieblich (1996) researched family lives in an Israeli kibbutz (a form of socialist community), reflecting on the way the book had an impact on those involved.

<< An older woman, Genia, who also read the first draft was the person I respected more than any other member of the kibbutz. After the joint meeting with all the 'readers', Genia asked to see me in private. 'I am shocked' she said, 'I cried so much' … she explained what caused her all the pain were the stories of her two daughters, which were included in the book. I realized that both of them said in so many words that Genia had been a 'bad mother'. During their childhood she dedicated all her time to the affairs of the kibbutz whilst they felt neglected and rejected. >>

Lieblich, A. (1996) 'Some unforeseen outcomes of conducting narrative research with people of one's own culture', in R. Josselson (ed.) *Ethics and Process in the Narrative Study of Lives*, London: Sage (cited in K. Plummer *Documents of Life* (2001) London: Sage, p. 225).

1 **Was it possible or desirable for Lieblich to have avoided upsetting Genia?**

always possible to anticipate them – see *Focus on research* on the previous page.

One of the reasons why sociologists rarely use experiments, for example, is that these may lead to the subjects being harmed by the experiment. In participant observational studies, where the researcher actually joins in with the group being studied (see Topic 3), the researcher can often become an important member of the group and may influence other members to behave in ways they would not normally.

Effects on the wider society

It is not only the people being studied who are potentially affected by the research. The families of those being researched may have information given about them that they wish to keep secret. Also, victims of crime may be upset by the information that researchers obtain about the perpetrators, as they may prefer to forget the incident.

Issues of legality and immorality

Finally, sociologists may be drawn into situations where they may commit crimes or possibly help in or witness deviant acts. While undertaking research on a prisoner in the USA, Kenneth Tunnell (1998) discovered that the prisoner had actually taken on the identity of someone else (who was dead), in order to avoid a much longer prison sentence. The prison authorities became suspicious and investigated the prisoner's background. Though Tunnell knew the truth, he felt that he owed the prisoner confidentiality and deliberately lied, stating that he knew nothing about the identity 'theft'. As a result, the prisoner was released many years early.

The relationship between theories and methods

Earlier we saw that research findings could be used either to generate new sociological theories, or to confirm or challenge existing theories. However, the relationship between research and theory is even more complicated than this. If a sociologist has a particular interest in a theoretical approach, then this may well influence their research methodology. There are areas in which theory has a strong influence on research – for example, the theoretical approach may:

1 direct people to explore certain areas of research
2 influence the actual techniques chosen
3 influence how researchers interpret the research findings.

Theory and choice of an area of research

One of the great joys of studying sociology is that the variety of different views and theories generates so many different opinions about society. However, when reading sociological research, you must always be aware that sociologists who hold strong theoretical beliefs about society are bound to study the topics that, in their eyes, are the most important, and to be less interested in other areas.

- **Feminist sociologists** see it as their role to examine the position of women in society, and to uncover the ways in which **patriarchy**, or the power of men, has been used to control and oppress women. Consequently, their choice of research projects will be influenced by this.
- **Marxist or critical sociologists** argue that the most important area of study is the question of how a relatively small group of people exploits the vast majority of the population. They will study issues such as the concentration of power and wealth, and the importance of social class divisions.
- **Functionalist-oriented sociologists** think that society is based on a general consensus of values. They are interested in looking at the ways in which society maintains agreement on values and solves social problems. Therefore, they will look at the role of religion or schools in passing on values.

Theory and techniques of study

Various theories may point to different areas of interest, but theories also nudge sociologists into different ways of studying society. Theories in sociology usually fall into two camps – **top-down** and **bottom-up** theories.

Top-down approaches

Top-down approaches, such as functionalism and Marxism, say that the best way to understand society is to view it as a real 'thing' which exists above and beyond us all as individuals. It shapes our lives and provides us with the social world in which we live. Our role is generally to conform. These sorts of theoretical approaches emphasize that any research ought to bear this in mind and that the researcher should be looking for general patterns of behaviour – which individuals may not even be aware of.

The favoured research methods used by these sociologists tend to be those that generate sets of statistics (such as questionnaires), known as **quantitative methods** (see Topic 2). Sociologists sympathetic to the use of these more 'scientific' methods are sometimes known as **positivists**.

Bottom-up approaches

Bottom-up approaches, such as interactionism, stress that the only way to understand society is to look at the world through the eyes of individuals, as it is their activities and beliefs that make up the social world. Research must start at 'the bottom' and work upwards. The sorts of research methods favoured by those who advocate this approach (known as **interpretive sociologists**) tend to be those that allow the researcher to see the world from the same perspective as those being studied (known as **qualitative methods**). An example is participant observation (see pp. 259–60).

The interpretation of research findings

The final impact of theory on research comes when interpreting the research findings. The research is completed and the results are all there in the computer. How does the researcher make sense of the results? This will depend, of course, on what they are looking for, and that, in turn, depends upon what theoretical approach the researcher sympathizes with. This is very different from bias or personal values – rather, it is a matter of choosing which results are most important, and this will always depend upon what best fits the theoretical framework of the researcher. A feminist researcher will be keen to understand the position of women; the Marxist will be looking for signs of class struggle; the functionalist will be looking at the key indicators to prove that a set of common beliefs exists.

The relationship between practical issues and research

So far we have looked at the ethical and theoretical issues which have an important influence on the research process. As you can see, these are quite difficult 'abstract' issues, which sometimes seem far removed from the reality of everyday life. However, just as important are a range of very down-to-earth influences on the research process.

Funding

All research has to be paid for by someone and those who pay for research have a reason for doing so. These funding organizations may vary from those who wish to extend knowledge about society and to improve the quality of life (such as the Joseph Rowntree Foundation), to private companies wanting to sell more products or services (such as market research organizations). Despite the differences between the funding organizations, each has an aim that constrains the research choices and activities of sociologists.

Probably the largest funder of sociological research in Britain is the government, which pays for a wide range of research into areas such as transport, health, crime and housing. However, anyone conducting research for the government signs a contract that restricts what they can say and publish about their findings.

focus on research

The British Sociological Association

The British Sociological Association is the official organization for academic sociologists engaged in research. It provides a set of ethical guidelines for its members. Below are some of the key points about the relationships between those who pay for the research (funders) and sociologists (members). You can find the full statement of ethics on the BSA website **www.britsoc.co.uk**

- Members should have a written contract with the funders.
- Members must be totally honest with the funders about their own qualifications and about the advantages/disadvantages of the chosen research methods.
- Members should not agree to research where the funding is dependent upon certain research results.
- Members need to know, before they start the research, that they have the right to publish their research and to let others know who funded it.

1 Take each of the points above and explain why it is important.

KEY TERMS

Bottom-up theories (generally called 'micro' or 'interpretive' approaches) sociological theories that analyse society by studying the ways in which individuals interpret the world.

Correlation a statistical relationship between two things. It does not necessarily mean that one causes the other.

Ethical issues moral concerns about the benefits and potential harm of research to the people being researched, to researchers themselves and to society.

Feminist sociology an approach within sociology that concerns itself with studying the way in which women are oppressed by men.

Functionalism an approach within sociology that stresses that society is based on a general agreement of values.

Interpretive sociology an approach favouring the use of qualitative methods, such as participant observation, that allow the researcher to see the world from the same perspective as those being studied.

Marxist or critical sociology an approach within sociology that stresses the exploitation of the majority of the population by a small and powerful 'ruling class'.

Patriarchy the oppression of women by men.

Positivism the view that sociology should try to use more 'scientific' approaches and methods, such as questionnaires and official statistics.

Qualitative methods methods, such as participant observation, which produce primarily written data and which allow

the researcher to see things from the same perspective as those being studied.

Quantitative methods methods, such as questionnaires, that produce primarily statistical data.

Sociological theory an explanation of how different parts of society or different events relate to one another.

Top-down theories (often called 'macro' or 'structural' approaches) sociological theories that believe it is important to look at society as a whole when studying it.

Academic specialism

Sociologists at university specialize in particular areas within sociology – for example, some will only study the family and others only health issues. Clearly, the research they will wish to undertake will be within their specialism.

Personal reasons

Sociologists, like everyone else, want to have successful careers, be promoted and become respected. Research choices are often influenced by these desires. If there are various areas of research to choose from, the ambitious sociologist chooses that one that may lead to promotion.

Appropriate methods

The research method is often dictated by the situation and the sociologist has no choice, even if they have misgivings. Generally, if a large number of people need to be studied, then the sociologist will use questionnaires or possibly interviews. If a few people need to be studied in depth, then some form of observation will be employed.

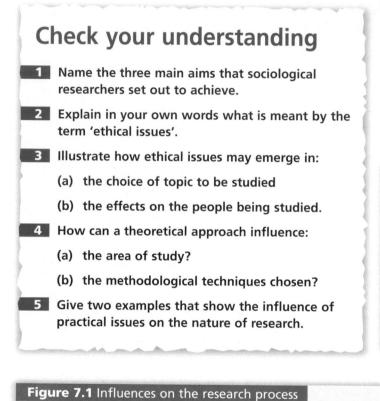

Check your understanding

1 Name the three main aims that sociological researchers set out to achieve.

2 Explain in your own words what is meant by the term 'ethical issues'.

3 Illustrate how ethical issues may emerge in:

(a) the choice of topic to be studied

(b) the effects on the people being studied.

4 How can a theoretical approach influence:

(a) the area of study?

(b) the methodological techniques chosen?

5 Give two examples that show the influence of practical issues on the nature of research.

research ideas

● Look in your school or college library for resources about drugs and alcohol. Who published the material? Can you suggest reasons why they published the material? Could this affect the content of the material in any way?

● Using any textbook of sociology, find one example of feminist research (use the index) and explain how the researcher's feminist approach might have affected the research in any way.

web.task

1 Go to the website of the British Sociological Association and find the section on 'The Statement of Ethical Practice'. Make a brief list of the key elements. Do you think they are all necessary?

How could 'informed consent' cause problems for studying young people or deviant groups?

Figure 7.1 Influences on the research process

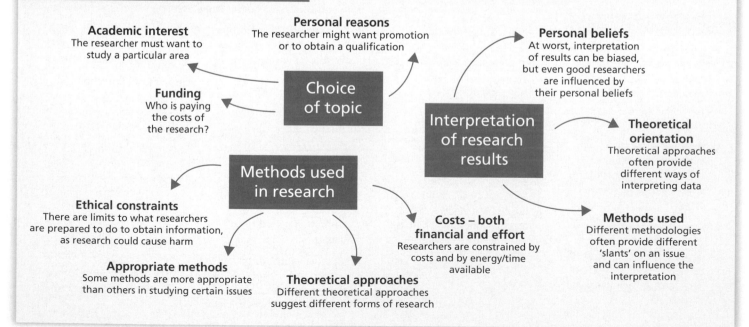

Academic interest
The researcher must want to study a particular area

Personal reasons
The researcher might want promotion or to obtain a qualification

Personal beliefs
At worst, interpretation of results can be biased, but even good researchers are influenced by their personal beliefs

Funding
Who is paying the costs of the research?

Choice of topic

Interpretation of research results

Theoretical orientation
Theoretical approaches often provide different ways of interpreting data

Ethical constraints
There are limits to what researchers are prepared to do to obtain information, as research could cause harm

Methods used in research

Costs – both financial and effort
Researchers are constrained by costs and by energy/time available

Methods used
Different methodologies often provide different 'slants' on an issue and can influence the interpretation

Appropriate methods
Some methods are more appropriate than others in studying certain issues

Theoretical approaches
Different theoretical approaches suggest different forms of research

Item A Suicide: the relationship between social 'facts', theory and method

Durkheim's famous study of suicide (1897) attempts to show how the cultures of different (European) societies could help explain the individual decision to commit suicide. The research was intended to prove that individual action can best be understood by examining social rather than individual differences. In doing so, it aimed to promote sociology as a science on a par with biology or chemistry. Durkheim gathered suicide statistics across various groups, religions and societies. He then interpreted these statistics as showing that the chances of individuals committing suicide vary according to their social group. Certain societies and groups have higher rates of 'social cohesion' – that is, people feel a greater sense of belonging than in others. For example, married people had lower rates of suicide. Durkheim's analysis was regarded by many as an excellent example of sociological research – gathering statistics across different countries to provide the basis for a clear theory.

However, in the 1960s and 1970s, sociologists who believed that the only way to understand society was by trying to see into the minds of individuals – the 'bottom-up' theorists – began to criticize Durkheim's acclaimed study, arguing that the statistics on which he had based his research were flawed. These sociologists said that in only a few cases can one know for certain if the death was suicide or not, as there are rarely suicide notes. Usually, a death is a 'suicide' when a coroner says it is. The real research, they argued, was in studying how coroners go about making their decision as to whether or not to classify a death as suicide.

Item B Feminist perspectives

<< The topic of Catrin's [research] very much evolved out of two fundamental concerns: women's health and women's imprisonment. Emma's interest, similarly, developed when she began to read a number of highly critical accounts of women's imprisonment ...

Both pieces of research were primarily influenced by what could loosely be termed a 'feminist' criminological perspective. In the 1970s and afterwards, feminist concern was directed at the misrepresentation and/or absence of women in conventional criminological research ... 'We were aware of the incomplete nature of this knowledge and were keen to address some of the gaps.' >>

Adapted from Smith, C. and Wincup, E. (2000) 'Breaking in: researching criminal justice institutions for women' in R.D. King and E. Wincup (eds), *Doing Research on Crime and Justice*, Oxford: OUP, pp. 332–3

Item C Ethical dilemmas

Carolyn Hoyle conducted research into domestic violence against women. She told victims what the research was about, how it was funded and how she would use the data. Hoyle describes how the violent husband and his victim were interviewed in separate rooms of their homes. The husbands were told that they were being asked the same questions as their wives. This was not true – they were misled as to the true nature of the questions asked of the wives.

Hoyle argues that this deception allowed the victims to speak freely and be assured that the husband/ perpetrator would not know what they were really asked. She believes that ethical principles are important but have to be weighed against other factors such as the need to obtain reliable evidence about a controversial topic, evidence which could help bring about an improvement in the lives of the research subjects – in this case, the wives. The greater the social problem, the more it may be justified to attach less weight to ethical principles.

Adapted from Hoyle, C. (2000) 'Being "a nosy bloody cow": ethical and methodological issues in researching domestic violence', in R.D. King and E. Wincup (eds), *Doing Research on Crime and Justice*, Oxford: OUP, pp. 401–2

1 Give one example of a 'bottom-up' perspective that believes sociology should 'see into the minds of individuals' (Item A). (2 marks)

2 Identify two reasons why Durkheim chose to study suicide in the way he did (Item A). (4 marks)

3 Suggest three situations (other than that described in Item C) where giving misleading information or withholding information from respondents might be justified. (Item B). (6 marks)

4 Identify and briefly explain two ways in which a researcher's feminist perspective might influence their research. (8 marks)

5 Using information from the Items and elsewhere, discuss the influence of theory on sociologists' choice of methods. (20 marks)

6 Using information from the Items and elsewhere, assess the importance of ethical issues in sociological research. (20 marks)

Quantitative research: getting 'the truth'?

Every year a survey called the Health Related Behaviour Questionnaire takes place. Young people are asked about their experiences of a range of health issues. According to the latest, conducted in 2002:

- Up to 21 per cent of 10 to 11 year olds had consumed an alcoholic drink during the previous week.
- 19 per cent of 15 year old males drank more than 11 units of alcohol in the previous week.
- Up to 65 per cent of young people will have smoked by year 10.
- About one in four pupils in year 10 have tried at least one illegal drug.
- Up to 8 per cent of 12 to 13 year olds have taken cannabis.

Schools Health Education Unit (2003), *Young people in 2002*, Exeter: SHEU

1 How can anyone make these claims? Did they ask every school student in Britain? If they didn't, how is it possible to arrive at these figures?

2 How honestly do you think pupils will answer these questions?

Sociologists choose different methods of research depending upon what method seems most appropriate in the circumstances, and the resources available to them. The approach covered in this topic is quantitative research. This stresses the importance of gathering statistical information that can be checked and tested. Quantitative research usually involves one or more of the following:

- **social surveys (cross-sectional research)**
- **experiments**
- **comparative research**.
- **case studies**.

Surveys

A social survey involves obtaining information in a standardized manner from a large group of people. Surveys usually obtain

this information through questionnaires or, less often, through interviews. The information is then analysed using statistical techniques. There are three possible aims of social surveys. They can be used:

- to find out 'facts' about the population – for example, how many people have access to the internet
- to uncover differences in beliefs, values and behaviour – for example, whether young people have a more positive view of the internet than older people
- to test 'a hypothesis' – for example, that women are less confident in using the internet than men.

A good example of a survey is the British Crime Survey, which takes place every two years and asks people about their experience of crime. This survey has helped sociologists gain a fuller understanding of patterns of crime. We now know a lot more about issues such as people's fear of crime, the factors affecting the reporting of crime and the likelihood of different social groups becoming victims of crime.

Before a full social survey is carried out, it is usual for a researcher to carry out a **pilot survey**. This is a small-scale version of the full survey, which is intended to:

- help evaluate the usefulness of the larger survey
- test the quality and the accuracy of the questions
- test the accuracy of the sample
- find out if there are any unforeseen problems.

Longitudinal surveys

Social surveys are sometimes criticized for providing only a 'snapshot' of social life at any one time. Sociologists often want to understand how people change over time and in these circumstances the typical **cross-sectional survey** (as these 'snapshot surveys' are sometimes called) is not appropriate. **Longitudinal surveys**, however, get around this problem by studying the same people over a long period of time (as the name suggests) – sometimes over as long as 20 years. Such surveys provide us with a clear, moving image of changes in attitudes and actions over time. The British Household Panel Survey is a longitudinal study that has studied over 10 000 British people of all ages, living in 5500 households. The interviewing started in 1991 and has continued every year since then. The information obtained covers a vast area including family change, household finances and patterns of health and caring. It is used by the government to help inform social policies.

Longitudinal surveys suffer from a number of problems, but the main one is that respondents drop out of the survey because they get bored with answering the questions, or they move and the researchers lose track of them. If too many people drop out, this may make the survey unreliable, as the views of those who remain may well be significantly different from the views of those who drop out.

Sampling

It is usually impossible for sociologists to study the entire population on the grounds of cost and practicality. Instead, they have to find a way of studying a smaller proportion of the population whose views will exactly mirror the views of the whole population. There are two main ways of ensuring that the smaller group studied (the sample) is typical – or **representative** – of the entire population:

1 some form of **random sampling**
2 **quota sampling**.

There are also other forms of sampling which are not representative but are sometimes used. These include:

3 **snowball sampling**
4 **theoretical sampling**.

Random sampling

This is based on the idea that, by choosing randomly, each person has an equal chance of being selected and so those

focuson**research**

The British Social Attitudes Survey: a cross-sectional survey

The British Social Attitudes Survey is a regular survey of the British population which aims to find out attitudes to a wide range of contemporary issues. The 2002 report covered areas as diverse as attitudes to public transport, saving and borrowing, drug use, education, and the importance of family and friends.

Some of the conclusions of the survey in 2002 were as follows:

1 Regular car users were not particularly enthusiastic about moving to public transport and it would be very difficult to change their behaviour without large increases in the costs of motoring.
2 There is growing support for allowing people to smoke cannabis – but not most other drugs.
3 People who have high levels of contact with other family members are less likely to seek friends or join clubs.

The sample consisted of 3287 respondents. The sample was chosen using the Postcode Address File which lists all the addresses held by the Post Office.

Selection was by stratified random sampling across Britain.

Each selected household was sent a letter asking for their help and explaining the purpose of the research.

Interviewers called at the selected addresses (they were not allowed to use other ones) and asked the chosen respondent to complete a questionnaire, which was then taken away by the interviewer.

Park, A., Curtice, J., Thompson, K., Lindsey, J. and Bromley, C. (2002) *British Social Attitudes* (The 19th Report), London: Sage

1 What sampling frame was used in this research?

2 How can 3287 people represent the views of the British population?

3 What problems for the survey may occur when researchers call at selected homes?

Some of the problems faced by interviewers...

chosen are likely to be a cross-section of the population. A simple random sample involves selecting names randomly from a list, known as a **sampling frame**. If the sampling frame is inaccurate, this can lead to great errors in the final findings. It therefore needs to be a true reflection of the sort of people whom the researcher wishes to study. Examples of commonly used sampling frames are electoral registers (lists of people entitled to vote, which are publicly available) or the Postcode Address File (see *Focus on research* on p. 253).

However, a simple random sample does not guarantee a representative sample – you may, for instance, select too many young people, too many males or too many from some other group. For this reason, many sociologists break down their list of names into separate categories (for example, males and females) and then select from those lists.

Types of random sampling

There are a number of commonly used types of random sampling which aim to guarantee a representative sample. These include:

- **Systematic sampling** – where every *n*th name (for example, every tenth name) on a list is chosen. It is not truly random – but it is close enough.
- **Stratified sampling** – where the population under study is divided according to known criteria (for example, it could be divided into 52 per cent women and 48 per cent men, to reflect the sex composition of the UK). Within these broad strata, people are then chosen at random. The strata can become quite detailed – for example, with further divisions into age, social class, geographical location.
- **Cluster sampling** – where the researcher selects a series of different places and then chooses a sample at random within the cluster of people within these areas. This method

is sometimes used where the population under study is spread over a wide area and it is impossible for the researcher to cover the whole area.

Quota sampling

This form of sampling is often used by market research companies and is used purely as the basis for interviews. Since the main social characteristics of the UK population (age, income, occupation, location, ethnicity, etc.) are known, researchers can give interviewers a particular quota of individuals whom they must find and question – for example, a certain proportion of women of different ages and occupations, and a certain proportion of men of different ages and occupations. The results, when pieced together, should be an accurate reflection of the population as a whole. This form of sampling can only be used where accurate information about the major characteristics of the population is available.

The major advantage of quota sampling over random sampling is the very small number of people needed to build up an accurate picture of the whole. For example, the typical surveys of voting preferences in journals and newspapers use a quota sample of approximately 1,200 to represent the entire British electorate.

Non-representative sampling

Sometimes researchers either do not want a cross-section of the population, or are unable to obtain one.

Snowball sampling

This method is used when it is difficult to gain access to a particular group of people who are the subjects of study, or where there is simply no sampling frame available. It involves making contact with one member of the population to be studied and then asking them to name one or more possible contacts. An example of this is McNamara's study of male prostitutes in New York (1994) where he simply asked prostitutes to identify others, gradually building up enough contacts for the research.

Theoretical sampling

Glaser and Strauss (1967) argue that sometimes it is more helpful to study non-typical people, because they may help generate theoretical insights. Feminist sociologists have deliberately studied very untypical societies where women occupy non-traditional roles in order to show that gender roles are socially constructed – if they were based on biology, we would expect to see the same roles in every society.

Experiments

Experiments are very commonly used in the natural sciences (e.g. physics and chemistry). An experiment is basically research in which all the variables are closely controlled, so that the effect of changing one or more of the variables can be understood. Experiments are widely used in psychology, but much less so in sociology.

This is because:

- it is impossible to recreate normal life in the artificial environment of an experiment
- there are many ethical problems in performing experiments on people
- there is the possibility of the experimenter effect, where the awareness of being in an experiment affects the behaviour of the participants.

Occasionally, sociologists use **field experiments**, where a form of experiment is undertaken in the community. Rosenhan (1973) sent 'normal' people to psychiatric institutions in the USA in the late 1960s to see how they were treated by the staff. (Rather worryingly, the staff treated ordinary behaviour in institutions as evidence of insanity!)

Comparative method

The sociological version of an experiment is the **comparative method**. When a sociologist is interested in explaining a particular issue, one way of doing so is by comparing differences across groups or societies, or across one society over time. By comparing the different social variables in the different societies and their effects upon the issue being studied, it is sometimes possible to identify a particular social practice or value which is the key factor in determining that issue. Emile Durkheim (1897/1952) used the comparative method in his classic study of the different levels of suicide in societies – concluding that specific cultural differences motivated people to commit suicide. In order to arrive at this conclusion, Durkheim collected official statistics from a number of different countries and then compared the different levels of suicide, linking them to cultural differences, including religion and family relationships, which varied across the different countries.

Case studies

A case study is a detailed study of one particular group or organization. Instead of searching out a wide range of people via sampling, the researcher focuses on one group. The resulting studies are usually extremely detailed and provide a depth of information not normally available. However, there is

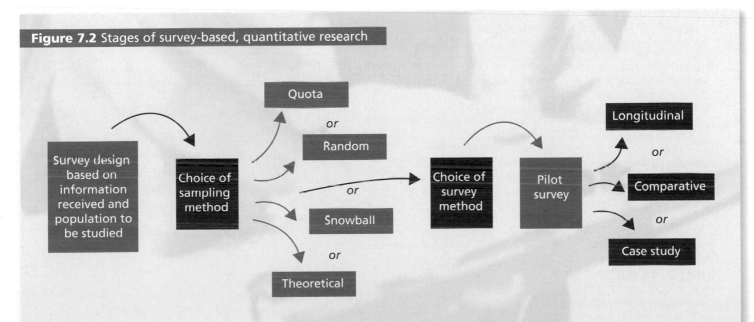

Figure 7.2 Stages of survey-based, quantitative research

always the problem that this intense scrutiny may miss wider issues by its very concentration. An example of a case study is Grieshaber's work (1997), where she conducted case studies of how families ate their meals, and the rules that the parents and their children negotiated.

Check your understanding

1. **What do we mean by quantitative research?**

2. **Explain in your own words the importance of sampling.**

3. **Why are random samples not always representative?**

4. **What is 'quota' sampling? What is the main drawback of this method?**

5. **Identify and explain, in your own words, three types of random sampling.**

6. **In what situations might a sociologist use:**

    (a) **snowball sampling?**

    (b) **theoretical sampling?**

7. **Why don't sociologists use experiments?**

8. **What is a case study?**

9. **Give one example of a research project that has used the comparative method.**

research ideas

- Work out the proportions needed in your sample if you were to do a quota sample of your school or college.

- Conduct a small survey to discover the extent of alcohol use among students (by age) at your school or college. Compare their use of alcohol with the use of illegal drugs identified in the 'Getting you thinking' exercise at the beginning of this topic (see p. 252).

web.tasks

1. Go to the website 'School Surveys' at www.schoolsurveys.co.uk, where you can organize your own online survey. You will need to get your teacher to register first.

2. Go to the 'Living in Britain' website (part of the government's National Statistics site) at www.statistics.gov.uk/lib2002 What is the General Household Survey and what methods does it use to collect information?

KEY TERMS

Case study a highly detailed study of one or two social situations or groups.

Cluster sampling the researcher selects a series of different places and then chooses a sample at random within the cluster of people within these areas.

Comparative method a comparison across countries or cultures; sociology's version of an experiment.

Cross-sectional survey (also known as **social survey** or **snapshot survey**) a survey conducted at one time with no attempt to follow up the people surveyed over a longer time.

Experiment a highly controlled situation where the researchers try to isolate the influence of each variable. Rarely used in sociology.

Field experiment an experiment undertaken in the community rather than in a controlled environment.

Longitudinal survey a survey carried out over a considerable number of years on the same group of people.

Pilot survey a small-scale survey carried out before the main one, to iron out any problems.

Quota sampling where a representative sample of the population is chosen using known characteristics of the population.

Random sampling where a representative sample of the population is chosen by entirely random methods.

Representative a sample is representative if it is an accurate cross-section of the whole population being studied.

Sampling frame a list used as the source for a random sample.

Snowball sampling where a sample is obtained using a series of personal contacts. Usually used for the study of deviant behaviour.

Stratified sampling where the population under study is divided according to known criteria, such as sex and age,

in order to make the sample more representative.

Survey a large-scale piece of quantitative research aiming to make general statements about a particular population.

Systematic sampling where every nth name (for example, every tenth name) on a list is chosen.

Theoretical sampling where an untypical sample of the population is chosen to illustrate a particular theory.

exploring quantitative methods

Item A A longitudinal study

The North-West Longitudinal Study involved following several hundred young people for five years between the ages of 14 and 18. The overall aim of this study was to assess how 'ordinary' young people, growing up in England in the 1990s, developed attitudes and behaviour in relation to the availability of illegal drugs, alongside other options such as alcohol and tobacco.

The main technique was a self-report questionnaire initially administered personally by the researchers (and then by post) to several hundred young people within eight state secondary schools in two non-inner-city boroughs of metropolitan north-west England.

At the start of the research the sample was representative of those areas in terms of gender, class and ethnicity. However, attrition (losing participants) partly reduced this over time with the disproportionate loss of some 'working-class' participants and some from Asian and Muslim backgrounds.

A longitudinal study is able to address issues of validity and reliability far more extensively than one-off snapshot surveys, but in turn must also explain inconsistent reporting that occurs over the years.

In general, the research provides a detailed account of how young people develop attitudes and behaviours through time.

Adapted from Parker, H., Aldrige, J. and Measham, F. (1998) *Illegal Leisure*, London: Routledge, pp. 48–9

Item B Research in Northern Ireland

Brewer and his colleagues studied the way in which local communities managed to control and limit crime, given that the police were often not welcome in certain areas of Belfast.

They worked through local community-based organizations in order to access general members of the public. Initial contact with the organizations was made possible by the network of contacts possessed by the authors and by the snowball technique. The authors believe that the organizations selected were an accurate political and social representation of the locality.

Adapted from Brewer, J.D., Lockhart, B. and Rodgers, P. (1998) 'Informal social control and crime management in Belfast', *British Journal of Sociology*, 49, December

1. Explain in your own words what is meant by a 'longitudinal study' (Item A). (2 marks)

2. Identify two problems the North-West Longitudinal Study would be likely to face (Item A). (4 marks)

3. Suggest three reasons why the sample in Item B may not have been representative of the people of Belfast. (6 marks)

4. Identify and briefly describe one advantage and one disadvantage of selecting a non-representative sample. (8 marks)

5. Examine the arguments for and against the use of experiments in sociological research. (20 marks)

6. Using information from Item A and elsewhere, assess the usefulness of longitudinal studies. (20 marks)

Understanding people: observation

gettingyouthinking

The extract on the right is from a research project which studies the lives and attitudes of door staff ('bouncers') working in night clubs. The researcher narrating the story is a student who has got a job as a bouncer as part of the research project.

1 What is your immediate reaction to the story?

2 Why do you think the girl was attacked by her friend?

3 Have you ever seen a fight outside a club at night? What happened? What did the doorstaff do?

4 Why do you think the researcher chose to get a job as a bouncer in order to study their lives? Could you think of a better way?

≪It's Friday evening outside a club in a city centre … one young woman has shouted an insult at another, the recipient of which has turned on her heel and begun to walk away. The first young woman continues to throw insults until the retreating young woman seemingly has a change of heart, turns, picks up an empty lager bottle from the street and hits the first young woman in the face with it.

A hush descends on the busy street. It isn't funny any more. Nobody is laughing; in fact there was a palpable 'Oh!' sound emitted from the spectators, mixed with the sound of thick glass crashing into tender flesh and bone. The injured young woman has her hand pressed to her mouth – she isn't screaming or crying, but instantly it is possible to tell that she is badly injured.

I snap out of my shocked state when I see Paul (bouncer and colleague) putting his arm around her back to support her unsteady steps … After some gentle coaxing, the woman releases her grip on the wound … blood spurts all over Paul's shirt. Her upper lip is split entirely, right up to her right nostril. It's a wide gash and through the resulting hole it becomes apparent that the woman has also lost at least three teeth. Blood is everywhere. Paul's shirt now appears tie-dyed red with blood.

Later when a policeman calls to take a statement, he informs me that I may be called as a witness in any resulting court case. When I ask how the young woman is, he informs me that 'She lost four teeth, 28 stitches to the upper lip, the usual bruising and swelling … Shame really. Pretty girl.' Turns out she's only 15.≫

Winlow, S., Hobbs, D., Lister, S. and Hadfield, P. (2001) 'Get ready to duck: bouncers and the realities of ethnographic research on violent groups', *British Journal of Criminology*, 41, pp. 536–48

Have you ever watched a sporting event on television and heard the commentator saying what a fantastic atmosphere there is? Yet, at home, you remain outside it. You know there is a fantastic atmosphere, you hear the roar of the crowd, yet you are not part of it. For the people actually in the stadium, the experience of the occasion is quite different. The heat, the closeness of thousands of others, the noise and the emotional highs and lows of the actual event, all combine to give a totally different sense of what is happening.

Some sociologists 'stay at home' to do their research. They may use questionnaires, interviews and surveys to obtain a clear, overall view. On the other hand, there are sociologists who are more interested in experiencing the emotions and sense of actually being there. These sociologists set out to immerse themselves in the lifestyle of the group they wish to study.

Because this form of research is less interested in statistics to prove its point (that is, quantitative research), and more interested in the qualities of social life, it is sometimes known as **qualitative research**. Qualitative approaches are based on the belief that it is not appropriate or possible to measure and categorize the social world accurately – all that is possible is to observe and describe what is happening and offer possible explanations.

The most common form of qualitative research consists of observational studies in which a particular group of people is closely observed and their activities noted. The belief is that, by exploring the lives of people in detail, insights may be gained that can be applied to the understanding of society in general. Observational studies derive from **ethnography**, which is the term used to describe the work of anthropologists who study simple, small-scale societies by living with the (usually tribal) people and observing their daily lives. However, strictly speaking, qualitative research can include a wide variety of other approaches, such as video and audio recording, in-depth interviews, analysis of the internet, or even qualitative analysis of books, magazines and journals.

Types of observation

Observational research is a general term that covers a range of different research techniques. Observational studies vary in two main ways:

1 the extent to which the researcher joins in the activities of the group – the researcher may decide to be a participant or not. The choice is between **non-participant observation** and **participant observation**
2 whether the researcher is honest and tells the group about the research, or prefers to pretend to be one of the group. The choice is between **overt** and **covert** research.

Participant observation

The most common form of observational study is participant observation, where the researcher joins the group being studied.

The advantages of participant observation

● *Experience* – Participant observation allows the researcher to join the group fully and see things through the eyes (and actions) of the people in the group. The researcher is placed in exactly the same situation as the group under study, fully experiencing what is happening. This results in the researcher seeing social life from the same perspective as the group.

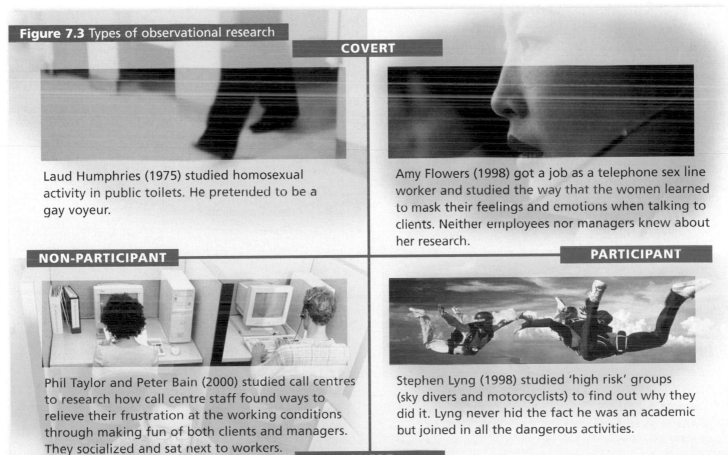

Figure 7.3 Types of observational research

COVERT

Laud Humphries (1975) studied homosexual activity in public toilets. He pretended to be a gay voyeur.

Amy Flowers (1998) got a job as a telephone sex line worker and studied the way that the women learned to mask their feelings and emotions when talking to clients. Neither employees nor managers knew about her research.

NON-PARTICIPANT

PARTICIPANT

Phil Taylor and Peter Bain (2000) studied call centres to research how call centre staff found ways to relieve their frustration at the working conditions through making fun of both clients and managers. They socialized and sat next to workers.

Stephen Lyng (1998) studied 'high risk' groups (sky divers and motorcyclists) to find out why they did it. Lyng never hid the fact he was an academic but joined in all the dangerous activities.

OVERT

- *Generating new ideas* – Often this can lead to completely new insights and generate new theoretical ideas, unlike traditional research, which undertakes the study in order to explore an existing theory or hypothesis.
- *Getting the truth* – One of the problems with questionnaires, and to a lesser extent with interviews, is that the respondent can lie. Participant observation prevents this because the researcher can see the person in action – it may also help them understand why the person would lie in a questionnaire or interview.
- *Digging deep* – Participant observation can create a close bond between the researcher and the group under study, and individuals in the group may be prepared to confide in the researcher on issues and views that would normally remain hidden.
- *Dynamic* – Questionnaires and interviews are 'static' – they are only able to gain an understanding of a person's behaviour or attitudes at the precise moment of the interview. Participant observation takes place over a period of time and allows an understanding of how changes in attitudes and behaviour take place.
- *Reaching into difficult areas* – Participant observation is normally used to obtain research information on hard-to-reach groups, such as religious sects and young offenders.

The disadvantages of participant observation

- *Bias* – The main problem lies with bias, as the observer can be drawn into the group and start to see things through their eyes. This may blind the observer to the insights that would otherwise be available.
- *Influence of the researcher* – The presence of the researcher may make the group act less naturally as they are aware of being studied. Of course, this is less likely to happen if the researcher is operating covertly.
- *Ethics* – If the researcher is studying a group engaged in deviant behaviour, then there is a moral issue of how far the researcher should be drawn into the activities of the group – particularly if these activities are immoral or illegal.
- *Proof* – Critics have pointed out that there is no way of knowing objectively whether the findings of participant observation are actually true or not, since there is no possibility of replicating the research. In other words, the results may lack **reliability**.
- *Too specific* – Participant observation is usually used to study small groups of people who are not typical of the wider population. It is therefore difficult to claim that the findings can be **generalized** across the population as a whole.
- *Studying the powerless* – Finally, almost all participant observational studies are concerned with the least powerful groups in society – typically groups of young males or females who engage in deviant activities. Some critics argue that the information obtained does not help us to understand the more important issues in society.

Non-participant observation

Some researchers prefer to withdraw from participation and merely observe.

Advantages of non-participant observation

- *Bias* – As the researcher is less likely to be drawn into the group, they will also be less likely to be biased in their views.
- *Influencing the group* – As the researcher is not making any decisions or joining in activities, the group may be less influenced than in participant observation.

Disadvantages of non-participant observation

- *Superficial* – The whole point of participant observation is to be a member of the group and experience life as the group experiences it. Merely observing leaves the researcher on the outside and may limit understanding.
- *Altering behaviour* – People may well act differently if they know they are being watched.

Covert and overt methods

Observational research is usually carried out amongst deviant groups or other groups who are unusual in some way, such as religious cults. Usually, these groups will not be very welcoming to a researcher. Before researchers begin their work, therefore, they must decide whether they wish to conduct the research in a covert or overt way.

The advantages of covert research

- *Forbidden fruit* – Researchers can enter forbidden areas, be fully accepted and trusted, and immerse themselves totally in the group to be studied. This can generate a real sense of understanding of the views of the group.
- *Normal behaviour* – The group will continue to act naturally, unaware that they are being studied.

The disadvantages of covert research

- *Danger* – If the researcher's true role is uncovered, they may place themselves in danger.
- *Ethical dilemmas* – First, there is the issue that it is wrong to study a group without telling them. Second, if the group engages in illegal or immoral activities, then the researcher may have to engage in these activities as well. They may then find themselves in possession of knowledge that it may be immoral to withhold from the authorities.

The advantages of overt observation

- *The confidante* – As someone who has no role within the group, the researcher may be in the position of the trusted outsider and receive confidences from group members.
- *Honest* – The researcher is also able to play an open, clear and honest role, which will help minimize ethical dilemmas.

- *Other methods* – Researchers can supplement their observation with other methods, such as interviews and questionnaires.

The disadvantage of overt observation

- *Outsider* – There will be many situations where only a trusted insider will be let into the secrets. Anyone else, even a sympathetic observer, will be excluded.

Doing ethnographic research

The process of doing ethnographic research involves solving some key problems.

Joining the group

Observational studies usually involve groups of people on the margins of society, and the first problem is actually to contact and join the group. The sociologist has to find a place where the group goes and a situation in which they would accept the researcher. Shane Blackman (1997) (see the *Exploring observation* activity on p. 263) studied a group of young homeless people, whom he met at an advice centre for young people. Sometimes sociologists make use of **gatekeepers** – members of the group who help the sociologist become accepted and introduce them to new people and situations. Andy Bennett describes how he gained entry to the local 'hip hop scene' in Newcastle (Bennett 1999):

≪ *My route 'into' the local hip hop scene in Newcastle was largely facilitated by a local breakdancer who also worked as an instructor at a community dance project. Through this contact, who essentially acted as a gatekeeper, I gained access to or learned of key figures in the local hip hop scene ... and accompanied the gatekeeper and a number of his dance students and other friends to around a dozen weekly hip hop nights held in a bar.* ≫

Acceptance by the group

There are often barriers of age, ethnicity and gender to overcome if the group are to accept the researcher. Moore (2004) researched young people 'hanging around'. He was initially unable to gain full acceptance because of his age. He overcame this by using young, female researchers.

Recording information

When researchers are actually hanging around with a group, it is difficult to make notes – particularly if engaged in covert research. Even if the group members are aware of the research, someone constantly making notes would disrupt normal activity and, of course, the researcher would also be unable to pay full attention to what was going on. In participant observational studies, therefore, researchers

Philippe Bourgois
In Search of Respect: Selling Crack in El Barrio

The biggest-selling research study in the USA in the last 20 years is Philippe Bourgois' study of the life of crack dealers in an impoverished and violent part of New York (East Harlem), known as El Barrio.

Bourgois moved into the area with his wife and young daughter, despite the strongly expressed concerns of their wider family and friends, and continued to live and research there for five years.

Bourgois had close contact with a number of crack dealers and spent a large part of his life in their company during this time – sometimes in very dangerous situations. Bourgois' main problem was that as the only white person in the area, he was often believed to be a policeman and so was at risk of attack.

Bourgois' study revealed that there was a thriving, dangerous, but functioning culture within El Barrio. He argued that street life, drug-dealing and violence in El Barrio were simply responses to the desperate poverty and inequality that these people faced in US society. They were trying to cope as best they could in an unequal society, and actually wanted to belong to mainstream US society, but quite simply had no chance of success in that legitimate world.

Their response was to create a culture of violence and drugs in which the sale and use of drugs, along with prostitution, became the central basis of their economy. The process of buying and selling drugs allowed dealers to make a living and they, in turn, spent the money on a range of goods and services in El Barrio. However, this illegal sale and widespread use of the drugs led to chaotic, violent lifestyles that, ironically, guaranteed their exclusion from the wider society.

1 Is it justifiable for the observer to get involved in dangerous and illegal activities?

2 Is it reasonable for Bourgois to make generalizations about wider society from the one case he has studied?

generally use a **field diary**. This is simply a detailed record of what happened, which the researcher writes up as often as possible. However, the research diary can also be a real weakness of the research.

Research diaries

Ethnographic researchers do not keep regular hours. Their observation may well go on into the night. It can be difficult to write up a diary each evening. Therefore, there is plenty of time to forget things and to distort them. Most observational studies include quotes, yet as it is impossible to remember the exact words, the quotes reflect what the researcher thinks the people said. This may be inaccurate.

Maintaining objectivity

In observational research, it is hard to remain objective. Close contact with the group under study means that feelings almost always emerge. In the introduction to Bourgois' (2003) study of crack cocaine dealers, he comments on how these dealers are his friends and how much he owes to the 'comments, corrections and discussions' provided by one particular dealer.

Influencing the situation

The more involved the researcher is with the people being studied, the greater the chance of influencing what happens. Stephen Lyng (1993) joined a group of males who engaged in 'edgework' – that is, putting their lives at risk through skydiving and (illegal) road motorcycle racing. Lyng became so entangled in this style of life that he actually helped encourage others into life-risking behaviour.

Check your understanding

1 What forms of observational studies are there?

2 What advantages does observational research have over quantitative methods?

3 Identify three problems associated with participant observation.

4 Suggest two examples of research where it would be possible to justify covert observation.

5 Suggest two examples of research situations where observational methods would be appropriate.

6 Suggest two examples of research situations where it might be more appropriate to undertake a survey.

research ideas

- Compare these two pieces of observation:

  - Go to your local library. Spend one hour watching how people behave. Write down as accurate a description as you can.
  - Then spend an evening at home 'observing' your family. Write down as accurate a description of home behaviour that evening as you can.

- Which study is likely to be more biased? Why? Does this make it any less accurate? Are you able to get greater depth studying your family? Why? Do you think it would make a difference if you operated in a covert rather than an overt way with your family?

KEY TERMS

Covert observation where the sociologist does not admit to being a researcher.

Ethnography describes the work of anthropologists who study simple, small-scale societies by living with the people and observing their daily lives. The term has been used by sociologists to describe modern-day observational studies.

Field diary a detailed record of events, conversations and thoughts kept by participant observers, written up as often as possible.

Generalizability the ability to apply accurately the findings of research into one group to other groups.

Gatekeeper person who can allow a researcher access to an individual, group or event.

Non-participant observation where the sociologist simply observes the group but does not seek to join in their activities.

Participant observational studies where the sociologist joins a group of people and studies their behaviour.

Qualitative research a general term for approaches to research that are less interested in collecting statistical data, and more interested in observing and interpreting the ways in which people behave.

Overt observation where the sociologist is open about the research role.

Reliability refers to the need for research to be strictly comparable (not a great problem with questionnaires and structured/closed-question interviews). This can pose a real problem in observational research, because of the very specific nature of the groups under study and therefore the difficulty of replicating the research.

Item A   Youth homelessness in Brighton

In 1992 Shane Blackman spent several months with a group of young homeless people in Brighton.

<< As the study proceeded my research role expanded to also include that of action researcher, drinking partner, friend, colleague and football player. In terms of techniques, I found that the conventional social research interview was an impossibility

with the individuals in the study, due to their suspicion of such forms of enquiry. The main research instrument was the field diary.

Where social research focuses on individuals and groups who are on the margins of society, the method through which data is collected is often of a highly intimate nature. The researcher is drawn into the lives of the

researched and the fieldworker feels emotions while listening to respondents' accounts of their own lives ...

Ethnographic descriptions are able to convey experience from the perspective of the subject of the research and to develop theories based on feeling.>>

Adapted from Blackman, S. (1997) 'An ethnographic study of youth underclass' in R. McDonald (ed.), *Youth, the Underclass and Social Exclusion*, London: Routledge

Item B   Moral issues and bias

In the late 1990's Fleisher spent a year with violent gang in Kansas City.

<< Genuine ethnography, spending six months to a year with informants in natural settings, creates a sort of 'marriage' between researcher and the researched. When I commit myself to a neighbourhood and its people, that commitment obtains the right to see things other

researchers never see, ask questions others never ask, get answers others never get. But that privilege has a dark side. That dark side is the personal damage that seeing kids in pain who inflict pain on others has caused me. I see child abuse and teenage prostitution, drug addiction and drug dealing and have even heard murder contracts and street-to-prison drug smuggling being arranged over

the phone. For this privilege I pay a heavy price.

My research and my bad dreams are worth it, only if my writing results in a better life for these people. But that's not up to me.>>

Adapted from Fleisher, M.S. (1998) 'Ethnographers, Pimps and the Company Store' in J. Ferrell and M.S. Hamm *Ethnography at the Edge*, Boston: Northeastern University Press

1. **Explain in your own words what is meant by a 'field diary' (Item A). (2 marks)**

2. **Identify two reasons why Blackman found it impossible to use conventional social research interviews for his research (Item A). (4 marks)**

3. **Give three reasons why Fleisher feels he has created 'a sort of marriage' (Item B). (6 marks)**

4. **Identify and briefly explain two problems in keeping a 'field diary' while undertaking participant observation. (8 marks)**

5. **Discuss the problem of values and bias in observational research. (20 marks)**

6. **Using information from the Items and elsewhere, assess the usefulness of participant observation to sociologists. (20 marks)**

web.task

Is it possible to do observational studies on the internet? Try observing a chat room or MSN Messenger. What behaviour occurs? Why?

Asking questions: questionnaires and interviews

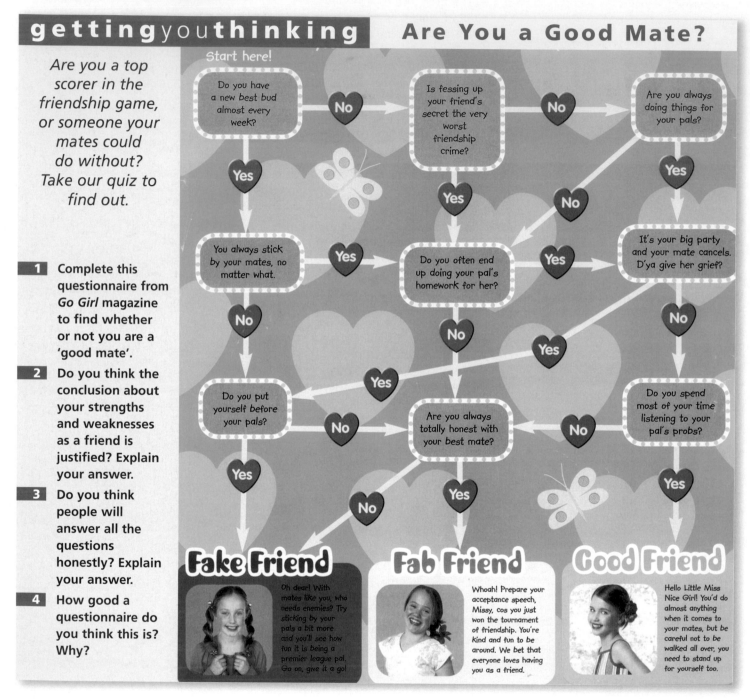

gettingyouthinking **Are You a Good Mate?**

Are you a top scorer in the friendship game, or someone your mates could do without? Take our quiz to find out.

Start here!

Do you have a new best bud almost every week?

Is fessing up your friend's secret the very worst friendship crime?

Are you always doing things for your pals?

You always stick by your mates, no matter what.

Do you often end up doing your pal's homework for her?

It's your big party and your mate cancels. D'ya give her grief?

Do you put yourself before your pals?

Are you always totally honest with your best mate?

Do you spend most of your time listening to your pal's probs?

Fake Friend

Oh dear! With mates like you, who needs enemies? Try sticking by your pals a bit more and you'll see how fun it is being a premier league pal. Go on, give it a go!

Fab Friend

Whoah! Prepare your acceptance speech, Missy, cos you just won the tournament of friendship. You're kind and fun to be around. We bet that everyone loves having you as a friend.

Good Friend

Hello Little Miss Nice Girl! You'd do almost anything when it comes to your mates, but be careful not to be walked all over; you need to stand up for yourself too.

1. **Complete this questionnaire from *Go Girl* magazine to find whether or not you are a 'good mate'.**
2. **Do you think the conclusion about your strengths and weaknesses as a friend is justified? Explain your answer.**
3. **Do you think people will answer all the questions honestly? Explain your answer.**
4. **How good a questionnaire do you think this is? Why?**

The most obvious way of finding out something is to ask questions. It is not surprising, then, to find that one of the most common methods of research used by sociologists is just to ask people questions about their attitudes and actions.

Sociologists ask questions in two main ways:

1. asking the questions face to face – the interview
2. writing the questions down and handing them to someone to complete – the questionnaire.

Which of the two methods is chosen depends upon which way of asking questions seems to fit the circumstances best – and has the best chance of gaining the information required.

Questionnaires

The essence of a good questionnaire

When constructing a questionnaire, the sociologist has to ensure that:

- it asks the right questions to unearth exactly the information wanted
- the questions are asked in a clear and simple manner that can be understood by the people completing the questionnaire
- it is as short as possible, since people usually cannot be bothered to spend a long time completing questionnaires.

When to use questionnaires

Questionnaires are used for reaching:

- a large number of people, since the forms can just be handed out
- a widely dispersed group of people, as they can simply be mailed out.

Self-completion questionnaires are also less time-consuming for researchers than interviewing, as they do not require the researcher to go and talk to people face to face.

Anonymous questionnaires are also very useful if the researcher wishes to ask embarrassing questions about such things as sexual activities or illegal acts. People are more likely to tell the truth if they can do so anonymously than if they have to face an interviewer.

Types of questionnaires

There are many different types of questionnaire. They vary in the way in which they expect the person to answer the questions set. At one extreme are 'closed' questionnaires, which have a series of questions with a choice of answers – all the respondent has to do is tick the box next to the most appropriate answer. At the other extreme are 'open' questionnaires that seek the respondent's opinion by leaving space for their response. Some questionnaires contain a mixture of both open and closed questions.

Issues in undertaking questionnaires

- Unfortunately, many people cannot be bothered to reply to questionnaires – that is, unless there is some benefit to them, such as the chance to win a prize. This is a serious drawback of questionnaires in research.
- A low **response rate** (the proportion of people who reply) makes a survey useless, as you do not know if the small number of replies is representative of all who were sent the questionnaire. Those who reply might have strong opinions on an issue, for example, whereas the majority may have much less firm convictions. Without an adequate number of replies, you will never know.
- It is difficult to go into depth in a questionnaire, because the questions need to be as clear and simple as possible.

- You can never be sure that the correct person answers. If you mail a questionnaire to one member of a household, how do you know that that person answers it?
- You can never be sure that the person who replies to the questionnaire interprets the questions in the way that the researcher intended, so their replies might actually mean something different from what the researcher believes they mean.
- Lying is also a danger. People may simply not tell the truth when answering questionnaires. There is little that the researcher can do, apart from putting in 'check questions' – questions that ask for the same information, but are phrased differently.

Figure 7.4 Types of survey questions

1 Quantity or information
In which year did you enrol on the part-time degree? _____

2 Category
Have you ever been, or are you now, involved almost full-time in domestic duties (i.e. as a housewife/househusband)?
☐ yes (currently) ☐ yes (in the past) ☐ never

3 List or multiple choice
Do you view the money spent on your higher education as any of the following?
☐ a luxury ☐ an investment ☐ a necessity ☐ a right
☐ a gamble ☐ a burden ☐ none of these

4 Scale
How would you describe your parents' attitude to higher education at that time? Please tick one of the options below:

very positive	positive	mixed/ neutral	very negative	negative	not sure
☐	☐	☐	☐	☐	☐

5 Ranking
What do you see as the main purpose(s) of your degree study? Please rank all those relevant in order from 1 downwards.
☐ personal development ☐ career advancement
☐ subject interest ☐ recreation
☐ fulfilling ambition ☐ keeping stimulated
☐ other (please specify) _____

6 Complex grid or table
How would you rank the benefits of your degree study for each of the following?

for:	very positive	positive	mixed/ neutral	negative	very negative	not sure
you						
your family						
your employer						
the country						
your community						
your friends						

7 Open ended
Please note down any further comments about your degree:

_____

_____

Source: Blaxter, L., Hughes, C. and Tight, M. (1996) *How to Research*, Buckingham: Open University Press, p. 161

Questionnaires and scientific method

Questionnaires – particularly closed questionnaires – are a favourite method used by positivist sociologists (see Topic 1, p. 248), as they can be used in large numbers and the answers can be codified and subjected to statistical tests.

Interviews

An interview can either be a series of questions asked directly by the researcher to the respondent or it can be conducted as a discussion.

When to use interviews

● Sociologists generally use interviews if the subject of enquiry is complex, and a questionnaire would not allow the researcher to probe deeply.
● Interviews are also used when researchers want to compare their observations with the replies given by the respondents, to see if they appear true or not.

Advantages of interviews

● The interviewer can help explain questions to the respondent if necessary.
● Researchers are also sure that they are getting information from the right person.
● They can be organized virtually on the spot and so can be done immediately – as opposed to preparing a questionnaire, finding a sampling frame and posting the questionnaires out.
● There is a much higher response rate with interviews than with questionnaires, as the process is more personal and it is difficult to refuse a researcher when approached politely.

Types of interviews

Interviews fall between two extremes: **structured** and **unstructured**. At their most structured, they can be very tightly organized, with the interviewer simply reading out questions from a prepared questionnaire. At the other extreme they can be unstructured, where the interviewer simply has a basic area for discussion and asks any questions that seem relevant. Interviews that have fall between the two extremes are known as 'semi-structured' interviews.

There are also individual and group interviews. Most people assume that an interview is between just two people, but in sociological research a group of people may get together to discuss an issue, rather than simply giving an answer to a question. Group interviews are commonly used where the researcher wants to explore the dynamics of the group, believing that a 'truer' picture emerges when the group are all together, creating a 'group dynamic'. An example of this is Mairtin Mac an Ghaill's *The Making of Men: Masculinities, Sexualities and Schooling* (1994), in which a group of gay students discuss their experiences of school.

Issues in undertaking interviews

Influencing the replies

Interviews are a form of conversation between people and, as in any conversation, likes and dislikes emerge. The problem is to ensure that the interviewer does not influence the replies provided by the respondent in any way – known as **interviewer bias**. For example, respondents may want to please the interviewer and so give the replies they think the interviewer wants. Influences that can affect the outcome of the interview include manner of speech, ethnic origin, sex or personal habits.

Lying

There is no reason why people should tell the truth to researchers, and this is particularly true when a sensitive issue is being researched. When questioned about sexual activities or numbers of friends, for example, people may exaggerate in order to impress the interviewer.

Interview reliability

The aim of the research process is to conduct enough interviews for the researcher to be able to make an accurate generalization. However, if interviews are actually different from each other as a result of the interaction, then it is wrong to make generalizations.

Recording the information

Unstructured interviews are generally recorded and usually require **transcribing** (writing up), which is time-consuming. Tizard and Hughes (1991) recorded interviews with students to find out how they went about learning – every hour of interview took 17 hours to transcribe and check! However, writing down the replies at the time is slow and can disrupt the flow of an interview.

Operationalizing concepts

Ideas that are discussed in sociology, such as 'sexual deviance', 'educational failure', or 'ill health', are all pretty vague when you spend a few moments thinking about them. Take educational failure – does this mean not having A levels? Perhaps it means having 'low' grades at GCSE (whatever the concept 'low grades' means)? Or only having one or two GCSEs? You can see that a concept as apparently simple as 'educational failure' is actually capable of having different meanings to different people.

However, concepts such as educational failure or ill health are used all the time in sociological research, so sociologists have had to find a way around this problem when they ask people questions about the concepts. For example, if you were to ask somebody if they 'suffered from ill health', the reply would depend upon the individual definition of ill health and different people might (in fact we know they *do*) use very different definitions of ill health.

In research, we need to use concepts such as sexual deviance, educational failure and ill health, but in a way which is valid and reliable (see p. 268). By this, we mean that the concepts are accurately measured (valid), and that each time we use them, we are sure that every respondent understands the concept in the same way (reliable).

When concepts are used in research, sociologists say that they are **operationalizing** them. So, if there is a piece of research to find out the levels of ill health amongst retired people, the concept 'ill health' will need to be operationalized. The problem when operationalizing' a concept is how to ensure that it is accurately and reliably measured.

Indicators

The answer is that sociologists use **indicators**. An indicator is something 'concrete' that stands in for the abstract concept, but which people can understand and sociologists can actually measure. Let us return to the example of 'ill health'. It is possible to ask people the following:

- whether they suffer from any specific diseases or any long-term disability
- whether they are receiving any specific medication
- how frequently they have attended a GP surgery or clinic in the last year.

Problems with indicators

An indicator then, is a short cut sociologists use to measure an abstract concept. Unfortunately, short cuts in any academic area of study bring problems. We need to remember **that what is actually being measured are the** *indicators, not the actual concept*. This may not be a problem if the indicators are a perfect reflection of the original concept, but this is rarely the case. Let's go back to ill health. One question used is how often people have visited the GP surgery in the last year. However, this does not necessarily tell us about *levels* of health, it may just tell us that some people tend to visit the GP (whether they need to or not) more than others. Someone might be very ill but refuse to visit a GP. For example, there is considerable evidence that older people visit GPs less often than their medical conditions warrant.

Furthermore, it is not the actual number of visits that could be considered important, but the reasons why they went. A younger person may be seeing a GP for contraceptive advice, while an older person may be concerned about a heart condition.

Coding

Using clear indicators in research allows answers to be *coded* – that is broken down into simple, distinct answers that can be counted. The researchers can simply add up the numbers of people replying to each category of indicator and then make statements such as '82 per cent of people have seen a doctor on their own behalf in 2002' (Department of Health 2003).

Questions about sex

A survey by the US National Opinion Research Center (Laumann *et al.* 1995) consisted of detailed questions about sexual behaviour. A sample of just under 3,500 people was used and methods consisted of a mixture of questionnaires, telephone and face-to-face interviews. In order to ensure a very high response rate, the researchers were prepared to pay some people up to $100 to 'bribe' them to reply to the questions.

The study sparked a very personal and heated debate in the *New York Review of Books* in which the sociologist Richard Lewontin heavily criticized the book. His main argument was that people simply lied to the interviewers and, in their replies to the questionnaires, male respondents were either engaged in wishful thinking or were lying to themselves. He points out, for example, that the total number of sexual partners claimed by the males added up to 75 per cent more than claimed by female respondents – he suggests that the numbers should more or less add up to the same totals. Furthermore, he expressed surprise that 45 per cent of males aged between 80 and 84 were still regularly engaging in sexual activity. Finally, he notes that people who belonged to organized religions had very much lower levels of homosexual and lesbian sex than those who were not religious. Lewontin suggests that they were simply 'hypocrites'.

The authors of the study replied that 'we went to great lengths to guarantee the privacy, confidentiality and anonymity of our respondents' answers'.

The issue that the debate raised was whether it is ever possible to get the truth about personal issues by asking people questions – whether through questionnaires or interviews.

1 Do you think that Lewontin's criticisms are correct and that people (males?) will lie about sexual activity?

2 What reasons could you suggest why people might lie?

3 If Lewontin is correct, what implications might this have for sociological research?

4 Can you suggest ways of 'getting around' the problems suggested by Lewontin?

Questions and values

Both questionnaires and interviews share the problem of the values of the researcher creeping into the questions asked. Two problems are particularly important – using leading questions and using loaded words.

Leading questions

Researchers write or ask questions that suggest what the appropriate answer is. For example, 'Wouldn't you agree that …?'

Loaded words and phrases

Researchers use particular forms of language that either indicate a viewpoint or will generate a particular positive or negative response – for example, 'termination of pregnancy' (a positive view) or 'abortion' (a negative view); 'gay' or 'homosexual'.

Check your understanding

1 **What are the three elements of a good questionnaire?**

2 **Why are response rates so important?**

3 **In what situations is it better to use self-completion questionnaires rather than interviews?**

4 **When would it be more appropriate to use open questions? Give an example of an open question.**

5 **Explain the difference between structured, semi-structured, unstructured and group interviews**

6 **What do we mean by 'transcribing'?**

7 **What do we mean when we talk about 'loaded questions' and 'leading questions'? Illustrate your answer with an example of each and show how the problem could be overcome by writing a 'correct' example of the same questions.**

Interviews and scientific methods

Interviews are used by all kinds of sociologists. The more structured the interviews, the more likely they are to be used in a quantitative way to produce statistics. The more unstructured the interviews (including group interviews), the more likely they are to be of use to interpretive sociologists.

Issues of validity and reliability

Validity

Questions asked should actually produce the information required. This is a crucial issue in sociological research and is known as the issue of **validity** (i.e. getting at the truth). The type of questions asked in the questionnaire or interview must allow the respondent to give a true and accurate reply.

Reliability

The researcher must ensure not only that the design of the question gets to the truth of the matter, but also that it does so consistently. If the question means different things to different people, or can be interpreted differently, then the research is not reliable. **Reliability**, then, refers to the fact that all completed questionnaires and interviews can be accurately compared.

web.task

1 **Go to the website of the opinion polling organization Market and Opinion Research International (www.mori.com). Find out how MORI go about asking questions.**

2 **Search the world wide web for other examples of questionnaires. Assess the strengths and weaknesses of the question design.**

KEY TERMS

Closed questions require a very specific reply, such as 'yes' or 'no'.

Indicator something easily measurable that can stand for a particular concept.

Interviewer bias the influence of the interviewer (e.g. their age, 'race', sex) on the way the respondent replies.

Open questions allow respondents to express themselves fully.

Operationalizing concepts the process of defining concepts in a way which makes them measurable.

Reliability quality achieved when all questionnaires and interviews have been completed consistently. This means that the data gathered

from each can be accurately compared.

Response rate the proportion of the questionnaires returned (could also refer to the number of people who agree to be interviewed).

Structured interview where the questions are delivered in a particular order and no explanation or elaboration of the questions is allowed by the interviewer.

Transcribing the process of writing up interviews that have been recorded.

Unstructured interview where the interviewer is allowed to explain and elaborate on questions.

Validity quality achieved when questions provide an accurate measurement of the concept being investigated.

Item A — Gaining trust

<< From my own experience in researching white British and Caribbean people with diabetes, I would argue that there is evidence suggesting that my own Caribbean background was a distinct advantage .... Rapport [a good relationship] with the Caribbeans developed fairly spontaneously ... We traded stories about how we ended up in England, what part of Jamaica or the Caribbean we are from and generally how we coped with the cold weather and lack of sunshine.

... The interviews with the white British sub-sample differed significantly. Initial conversations were polite and were confined to matters relating to the interview .... Generally, there was no sharing of personal details and the interviewees did not elaborate on the issues of the research in the way that the Caribbean sample had. >>

Scott, P. (1999) 'Black people's health: ethnic status and research issues' in S. Hod, B. Mayall and S. Oliver, *Critical Issues in Social Research*, Buckingham: Open University Press

Item B — Telling the truth?

<< The first time we had this questionnaire, I thought it was a bit of a laugh. That's my memory of it. I can't remember if I answered it truthfully or not ... It had a list of drugs and some of them I'd never heard of, and just the names just cracked me up. >>

Youth quoted in Parker, H., Aldrige, J. and Measham, F. (1998) *Illegal Leisure*, London: Routledge, pp. 46 7

1 **Explain in your own words what is meant by 'interviewer bias'.** (2 marks)

2 **Identify one advantage and one disadvantage of the rapport identified in Item A.** (4 marks)

3 **Suggest three problems of using questionnaires to collect sensitive information.** (6 marks)

4 **Identify and briefly explain one advantage and one disadvantage of the researcher in Item A using a questionnaire rather than an interview.** (8 marks)

5 **Using information from Item A and elsewhere, examine the ways in which different types of interviews have been used in sociological research.** (20 marks)

6 **Using information from Item B and elsewhere, assess the usefulness of questionnaires in sociological research.** (20 marks)

research ideas

- Your aim is to find out about a sample of young people's experience of schooling. Draft a closed questionnaire to collect this data. Collect and analyse the data quantitatively.

  Now draft guide questions for an unstructured interview to find out about the same issue. Conduct two or three of these interviews, either taping or making notes of the responses.

  Compare the two sorts of data. What differences are there? Why do those differences occur? Which method do you think was most effective for that particular purpose? Why? (This task is particularly suitable as a pair or group activity.)

- Working with a partner of the opposite sex, draft guide questions for an unstructured interview with young men about their attitudes to sex. Each partner should then conduct three of these interviews.

  Discuss the different ways interviewees responded. Are the young men more honest and open with a male or female interviewer or is there no difference? Do you think that one of the interviewers obtained more valid results? If so, what reasons can you suggest for this?

Secondary sources of data

gettingyouthinking

Lucy Moore, in *The Thieves' Opera,* wrote a social history about people living in London in the early to mid 18th century. One chapter is devoted to death by hanging – the penalty for any theft worth more than one shilling (equivalent in value to £10 today). Read the extract on the right and then answer the questions below.

1 List the aspects of 18th-century punishment noted in this extract that you didn't already know.

2 Do you think that the extract is true? How could you prove it?

3 If you wanted to find out more about public executions, what would you do?

4 If we told you that the person who wrote the book from which we took the extract was strongly against capital punishment, would that alter your view at all? (We don't actually know what the author's views are.)

<< According to Bleakely ... when the cart stopped at Tyburn and the hangman began his preparations, Jack held out a pamphlet called *A Narrative of All the Robberies, Escapes etc. of John Sheppard, written by himself* ... He declared that this should be published as his official confession. He agreed to publicize the account of his life in return for an assurance by the publisher that he would arrange his 'rescue', a common practice that involved waiting to collect the near-dead body once it had hung for the mandatory fifteen minutes, and taking it to the doctor who would try to revive it with warm blankets and wine.

Until the automatic drop was introduced in 1760, hanging more often resulted in unconsciousness than death. By tradition, if the first hanging was unsuccessful, a condemned man could go free because his survival was a sign of divine favour.

At last Jack was subdued and obedient. Once the noose was fastened around his neck, the cart moved out from beneath his feet and he was left dangling beneath the gibbet. Because he was so slight, it took several minutes for him to lose consciousness. He did not weigh enough to force his body to drop sharply and thus break his neck. He writhed and twisted on the end of the rope with people in the crowd pulling at his legs hoping to ease his pain by breaking his neck, until finally he grew limp and still.

After the allotted fifteen minutes were up, the hearse ordered by Defoe and Applebee to take Jack away and try to resuscitate him approached the dangling body. The crowd, fearing that the hearse was about to take him off to be dissected for anatomical research, pelted the driver with stones and surged forward to protect the body.

Being dissected was the overriding terror of men condemned to death.

Foremost in the minds of the crowd was the awareness that the dead man might just as easily have been them. They were compelled by a sense of solidarity with the victim as well as traditional religious beliefs in the sanctity of the corpse because of the soul's resurrection on Judgement Day.>>

Moore, L. (1997) *The Thieves' Opera,* Harmondsworth: Penguin

Not all research uses primary sources – that is, observing people in real life, sending out questionnaires or carrying out interviews. Many sociologists prefer to use material collected and published by other people. This material is known as **secondary data**.

Secondary data consist of a very wide range of material collected by organizations and individuals for their own purposes, and include sources as complex as official government statistics at one extreme and as personal as diaries at the other. These data include written material, sound and visual images. Such material can be from the present day or historical data. Finally, and most commonly, secondary sources include the work of sociologists, which is read, analysed and commented on by other sociologists.

Secondary sources are invaluable to sociologists, both on their own and in combination with primary sources. It is unheard of for a researcher not to refer to some secondary sources.

Why sociologists use secondary sources

Some of the main reasons for using secondary sources include:

- The information required already exists as secondary data.
- Historical information is needed, but the main participants are dead or too old to be interviewed.
- The researcher is unable for financial or other reasons to visit places to collect data at first hand.
- The subject of the research concerns illegal activities and it is unsafe for the researcher to collect primary data.
- Data need to be collected about groups who are unwilling to provide accounts of their activities – for instance, extreme religious sects who do not want their activities to be open to study.

Errors and biases

Whenever sociologists use a secondary source, they must be aware that the person who first created the source did so for a specific reason, and this could well create **bias**. A diary, for example, gives a very one-sided view of what happened and is bound to be sympathetic to the writer. Official statistics may have been constructed to shed a good light on the activities of the government – for example, so that they can claim they are 'winning the war against crime'. Even the work of previous sociologists may contain errors and biases.

Types of secondary data

The most common types of secondary data used by sociologists include:

- previous sociological research
- official publications, including statistics and reports

- diaries and letters
- novels and other works of fiction
- oral history and family histories
- the media.

Previous sociological research

Previous studies as a starting point

Whenever sociologists undertake a study, the first thing they do is to carry out a **literature search** – that is, go to the library or the internet and look up every available piece of sociological research on the topic of interest. The sociologist can then see the ways in which the topic has been researched before, the conclusions reached and the theoretical issues thrown up. Armed with this information, the researcher can then construct the new research study to explore a different 'angle' on the problem or simply avoid the mistakes made earlier.

However, there are sometimes methodological errors in published research, as well as possible bias in the research findings. There have been many examples of research that has formed the basis for succeeding work and that only many years later has been found to be faulty. A famous piece of anthropological research that was used for 40 years before it was found to be centrally flawed was Mead's *Coming of Age in Samoa* (1928). Mead made a number of mistakes in her interpretation of the behaviour of the people she was studying, but as no one knew this, many later studies used her (incorrect) findings in their work.

Reinterpreting previous studies

Often sociologists do not want to carry out a new research project, but prefer instead to examine previous research in great detail in order to find a new interpretation of the original research results. Secondary data then provides all the information that is needed.

Official publications

Statistics

Statistics compiled by governments and reputable research organizations are particularly heavily used by sociologists. These statistics often provide far greater scale and detail than a sociologist could manage. It is also much cheaper to work on statistics already collected than repeating the work.

The government will usually produce these statistics over a number of years (for example, the government statistical publication *Social Trends* has been published for 30 years), so comparisons can be made over a long period of time.

However, while these official statistics have many advantages, there are also some pitfalls that researchers have to be aware of. The statistics are collected for administrative reasons and the classifications used may omit crucial information for sociologists. For example, sociologists may be interested in exploring issues of 'race' or gender, but this information might be missing from the official statistics.

Official statistics may be affected by political considerations, such as when they are used to assist the image of the government of the day. They may also reflect a complex process of interaction and negotiation – as is the case with crime statistics – and may well need to be the focus of investigation themselves!

Reports and government inquiries

The civil service and other linked organizations will often produce official reports which investigate important problems or social issues. However, although they draw together much information on these issues, they are constrained by their 'remit', which states the limits of their investigations. The government and other powerful bodies are therefore able to exclude discussion of issues that they do not want to become the centre of public attention. Government discussions on issues related to drugs, for example, are usually carefully controlled so that legalization of drugs is simply not discussed.

Diaries and letters

It is difficult to understand a historical period or important social events if the researcher has no way of interviewing the people involved. Usually, only the official information or media accounts are available. Using such things as letters and diaries helps to provide an insight into how participants in the events felt at the time.

However, problems can occur, as the writers may have distorted views of what happened, or they may well be justifying or glorifying themselves in their accounts. Almost any politician's memoirs prove this.

Novels

Novels can give an insight into the attitudes and behaviour of particular groups, especially if the author is drawn from one of those groups. However, they are fiction and will exaggerate actions and values for the sake of the story. Also, writing books is typically a middle- or upper-class activity, which may limit the insight that can be gained about the particular group featured.

Oral history and family histories

The events to be studied may have taken place some considerable time ago, but there may be older people alive who can recall the events or who themselves were told about them. There may be recordings available of people (now dead) talking of their lives. People often have old cine-film or family photos of events of interest. All of these can be collected and used by the researcher to help understand past events. Of course, the best of all these methods is the interview, with the older person recalling events of long ago (although quite where the line can be drawn between this as secondary research and as a simple interview is rather unclear).

These approaches do all share the usual problems that events may be reinterpreted by older people or by families to throw a positive light on their actions and, of course, to hide any harm they did to others.

What are the advantages and disadvantage of using novels, such as those of Jane Austen, to understand life in the past?

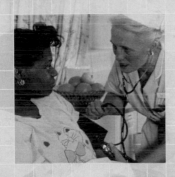

Research based on secondary data discovered that differences in health between ethnic groups are closely linked to social class and income

George Davey Smith *et al.*

The health of ethnic minorities: a meta-study

George Davey Smith and his colleagues were concerned that there was relatively little information on the health of ethnic minorities in Great Britain. They therefore conducted a **meta-study** to try to provide an overall picture of health care. They looked at data from a range of surveys including official publications, small-scale surveys and earlier sociological studies. Putting all of this together, they provided a picture of standards of health for different ethnic groups in Britain, taking into account the impact of social class. In order to do this, they also had to review a wide range of theoretical and methodological books and articles. The study therefore includes secondary research, which is based upon both theoretical and statistical studies, from government as well as academic sources.

They found that, overall, the health standards of ethnic minorities in Britain were worse than those of the general population, and that these differences were most apparent in childhood and old age. They found that most previous studies tended to explain any differences in health between ethnic minorities and the majority population in terms of cultural, dietary or genetic differences. However, they concluded that ethnicity by itself does not explain these differences. They suggest instead that differences in health are closely linked to social class and income.

Davey Smith, G., Chaturverdi, N., Harding, S., Nazroo, J. and Williams, R. (2003) *Health Inequalities: Lifecourse approaches*, Bristol: Policy Press

1 Why did the researchers use a meta-study?

2 How did the use of secondary sources allow them to reach different conclusions from earlier research?

The media and content analysis

A huge amount of material is available from newspapers, the internet, magazines and television. In fact, so much material is available that one of the major problems of using the mass media as secondary data lies with the selection of material: on exactly what grounds are items included or excluded? Researchers have to be very careful to include all relevant material and not to be biased in their selection in order to 'prove' their point. Two of the best-known studies using **content analysis** have been strongly criticized for just this. The Glasgow University Media Group's publications have explored a range of topics including television news, representations of mental illness in the media and the portrayal of the 1991 Iraq war; critics claim that they were selective in their choice of material and that they applied their own interpretations to the selections.

However, trying to understand and interpret accurately the printed and broadcast media is not just a matter of watching out for bias; there is also the issue of how to *interpret* the material. When we look at pictures or read a story in a magazine, different people find different meanings in the material. There are many factors influencing this, but one crucial factor is our own beliefs and attitudes towards the subject that we are reading about. The importance of this for research using secondary data is that we must not assume that what we read or see is the same as it was for the original readers or viewers.

Check your understanding

1 **What are secondary data?**

2 **Why do sociologists use secondary sources?**

3 **What are the disadvantages of using secondary sources?**

4 **What are the advantages and disadvantages of using official statistics and other government documents?**

5 **What are the advantages and disadvantages of using qualitative secondary data such as diaries?**

Bias where the material reflects a particular viewpoint to the exclusion of others. This may give a false impression of what happened. This is a particularly important problem for secondary sources.

Content analysis exploring the contents of the various media in order to find out how a particular issue is presented.

Literature search the process whereby a researcher finds as much published material as possible on the subject of interest. Usually done through library catalogues or the internet.

Meta-study a secondary analysis using all or most of the published information on a particular topic

Secondary data data already collected by someone else for their own purposes.

research ideas

- Watch *Eastenders, Coronation Street, Hollyoaks* or another 'soap' of your choosing. If sociologists were to watch this soap 50 years in the future, how accurate a picture of life today do you think it would give?

- Collect postcards sent to you, your friends and family. Look at their contents. Is there a pattern? Are they all positive? What sort of representation do postcards give of holidays? How accurate are they in representing holidays?

web.task

1 **Go to the government's National Statistics website (www.statistics.gov.uk) Find one set of statistics that you think is likely to be accurate and one set that you think is less likely to be accurate. What are they? Why should different official statistics be more or less accurate?**

2 **Find the website 'Corporate Watch' (www.corporatewatch.org.uk). Look up information about any two huge corporations (for example, Microsoft or Disney). Then go to the website belonging to that corporation. What are the differences between the information given? Which do you think is more accurate? Why?**

exploring secondary sources of data

Item A Forest

Forest is a pressure group that supports the right of people to smoke cigarettes. It is largely supported by funding from the tobacco industry. In May 2004, it produced the results of a report, a random sample of 10,000 adults aged 18+ in eight cities. Below are the answers to one question asked and the summary by the report.

<<Which one of the following statements is closest to your view about the way smoking should be dealt with in pubs, clubs and bars?>>

- Smoking should be allowed throughout all pubs, clubs and bars   6%
- All pubs, bars and clubs should be mainly smoking with separate non-smoking areas   19%
- All pubs, bars and clubs should be mainly non-smoking with separate areas for smoking   49%
- Smoking should be banned completely in all pubs, bars and clubs   24%
- Don't know   1%

ALL (10,000)

Source: Forest (2004) *Smoking in Public Places*

The replies were summarized in the report as follows:

<<Presented with four options of how smoking should be handled in pubs, clubs and bars – 74 per cent prefer to retain some smoking facility rather than banning it altogether, with 24 per cent agreeing with a complete ban on smoking. Just over two-thirds of non-smokers (67 per cent) agreed with one of the options that would retain some smoking facility, compared with 90 per cent of smokers. The proportion of non-smokers opting for a complete ban was 32 per cent compared with only 24 per cent of smokers. Of those visiting pubs frequently or often, only 19 per cent would prefer to see a ban.>>

Item B My Aunt Esther

Stephen Bourne grew up in London in the 1960s and his family was regularly visited by his Aunt Esther, a black woman. Stephen Bourne thought nothing about this until he saw a television programme about black people in Britain and he also found some old family photos showing his aunt and his mother's family when they were young.

<< The point of departure for me came in 1974 when I watched ... *The Black Man in Britain 1550–1950*. This documented the history of black people in Britain over 400 years ... By this time I had discovered a shoe box in Mum's wardrobe which was full of old family photographs. Several featured Aunt Esther ... Hungry for information, I was disappointed to find that, apart from the slave trade there was no mention of black people in our school history books ... However, through inter-library loans, I accessed two books then available on the subject: James Walvin's *Black and White: The Negro and English Society 1555–1945* (1973) and Folarin Shyllon's *Black People in Britain 1555–1833* (1977) ... I realized that my quest for knowledge would have to come from first-hand accounts, so I began to ask Aunt Esther questions ...

Aunt Esther – who worked as a seamstress – gave me first-hand accounts of what life was like for a working-class black Londoner throughout the century ... In 1992 we published her life story ... For this we received the Raymond Williams Prize for Community Publishing ... However, although the black media and women's press gave the book excellent coverage ... book editors on the broadsheet newspapers completely ignored us. >>

Bourne, S. (2000) 'My Aunt Esther', *History Today*, February, pp. 62–3

1 Explain what is meant by the term 'first-hand accounts' (Item B). (2 marks)

2 Identify two ways in which the summary of the results in Item A might be criticized. (4 marks)

3 Suggest three criticisms of the data gathered from Aunt Esther (Item B). (6 marks)

4 Identify and briefly explain two problems the author of Item B may have experienced in interviewing Aunt Esther. (8 marks)

5 Discuss the advantages and disadvantages of using official statistics in sociological research. (20 marks)

6 Using material from Items A and B, and elsewhere, evaluate the usefulness of personal and historical documents for sociologists. (20 marks)

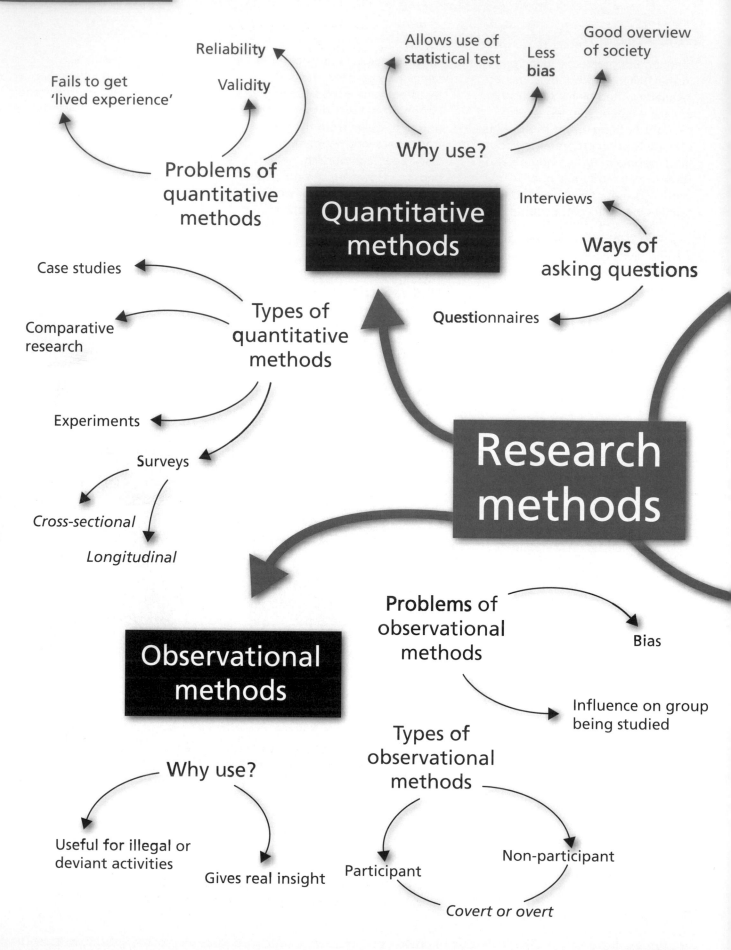

Reliability

Validity

Fails to get
'lived experience'

Allows use of
statistical test

Less
bias

Good overview
of society

Problems of
quantitative
methods

Why use?

Quantitative
methods

Interviews

Ways of
asking ques**tions**

Case studies

Comparative
research

Types of
quantitative
methods

Questionnaires

Experiments

Surveys

Research
methods

Cross-sectional

Longitudinal

Problems of
observational
methods

Bias

Observational
methods

Influence on group
being studied

Types of
observational
methods

Why use?

Useful for illegal or
deviant activities

Gives real insight

Participant

Non-participant

Covert or overt

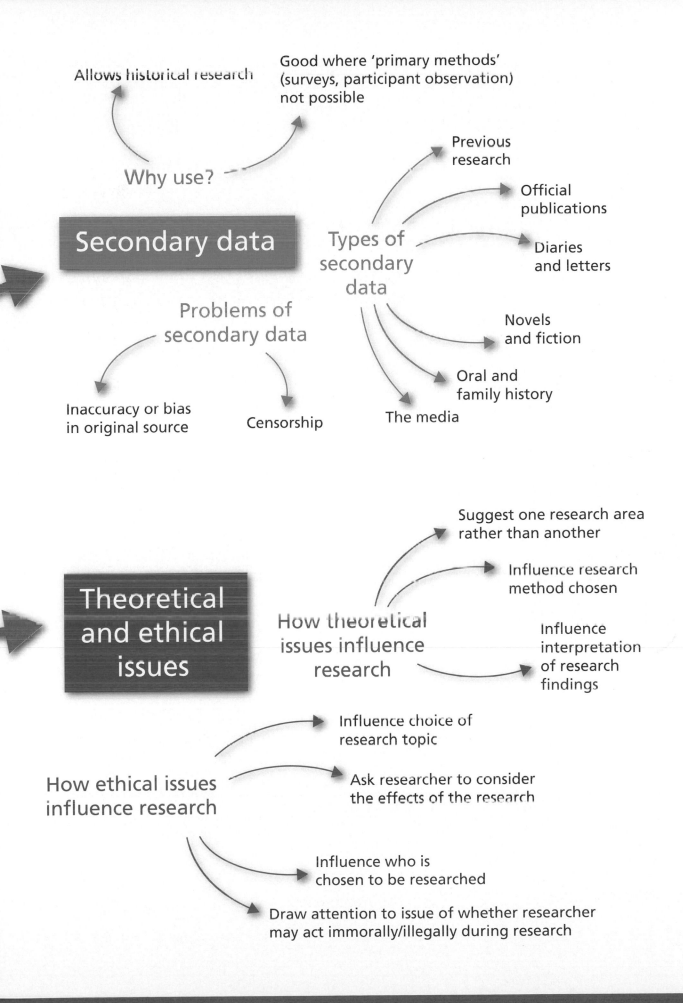

Allows historical research

Good where 'primary methods'
(surveys, participant observation)
not possible

Why use?

Secondary data

Types of
secondary
data

Previous
research

Official
publications

Diaries
and letters

Novels
and fiction

Oral and
family history

Problems of
secondary data

Inaccuracy or bias
in original source

Censorship

The media

Suggest one research area
rather than another

Influence research
method chosen

**Theoretical
and ethical
issues**

How theoretical
issues influence
research

Influence
interpretation
of research
findings

Influence choice of
research topic

Ask researcher to consider
the effects of the research

How ethical issues
influence research

Influence who is
chosen to be researched

Draw attention to issue of whether researcher
may act immorally/illegally during research

YES – YOU'VE ENJOYED STUDYING AS-LEVEL SOCIOLOGY. Yes – the issues you've covered have been interesting. Yes – you've learned a lot about society today. Yes – you feel more confident in discussions about social issues. But in the end, you know that your feelings about the course will probably depend on how well you get on in the exam board assessments that measure the standard of your work.

Your performance in the AQA AS-level course will be judged either totally by exams or through a combination of exams and coursework. Either way, you need to be completely confident about the organization of the exams: how long they last, how the questions are phrased and what knowledge and skills are being tested. You also need to be aware of the nature of the coursework task, how it is broken down and how marks are allocated.

This unit guides you through both AQA exams and AQA coursework. It provides essential information about the content and assessment of the course, including some really useful tips for both exams and coursework. After working through this unit, you should feel a lot more confident about the way your performance will be judged and be in a good position to get full value for all the work you've put in to your AS-level Sociology course.

Preparing for the AS exam

Preparing for the AQA AS-level exam

As well as being a sound introduction to the study of sociology, the AS course leads to a qualification in its own right. It is also an essential grounding for those wishing to continue for a further year of A-level study.

The AS course is sufficiently flexible to allow a choice of topic areas within Units 1 and 2 and the choice of a written examination or a coursework task based on a research proposal for Unit 3. It also ensures a thorough coverage of sociological perspectives and of the two core themes:

- socialization, culture and identity
- social differentiation, power and stratification.

These core themes are required elements of any AS/A-level sociology specification.

The knowledge and skills acquired in this course should enable you to take a more informed and critical look at many aspects of your own society and how they relate to your own life, while at the same time enabling you to develop and practise the skills of informed debate and critical analysis. The skills acquired in a sociology course can be of life-long benefit.

What will I study?

Aims of the course

The AQA specification in AS/A-level sociology offers you:

- the opportunity to acquire knowledge and understanding of key aspects of sociological thought
- a sound introduction to sociological research methods
- the opportunity to study a number of different areas of social life in depth.

Modules of study and units of assessment

The AQA AS course is divided into three modules of study, which lay out what you should know. When you enter for an examination, the module becomes a unit of assessment. Modules 1 and 2 each contain three topic areas, and each topic area forms the basis of a question in the written examination for the first two units of assessment. Module 3 covers only one area of study, namely: sociological methods. You are given a choice regarding the assessment of this unit.

Table 8.1 Modules of study and units of assessment

Module of study	Topics	Unit of assessment	Forms of assessment
1	• Families and households • Health • Mass media	**1**	Written examination of 1 hour 15 minutes; one data-response question per topic area
2	• Education • Wealth, poverty and welfare • Work and leisure	**2**	Written examination of 1 hour 15 minutes; one data-response question per topic area
3	• Sociological methods	**3**	**Either:** written examination of one hour consisting of one data-response question, **or:** coursework task based on structured proposal for a piece of research

How will I be assessed?

Skills

The skills you will acquire and develop in your AS course are tested in the examination by two assessment objectives, each of which counts for half of the available marks.

Assessment objective 1 (AO1): knowledge and understanding

This requires you to demonstrate your knowledge and understanding of the chosen topic area which forms the basis of the assessment. It covers knowledge and understanding of relevant sociological theories and perspectives, concepts, studies and social policies. You should also be able to make reference to relevant issues and events. Also included in AO1 is the skill of communication. While this is not assessed separately, and therefore does not carry a particular mark weighting, it is an important skill, as poor communication will prevent you from showing the examiner clearly what you mean.

Assessment objective 2 (AO2): identification, analysis, interpretation and evaluation

This range of skills together counts for half of the available marks. To demonstrate them successfully you will need to be able to identify perspectives, reasons, examples, criticisms and so on, as required by the particular question. The skill of interpretation covers your ability to work out and respond to what the question is requiring you to do and to interpret different types of evidence, including research studies and statistical data, by discussing what they can tell us. Good analysis is shown by presenting an informed, detailed and accurate discussion of a particular theory, perspective, study or event, and also by the ability to present your arguments and evidence in a clear and logically structured manner. Evaluation refers to your ability to recognize and discuss the strengths and weaknesses of theories and perspectives, studies, sociological methods and data presented in a variety of forms.

Exams

The basic structure of the units of assessment is shown in Table 8.1 on the left and the question structure is discussed in more detail in the next section. The weighting given to each of the three AS units is given in Table 8.2, which shows the percentage of the marks allocated to each unit in terms of both the AS and the full A level.

Coursework

The AS coursework task is offered in Unit 3 as an alternative to the written examination. It takes the form of a highly structured research proposal which may, if you wish, form the basis of an actual research project in the second year of the course. Further details of the AS coursework are given in the 'How can I do well in the coursework task?' section (p. 282).

Table 8.2 Weighting given to AS units at AS- & A-level

Unit of Assessment	AS-level weighting	A-level weighting
Unit 1	35% of the total AS-level marks	17.5% of the total A-level marks
Unit 2	35% of the total AS-level marks	17.5% of the total A-level marks
Unit 3	30% of the total AS-level marks	15% of the total A-level marks

How can I do well in the written exams?

Question style and structure

AS-level questions are data-response questions. Each question has typically two Items of information. The Items have a dual purpose. They provide the basis for some of the shorter questions, for example when you are asked to explain the meaning of a concept or phrase which occurs in the Item or to interpret some statistical data from a graph or table, and they also provide helpful information to assist you in answering the longer, higher-mark questions.

Each question is marked out of 60, and it might be helpful to think of the 60 marks being allocated in three groups of 20 marks.

Short-answer questions (a), (b), (c) and (d)

The first 20 marks are awarded for a series of short-answer questions, namely (a), (b), (c) and (d) – typically carrying 2, 4, 6 and 8 marks respectively.

- The 2-mark question will usually ask you to explain the meaning of a concept or phrase taken from one of the Items. You should do this in your own words. If the phrase has several elements, such as 'infant mortality rate', make sure your answer explains all the parts: what is infant, what is mortality, and what is a rate? Here, the answer should be 'the number of deaths, per year, of young children (under the age of 1), per thousand born'.

- The 4- and 6-mark questions will ask you to do two or three things, each of which will carry 2 marks. Typical questions would be:

  - *give two reasons why …*
  - *give three examples of …*
  - *suggest two explanations of …*
  - *identify three criticisms which could be made of …*.

  If asked for two things, make sure you give two distinct things. If asked for three, make sure you give three. Less means you cannot score all the marks available, more means you are wasting time.

- The 8-mark question will typically carry the instruction: *Identify and briefly explain **two** ....* The 'two' could refer to criticisms, reasons why, disadvantages of, etc. As you have been asked to do two things (identify and briefly explain), and you have been asked to do these for each of two different things (criticisms, reasons why, disadvantages of, etc.), the marks are awarded as 2 + 2 + 2 + 2 (assuming that you do everything correctly!). In other words, you get 2 marks for each of the two 'things' correctly identified, and a further 2 marks for each of these successfully explained.

Longer-answer questions (e) and (f)

- The (e) question carries 20 marks, and will typically ask you to *discuss* or *examine* something. It is important to understand that this question carries 14 of the 20 available marks for knowledge and understanding (AO1) and the remaining 6 marks for the AO2 skills. This question will usually not be based on one of the Items, but will focus on a different aspect of the topic area than that covered in the Items, allowing you to demonstrate a breadth of knowledge.
- The (f) question also carries 20 marks, and will typically ask you to *assess* something. It is important to understand that this question carries 14 of the 20 available marks for the AO2 skills, particularly analysis and evaluation, and the remaining 6 marks for knowledge and understanding. Since you are being asked to assess something, it is reasonable to spend a *short* time describing *briefly* what it is you are assessing, but the bulk of the answer must be the evaluation. This usually involves either empirical evidence for and against a point of view or a consideration of other theories. Attempt to be *balanced*. Give both sides equal weight and equal time, if possible. At the end try to come to a conclusion that is based on the information you have given in your answer. Sitting on the fence and saying both sides might be right, does not always follow from what the rest of the essay suggests.

The two longer-answer questions do not allocate specific marks for each of the two assessment objectives, that is, you do not get a mark out of 14 and a mark out of 6. Marks are allocated between three broad bands, and are awarded on the basis of descriptions of typical answers. The greater focus of the (e) mark scheme is on the relevant knowledge and understanding displayed, while in the (f) mark scheme the emphasis is on the AO2 skills shown in the answer.

How can I do well in the coursework task?

Requirements

The AS-level coursework task requires you to submit a proposal for a piece of sociological research, based on the collection of primary or secondary data. Your proposal has to be presented under four set headings, as shown in Table 8.3. There is an overall word limit of 1200 words, and each of the

Exam tips

- Read both the Items and the whole question very carefully before you begin to answer. The Items will contain information that is essential, helpful or both, and reading the whole question will give you an understanding of which aspects of the topic have been covered.

- Keep an eye on the time. Remember that the (e) and (f) questions together count for 40 of the 60 marks available, so it is very important that you allow sufficient time for these, and are able to write more than just a few paragraphs. It is quite acceptable, in questions in which you are asked to give two reasons, or give three examples, to do just that, using bullet points if you wish. There is no need in such questions to write a long paragraph.

- In the 8-mark (d) questions, separate out your answer into two parts, so that you identify and briefly explain one thing, and then leave a line and go on to identify and briefly explain a second thing. This makes it less likely that you will forget to do both parts of the question.

- Read the whole question and plan the answers to parts (e) and (f) before you begin any writing. As you go through the other answers you may well remember elements that you will wish to slot into these answers.

- If you find you are using the same information in different answers, check carefully that you are answering the question set. The examiner attempts to cover as much of the specification as possible and is unlikely to be asking the same question twice.

  Particularly in the 20-mark questions, refer to appropriate theories, perspectives, studies and evidence to support and inform your answer. Where possible, bring in examples of recent or current events or social policies to illustrate the points you are making. Make quite sure that in the (f) question you have given sufficient demonstration of the AO2 skills, particularly analysis and evaluation.

- Finally, make sure that you answer the question that the examiner has set, rather than the one that you wished had been set! This is a serious point – many candidates fail to achieve marks because they have not kept to the focus of the question. No question is likely to ask you simply to write everything you know about a certain topic and yet this is what some students do.

four sections has its own word limit, which has to be shown on the proposal. Your proposal does not have to be for research that would be capable of being conducted by a 17-year-old student. However, if you think that you may wish to develop your AS proposal and use it as the basis for an actual

Table 8.3 Requirements of coursework

Section	Outline requirements	Maximum no. of words	Total marks for that section
Hypothesis/ aim	Identify an appropriate sociological area or issue and develop a hypothesis or aim to form the basis of your research, explaining its sociological significance.	100	8
Context and concepts	Identify and briefly describe two pieces of material that would form appropriate contexts for the proposed research. Choose two concepts that would be useful in the collection and/or analysis of the data.	400	20
Main research method and reasons	Choose a single research method for the collection of data, saying why you think it is appropriate for testing/exploring your hypothesis or aim. Give supporting information regarding the implementation of the method.	400	20
Potential problems	Identify some problems which a sociologist would need to be aware of if the proposed research were carried out, explaining why these problems might arise.	300	12
	Total	**1200**	**60**

research project in A2, then you would have to bear in mind when framing your AS proposal the obvious limitations of time, cost, access to informants, data and so on that you would have to deal with at A2. Table 8.3 above shows you in outline what you have to do.

Coursework tips

- Make sure that your research has a clear sociological focus.

- Do not be overambitious and do not make your hypothesis or aim too broad – this will lead to problems in the later sections.

- Keep referring back to your hypothesis or aim – all the other sections should show a clear link to this.

- Make sure that you spend time choosing appropriate pieces of context and show how and why these provide an appropriate context for the proposed research.

- Choose only one method to use as the main method of data collection.

- Remember to give clear reasons for all your choices and decisions.

- Allow sufficient time to draft and redraft your proposal – it is seldom possible to get everything right the first time. Make sure that you are aware of, and meet, the set deadline.

- Stick to the word limit!

What will the A2 course be like?

Modules of study and units of assessment

The A2 part of the course is also divided into three modules of study/units of assessment.

- Module 4 contains three topics: *power and politics*, *religion*, and *world sociology*. Each of these will form the basis of a question in the written examination. This unit carries 15 per cent of the total A-level marks.
- Module 5 is based on *theory and methods*, and you have a choice between a written examination of this topic, and submitting a piece of coursework with a maximum word length of 3500 words. This unit carries 15 per cent of the total A-level marks.
- Module 6 is the synoptic module (see below) and is assessed by a written examination. This unit carries 20 per cent of the total A-level marks.

Synoptic assessment

Unit 6 is the synoptic unit, which will test your knowledge and understanding of the links between all the sections of the course that you have studied. The two topic areas that form the basis of synoptic assessment are: *crime and deviance*, and *stratification and differentiation*. There will be a question on each of these on the examination paper. You will answer a question on one of these topics only. The questions on this paper will require you to show an informed and critical knowledge and understanding of your chosen synoptic topic and its links with sociological theory, sociological methods, and the other topic areas you have studied over the two years of the course.

REFERENCES

Abraham, J. (1996) *Are Girls Necessary? Lesbian Writing and Modern Histories*, London: Routledge

Ali, S. (2002) 'Interethnic Families', *Sociology Review*, 12(1)

Alford, R.R. (1975) *Health Care Politics: Ideological and interest group barriers to reform*, Chicago: The University of Chicago Press

Allan, G. (1985) *Family Life: Domestic roles and social organization*, London: Blackwell

Althusser, L. (1971) 'Ideology and ideological state apparatuses', in *Lenin and Philosophy and Other Essays*, London: New Left Books

Anderson, C.A. and Dill, K.E. (2000) 'Video games and aggressive thoughts, feelings, and behavior in the laboratory and in life', *Journal of Personality and Social Psychology*, 78(4), pp. 772–90

Anderson, M. (1971) 'Family, household and the Industrial Revolution', in M. Anderson (ed.) *The Sociology of the Family*, Harmondsworth: Penguin

Annandale, E. (1998) *The Sociology of Health and Illness*, Cambridge: Polity Press

Aries, P. (1962) *Centuries of Childhood*, London: Random House

Arnot, M., David, D. and Weiner, G. (1999) *Closing the Gender Gap*, Cambridge: Polity Press

Bagdikian, B. (2000) *The Media Monopoly* (6th edn), Boston: Beacon Press

Bagdikian, B. (2004) *The New Media Monopoly*, Boston: Beacon Press

Bain. P. and Taylor, P. (2000) 'Entrapped by the "electronic panopticon"? Worker resistance in the call centre', *New Technology, Work and Employment*, 15(1)

Ball, S. (2002) *Class Strategies and the Education Market: The Middle Classes and Social Advantage*, London: RoutledgeFalmer

Ball, S. (2003) Inaugural lecture as Karl Mannheim professor of sociology of education at London University's Institute of Education.

Ball, S. *et al.* (1994) 'Market forces and parental choice', in S. Tomlinson (ed.) *Educational Reform and Its Consequences*, London: Rivers Oram Press

Bandura, A., Ross, D. and Ross, S.A. (1963) 'The imitation of film mediated aggressive models', *Journal of Abnormal and Social Psychology*, 66(1), pp. 3–11

Barber, B. (1963) 'Some problems in the sociology of professions', *Daedalus*, 92(4)

Barrett, M. and McIntosh, M. (1982) *The Anti-social Family*, London: Verso

Bauman, Z. (1990) *Thinking Sociologically*, Oxford: Blackwell

Beck, U. (1992) *Risk Society: Towards a New Modernity*, London: Sage

Beck, U. and Beck-Gernsheim, E. (1995) *The Normal Chaos of Love*, Cambridge: Polity Press

Becker, H. (1963) *Outsiders: Studies in the Sociology of Deviance*, London: Macmillan

Becker, H. (1971) 'Social class variations in the teacher–pupil relationship', in B. Cosin (ed.) *School and Society*, London: Routledge & Kegan Paul

Bennett, A. (1999) 'Rappin' on the Tyne: White hip hop culture in Northeast England – an ethnographic study', *Sociological Review*, 47(1), pp. 1–24

Benston, M. (1972) 'The political economy of women's liberation', in N. Glazer-Malbin and H.Y. Waehrer (eds) *Women in a Man-Made World*, Chicago: Rand McNally

Bernard, J. (1982, originally 1972) *The Future of Marriage*, Yale: Yale University Press

Berthoud, R. (2000) 'Family formation in multi-cultural Britain: three patterns of diversity', *Working Paper of the Institute for Social and Economic Research*, Colchester: University of Essex

Berthoud, R. (2003) Lecture at ATSS Conference 2004, based on research conducted in 2003

Berthoud, R. and Gershuny, J. (2000) *Seven Years in the Lives of British Families: Evidence on the dynamics of social change from the British Household Panel Survey*, Bristol: The Policy Press

Best, L. (1993) 'Dragons, dinner ladies and ferrets', *Sociology Review*, February

Billington, R., Hockey, J. and Strawbridge, S. (1998) *Exploring Self and Society*, Basingstoke: Macmillan

Blaxter, M. (1990) *Health and Lifestyles*, London: Tavistock

Blumler, J.G. and McQuail, D. (1968) *Television in Politics: Its Uses and Influence*, London: Faber & Faber

Bourdieu, P. and Passeron, J. (1977) *Reproduction in Education, Society and Culture*, London: Sage

Bourgois, P. (2003) *In Search of Respect* (2nd edn), Cambridge: Cambridge University Press

Bowles, S. and Gintis, H. (1976) *Schooling in Capitalist America: Educational Reform and the Contradictions of Economic Life*, New York: Basic Books

Bradshaw, J. and Ernst, J. (1990) *Establishing a Modest but Adequate Budget for a British Family*, Family Budget Unit

Brannen, J. (2003) 'The age of beanpole families', *Sociology Review*, September

British Film Institute (2001) *The Stats*, British Film Institute

Broadcasters' Audience Research Board (2204) *see* www.barb.co.uk

Brown, C. (1979) *Understanding Society*, Harlow: Longman

Brown, G.W., Harris, T.O. and Hepworth, C. (1995) 'Loss, humiliation and entrapment among women developing depression', *Psychological Medicine*, 25, pp. 7–21

Buckingham, D. (ed.) (1993) *Reading Audiences: Young people and the media*, Manchester: Manchester University Press

Burghes, L. (1997) *Fathers and Fatherhood in Britain*, London: Policy Studies Institute

Burghes, L. and Brown, M. (1995) *Single Lone Mothers: Problems, prospects and policies*, York: Family Policy Studies Centre with the support of the Joseph Rowntree Foundation

Burns, J. and Bracey, P. (2001) 'Boys' underachievement: Issues, challenges and possible ways forward', *Westminster Studies in Education*, 24, pp. 155–66

Busfield, J. (1988) 'Mental illness as a social product or social construct: a contradiction in feminists' arguments?', *Sociology of Health and Illness*, 10, pp. 521–42

Buswell, C. (1987) *Training for Low Pay*, Basingstoke: Macmillan

Campbell, B. (2000) *The Independent*, 20 November 2000

Chamberlain, M. and Goulborne, H. (1999) *Caribbean Families in Britain and the Trans-Atlantic World*, Basingstoke: Macmillan

Charlesworth, S. (2000) *A Phenomenology of Working Class Experience*, Cambridge: Cambridge University Press

Charlton, T., Gunter, B. and Hannan, A. (2000) *Broadcast Television Effects in a Remote Community*, Hillsdale, NJ: Lawrence Erlbaum

Chesler, P. (1972) *Women and Madness*, New York: Doubleday

Clark, J. and Hein, J. (2000) 'The Political Economy of Welfare Reform in the United States' in J. Clark et al. (eds) *Welfare, Work and Poverty*, London: Institute for the Study of Civil Society

Clarke, J. N. (1992) 'Cancer, heart disease and AIDS: What do the media tell us about these diseases?', *Health Communication*, 4(2)

Coard, B. (1971) *How the West-Indian Child is Made Educationally Sub-normal in the British School System*, London: New Beacon Books

Cohen, P. (1984) 'Against the new vocationalism', in L. Bates, J. Clarke, P. Cohen, R. Moore and P. Willis, *Schooling for the Dole*, Basingstoke: Macmillan

Connect Research (2003) *Connecting with Black and Asian Viewers*, Connect Research

Connolly, P. (1998) *Racism, Gender Identities and Young Children*, London: Routledge & Kegan Paul

Coward, R. (1989) *The Whole Truth; The Myth of Alternative Health*, London: Faber

Crosland, C.A.R. (1956) *The Future of Socialism*, London: Jonathan Cape

Cumberbatch, G. (2004) *Video Violence: Villain or Victim?* Report for the Video Standards Council available at www.videostandards.org.uk/video_violence.htm

Davey Smith, G., Shipley, M.J. and Rose, G. (1990) 'The magnitude and causes of socio-economic differentials in mortality: further evidence from the Whitehall study', *Journal of Epidemiology and Community Health*, 44, pp. 265–70

De'ath, E. and Slater, D. (eds) (1992) *Parenting Threads: Caring for children when couples part*, Stepfamily Publications

Delphy, C. (1984) *Close to Home*, London: Hutchinson

Dennis, N. and Erdos, G. (2000) *Families Without Fatherhood* (3rd edn), London: Civitas

Dex, S. (2003) *Families and Work in the Twenty-first Century*, York: Joseph Rowntree Foundation

DfES (2002) *Youth Cohort Study: Activities and Experiences of 18 Year Olds: England and Wales 2002*, London: DFeS www.dfes.gov.uk/rsgateway/DB/SFR/s000382/V4sfr04-2003.pdf

DfES (2003) *Statistical Bulletin: Permanent Exclusions from Maintained Schools in England 2001/02* (ref 08/2003), London: DFeS

Dietz, T. (1998) 'An examination of violence and gender role portrayals in video games: Implications for gender socialization and aggressive behavior', *Sex Roles*, 38, pp. 425–42

Doyal, L. (1979) *The Political Economy of Health*, London: Pluto

Drew, D. (1995) *Race, Education and Work: The Statistics of Inequality*, Aldershot: Avebury

Dryden, C. (1999) *Being Married Doing Gender*, London: Routledge

Duncombe, J. and Marsden, D. (1995) 'Women's "triple shift": paid employment, domestic labour and "emotion work"', *Sociology Review* 4(4)

Dunne, G. A. (ed.) (1997) *Lesbian Lifestyles: Women's Work and the Politics of Sexuality*, Basingstoke: Macmillan

Durkheim, E. (1897/1952) *Suicide: a Study In Sociology*, London: Routledge

Edgell, S. (1980) *Middle-class Couples*, London: Allen & Unwin

Eisenberg, L. (1977) 'Disease and illness: distinction between professional and popular ideas of sickness', *Culture, Medicine and Psychiatry*, 1, pp. 9–23

Elias, N. (1978) *The Civilising Process*, Oxford: Blackwell

Equal Opportunities Commission (2005) *Sex and Power: Who Runs Britain? 2005*, Equal Opportunities Commission

Esping-Andersen, G. (1990) *The Three Worlds of Welfare Capitalism*, Cambridge: Polity Press

Essex University Study (2000) *Family Formation in Multicultural Britain: Three Patterns of Diversity*, Institute for Social and Economic Research, Essex University (author: Richard Berthoud)

Ferguson, M. (1983) *Forever Feminine: Women's Magazines and the Cult of Femininity*, London: Heinemann

Fesbach, S. and Sanger, J.L. (1971) *Television and Aggression*, San Francisco: Jessey-Bass

Field, F. (1989) *Losing Out: The Emergence of Britain's Underclass,* Oxford: Blackwell

Finkelstein, V. (1980) *Attitudes and Disabled People: Issues for Discussion,* New York: World Rehabilitation Fund

Finn, D. (1987) *Training without Jobs,* Basingstoke: Macmillan

Flowers, A. (1998) *The Fantasy Factory: An insider's view of the phone sex industry,* Philadelphia: University of Pennsylvania Press

Ford, R. and Millar, J. (eds) (1998) *Private Lives and Public Costs: Lone parents and the state,* London: Policy Studies Institute

Forest (2004) *Smoking in Public Places: An Independent Survey Of Public Attitudes to Smoking in Pubs, Bars And Clubs,* www.forestonline.org/files/pdf/FOREST_Booklet_V6.pdf

Forsyth, A. and Furlong, A. (2003) *Socioeconomic Disadvantage and Experience in Further and Higher Education,* Bristol: Policy Press

Foster, J. (1990) *Villains: Crime and Community in the Inner City,* London: Routledge

Foucault, M. (1965) *Madness and Civilization,* New York: Random House

Foucault, M. (1976) *The Birth of the Clinic,* London: Tavistock

Fox Harding, L. (1996) *Family, State and Social Policy,* Basingstoke: Macmillan

Francis, B. (1998) *Power Plays: Primary School Children's Constructions of Gender, Power and Adult Work,* Stoke-on-Trent: Trentham Books.

Friedson, E. (1965) 'Disability as social deviance', in M.B. Sussman (ed.) *Sociology of Disability and Rehabilitation,* Washington, DC: American Sociological Association

Fuller, M. (1984) 'Black girls in a London comprehensive', in R. Deem (ed.) *Schooling for Women's Work,* London: Routledge

Future Foundation Survey (2000) 'Complicated lives' (conducted by William Nelson)

Galtung, J. and Ruge, M. (1973) 'Structuring and selecting news', in S. Cohen and J. Young (eds) *The Manufacture of News, Social Problems, Deviance and the Mass Media,* London: Constable

Gauntlett, D. (2002) *Media, Gender and Identity: An Introduction,* London: Routledge

Gershuny, J. (2000) ISER, University of Essex with the Future Foundation for Abbey National

Gewirtz, S. (2002) *The Managerial School: Post-welfarism and social justice in education,* London, Routledge

Giddens, A. (1991) *Modernity and Self-Identity: Self in Society in the Late Modern Age,* Cambridge: Polity

Giddens, A. (1999) *The Third Way: The Renewal of Social Democracy,* Cambridge: Polity Press

Gillborn, D. (1990) *'Race', Ethnicity and Education: Teaching and Learning in Multi-ethnic Schools,* London: Unwin Hyman

Gillborn, D. and Gipps, B. (1996) *Recent Research in the Achievement of Ethnic Minority Pupils,* London: HMSO

Gillborn, D. and Mirza, H.S. (2000) *Educational Inequality: Mapping Race and Class,* OFSTED.

Gillborn, D. and Youdell, D. (1999) *Rationing Education: Policy, Practice, Reform and Equity,* Milton Keynes: Open University Press

Ginsberg, N. (1998) 'The socialist perspective', in P. Alcock, A. Erskine and M. May (eds) *The Student's Companion to Social Policy,* Oxford: Blackwell

Glaser, B. and Strauss. A. (1967) *The Discovery of Grounded Theory,* Chicago: Aldine

Glasgow University Media Group (2000) *Viewing the World: News Content and Audience Studies,* DFID: London (web site: www.dfid.gov.uk)

Glasgow University Media Group and Eldridge, G. (ed.) (1993) *Getting the Message: News, Truth and Power,* London: Routledge

Glendinning, C. and Millar, J. (1992) *Women and Poverty in Britain: The 1990s* (2nd edn), Hemel Hempstead: Harvester Wheatsheaf

Goffman, E. (1959) *The Presentation of Self in Everyday Life,* Harmondsworth: Penguin

Goffman, E. (1961) *Asylums,* Harmondsworth: Penguin

Goffman, E. (1963) *Stigma: Notes on the Management of Spoiled Identity,* New York: Prentice Hall

Gordon, D., Adelman, L., Ashworth, K., Bradshaw, J., Levitas, R., Middleton, S., Pantazis, C., Patsios, D., Payne, S., Townsend, P. and Williams, J. (2000) *Poverty and Social Exclusion in Britain,* York: Joseph Rowntree Foundation

Gottman, J.S. (1990) 'Children of gay and lesbian parents', in F.W. Bozett and M.B. Sussman (eds) *Homosexuality and Family Relations,* New York: Harrington Press

Gove, W.R. (1982) 'The current status of the labeling theory of mental illness', in W.R. Gove (ed.) *Deviance and Mental Illness* (pp. 273–300), Beverly Hills, CA: Sage Publications

Graham, H. (2002) 'Inequality in Men and Women's Health', in S. Nettleton and U. Gustafsson (eds) *The Sociology of Health and Medicine,* Cambridge: Polity

Grieshaber, S. (1977) 'Mealtime rituals: power and resistance in the construction of mealtime rules', *British Journal of Sociology,* 48(4)

Griffin, C. (1985) *Typical Girls: Young Women from School to the Job Market,* London: Routledge & Kegan Paul

Hakim, C. (1996) *Key Issues in Women's Work,* London: Athlone

Hall, S. and Jefferson, S. (1976) *Resistance through Rituals: Youth Subcultures in Post-war Britain,* London: Hutchinson

Hall, S., Critcher, C., Jefferson, A., Clarke, J. and Robert, B. (1978) *Policing the Crisis: Mugging, the State and Law and Order,* London: Palgrave Macmillan

Ham, C. (1999) *Health Policy in Britain,* Basingstoke: Palgrave

Haque, Z. and Bell, J.F. (2001) 'Evaluating the performances of minority ethnic pupils in secondary schools', *Oxford Review of Education,* 27(3), pp.359–68

Haralambos, M. and Holborn, M. (2004) *Sociology: Themes and Perspectives* (6th edn), London: Collins Education

Hardey, M. (1998) *The Social Context of Health*, Buckingham: Open University Press

Hargreaves, D.H. (1967) *Social Relations in a Secondary School*, London: Routledge & Kegan Paul

Hart, N. (1976) *When Marriage Ends*, London: Tavistock

Haskey, J. (2002) *Report for the Office for National Statistics*, London: ONS

Hills, J. (1998) *Income and Wealth: The latest evidence*, York: Joseph Rowntree Foundation

Himmelweit, H. (1958) *TV and the Child*, Oxford: Oxford University Press

Humphreys, L. (1975) *Tearoom Trade: Impersonal sex in public places*, New York: Aldine De Gruyter.

Illsley, R. (1986) 'Occupational class, selection and the production of inequalities in health', *Quarterly Journal of Social Affairs*, 2(2), pp. 151–64

Jackson, M. (2000) 'From South Fork to South Park', The Fleming Lecture 2000, 10 May

Jackson, M. (2001) 'Channel 4: The Fourth Way', New Statesman Media Lecture 2001, 31 October

Jasper, L. (2002) 'School system failing black children', *Guardian*, 16 March

Jefferis, B., Power, C. and Hertzman, C. (2002) 'Birth weight, childhood socioeconomic environment, and cognitive development in the 1958 British birth cohort study', *British Medical Journal*, 325, p.305

Jhally, S. and Lewis, J. (1992) *Enlightened Racism. The Cosby Show, Audiences and the Myth of the American Dream*, Oxford: Westview Press

Joseph Rowntree Foundation Survey (1999, 2002) *Monitoring Poverty and Social Exclusion*, York: Joseph Rowntree Foundation

Jowell, R., Curtice, J. Park, A., Brook, L. and Ahrendt, A. (eds.) (1995) *British Social Attitudes: the 12th Report*, Aldershot: Dartmouth

Kenway, J. (1997) 'Taking stock of gender reform policies for Australian schools: past, present, future', *British Educational Research Journal*, 23, pp. 329–44

Kinder, M. (1999) *Kid's Media Culture*, Durham, North Carolina: Duke University Press.

Klapper, J.T. (1960) *The Effects of Mass Communication*, New York: The Free Press

Krause, I.B. (1989) 'Sinking heart: a Punjabi communication of distress', *Social Science and Medicine*, 29, pp. 563–75

Laslett, P. (1972) 'Mean household size in England since the sixteenth century', in P. Laslett (ed.) *Household and Family in Past Time*, Cambridge: Cambridge University Press

Laumann, E.O., Gagnon, J.H., Michael, R.T. and Michaels, S. (1995) *The Social Organization of Sexuality: Sexual Practices in the United States*, Chicago: University of Chicago Press

Le Grand J. (1982) *The Strategy of Equality: Redistribution and the Social Services*, London: Allen & Unwin

Legal & General Survey (2000) 'The value of a mum'

Leighton, G. (1992) 'Wives' paid and unpaid work and husbands' unemployment', *Sociology Review*, 1(3)

Lewis, O. (1966) *La Vida*, New York: Random House

Liddiment, D. (2001) The McTaggart Lecture, Guardian Edinburgh International Television Festival

Link, B. and Phelan, J. (1995) 'Social conditions as fundamental cause of disease', *Journal of Health and Social Behaviour*, pp. 80–94

Low Pay Commission (2003) *The National Minimum Wage: Building on Success. Fourth Report of the Low Pay Commission*, London: Low Pay Commission

Lupton, D. (1994) *Medicine as Culture: Illness, Disease and the Body in Western Societies*, London: Sage

Lyng, S. (1998) 'Dangerous methods: risk taking and the research process', in J Ferrell and M.S. Hamm (eds) *Ethnography at the Edge: Crime, Deviance and Field Research*, Boston: Northeastern University Press

Mac an Ghaill, M. (1994) *The Making of Men: Masculinities, Sexualities and Schooling*, Milton Keynes: Open University Press

McAllister, F. with Clarke, L. (1998) *Choosing Childlessness*, York: Family Policy Studies Centre and Joseph Rowntree Foundation

McGlone, F., Park, A. and Smith, K. (1998) *Families and Kinship*, York: Family Policy Studies Centre in association with the Joseph Rowntree Foundation

MacIntyre, S. (1993) 'Gender differences in the perceptions of common cold symptoms', *Social Science and Medicine*, 36(1), pp. 15–20

Mack, J and Lansley, S. (1993) *Breadline Britain*, London: Unwin Hyman

McNamara, R.P. (1994) *The Times Square Hustler: Male prostitution in New York City*, Westport: Praeger

Marcuse, H. (1964) *One Dimensional Man*, London: Routledge and Keegan Paul

Marshall, G., Newby, H., Rose, D. and Vogler, C. (1988) *Social Class in Modern Britain*, London: Hutchinson

Marsland, D. (1996) *Welfare or Welfare State?*, Basingstoke: Macmillan

Mead, M. (1928) *Coming of Age in Samoa*, New York: Morrow

Mirrlees-Black, C. (1999) 'Domestic violence: findings from a new British Crime Survey self-completion questionnaire', *Home Office Research Study 191*

Mirza, H. (1992) *Young, Female and Black*, London: Routledge

Modood, T. (1997) *Ethnic Minorities in Britain: Diversity and Disadvantage*, London: Policy Studies Institute

Moore, S. (2004) 'Hanging around: the politics of the busstop', *Youth and Policy*, 82, pp. 47–59

Morgan, P. (2000) *Marriage-Lite: the Rise of Cohabitation and its Consequences*, London: Civitas

Morley, D. (1980) *The Nationwide Audience*, London: BFI

Morrison, D.E. (1999) *Defining Violence: The Search for Understanding*, Luton: University of Luton Press

Morrow, V. (1998) *Understanding Families: Children's Perspectives*, York: National Children's Bureau in association with the Joseph Rowntree Foundation

Moser, K., Goldblatt, P., Fox, J. and Jones, D. (1990) 'Unemployment and mortality', in P. Goldblatt (ed.) *Longitudinal Study: Mortality and Social Organisation*, London: HMSO

Mulvey, L. (1975) 'Visual pleasures and narrative cinema', *Screen*, 16(3)

Murdock, G.P. (1949) *Social Structure*, New York: Macmillan

Murray, C. (1990) *The Emerging British Underclass*, London: IEA

Murray, C. (1994) *Underclass: The Crisis Deepens*, London: IEA

Myers, J. (1975) 'Life events, social integration and psychiatric symptomatology', *Journal of Health and Social Behaviour*, 16, pp. 121–7

Myers, K. (2000) *Whatever Happened to Equal Opportunities in Schools?*, Buckingham: Open University Press.

Myhill, D. (1999) 'Bad boys and good girls: patterns of interaction and response in whole class teaching', Exeter University School of Education paper

National Survey of NHS Patients (2003), Department of Health

Navarro, V. (1977) *Medicine under Capitalism*, London: Martin Robertson

Nazroo, J. (1999) 'Uncovering gender differences in the use of marital violence: the effect of methodology' in G. Allan (ed.) *The Sociology of the Family: A Reader*, Oxford: Blackwell

Nazroo, J.Y. (2001) *Ethnicity, Class and Social Health*, London: PSI

Newbold, C., Boyd-Barrett, O. and Van Den Bulk, H. (2002) *The Media Book*, London: Arnold

Newsom, E. (1994) 'Video violence and the protection of children', *The Psychologist*, June

Oakley, A. (1986) 'Feminism, motherhood and medicine – Who cares?', in J. Mitchell and A. Oakley (eds) *What is Feminism?*, Oxford: Blackwell

O'Connor, J. (1973) *The Fiscal Crisis of the State*, Basingstoke: Macmillan

O'Donnell, M. (1991) *Race and Ethnicity*, Harlow: Longman

Oliver, M. (1990) The Politics of Disablement, Basingstoke: Macmillan

Oliver, M. (1996) *Understanding Disability*, London: Macmillan

Orbach, S. (1991) *Fat is a Feminist Issue*, London: Hamlyn

Packard, V. (1957) *The Hidden Persuaders*, Harlow: Longman

Pahl, R.E. (1988) 'Some remarks on informal work, social polarisation and the class structure', *International Journal of Urban and Regional Research*, 12(2), pp. 247–67

Palmer, G., Carr, J. and Kenway, P. (2004) *Monitoring Poverty and Social Exclusion 2004*, York: Joseph Rowntree Foundation

Parsons, T. (1955) 'The social structure of the family', in T. Parsons and R.F Bales (eds) *Family, Socialization and Interaction Process*, New York: The Free Press

Parsons, T. (1965) 'The normal American family', in S.M. Farber (ed.) *Man and Civilization: the Family's Search for Survival*, New York: McGraw Hill

Parsons, T. (1975) 'The sick role and the role of the physician reconsidered', *Millbank Memorial Fund Quarterly: Health and Society*, 53, pp 257–78

Phillips, M. (1997) *All Must Have Prizes*, London: Little Brown

Philo, G. and Berry, M. (2004) *Bad News from Israel*, London: Pluto Press

Pilgrim, D. and Rogers, A. (1999) *A Sociology of Mental Health and Illness* (2nd edn), Buckingham: Open University Press

Postman, N. (1982) *The Disappearance of Childhood*, New York: Delacorte Press

Power, S. *et al.* (2003) *Education and the Middle Class*, Milton Keynes: Open University Press

Pryke, R. (2000) 'Poverty-wallahs, the underclass and incentives', in J. Clark, N. Dennis, J. Hein, R. Pryke and D. Smith (eds) *Welfare, Work and Poverty*, London: Institute for the Study of Civil Society

Putnam, R. (2000) *Bowling Alone*, New York: Simon and Schuster

Rapoport, R.N., Fogarty, M.P. and Rapoport, R. (eds) (1982) *Families in Britain*, London: Routledge

Rees, T. (1999) *Mainstreaming Equality in the European Union*, London: Routledge

Reynolds, T., Callender, C. and Edwards, R. (2003) *Caring and Counting: The impact of mothers' employment on family relationships*, Bristol: The Policy Press

Rikowski, G. (2001) *The Battle in Seattle: Its Significance for Education*, London: Tufnell Press

Riseborough, G. (1993) 'The gobbo barmy army: one day in the life of YTS boys', in I. Bates (ed.) *Youth and Inequality*, Milton Keynes: Open University Press

Rosenhan, D.L. (1973/1982) 'On being sane in insane places', *Science*, 179, pp. 250–8; also in M. Bulmer (ed.) (1982) *Social Research Ethics*, London: Holmes and Meier

Rosenthal, R. and Jacobson, L. (1968) *Pygmalion in the Classroom*, New York: Holt, Rinehart & Winston

Rowntree, S. (1901) *Poverty: A Study of Town Life*, London: Macmillan

Rutherford, J. (1988) 'Who's that man?', in R. Chapman and J. Rutherford (eds) *Male Order: Unwrapping Masculinity*, London: Laurence & Wishart

Scambler, G. and Hopkins, A. (1986) 'Being epileptic; coming to terms with stigma', *Sociology of Health and Illness*, 8, pp. 26–43

Scheff, T. (1966) *Being Mentally Ill: A Sociological Theory*, Chicago: Aldine

Schlesinger, P. (1978) *Putting Reality Together*, London: Constable

Sclater, S.D. (2000) *Access to Sociology: Families*, London: Hodder Arnold

Scott, S. (2003) 'Symbolic interactionism and shyness', *Sociology Review*, 12(4)

Sewell, T. (1996) *Black Masculinities and Schooling*, Stoke on Trent: Trentham Books

Sewell, T. (2000) 'Identifying the pastoral needs of African-Caribbean students: a case of "critical antiracism"', *Education and Social Justice*, 3(1)

Sharpe, S. (1976) *Just Like a Girl*, Harmondsworth: Penguin (2nd edn 1994)

Shaw, M., Dorling, D., Gordon, D. and Davey Smith, G. (1999) *The Widening Gap*, Bristol: Policy Press

Smart, C. and Stevens, P. (2000) *Cohabitation Breakdown*, London: The Family Policy Studies Centre

Smith, J. (1989) *Mysogenies*, London: Faber & Faber

Smith, J. (2001) *Moralities, Sex, Money and Power in the 21st Century*, Allen Lane

Stanko, E. (2000) 'The day to count: a snapshot of the impact of domestic violence in the UK', *Criminal Justice*, 1(2)

Stone, M. (1981) *The Education of the Black Child in Britain*, Glasgow: Fontana

Strinati, D. (1995) *An Introduction to Theories of Popular Culture*, London: Routledge

Swann Report (1985) *Education for All*, London: HMSO

Swingewood, A. (2000) *A Short History of Sociological Thought*, Basingstoke: Macmillan

Szasz, T. (1973 first published 1962) *The Myth of Mental Illness*, London: Paladin

Taylor, S. (1999) 'Postmodernism: a challenge to sociology', *'S' Magazine*, 4

Thornes, B. and Collard, J. (1979) *Who divorces?*, London: Routledge & Kegan Paul

Tizard, B. and Hughes, M. (1991) 'Reflections on young people learning', in G. Walford (ed.) *Doing Educational Research*, London: Routledge

Townsend, P. (1979) *Poverty in the United Kingdom*, Harmondsworth: Penguin

Tuchman, G., Kaplan Daniels, A. and Benit, J. (eds) (1978) *Hearth and Home: Images of Women in the Mass Media*, New York: Oxford University Press

Tunnell, K.D. (1998) 'Honesty, secrecy, and deception in the sociology of crime: confessions and reflections from the backstage', in J. Ferrell and M.S. Hamm (eds), *Ethnography at the Edge*, Boston: Northeastern University Press

van Dijk, T. (1991) *Racism and the Press*, London: Routledge

Viewing the World (2000) Department for International Development

Virdee, S. (1997) 'Racial harassment', in T. Moddod, R. Berthoud, J. Lakey, J. Nazroo, P. Smith, S. Virdee and S. Beishon (eds) *Ethnic Minorities in Britain: Diversity and Disadvantage*, London: PSI

Waitzkin, H. (1979) 'Medicine, superstructure and micropolitics', *Social Science and Medicine*, 13a, pp. 601–9

Walter, N. (1999) *The New Feminism*, London: Virago

Warin, J., Solomon, Y., Lewis, C. and Langford, W. (1999) *Fathers, Work and Family Life*, York: Joseph Rowntree Foundation

Wertz, R.W. and Wertz, D.C. (1981) 'Notes on the decline of midwives and the rise of medical obstetricians', in P. Conrad and R. Kerns (eds) *The Sociology of Health and Illness. Critical Perspectives*, New York: St Martin's Press

West, A. and Hind, A. (2003) *Secondary School Admissions in England: Exploring the extent of overt and covert selection*, Centre for Educational Research, Department of Social Policy, London School of Economics and Political Science.

Wilkinson, H. (1994) *No Turning Back: Generations and the Genderquake*, London: Demos

Willis, P. (1977) *Learning to Labour*, Aldershot: Ashgate

Winship, J. (1987) *Inside Women's Magazines*, London: Pandora Press

Witz, A. (1992) *Professions and Patriarchy*, London: Routledge

Wolf, N. (1990) *The Beauty Myth*, London: Vintage

Wood, J. (1993) 'Repeatable pleasures: notes on young people's use of video', in D. Buckingham (ed.) *Reading Audiences: Young People and the Media*, Manchester: Manchester University Press

Woods, P. (1983) *Sociology and the School: An Interactionist Viewpoint*, London: Routledge & Kegan Paul

Working Group on 14–19 Reform (2004) *14–19 Curriculum and Qualifications Reform: Final report of the working group on 14–19 reform*, London: DfES

Wright, C. (1992) 'Early education: multi-racial primary classrooms', in D. Gill, B. Mayor and M. Blair (eds) *Racism and Education: Structures and Strategies*, London: Sage

Young, M. and Willmott, P. (1957) *Family and Kinship in East London*, Harmondsworth: Penguin

Young, M. and Willmott, P. (1973) *The Symmetrical Family*, Harmondsworth: Penguin

INDEX

Note: page numbers in **bold** refer to definitions/explanations of key terms.

Sociology AS for AQA

top-down theories 248, **249**
Townsend, P. 214
transcribing 266, **268**
transnational companies 28, **29**, 117

U

underclass 8, **9**, 47, 225–6, **228**, 229, 231
unemployment 90, 220, 227, 232–3
universalism 238, **240**
unstructured interviews 266, **268**
upward social mobility 7, **9**
urbanization 26–7, **29**
uses and gratifications model 133, **134**, 138

V

validity **268**
values 3–4, **4**
   consensus 13–14, **14**
   education 164
   family 36
   functionalism 14–15
   questionnaires and interviews 268
van Dijk, T. 148
VAT (value-added tax) 209, **210**
vertical integration 117, 119, **120**
violence 72–3, 136–41, 144–5
vocational education 163, **166**, 170–1, **172**, 198–201, **200**
vocational training 199, **200**
voluntary organizations **240**

W

Walter, Natasha 18
watchdog **120**
wealth 17, 206–11, **210**
Weber, Max 18, 107–8, 210
welfare benefits 209, **234**
   development of the welfare state 237–41
   family 36, 38, 41, 47, 59
   poverty 225–7
welfare regime **240**
welfare state 230–5, **234**, 236–41
Willis, Paul 165, 167, 193, 194
Willmott, P. 42, 45, 70
work
   childhood 65–7
   conflict of interest 16
   division of labour 13
   education 163–5, 187
   family 71–2
   fatherhood 72
   gender 91, 187
   health 90–1, 108

   industrialization 41
   job insecurity 209
   Marxism 17–18
   mothers 72
   postmodernity 27–8
   social differentiation 6–7
   welfare state 232
working class extended family 60, **62**
working mothers 47–9, 54–5, 71
Working Tax Credits **234**
Wright, C. 183

Y

Youdell, Deborah 173, 183, 185
Young, M. 42, 45, 70, 71
YTS (Youth Training Scheme 193, **196**, 199